DATE DUE

SMART SENTENCING

SMART SENTENCING

The Emergence of
Intermediate Sanctions

edited by

James M. Byrne
Arthur J. Lurigio
Joan Petersilia

 SAGE Publications
International Educational and Professional Publisher
Newbury Park   London   New Delhi

For information address:

 SAGE Publications, Inc.
2455 Teller Road
Newbury Park, California 91320

SAGE Publications Ltd.
6 Bonhill Street
London EC2A 4PU
United Kingdom

SAGE Publications India Pvt. Ltd.
M-32 Market
Greater Kailash I
New Delhi 110 048 India

Printed in the United States of America

Library of Congress Cataloging-in-Publication Data

Main entry under title:

Smart sentencing: the emergence of intermediate sanctions / edited by
    James M. Byrne, Arthur J. Lurigio, Joan Petersilia.
        p.   cm.
    Includes bibliographical references and index.
    ISBN 0-8039-4164-1.—ISBN 0-8039-4165-X (pbk.)
    1. Alternatives to imprisonment—United States. I. Byrne, James M.
    II. Lurigio, Arthur J. III. Petersilia, Joan.
    HV9304.S56 1992
    364.6'8—dc20   92-20279

                94 95 96 10 9 8 7 6 5 4 3

Sage Production Editor: Astrid Virding

Contents

Part VI. A Look at the Future

Introduction:
The Emergence of Intermediate Sanctions

Joan Petersilia

Arthur J. Lurigio

James M. Byrne

Crime is a major social problem in the United States. Until recently, this country had few sentencing options for punishing criminals. Offenders were either incarcerated or given ordinary probation, which in larger jurisdictions often equated with perfunctory supervision. Because the range of seriousness of crimes does not fall neatly into these two categories of punishment, sentencing commonly erred in one direction or the other. It was either too harsh, putting behind bars offenders whose crimes and criminality did not warrant prison, or too lenient, giving probation to offenders whose crimes and criminality deserved stronger punishment.

In search of remedies, many states began to experiment with *intermediate sanctions,* punishments that lie somewhere between prison and routine probation with respect to their harshness and restrictiveness. Intermediate sanctions offer an alternative to the "either/or" sentencing policy found in many states, that is, *either* prison *or* probation. Various intermediate sanctions have been developed in recent years, including house arrest, electronic monitoring, intensive supervision, boot camps, split sentences, day reporting centers, day fines, and community service sentences. The stated, or public, purposes of current intermediate sanctions are as follows:

- to *save* taxpayers money by providing cost-effective alternatives to incarceration for prison and jail-bound offenders
- to *deter* offenders (specifically) and the public (generally) from crime
- to *protect* the community by exerting more control (than does traditional probation) over offender behavior

- to *rehabilitate* offenders by using mandatory treatment requirements, which are then reinforced by mandatory substance abuse testing and the swift revocation of violators

While most intermediate sanctions have been "sold" to the public through the promise of these results, it has been argued that these programs also have a number of other important (but unstated) purposes (see Morris & Tonry, 1990), for example:

- to create an "appearance" of correctional reform
- to institute a mechanism for reclaiming limited correctional resources for probation and parole
- to provide probation administrators (and legislators) with an effective response to the more punitive orientation of the public

Whether intermediate sanctions fulfill any or all of these purposes is debatable. Most intermediate sanctions were developed or greatly expanded during the mid-1980s, when prison crowding reached epidemic proportions. Program descriptions and evaluations are scarce and not well publicized. Consequently, many states and jurisdictions are not aware of alternative sanction models that can offer some guidance—negative as well as positive—for developing their own programs.

This book is intended to redress the relative dearth of information on intermediate punishments. Specifically, the current collection of chapters is intended to help policymakers and correctional managers better understand intermediate sanctions by describing some of the best known and most emulated programs, and then presenting and critically commenting on data assessing program costs and effects. The book also discusses the broader implications of intermediate sanctions for criminal justice policy, while highlighting the critical issues local, county, state, and federal decision-makers still need to resolve.

Overview of Contents

This book consists of 20 chapters organized in six parts. Parts I through IV review specific intermediate sanction *programs*, while Parts V and VI, respectively, discuss *issues and controversies* and *future considerations*. Although Parts I through IV give the impression that different types of intermediate sanctions are clearly distinguishable, it is also true that these punishments do not generally operate in isolation. Intensive probation supervision and house arrest programs often utilize electronic monitoring to measure compliance; electronic monitoring is seldom a punishment in itself. Fines and community service sentences are often combined with other punishments. Split sentencing and boot camps commonly incorporate an intensive supervision phase that may also utilize electronic monitoring. And so, in practice, these programs are not as distinct as our separate sections may lead the reader to believe.

Part I is devoted to intensive probation supervision (IPS), the most widely utilized intermediate sanction in the United States. In Chapter 1, Lurigio and Petersilia place IPS programs in historical context, describe common IPS program features, and summarize existing descriptive data on program performance. Petersilia, Turner, and Deschenes, in Chapter 2, report on the results of an experiment designed to apply IPS to drug-involved offenders. Their evaluation assesses IPS's impact on recidivism, program participation, and system costs.

Part II focuses on home confinement and electronic monitoring. Renzema presents a historical overview of home confinement programs in Chapter 3, and describes the extensiveness of such programs in the United States. In Chapter 4, Baumer and Mendelsohn provide information on the types and features of commonly used monitoring systems, identify organizational features that enhance successful program implementation, and summarize the available evidence regarding the effects of electronic monitoring on offender performance.

Watts and Glaser report in Chapter 5 on an evaluation of an electronic monitoring demonstration project for drug offenders in Los Angeles County. They utilize official record data as well as offender interviews to assess program impact. Their chapter highlights the difficulties of implementing electronic monitoring programs and lends practical guidance to probation managers thinking of utilizing such equipment. The final chapter in Part II is by Corbett and Marx, who question the widespread expansion of electronic monitoring systems, absent any evidence demonstrating their effectiveness in reducing offender recidivism or system costs.

Part III examines shock incarceration programs, commenting on the recent increase of boot camps as a sentencing option for young adult offenders. In Chapter 7, MacKenzie and Parent summarize the recent growth and interest in boot camps, describe common program features, and critically summarize the existing data on effectiveness. They caution that boot camps, like other intermediate sanctions, are proliferating at a faster rate than might be justified by the available data.

Part IV describes a number of other approaches to intermediate sanctions, including day fines, day reporting centers, residential community correction centers, and community service orders. For the most part, such programs are new and, as a result, descriptive and evaluative data are limited. In Chapter 8, Hillsman and Greene describe the U.S. and Western European experiences with imposing and collecting fines and suggest that expanding the use of fines may become an integral component of U.S. sentencing policy. In Chapter 9, Cole discusses the difficulties of fine enforcement and compliance. He outlines current organizational and political barriers to the effective collection of monetary sanctions and offers a number of practical approaches to addressing current difficulties.

McDevitt and Miliano discuss the innovative concept of day reporting centers in Chapter 10. These authors explore the experience of the state of Massachusetts in designing and operating several centers, and detail different program characteristics and impacts. They suggest that such centers may be applicable to a broad range of settings and clientele.

In Chapter 11, Latessa and Travis examine one of the older intermediate sanctions, residential community correction centers or halfway houses. They review the history and effectiveness of such programs and examine how they are being restructured in response to current trends and offender populations. McDonald provides similar information in Chapter 12 with respect to community service sentencing and also estimates the relative costs of this sanction relative to incarceration. In the final chapter in Part IV, Lilly draws on his English experiences to consider the impact of intermediate treatment for juvenile offenders.

Part V discusses some of the major issues and controversies surrounding intermediate sanctions. In Chapter 14, von Hirsch observes that while intermediate sanctions are growing rapidly, little thought is being given to matching offenders to punishments and to calibrating the severity of the punishment to the severity of the offense. He contrasts two punishment scaling schemes—one based on desert principles and the other on preventive and retributive elements—and discusses the implications of these different schemes for identifying populations that should be targeted for intermediate punishments. Robinson, in Chapter 16, is also concerned with targeting offenders for intermediate sanctions, and presents data on the availability of intermediate sanction programs for females.

In Chapter 15, Palumbo, Clifford, and Snyder-Joy question whether intermediate sanctions may simply widen the scope of social control, particularly over the minority population, "who are being sentenced to prison and also to the newer alternatives in proportions far greater than their representation in the overall population" (p. 242). Using a house arrest program in Arizona as an example, these authors conclude that net widening (and increased costs) did occur, although this was contrary to the program's intent. They caution that similar scenarios are likely to occur if current intermediate sanction trends continue. Byrne and Pattavina reach similar conclusions in Chapter 18, after reviewing the available evidence on the effects of intermediate sanctions on costs, diversion, and recidivism. They report that, contrary to expectations and early claims, the latest wave of *surveillance-*oriented intermediate sanction programs do not reduce recidivism, prison crowding, and/or the cost of corrections. We conclude the "issues and controversy" section by focusing on the utilization of intermediate sanctions at the federal level. In Chapter 17, Klein-Saffran provides an overview of the federal role in the development of intermediate sanctions, highlighting a range of programs designed specifically for the federal offender population.

Part VI considers the future of intermediate sanctions. In Chapter 19, Cochran focuses on the critical importance of information systems in the design, implementation, and evaluation of the next wave of intermediate sanction programs. In Chapter 20, Clear and Byrne call the 1990s the "decade of intermediate sanctions," and state that they believe that how we develop, implement, and evaluate such programs today will set the stage for their future development. They caution that if we fail to define program goals, staff orientation, and appropriate clientele, these programs may fall by the wayside, as many "alternatives" have in the past. If, however, we use these programmatic options to match sanctions closely with offender risk, they may pave the way for restructuring the entire criminal sentencing system.

Concluding Remarks

The criminal justice system has been reeling continually from one sort of crisis or another in the years since World War II. As a result, innovations tend to be seen as "quick fixes" rather than as suggestive models that need time to mature and adapt to local settings, needs, priorities, and resources. One after another, most of these proposed innovations have been tried and found wanting. For example, pre-release centers proliferated in the 1970s, when federal funds were plentiful and faith in the rehabilitative ideal was strong. As the

nation became more punitive, and more convinced that rehabilitation programs "didn't work," funding for such centers became increasingly difficult to secure; the programs began to disappear. The
same is likely to happen to intermediate sanction programs if jurisdictions fail to address some of the key questions raised in this book.

Jurisdictions must consider what their own correctional systems
demand, and what kinds of offenders are on the caseloads. How
many of them could be safely supervised in various types of intermediate sanctions? What are the goals of the different programs?
And, most important, should intermediate sanctions be developed
even if they offer no tangible evidence of effectiveness, in terms of
cost, diversion, or recidivism?

If jurisdictions are interested primarily in gaining much-needed
flexibility in sentencing decisions by imposing intermediate punishments that more closely fit offenders' crimes, then intermediate
sanctions hold promise. If, however, they are interested primarily in
reducing costs and recidivism, then most of today's intermediate
sanctions will likely fall short. The reason for this gloomy assessment
can be linked to the surveillance/control orientation of these programs. Although most intermediate sanction programs have been
"sold" to legislators and the public at large based on their surveillance (and control) components, it now appears that it is the *treatment*
component of these programs that results in changes in the subsequent criminal behavior of offenders. Unless policy makers and
program developers recognize this fact by providing resources for
both offender control and treatment, intermediate sanction programs
will *not* be viewed as examples of "smart" sentencing; they will be
viewed as simply further evidence that "nothing works."

The future viability of these programs must depend on a realistic
reappraisal of what they can be expected to accomplish. Proponents
suggest that intermediate punishments can relieve prison crowding,
enhance public safety, and rehabilitate offenders—and all at a cost
savings. It is doubtful that the current wave of intermediate sanctions can accomplish such far-reaching and lofty goals. If community
sanctions are made more effective through an emphasis on public
safety and offender accountability, then an increase in program costs
is likely. On the other hand, developing an array of sentencing
options is an important and necessary first step toward a more
comprehensive and graduated sentencing structure, where the punishment more closely matches the crime. To many observers, the goal
of restoring the principle of just deserts to the criminal justice system
is justification enough for the continued development of intermedi-

ate sanctions. But if we expect something more than just deserts, then careful attention to the issues raised in this collection is certainly in order.

For Further Reading

Ball, R. A., Huff, C. R., & Lilly, J. R. (1988). *House arrest and correctional policy: Doing time at home.* Newbury Park, CA: Sage.

Byrne, J. M., Lurigio, A. J., & Baird, S. C. (1989). *The effectiveness of the new intensive supervision programs* (Research in Corrections, No. 5). Washington, DC: National Institute of Corrections.

Lurigio, A. J. (Ed.). (1990). Intensive probation supervision: An alternative to prison in the 1980s [Special issue]. *Crime and Delinquency, 36*(1).

McCarthy, B. R. (Ed.). (1987). *Intermediate punishments: Intensive supervision, home confinement, and electronic surveillance.* Monsey, NY: Criminal Justice Press.

Morris, N., & Tonry, M. (1990). *Between prison and probation: Intermediate punishments in a rational sentencing system.* New York: Oxford University Press.

Palmer, T. (1992). *The re-emergence of correctional intervention.* Newbury Park, CA Sage.

Petersilia, J. (1987). *Expanding options for criminal sentencing* (Publication No. R-3544-EMC). Santa Monica, CA: RAND Corporation.

U.S. General Accounting Office. (1990). *Intermediate sanctions: Their impacts on prison crowding, costs, and recidivism are still unclear* (Publication No. GAO/PEMD-90-21). Gaithersburg, MD: Author.

PART I

Intensive Probation Supervision

1. The Emergence of Intensive Probation Supervision Programs in the United States

Arthur J. Lurigio

Joan Petersilia

This chapter describes one of the most popular and widely studied intermediate sanctions in the United States: intensive probation supervision (IPS). The present discussion of IPS is organized in three sections. The first reviews some of the events that provided the major thrust for IPS projects, namely, prison overcrowding and the sentencing of high-risk felons to probation. The second section addresses the theoretical foundations of IPS, current IPS program models, and the tremendous divergence among IPS projects. The final section offers a few observations on the future of IPS.

Background

PRISON OVERCROWDING
AND THE NEED FOR ALTERNATIVES

Prison overcrowding has created a crisis in corrections. From 1970 to 1988, the incarceration rate in the United States doubled in state and federal institutions; it is already higher than that of any Western European country (Morris & Tonry, 1990). Sweeping revisions in sentencing legislation and a proliferation of stricter laws led to a higher percentage of offenders being sent to prison for longer terms and with fewer hopes for parole (Irwin & Austin, 1987; Skogan, 1990). The "get tough" movement in criminal justice policy included such reforms as the abolition of early release, mandatory minimum

3

sentences, determinate sentencing, and sentencing enhancements (Cullen, Clark, & Wozniak, 1985). As a consequence, approximately half of all convicted felons now are sentenced to prison (Bureau of Justice Statistics, 1989).

The nation's prison population grew to a record 46,000 new inmates in the first six months of 1989, reaching an unprecedented total of 673,565 persons (Bureau of Justice Statistics, 1990). More than 30 states are currently under federal district court orders to alleviate prison overcrowding and its attendant problems (Morris & Tonry, 1990). Furthermore, precipitous prison growth and inmate "overflow" have resulted in a concurrent jail overcrowding problem (Byrne & Kelly, 1989; Petersilia, 1987). At any given time, between 10,000 and 20,000 inmates are being held in local jails because of lack of prison space or delays in transferring convicted, prison-bound offenders (Abadinsky, 1991). If the current trend in prison use continues, the aggregate number of inmates will climb an additional 21% by 1995 (Austin & Tillman, 1988), when an estimated 440 Americans per 100,000 will be incarcerated (Morris & Tonry, 1990).

Prisons are prohibitively expensive to build and operate. On the average, the construction of one cell costs $60,000, and the housing of a single inmate costs $14,000 a year (McDonald, 1989). During 1988 alone, $2.5 billion was spent across the country to construct new prison facilities or additions (Durham, 1989). Indeed, corrections has become the fastest-growing component of many state budgets (Austin, 1990; Petersilia, 1987). For example, the exorbitant costs of prisons were a major factor in the growth of California's corrections budget. With a rated capacity of approximately 47,000, California prisons are currently operating at 170% over design capacity, ranking California first among all states in percentage of overcrowding (Bureau of Justice Statistics, 1990). Experts acknowledge that by 1994—after the state has created an additional 37,000 prison and jail beds costing more than $5.2 billion—California's correctional institutions will have become even more crowded (California Commission on Inmate Population Management, 1990).

California is not alone. The continuing upward spirals of prison populations and correctional outlays can be found nationwide. Nonetheless, more prison space and longer prison terms have had little favorable impact on crime or public safety. Despite an enormous investment in prisons, the level of violent crime is substantially higher today than it was a decade ago (Jamieson & Flanagan, 1989).

THE USE OF PROBATION TO RELIEVE OVERCROWDING

Probation has been used increasingly as a tentative solution to the crowding crisis. Placing offenders on probation is deemed an expeditious way to lower inmate populations and to avoid building new prisons. Hence nearly two-thirds of all convicted adult offenders are sentenced to probation, which is growing each month at the rate of 9,000 new cases (Byrne, 1987).

The push to alleviate institutional crowding also has resulted in the sentencing of more serious offenders to probation, which is no longer reserved for first-time misdemeanants or petty criminals. Current caseloads in many jurisdictions include high-risk felons who previously would not have been considered for probation. For example, Petersilia, Turner, Kahan, and Peterson (1985) discovered that 65% of the felony probationers in Los Angeles and Alameda counties (California) were rearrested during probation—many of them for serious offenses such as burglary, assault, and robbery. In addition, they found that the conviction offenses and criminal histories of 25% of the probationers were indistinguishable from those of prison inmates.

Despite rising numbers of high-risk offenders, burgeoning caseloads, and soaring rates of recidivism, probation expenditures in many jurisdictions have been dramatically reduced (Jacobs, 1987). Ironically, most of the fiscal cutbacks in community corrections were made to supplement prison construction and resources (Petersilia, 1987). Over the last 10 years in California, for example, the number of probationers has increased by 50%, while the number of probation officers has declined 20%. Caseloads have grown so large and unmanageable that several county probation departments in the state can render active supervision to less than one-third of their probationers. Under these circumstances, offenders receive rather perfunctory surveillance, and the enforcement of probation conditions is spotty at best (Petersilia, 1990). Therefore, the failure to increase probation budgets to keep pace with the size and seriousness of caseloads has greatly diminished probation's capacity to monitor offenders.

The Appearance of
Intensive Probation Supervision Programs

Rampant prison overcrowding and the public threat posed by serious felons on probation eventually led to the development of

intermediate sanctions, which accord judges a longer menu of sentencing options beyond the limited choices of probation and prison
(McCarthy, 1987; Tonry & Will, 1988; see also the introduction to this
volume). Intensive probation supervision is the most prevalent intermediate sanction, and is regarded widely as the best hope for relieving
prison crowding and ensuring public safety (Petersilia, 1990).

As its name implies, IPS is more severe than routine probation.
Typically, IPS offenders have multiple weekly contacts with their
probation officers. They also are held stringently to curfews and
other conditions of release, are subjected to unscheduled drug tests,
and are ordered to perform community service (Byrne et al., 1989).
IPS is designed to divert offenders from incarceration, thereby saving money and reducing the prison population. Furthermore, IPS
strenuously monitors serious offenders to protect the community
and to ensure that such offenders are being sufficiently punished and
controlled (Lurigio, 1987). In short, "intensive supervision is designed to hold the middle ground between incarceration and regular
probation, in terms of punitiveness, the degree of safety afforded the
public, and cost" (Petersilia, 1990, p. 3).

The apparent promise of IPS programs led some criminal justice
researchers to conclude as early as 1985 that

> intensive community surveillance/supervision programs will be the
> most significant experiment made by the criminal justice system in the
> next decade. We expect to see such programs adopted in jurisdictions
> across the country. If [the programs] prove successful over time and
> across jurisdictions, they would not only restore probation's credibility,
> but they could also reduce incarceration rates without increasing crime.
> And perhaps most important, such programs may well rehabilitate at
> least some of the offenders who participate. (Petersilia et al., 1985, p. 77)

Since that time, jurisdictions in 40 states (plus Washington, D.C.)
have implemented IPS programs (Byrne, 1990). The vast majority of
operational programs (85%) are administered under the states' departments of corrections or the circuit courts. Approximately 25,000
offenders, or nearly 3% of all probationers in the United States, are
on IPS (Byrne et al., 1989).

EARLY IPS PROJECTS TO ASSESS CASELOAD SIZE

Although IPS is being hailed as the panacea of modern corrections,
veteran correctional administrators may well be asking, "Why all the

excitement?" About 25 years ago, dozens of intensive probation programs were developed, primarily with funds from the Law Enforcement Assistance Administration (LEAA) (Petersilia, 1990). These early IPS projects were largely probation-management tools, designed to determine the ideal caseload size for achieving rehabilitation.

Most probation staff at that time supported the medical model, which assumed that offenders were sick, disadvantaged, or otherwise needy. The probation officer's task was to diagnose the trouble and provide appropriate treatment (either directly or by referral to another agency). In this context, the officer was seen as the probationer's advocate or counselor. The obligation to enforce court-ordered conditions was acknowledged, but aspects of control, monitoring, and surveillance remained secondary. Probation officers in the 1960s assumed that smaller caseloads would lead to increased contact between probation officers and clients, which, in turn, would result in improved service delivery, more efficient treatment, and enhanced rehabilitation (Carter & Wilkins, 1984).

One of the best known and earliest studies of probation caseloads was the so-called San Francisco project, conducted by the University of California, Berkeley, from 1964 to 1966. For research purposes, federal probation authorities assigned offenders to four levels of supervision: "ideal" (caseloads of 50 offenders per officer), "normal" (caseloads of 70 to 130), "intensive" (caseloads of 20), and "minimum" (caseloads of several hundred). After two years, it was shown that smaller caseloads did little except generate more technical violations. Crime rates were about the same for all categories of supervision (Carter, Robinson, & Wilkins, 1967).

Similar conclusions were reached by Banks, Porter, Rardin, Silver, and Unger (1977), who performed a contemporary and comprehensive review (sponsored by the U.S. General Accounting Office) of IPS evaluations. After examining information on 46 separate programs and conducting site visits to 20 of these projects, the researchers concluded that "the studies reviewed contained such poor research designs, and such unclear operational definitions of key variables, that the effect of reduced caseloads on offender recidivism remains unknown" (p. 7). With this caveat in mind, Banks et al. (1977) summarized the apparent implications of these evaluations:

- Smaller caseloads often failed to produce more contacts between officer and client; that is, the projects failed to become "intensive."
- Intensive supervision, especially with adults, either had no effect on failure rates or seemed to *increase* them.

- Projects designed as alternatives to incarceration consistently failed to attract a target group of true diversions and instead "widened the net" by granting IPS to offenders who otherwise would have received regular probation.

As similar evidence accumulated, federal funding for criminal justice projects began to evaporate. And in 1975, the now-famous Martinson review of the effectiveness of correctional treatment programs contended that "with few and isolated exceptions, the rehabilitative efforts that have been reported so far have had no appreciable effect on recidivism" (Lipton, Martinson, & Wilks, 1975). There were 18 IPS projects included in this review, and the results were consistent with the "nothing works" commentary. Under these circumstances, most of the earlier IPS projects were dismantled; they remained dormant until the early 1980s.

THE NEW SURVEILLANCE-ORIENTED IPS PROGRAMS

Theoretical Foundation

In view of the above evidence, one might reasonably ask: "Why the resurgence of support for intensive probation supervision?" Indeed, Clear, Flynn, and Shapiro (1987) observe: "The new call for intensive probation is not based on a firm grounding of social science . . . which is at best only promising, and at worst downright shaky" (p. 33). It is acknowledged commonly that if prison crowding disappeared tomorrow, thereby eliminating the need to create less expensive sanctions, so would the incentive to develop intensive supervision (Petersilia, 1987). Thus the crisis of prison crowding added new vitality to the relatively old concept of intensive supervision and is the major impetus behind today's programs. Along these lines, Clear and Hardyman (1990) note:

> Without jail and prison crowding, it is hard to imagine that the current support for IPS would have materialized of its own accord. In most jurisdictions in the United States, courts are imposing levels of control or punishment for which the system lacks resources, and IPS is presented as an alternative that occupies the crevice between available resources and demands for them. (p. 45)

Yet IPS programs are not devoid entirely of a theoretical foundation. They rely heavily on a sentencing model that underscores specific deterrence and incapacitation and places less weight on rehabilitation (Blumstein, Cohen, & Nagin, 1978). Deterrence-based programs attempt to change the offenders' perceptions of the costs of crime. There is a long-held notion that offenders assess the consequences of their actions, both positive and negative, and commit crimes only when such actions are in their self-interest. Jeremy Bentham expressed the point this way:

> The profit of the crime is the force which urges a man to delinquency; the pain of the punishment is the force employed to restrain from it. If the first of these forces is the greater, the crime will be committed; if the second, the crime will not be committed. (quoted in Zimring & Hawkins, 1973, p. 75)

Such classical interpretations of deterrence are at the core of IPS supervision. Administrators hope that IPS—its case monitoring, coupled with threats of detection and subsequent incarceration—will influence the crime-related choices made by individuals participating in the program. The increased monitoring and surveillance in IPS programs are designed to boost offenders' perceptions of the effectiveness of the system in detecting and punishing their criminal behavior.

An important assumption of IPS programs is that close supervision should increase the probability of detecting and arresting offenders who are not deterred by the program and who continue to commit crimes. Speedy revocation to custody results in incapacitation, and, because IPS participants are encouraged to be employed and to attend counseling sessions, rehabilitation *may* occur. However, newer IPS programs do not count on rehabilitation to ensure public safety.

Programs based on deterrence and incapacitation have a narrow and short-term crime control focus. In this respect they are quite different from rehabilitation programs, which attempt to achieve longer-term offender change (e.g., desistance from crime). An emphasis on deterrence and incapacitation, on the one hand, and rehabilitation on the other is often referred to as the "control versus cure" debate (Harland & Rosen, 1987). Most IPS models advocate control. As Byrne et al. (1989) state, "IPS is quite compatible with broad changes in correctional policies that emphasize community protection over offender rehabilitation" (p. 8). In essence, IPS has become a way for probation administration to combat long-standing negative perceptions, to restore public and judicial confidence in probation as a meaningful and "tough" sentence, and to "revitalize probation, establishing it again as a powerful cog in the machinery of justice" (Clear & Hardyman, 1990, p. 47).

Rather than giving priority to offenders' needs for services, newer IPS programs concentrate on the community's need for protection. Program developers hope that IPS will be able to deter and incapacitate offenders, even if it fails to rehabilitate them. Conrad (1986) expresses these sentiments as follows:

> I am a believer. The strength of newer IPS programs lies in realism about the punitive nature of the experience of surveillance. We are no longer deceiving ourselves and attempting to deceive the probationers about the therapeutic benefits of the relationship between the officer and the offender. (p. 85)

Current IPS Models

Although the general objectives of IPS are widely accepted, practices vary considerably from program to program. Recent national surveys of IPS programs have found that no two are exactly alike (Byrne, 1986, 1990; Petersilia, 1987). To begin, IPS programs differ in their specific goals. Georgia's IPS program, for example, is a "front-end" release mechanism for prison-bound offenders. Its goal is to prevent offenders from entering prison in the first place. Program officers conduct eligibility reviews of offenders after sentencing to incarceration but prior to imprisonment. Based on these evaluations, officers may ask judges to rescind prison orders and consider IPS as an alternative (Erwin, 1987).

In contrast, New Jersey's program admits offenders through a "back-end" or early-release mechanism for persons already in prison. Its goal is to relieve institutional crowding explicitly for the purposes of conserving scarce prison resources and saving public monies. The program involves a lengthy intake process initiated by prisoners after they have served a minimum time of incarceration. If deemed eligible, offenders can leave prison before their anticipated dates of release (Pearson & Harper, 1990).

A third type of IPS program, administered in Massachusetts, is for felony offenders already sentenced to regular probation. Probationers are assigned to IPS on the basis of their scores on a risk scale that forecasts their potential to commit future crimes. The goal of IPS here is to enhance a regular probation or case management program (Byrne & Kelly, 1989).

Proponents of prison-diversion and early-release IPS claim that they can reduce prison crowding and save public funds by replacing expensive imprisonment with less expensive IPS, while protecting the public through strict surveillance. In contrast, case management IPS does not profess to be an alternative to incarceration and only indirectly serves as a means to reduce prison crowding or to save public monies (by preventing crimes through close monitoring, thereby reducing the future need for prison beds).

IPS programs also may serve hidden or latent goals. Tonry (1990) identifies three unstated functions of IPS that underlie the inauguration and continuation of programs. The first involves *institutional aims*. As discussed earlier, probation has had a long-standing image problem; it has been referred to as "a slap on the wrist" (Duffie, 1987, p. 125) and "a kind of standing joke" (Martinson, 1976, p. 47). IPS has helped to bolster probation's flagging public relations image; it claims to be tough on offenders and a truly safe alternative to prison. The second unstated function involves *professional aims*. IPS has eventuated in more resources and enhanced esteem for program probation officers who "get to do probation work the way it ought to be done" and who "work closely with just a few people so [they] can make a difference in their lives" (Pearson, 1987, p. 105). The third unstated function involves *political aims*. IPS permits probation to strike a responsive chord with the public's harsher attitudes toward crime and criminals, and it does so while attending to fiscal constraints. Hence IPS is infinitely salable to the public.

IPS programs also differ in their definitions of *intensive* (Byrne, 1990; Byrne et al., 1989; Petersilia, 1987). For some programs, *intensive* means multiple face-to-face visits with probation officers; for others it means electronically monitored home confinement, curfew checks, periodic imprisonment, collateral visits with employers and family members, and the payment of restitution to victims (Byrne, 1990). In a national survey of IPS programs, Byrne (1986) found that they not only varied in type of contact, but also in frequency of contact (e.g., from 1 per day to 4 per month) and in duration of the sentence, that is, the length of mandated program participation. Moreover, although many IPS programs are conducted by specially selected and trained officers, a number are run by traditional probation officers adopting standard caseload management strategies. In fact, early evaluations of IPS programs revealed that their levels of surveillance were no more intense than those of routine probation (Banks et al., 1977). In addition, caseload sizes can range from 12 per officer to 40 or more per officer (Tonry & Will, 1988). Finally, programs that appear similar on the surface may emphasize certain elements of casework practices (e.g., treatment) over others (e.g., surveillance), and may initiate divergent responses to probation violators (Byrne, 1990; Tonry & Will, 1988).

The third basic difference among IPS programs, which is in part a corollary of the first, is in their disparate target populations. Even if all IPS programs were actually performing the same procedures, they would probably be doing them with markedly different offender groups. According to Byrne, McDevitt, and Pattavina (1986), "There is no *one* answer to the question, 'Who will be placed on intensive probation supervision?' " (p. 5). Overall, offenders sentenced to prison (as in back-door IPS programs) have committed more serious offenses and have lengthier criminal histories than those sentenced directly to IPS (as in front-end IPS programs) or those drawn from existing probation caseloads (as in probation-enhancement IPS programs). As a group, IPS programs accept a broad range of participants, including violent and nonviolent offenders, high- and low-risk offenders, probation and parole violators, and drug offenders (Byrne, 1986).

To illustrate more specifically: Some programs exclude offenders with drug and alcohol problems, while others consider them target groups. For example, the program in Montgomery County, Maryland, selects persons who are "first offender felons with alcohol, drug or mental health problems." Other programs are designed for offenders with particular needs. For example, the Monroe County, New York, program selects "unemployed or underemployed probationers," while the Suffolk County, New York, program concentrates on "persons with repeated convictions for driving while under the influence of intoxicants" (Petersilia, 1990).

The Future Course of IPS Programs

Even if the public accepts the arguments in favor of IPS, the long-term viability of these programs may depend on a realistic reappraisal of what they can accomplish, a shift in their emphasis, and a consideration of different criteria for judging their effectiveness.

REALISTIC GOALS FOR IPS

What IPS programs can accomplish depends largely on the nature of the "candidate pool" and other aspects of the corrections environment. IPS probably is not going to deter many high-risk offenders.

Furthermore, it will not be able to incapacitate them unless the local jail has more space than most jurisdictions currently can provide. In this type of environment, IPS programs function primarily as a way to impose conditions that come closer than routine probation to achieving the just deserts goal of sentencing.

Because they have better access to treatment programs and job placement services, IPS programs also have some potential for rehabilitating offenders. This is ironic, considering that rehabilitation has been a traditional focus of probation, whereas surveillance and restriction have been the fundamental objectives of IPS. The most recent studies of IPS have demonstrated that offenders who receive counseling, who are employed and in drug programs, and who perform community service have less chance of recidivism (e.g., Petersilia, 1990; see also Byrne & Pattavina, chap. 18, this volume). Recent research also indicates that IPS programs may afford a particularly effective context for drug treatment. In a review of the effectiveness of major drug treatment modalities, Anglin and Hser (1990) conclude:

> Despite less favorable preadmission characteristics, legally coerced clients (e.g., probationers) benefitted from treatment as much as other clients, and their addiction-related behaviors markedly improved after entry into treatment. . . . The evidence generally supports the proposition that a collaborative relationship between the criminal justice system and community-treatment delivery systems produces, at an aggregate level, enhanced treatment outcomes. (p. 143)

SHIFTING THE EMPHASIS OF IPS

The prevalence of drug involvement of offenders raises another issue—the emphasis IPS places on conditions and technical violations. Drug use is one of the major reasons for the high revocation and recidivism rates of serious offenders. Most serious criminals in this country have drug histories and/or drug-related problems. If drug users are excluded from IPS eligibility, the candidate pool will virtually dry up. If they are not excluded, and drug testing is included in the IPS program, violation rates will probably be high. If a program responds rigorously to violations, it will have high incarceration rates.

A concentration on technical violations basically reflects the assumption that such violations are proxies for criminal behavior. In other words, technical violations predict or signal that offenders are "going bad." Thus, if an IPS officer discovers violations and an offender's probation consequently is revoked, the system may be preventing crimes. However, Petersilia (1990) found that IPS offenders who had technical violations were no more likely to have new arrests than offenders who did not.

Because technical violations are evidently not proxies for criminal behavior, it seems reasonable to question IPS programs' focus on them—especially the practice of sending offenders to prison for technical violations. The effort and resources spent on monitoring and incarcerating offenders for technical violations might be better spent elsewhere (e.g., on more drug/alcohol treatment and job placement efforts).

One argument against deemphasizing technical violations is that this would effectively reduce IPS's punitiveness. The conditions of curfew, drug testing, reporting, and the like embody IPS's purpose and its departure from routine probation. If a program does not monitor its conditions or revoke participation for failure to meet those conditions, why should offenders be expected to comply? If the conditions are merely paper requirements, how does IPS differ from routine probation? If it does not differ, what happens to just deserts?

It seems more equitable to impose only conditions that are relevant to an individual's case rather than to set standard conditions for all offenders in a particular program, which is common practice. Moreover, imposing only relevant conditions does not mean offenders are watched less closely. Instead, monitoring fixes on the limited conditions imposed and on offenders' general behavior. If IPS programs were to discontinue monitoring behavior closely and imposing sanctions for violations, they would no longer be providing *intensive probation supervision*. They would not be holding offenders accountable to ensure public safety, and they would be no more stringent than routine probation.

RETHINKING THE CRITERIA FOR SUCCESS

To date, IPS programs in general have focused primarily on surveillance. As these programs move away from rehabilitation and toward control, some might contend that higher arrest rates should be seen as a criterion of program *success*, not failure, especially when dealing with high-risk offenders. Barry Nidorf, chief probation officer of Los Angeles County, recently reflected:

As I begin to look at the effectiveness of my IPS program, I question whether recidivism rates—the number of offenders who return to crime—are really an appropriate outcome measure. When rehabilitation was our primary purpose, recidivism rates seemed appropriate. However, if control and community protection are IPS goals, then a "success" might be viewed as the identification and quick revocation of persons who are committing crimes. After all, the police are in the business of surveillance and control, and they judge an "arrest" a success, whereas we deem it as a failure.

If community safety is the primary goal, then perhaps an arrest and revocation should be seen as a success and not a failure. Yet we continue to judge these programs by how many offenders have "rehabilitated." It seems to me that serious rethinking about how to judge the effectiveness of these new programs is in order. (personal communication, September 1990)

It is particularly important for jurisdictions to understand how the public perceives the objectives of IPS. If the public expects and demands deterrence, and the jurisdiction has a high-risk candidate pool, public support is not likely to be immediately forthcoming. However, a number of recent studies have examined the public's attitudes about crime and punishment and have discovered that Americans strongly favor increasing the use of alternatives to incarceration, except for violent offenders. Support for the use of alternatives further increases as the public learns about the costs of incarceration (Doble, 1987).

References

Abadinsky, H. (1991). *Probation and parole: Theory and practice* (4th ed.). Englewood Cliffs, NJ: Prentice-Hall.

Anglin, D. M., & Hser, Y. (1990). Treatment of drug abuse. In M. Tonry & J. Q. Wilson (Eds.), *Drugs and crime* (pp. 393-460). Chicago: University of Chicago Press.

Austin, J. (1990). *America's growing correctional-industrial complex.* San Francisco: National Council on Crime and Delinquency.

Austin, J., & Tillman, R. (1988). *Ranking the nation's most punitive states.* San Francisco: National Council on Crime and Delinquency.

Banks, J., Porter, A. L., Rardin, R. L., Silver, T. R., & Unger, V. E. (1977). *Summary phase I evaluation of intensive special probation project.* Washington, DC: National Institute of Law Enforcement and Criminal Justice.

Blumstein, A., Cohen, J., & Nagin, D. (Eds.). (1978). *Deterrence and incapacitation: Estimating the effects of criminal sanctions on crime rates.* Washington, DC: National Academy of Science.

Bureau of Justice Statistics. (1989). *Prisoners in 1988: BJA bulletin*. Washington, DC: U.S. Department of Justice.

Bureau of Justice Statistics. (1990). *Prisons*. Washington, DC: U.S. Department of Justice.

Byrne, J. M. (1986). The control controversy: A preliminary examination of intensive probation supervision programs in the United States. *Federal Probation, 50*, 4-16.

Byrne, J. M. (1987). *Probation*. Washington, DC: National Institute of Justice.

Byrne, J. M. (1990). *Assessing what works in the adult community correction system*. Paper presented at the annual meeting of the Academy of Criminal Justice Sciences, Denver.

Byrne, J. M., & Kelly, L. (1989). *Restructuring probation as an intermediate sanction: An evaluation of the Massachusetts Intensive Probation Supervision program*. Final report to the National Institute of Justice, Research Program on the Punishment and Control of Offenders.

Byrne, J. M., Lurigio, A. J., & Baird, S. C. (1989). *The effectiveness of the new intensive supervision programs* (Research in Corrections, No. 5). Washington, DC: National Institute of Corrections.

Byrne, J. M., McDevitt, J., & Pattavina, A. (1986). *What does intensive supervision really mean?* Paper presented at the Probation With Conditions Meeting, National Institute of Corrections, Washington, DC.

California Commission on Inmate Population Management. (1990). *Final report*. Sacramento: California State Legislature.

Carter, R. M., Robinson, J., & Wilkins, L. T. (1967). *The San Francisco Project: A study of federal probation and parole—final report*. Berkeley: University of California Press.

Carter, R. M., & Wilkins, L. T. (1984). Caseloads: Some conceptual models. In R. M. Carter & L. T. Wilkins (Eds.), *Probation, parole, and community correction* (pp. 34-56). New York: John Wiley.

Clear, T. R., Flynn, S., & Shapiro, C. (1987). Intensive supervision in probation: A comparison of three projects. In B. R. McCarthy (Ed.), *Intermediate punishments: Intensive supervision, home confinement, and electronic surveillance* (pp. 31-51). Monsey, NY: Criminal Justice Press.

Clear, T. R., & Hardyman, P. L. (1990). The new intensive supervision movement. *Crime and Delinquency, 36*, 42-61.

Conrad, J. P. (1986). Research and development in corrections. *Federal Probation, 50*(2).

Cullen, F. T., Clark, G. A., & Wozniak, J. F. (1985). Explaining the get tough movement: Can the public be blamed? *Federal Probation, 49*, 16-24.

Doble, J. (1987). *Crime and punishment: The public's view*. New York: Public Agenda Foundation.

Duffie, H. C. (1987). Probation: The best-kept secret around. *Corrections Today, 47*, 122-126.

Durham, A. M. (1989). Rehabilitation and correctional privatization: Observation on the 19th century experience and implications for modern corrections. *Federal Probation, 53*, 43-52.

Erwin, B. S. (1987). *Evaluation of intensive probation supervision in Georgia*. Atlanta: Georgia Department of Corrections.

Harland, A., & Rosen, C. J. (1977). Sentencing theory and intensive supervision caseload. *Federal Probation, 51*, 33-42.

Irwin, J., & Austin, J. (1987). *It's about time: Solving America's prison crowding problem*. San Francisco: National Council on Crime and Delinquency.

Jacobs, J. B. (1987). *Inside prisons*. Washington, DC: National Institute of Justice.

Jamieson, K. M., & Flanagan, T. J. (Eds.). (1989). *Sourcebook of criminal justice statistics: 1988*. Washington, DC: U.S. Department of Justice.

Lipton, D., Martinson, R., & Wilks, J. (1975). *The effectiveness of correctional treatment: A survey of treatment evaluation studies*. New York: Praeger.

Lurigio, A. J. (1987). Evaluating intensive probation supervision: The Cook County experience. *Perspectives, 11*, 17-19.

Martinson, R. (1976). What works: Questions and answers about prison reform. In R. Martinson, T. Palmer, & S. Adams, *Rehabilitation, recidivism, and research*. Hackensack, NJ: National Council on Crime and Delinquency.

McCarthy, B. R. (Ed.). (1987). *Intermediate punishments: Intensive supervision, home confinement, and electronic surveillance*. Monsey, NY: Criminal Justice Press.

McDonald, D. C. (1989). The cost of corrections: In search of the bottom line. *Research in Corrections, 2*(1), 1-25.

Morris, N., & Tonry, M. (1990). *Between prison and probation: Intermediate punishments in a rational sentencing system*. New York: Oxford University Press.

Pearson, F. S. (1987). *Research on New Jersey's Intensive Supervision Program*. Final report submitted to the National Institute of Justice under Grant No. 83-IJ-CX-K027.

Pearson, F. S., & Harper, A. G. (1990). Contingent intermediate sentences: New Jersey's Intensive Supervision Program. *Crime and Delinquency, 36*, 75-86.

Petersilia, J. (1987). *Expanding options for criminal sentencing* (Publication No. R-3544-EMC). Santa Monica, CA: RAND Corporation.

Petersilia, J. (1990). *Intensive supervision probation for high-risk offenders: Findings from three California experiments*. Santa Monica, CA: RAND Corporation.

Petersilia, J., Turner, S., Kahan, J., & Peterson, J. (1985). *Granting felons probation: Public risks and alternatives*. Santa Monica, CA: RAND Corporation.

Skogan, W. G. (1990). Crime in the American states. In V. Gray, H. Jacob, & R. Albritton (Eds.), *Politics in the American states* (pp. 343-386). Chicago: University of Chicago Press.

Tonry, M. (1990). Stated and latent features of IPS. *Crime and Delinquency, 36*, 174-191.

Tonry, M., & Will, R. (1988). *Intermediate sanctions: Preliminary report to the National Institute of Justice*. Washington, DC: National Institute of Justice.

Zimring, F., & Hawkins, G. J. (1973). *Deterrence: The legal threat in crime control*. Chicago: University of Chicago Press.

2. Intensive Supervision Programs for Drug Offenders

Joan Petersilia

Susan Turner

Elizabeth Piper Deschenes

The Office of National Drug Control Policy has recently identified intensive supervision programs (ISPs) as one of the few sanctions that promise both punishment and rehabilitation for drug-involved offenders (Office of Drug Control Policy, 1989). This endorsement reflects growing national interest over the last decade in ISPs as an intermediate sanction for high-risk offenders in general. By 1990, jurisdictions in all 50 states had instituted forms of ISPs, some of which focused specifically on drug offenders. Early results indicated that ISPs did have lower recidivism rates than traditional probation programs, and those results helped foster beliefs in their potential for controlling and rehabilitating drug offenders.

As part of its Intensive Supervision Demonstration, the Bureau of Justice Assistance (BJA) provided funding in 1987 to give that potential a rigorous, experimental test.[1] Seven jurisdictions in five states received support to develop highly structured, noncustodial programs that were more stringent than traditional probation or parole, but less severe than prison. These programs were to target serious drug offenders, on probation or parole, who would normally have high rates of recidivism. Participants were randomly assigned to the intensive supervision program or the control program. Such a research design helps ensure that outcomes result from program—not

AUTHORS' NOTE: Research reported here was supported by the Bureau of Justice Assistance, U.S. Department of Justice, Grant Number 87-DD-CX-0044.

participant—differences. RAND was selected to evaluate these Drug-ISPs, which ran from 1987 through 1990 and involved more than 500 offenders. This chapter summarizes the major evaluation findings in terms of program implementation and recidivism outcomes. Future reports will analyze the costs of intensive versus routine supervision; assess the implementation and effectiveness of drug testing in the ISPs; explore the relationships among contact levels, technical violations, and recidivism; and identify the type of offender who performs best in ISPs.

Overall, the data for the seven Drug-ISP sites indicate that both the experimental research design and the ISPs were successfully implemented. The offenders assigned to the experimental and control groups showed no major differences in background characteristics or offense variables. Participants assigned to the ISP were tested more frequently for drug use and had more face-to-face and telephone contacts with their probation/parole officers than their counterparts assigned to routine supervision.[2] However, the 12-month follow-up study indicates that intensive supervision, as implemented in these sites, was no more effective than routine supervision in curbing the offender's subsequent recidivism (as measured by official records). With few exceptions, no significant variations were found among the ISP and routine probationers/parolees in terms of (a) the proportion rearrested, (b) the average number of arrests during the follow-up period, (c) the nature of the new offenses, or (d) the rate of arrests, controlling for street time (i.e., time not incarcerated).

Even though no differences in recidivism outcomes were observed between the ISP and routine supervision cases within a site, vast differences exist in recidivism measures *across* sites—and these relationships were often not in the expected directions. For example, in Waycross, Georgia, where 83% of the offenders were predicted to have a "high" rate of recidivism, the subsequent rearrest rates for both ISP and control groups were among the lowest of all sites studied, less than 15%. Yet in Seattle, where 60% of the offenders were predicted to have a "high" risk of recidivism, about 40% were rearrested during the one-year follow-up. Furthermore, when rather similar offenders were subjected to rather similar supervision strategies, the observed outcomes differed greatly across sites. We speculate that such wide variations in outcomes may reflect agency performance more than offender behavior, and may be heavily affected by what agencies choose to record or, alternatively, tolerate without taking action. Thus the impact of intensive supervision on *actual* offender behavior (as opposed to what is officially recorded) remains inconclusive.

What ISPs Are Expected to Accomplish

Drugs and drug offenders constitute a serious threat to public safety and a serious drain on public resources. Recent statistics indicate that nearly 70% of people arrested in major metropolitan areas have used drugs within the preceding 72 hours (Wish & O'Neil, 1989). Both this drug/crime nexus and the violence associated with the drug market have generated public demand for authorities to get tough with drug offenders. That demand led to creation of the Office of National Drug Control Policy with a mandate to mastermind the "war on drugs." It also caused a tremendous growth in prison sentences for drug offenders. Until 1986, drug offenders accounted for about 10% of the prison population; now, they account for 20-35% across the country (Austin & McVey, 1989).

This more stringent treatment of drug offenders exacerbates the already serious problem of prison crowding. The nature, causes, and effects of that problem are too well documented and publicized to require discussion here. Suffice it to say that the system no longer has the space to incarcerate all serious, high-risk offenders. Nor does it have the resources to build its way out of the prison crowding problem—even if everyone agreed that imprisoning these people is a desirable, or possibly the only, solution.

Under the circumstances, it seems particularly impractical, on the one hand, to use prison space for drug-involved offenders—unless their records and conviction crimes are violent. On the other hand, it seems hardly just or prudent to place repeat, high-risk offenders on routine probation and parole. The latter are sanctions in name only in many of the jurisdictions that have the greatest numbers and highest proportions of serious offenders under community supervision. Thus the keen interest in ISP as an intermediate sanction.

ISPs have three basic goals: to reduce prison crowding at less cost than building more prisons, to ensure community safety through close surveillance and monitoring of probationers' behavior, and to give serious offenders an intermediate sanction that is more severe (thus more "just") than routine probation. ISPs for drug offenders have a fourth objective: to help offenders overcome their drug addictions. To achieve these objectives, ISPs generally involve curfews, drug testing, mandatory community service, frequent reporting and contacts, and unannounced home visits. For drug offenders, they often require participation in various types of drug treatment.

Underlying these features are three basic assumptions. First, these conditions impose a greater risk of detection and revocation than does routine probation or parole. Second, offenders will recognize this and be deterred from future crime (i.e., recidivism)—thus lessening the risk to the community. Third, treatment (coupled with counseling and employment) may rehabilitate offenders—which would have long-term benefits for society.

The Need for Experimental Testing of ISPs

Published outcomes of early ISPs raised high hopes for their success. Recidivism rates in those programs were low, and the majority of new arrests were for technical violations rather than new crimes.[3] Despite this apparent success, many people have questioned whether ISPs are responsible for the observed outcomes. Most programs limited participation to property offenders with minor criminal records, which undoubtedly helped explain the low rearrest rates. In the absence of an experiment that randomly assigned offenders to treatment and control groups, it was impossible to know whether the outcomes resulted from the nature of the programs or the nature of the offenders assigned to them.

The Purpose and Nature
of the Demonstration/Evaluation

The purpose of the BJA effort was to test the assumptions underlying ISPs by randomly assigning drug-involved offenders either to routine probation and parole or to ISPs designed particularly for them. The ISPs were to include state-of-the-art risk assessment, appropriate counseling and treatment services, and team supervision. Emphasis was to be placed on surveillance, urinalysis, and appropriate treatment. The sites were also required to design and implement an ISP following a general model developed in Georgia, to participate in several training conferences and technical assistance activities, and to participate in an independent evaluation by RAND.[4]

The BJA selected seven sites to receive funding for 18 to 24 months at a level of $100,000 to $150,000 per site. The sites were Seattle, Washington; Des Moines, Iowa; Santa Fe, New Mexico; Atlanta, Macon, and Waycross, Georgia; and Winchester, Virginia.

The purpose of the evaluation was to assess the effectiveness of ISPs by comparing their results with the results for the control programs, specifically answering the following questions:

- What were the key components of the Drug-ISPs, as designed by the local sites?
- As implemented, in what ways did intensive supervision differ from routine supervision?
- What was the nature of the ISP candidate pool?
- Were Drug-ISP participants more likely than those on routine supervision to participate in treatment programs?
- Was participation in the Drug-ISP associated with reductions in recidivism, as measured by the incidence, type, and rate of technical violations and new arrests?

The Sites and Their Programs

There is no generic ISP sanction, but the newer ISPs generally provide closer supervision of offenders than do traditional probation/parole programs, through some combination of curfew, multiple weekly contacts of participants with probation/parole officers, unscheduled drug testing, strict enforcement of program conditions, and counseling referrals. Some ISPs also involve house arrest and/or electronic monitoring.

The BJA encouraged individual agencies to tailor their ISPs to their local clienteles' needs and risks, their own financial resources, and internal and external political contexts. Thus the sites all operationalized the general ISP protocol slightly differently. However, it is important to note that all the ISPs were *enhancement* programs, designed to increase the supervision received by offenders placed on routine probation or parole (as opposed to prison *diversion* ISPs), and all dealt with adults only. The characteristics of the *planned* ISP in each site are described below.

SEATTLE, WASHINGTON

Seattle's Drug-ISP was operated by the Division of Community Services, Washington Department of Corrections. Specific goals for the ISP included helping the offender abstain from drugs and crime, and assisting in his or her long-term addiction recovery. The ISP officers stressed participation in treatment programs and employment. They also utilized frequent urinalysis testing to monitor drug use, and worked closely with Seattle police to monitor new arrests.

The Drug-ISP focused on offenders (a) who were currently convicted of a felony drug (or drug-related) offense and (b) whose presentence investigation reports indicated drug dependency and recommended probation sentences.[5] Persons meeting these criteria were considered "ISP eligible" and were randomly assigned to routine community supervision or the Drug-ISP.

ISP caseloads were limited to 20, and offenders were to move through five phases of supervision, with decreasing levels of contacts and drug testing. The complete program was designed to last one year. In Phase 1 (first four months), program participants were to receive 12 face-to-face contacts and 8 drug tests per month, 4 law enforcement monitoring checks, and counseling and job referrals. ISP offenders were monitored by a unit composed of ISP officers, two Seattle police officers (one from the narcotics division), and a community worker responsible for providing local drug treatment.

The control program in Seattle was routine community supervision, where caseloads average 85:1 and have the requirement of 4 face-to-face contacts per month, with all other contacts and testing at the officer's discretion.

DES MOINES, IOWA

The Des Moines Drug-ISP was operated by the Iowa Department of Corrections through its Fifth Judicial District Department of Correctional Services. The Drug-ISP placed strong emphasis on urinalysis testing, unannounced visits, and collateral contacts with "significant others." Drug and alcohol treatment and employment development were also mandatory requirements for all ISP clients and were strictly monitored. The Drug-ISP had a surveillance officer who worked at all hours of the day and night as well as weekends. Des Moines's ISP staff were particularly proud of their system of rewarding their successes as well as hoping to provide for speedy sanctions for their failures. For example, when an offender graduated to Phase 2 of the program, he or she received a letter of congratulations outlining the accomplishments achieved during Phase 1 and defining new goals to be reached in Phase 2. The Drug-ISP emphasized job training and education, and worked closely with staff from the State Job Services and the Department of Education.

The Drug-ISP accepted probationers and parolees who were (a) currently convicted of a drug offense or (b) currently convicted of burglary, but had serious drug abuse histories (determined through risk/need assessment). Probationers facing direct sentencing or revocation, as well as incarcerated offenders referred directly by the Parole Board or parolees facing revocation, were considered eligible for the ISP.

Caseloads were limited to 35 offenders, who were supervised by an ISP team of three officers. The complete program was designed to last 6-12 months. In Phase 1 (first 3 months), ISP participants were to receive 16 face-to-face and 4 telephone contacts per month and 8 drug tests per month, had to observe nighttime curfews, and had to show verification of employment (e.g., paycheck stubs) or attempts at employment. ISP offenders also were to spend a minimum of 42 days on electronic monitoring during Phase 1.

The control program in Des Moines was routine supervision. Offenders were monitored on a mixed caseload of 70:1, where contact levels were determined by a classification system. The control offenders were most often on the intensive level of supervision, where contacts equaled 2 face-to-face and 2 collateral contacts per month, and 1 home visit every 6 months. Drug and alcohol testing were ordered at the officer's discretion, and electronic monitoring was infrequently used.

SANTA FE, NEW MEXICO

The Drug-ISP was supervised by the Santa Fe office of the Probation and Parole Division, New Mexico Corrections Department. More so than the other Drug-ISPs, the Santa Fe program stressed a therapeutic approach, emphasizing counseling and job development. In addition to the usual frequent face-to-face and collateral contacts, community service requirements, and urinalysis testing, clients were also required to attend group therapy sessions during the first two phases of the program. The outpatient chemical abuse treatment program placed strong emphasis on art therapy and drug counseling. Clients were also referred to individual counseling on a case-by-case basis. Job development was also required of offenders who were unable to locate employment, and the Department of Corrections obtained 10 slots from the Department of Labor for employment for its ISP clients under the Job Partnership Training Act.

The ISP accepted both probationers and parolees who were being sentenced for new crimes or being considered for revocation of their current probation/parole sentences. From this group, offenders were identified who (a) scored as high or intensive risks on a local risk-of-recidivism assessment or (b) scored 20 or more on a local needs assessment. Offenders meeting these criteria were considered eligible for ISP and randomly assigned to the experimental or control group.

ISP caseloads were limited to 35 offenders who were supervised by a team of two officers. In Phase 1 (first three months), offenders were required to have 12 face-to-face contacts per month, 8 unannounced home visits per month, and 4 urinalysis tests per month. ISP offenders were also required to attend three group therapy sessions per week during Phase 1 of the program, and clients were also frequently referred to individual counseling.

The control program in Santa Fe was routine supervision, where caseloads were 60:1, required contacts for maximum-level cases were 2 face-to-face and 1 office visit per month, and referral to treatment and drug and alcohol testing was at the officer's discretion.

ATLANTA, MACON, AND WAYCROSS, GEORGIA

Georgia used the BJA demonstration to augment its existing ISP and test whether different forms of surveillance would provide additional benefits. In the three Georgia sites, the control program was not routine supervision, but the already-existing ISP. By design, the only difference between the ISP and control programs in the Georgia sites was increased surveillance (passive and electronic monitoring in Atlanta and Macon, and increased drug testing in Waycross). All the Georgia programs were designed to last one year and were divided into three phases, with the intensity of supervision decreasing with each successive phase. Enhanced ISP caseloads averaged 40 offenders per three-person teams (consisting of one probation officer and two surveillance officers). Both the existing and new ISPs were operated by each county's Probation Division, within the Georgia Department of Corrections. Program goals included (a) testing the differential effects of human versus electronic surveillance, (b) testing the differential effects of passive and active electronic surveillance, (c) testing the efficacy of in-house drug treatment for substance abuse, and (d) identifying subgroups of offenders who were responsive to varying combinations of supervision intrusiveness and increased drug testing frequency.

The Georgia programs focused on nonviolent offenders who were (a) directly sentenced by judges to the ISP, (b) sentenced prisoners deemed ISP eligible by staff and for whom judges rescinded prison orders, and (c) probationers revoked to prison for whom judges agreed to rescind the orders and place the offenders in the ISP. In addition, offenders had to have scored medium or high on a local "needs" scale, and to have been drug or alcohol involved.

All three experimental ISPs imposed highly structured daily supervision, the provision of rehabilitative services with constant, specific follow-up, emphasis on employment and development of employment potential, frequent urinalysis testing, and constant monitoring of whereabouts and activities.

Atlanta's enhanced ISP utilized a "voice verification" system, or what is commonly referred to as passive electronic monitoring, in which an offender speaks into a computerized device attached to his or her home phone that verifies the offender's voice and the fact that he or she is in the residence and observing curfews. Atlanta's voice verification system also included a breathalizer or alcosensor to monitor the offender's sobriety. The ISP staff called the offenders on a random basis.

Macon used an active electronic monitoring system with its ISP. The system, like other typical active systems, constantly monitors the offender's presence in his or her home by transmitting information over the telephone lines to a central computer.

The enhanced ISP in Waycross utilized a strong drug-therapeutic approach, combined with home curfews monitored by surveillance officers during all hours of the day/night and weekends. The counseling included in-house Narcotics Anonymous and Alcoholics Anonymous group therapy sessions, held several times a week, with a staff therapist.

Both the existing ISP and the enhanced ISPs utilized a three-phase system. In Phase 1, offenders were to have 12 face-to-face and 10 telephone contacts per month as well as weekly employment verification and random drug and alcohol tests.

WINCHESTER, VIRGINIA

The Winchester ISP was administered by the Virginia Department of Corrections, through the Adult Community Corrections Division. The ISP targeted high-risk probationers and parolees with current drug or drug-related convictions, and/or prior histories of drug abuse. Offenders facing revocation for infractions or those currently on probation/parole caseloads were eligible. A single officer supervised up to 24 offenders in the ISP.

The ISP lasted a minimum of six months, with graduated supervision phases. Phase 1 (first two to three months) consisted of 12 face-to-face contacts, 4 telephone contacts, and 4 monitoring checks per month, as well as urine testing, with frequency as ordered by ISP staff. In addition, all ISP clients were referred to an outside agency for substance abuse evaluations. Recommendations were made by the outside agency for subsequent group or individual counseling. The program utilized a graduated sanctions approach to program violations, ranging from increased contacts, increased urine screenings, and evening curfews (among others) to full revocation proceedings as the ultimate sanction. Other sanctions included residential placement at a local halfway house facility, placement at a local detox facility prior to inpatient treatment, and intensified outpatient or inpatient treatment.

The control program in Winchester was routine supervision, where caseloads were 80:1 and contacts consisted of 2 face-to-face and 2 telephone contacts per month; all other contacts and testing were at the officer's discretion.

Experimental Design and Data Collection

As noted above, each site developed its own ISP eligibility criteria, and each was responsible for determining whether offenders met those criteria. Once a site determined that an offender was eligible for inclusion, RAND staff randomly assigned the offender to either the experimental program (ISP) or the control program. The study-assignment period began in December 1987 and continued through May 1989. The 12-month follow-up period was defined individually for each participant, beginning on the day of assignment to a program, and hence was completed by May 1990.

For each offender, staff were required to fill in three data collection forms, using official records (e.g., presentence investigation reports, supervision chronological notes). The Background Assessment Form recorded the offender's prior record, demographics, current offense, and various items relating to risk of recidivism and need for treatment. Reviews at 6 and 12 months then documented the services the offender had received in the program (e.g., the number of contacts, number of counseling sessions, and number of drug tests), as well as technical violations and new arrests, employment, restitution, and fee payment.

To record "time at risk" (or "street time") information, the data collection forms also included a "status calendar," which was completed at the end of 6 months and at the end of 12 months. The calendar recorded the dates the offender was placed on and removed from ISP or routine probation, as well as the dates of entry into and release from jail, residential placement, or prison.

Results of the Evaluation

WHO PARTICIPATED IN
BJA'S DRUG-ISP DEMONSTRATION PROJECT?

Selected offenders in the five states were predominantly male. Racial/ethnic compositions differed widely across the jurisdictions.

In Des Moines, Waycross, and Winchester, the majority of offenders were white, whereas in Seattle, Atlanta, and Macon, the majority were black. In Santa Fe, Hispanic offenders constituted almost 90% of the sample. Offenders ranged from a mean age of 26 years in Waycross to 30 years in Des Moines and Santa Fe.

THE ISPs HANDLED A GROUP OF SERIOUS DRUG OFFENDERS

As Table 2.1 shows, the Drug-ISPs faced a formidable challenge: Judged by conviction crimes, prior criminal records, drug treatment needs, and risk scores, this was a group of serious drug-involved offenders. In all but two of the sites the majority of offenders evidenced dependency upon drugs; however, in only three of the seven sites was the dependency so great as to indicate "high" drug treatment needs for the majority of offenders.[6] "Risk," as calculated using primarily prior record information from the offender background form, indicated that more than two-thirds of the offenders in the individual sites were either "high" or "moderate" risk.[7] However, differences were apparent across sites in terms of the relative seriousness of offenders. Offenders in Des Moines, Santa Fe, and Waycross appeared to be more serious in terms of risk than offenders in the other sites.

The nature of conviction offenses varied across the sites. In Waycross and Santa Fe, the current conviction offense was often a probation/parole revocation. In the other sites, the current conviction offenses were commonly theft and drug sale/possession. Only in Seattle were the majority of offenders currently sentenced for drug offenses.[8]

When the backgrounds of the ISP and routine supervision offenders were compared for the characteristics in Table 2.1, only two differences emerged: In Winchester, a higher percentage of ISP offenders than controls were on probation rather than parole. And in Iowa, more ISP offenders had "high" drug treatment needs. Thus the random assignment procedures were implemented successfully in all sites, creating control and experimental groups that were similar prior to the ISP intervention.

ISP OFFENDERS DID RECEIVE MORE SURVEILLANCE

One of the most consistent findings of previous ISP evaluations is that the mere establishment of smaller caseloads does not guarantee a more intensive level of supervision. That was not true here: As

TABLE 2.1 Offender Characteristics, JSP and Control Offenders Combined[a] (in percentages)

	Seattle, WA (N = 173)	Des Moines, IA (N = 115)	Santa Fe, NM (N = 58)	Atlanta, GA (N = 50)	Macon, GA (N = 50)	Waycross, GA (N = 50)	Winchester, VA (N = 53)
Current conviction crime							
violent[b]	7	6	12	10	24	0	4
burglary/theft	26	74	31	8	40	26	28
drug sale/possession	66	15	17	48	32	16	40
other[c]	1	5	40	34	4	58	28
Prior prison term	21	47	33	22	16	6	25
Drug dependency	99	97	98	36	56	100	96
High drug treatment need	78	74	47	38	—[d]	54	17
Offender risk score[e]							
low	7	0	2	10	4	2	13
moderate	33	18	16	31	23	15	40
high	60	82	82	58	73	83	47
Current sentence							
probation	92	21	71	100	100	100	55
parole	0	76	29	0	0	0	43
other[f]	8	4	0	0	0	0	2

NOTES: a. Characteristics of ISP and routine supervision cases were examined for differences. In Iowa, more ISP offenders had "high" drug treatment needs; in Winchester, a greater percentage of ISP offenders were on probation.
b. Homicide, rape, kidnap, assault, robbery.
c. Includes probation or parole revocations.
d. More than 50% missing data for this item.
e. Risk score was constructed from the following variables: drug treatment needs, age at first or current conviction, prior probation terms, prior probation and parole revocations, prior felony convictions, and type of current offense.
f. Other sentences includes prison, pending, and jail only.

29

shown in Table 2.2, the ISPs for which the stated protocols dictated more frequent contacts involved significantly more face-to-face contacts, telephone and collateral contacts, and drug tests than the control programs did. And in Atlanta, Macon, and Des Moines, ISP offenders were more often supervised using electronic monitoring equipment.

Across sites, the level of delivered contacts for ISPs varied widely, reflecting the differences in the planned levels in the program protocols. The average number of monthly face-to-face contacts ranged from about 3 in Seattle to just under 23 in Waycross, Georgia. Telephone and other collateral contacts ranged from under 1 per month in Macon to just under 10 in Atlanta and Winchester. Drug tests ranged from fewer than 1 a month in Seattle to about 6 per month in Macon, Georgia. Considering all types of contacts, the three Georgia sites generally delivered the most intensive supervision found in the seven sites studied. In the three Georgia sites, however, the contact levels for the enhanced ISPs were not significantly different from those for the in-house ISPs.[9]

TREATMENT PARTICIPATION VARIED ACROSS PROGRAMS

Overall, offender participation in counseling differed across sites, from a high of 100% in Waycross to a low of 12% in Winchester (see Table 2.3). ISP offenders in Seattle, Des Moines, and Santa Fe participated more often in relevant counseling programs than did their counterparts on routine supervision. Our data collection form also recorded the number and type of counseling sessions in which an offender participated (not shown here). Again, Waycross's commitment to counseling is shown: All of the ISP participants received some counseling, and the average number of sessions per offender during the 12-month follow-up was 77 sessions, more than once a week.

NO SIGNIFICANT DIFFERENCES
IN OUTCOMES FOR ISP AND CONTROL

A primary goal of ISPs is to reduce recidivism—that is, the offender's return to crime. To be as comprehensive as possible, the study collected multiple indicators of recidivism. All of the measures, however, are derived from official records rather than offender self-reports.

Table 2.4 categorizes each individual according to the "most serious" recidivism event he or she experienced during the 12-month

TABLE 2.2 Monthly ISP and Routine Supervision Contact Levels (means averaged over the one-year follow-up)

| | Seattle, WA | | Des Moines, IA | | Santa Fe, NM | | Atlanta, GA | | Macon, GA | | Waycross, GA | | Winchester, VA | |
| | ISP | Control | ISP | Control | ISP | Control | ISP | Control | ISP | Control | ISP | Control | ISP | Control |
	(N = 89)	(N = 84)	(N = 59)	(N = 56)	(N = 29)	(N = 29)	(N = 26)	(N = 24)	(N = 26)	(N = 24)	(N = 24)	(N = 26)	(N = 28)	(N = 25)
Face-to-face contacts	3.4*	0.8	5.8*	3.8	10.6*	2.8	12.5	14.9	16.1	17.7	22.8	22.4	8.1*	1.9
Telephone contacts	0.8*	0.4	2.3	2.1	2.6*	0.7	7.0	5.5	0.2	0.1	0.6	0.4	1.2*	0.6
Collateral monitoring	3.2*	1.2	6.4*	4.1	4.4*	1.3	1.8	0.6	0.5	0.5	2.2	1.8	8.5*	1.7
Alcohol tests taken	0.0	0.0	0.1*	0.0	2.8*	1.0	7.2	4.4	6.6	7.0	0.2	0.2	0.5	0.2
Drug tests taken	0.4*	0.1	2.8*	1.0	2.9*	1.1	4.8	4.9	5.8*	3.7	4.2*	1.6	1.5*	0.4
Days on electronic monitoring	NA	NA	55.8*	5.4	NA	NA	32.3*	0.0	80.5*	0.0	NA	NA	NA	NA

NOTE: Rates are averaged for the total time under supervision and are not directly comparable to the planned rates for different phase levels discussed in the text. All rates were rounded to the nearest tenth; those that were greater than zero and less than .049 are represented by 0.0.
*ISP and control groups are significantly different at $p < .05$, using t tests.

31

TABLE 2.3 Offender Participation in Counseling During 12-Month Follow-Up (in percentages)

	Seattle, WA		Des Moines, IA		Santa Fe, NM		Atlanta, GA		Macon, GA		Waycross, GA		Winchester, VA	
	ISP	Control	ISP	Control	ISP	Control	ISP	Control	ISP	Control	ISP	Control	ISP	Control
Received any counseling	41.6*	14.3	59.3*	41.1	100.0*	58.6	48.0	47.8	65.4	50.0	100.0	88.5	32.1	12.0
personal/family	0.0	0.0	32.2*	14.3	96.6*	24.1	15.4	12.5	7.7	8.3	4.2	0.0	3.6	0.0
drug	41.6*	13.1	50.9	37.5	100.0*	44.8	32.0	30.4	53.8	29.2	100.0	88.5	32.1	12.0
alcohol	0.0	2.4	32.2	26.8	20.7	37.9	28.0	30.4	23.1	16.7	100.0	88.5	14.3	12.0

NOTE: *ISP and control groups are significantly different at $p < .05$, using chi-square tests.

TABLE 2.4 Comparative Outcomes for ISP and Control Groups, One-Year Follow-Up (in percentages)

	Seattle, WA		Des Moines, IA		Santa Fe, NM		Atlanta, GA		Macon, GA		Waycross, GA		Winchester, VA	
	ISP	Control	ISP	Control	ISP	Control	ISP	Control	ISP	Control	ISP	Control	ISP	Control
Most serious recidivism[a]														
none	20.2*	39.3	37.3	37.5	27.6	37.9	23.1	50.0	0.0	0.0	62.5	69.2	28.6*	68.0
technical violation	33.7*	25.0	39.0	33.9	24.1	34.5	65.4	45.8	57.7	62.5	25.0	15.4	42.9*	20.0
new arrest	46.1*	35.7	23.7	28.6	48.3	27.6	11.5	4.2	42.3	37.5	12.5	15.4	28.6*	12.0
violent	9.0	8.3	3.4	3.6	13.8	6.9	0.0	0.0	3.8	12.5	0.0	3.8	7.1	0.0
property	15.7	9.5	8.5	19.6	20.7	10.3	3.8	4.2	15.4	8.3	4.2	3.8	7.1	4.0
drug	11.2	10.7	3.4	1.8	0.0	3.4	7.7	0.0	11.5	12.5	4.2	3.8	10.7	8.0
other	10.1	7.1	8.5	3.6	13.8	6.9	0.0	0.0	11.5	4.2	4.2	3.8	3.6	0.0
System response														
new conviction	19.1	20.2	15.2	21.4	17.2	13.8	7.7	0.0	19.2	25.0	0.0	0.0	10.7	4.0
jail or prison time from technical violations	66.3*	40.5	40.7	25.0	51.7	44.8	42.3	29.2	76.9	87.5	16.7	19.2	35.7	20.0
jail or prison time from arrest	16.8	19.1	11.9	16.1	10.3	13.8	7.7	4.2	15.4	16.7	4.2	0.0	14.3	4.0

NOTES: a. Recidivism is categorized from least serious (none), to medium serious (technical violations), to most serious (arrests).
*ISP and control groups are significantly different at p < .05, using t tests.

follow-up.[10] With very few exceptions, there are no statistically significant differences in outcomes between the ISP and routine supervision offenders.[11] Although not statistically significant, the trend within the sites is that ISP participants generally had *higher* rates of technical violations and arrests than those on routine supervision.

A number of other recidivism analyses (not shown here) were also performed, and the results were consistent with those shown in Table 2.4: No significant differences between the ISP-experimental and control groups were evidenced in (a) the arrest rate, calculated as the mean number of arrests per year of street time,[12] or (b) the seriousness of the arrest crimes.

The proportion of ISP offenders arrested for new crimes ranged from a low of about 11% in Atlanta to a high of just over 48% in Santa Fe. Among those arrested, the most serious type of arrest (e.g., violent, property, drug, or other offense type) was generally similar for ISP and control offenders.

It appears that the ISPs did not reduce recidivism during the follow-up period, as measured by official records. But the impact an ISP had on the *actual* number of crimes an offender committed during the study period remains unclear for at least two reasons. As indicated earlier, wide variations in recidivism outcomes *across* sites may be heavily affected by what agencies chose to record. Additionally, within a site, the recidivism measures may not accurately reflect differential involvement in criminal activity by ISP and routine supervision offenders. The major outcome measure in this study (as in most corrections evaluations)—officially recorded recidivism—is a product of the offender's crime rate and his or her arrest probability. When a crime was committed, police might have been more aware of the whereabouts of ISP offenders, and therefore may have had a greater chance of connecting one of them to a crime, hence raising those individuals' arrest probability.[13] Even if ISP offenders did have a lower rate of crime than controls, if their probability of arrest was higher than that of controls, this would result in the similarity of arrest rates that we see here. The data available for this study did not permit us to evaluate the extent to which this may have occurred (for a more complete discussion of this point, see Petersilia & Turner, 1990).

Conclusions and Implications
for Future Drug-ISPs

This demonstration has made an important contribution to our knowledge about treating drug offenders in the community. While

BJA encouraged sites to customize their ISPs to local conditions, the wide variation represented here—in program design, targeted clientele, and policies regarding noncompliance—confirms the notion that there is no generic ISP sanction.

Despite such wide program variation, the results were surprisingly consistent in terms of effects: In no instance did an ISP reduce the (officially recorded) recidivism rates of participants. This finding occurs despite the fact that ISP offenders not only received more surveillance-oriented contacts but in many instances were more involved in treatment-oriented programs as well.[14] And, in the Georgia sites, which were testing the benefits of adding electronic monitoring to the state's already-existing ISP, there was no evidence that electronically monitored surveillance was more effective than human monitoring in curbing recidivism.[15]

Nonetheless, the programs were able to achieve another of their stated goals, that of imposing an intermediate punishment, for which the court-ordered conditions were more credibly monitored and enforced than was possible with routine supervision. It appears that the ISP, rather than rehabilitating the *offender*, rehabilitated the *system*. In the long run, such intermediate sanctions should escalate the cost of crime to the offender and help restore the principle of just deserts to the criminal justice system. And bridging the middle ground with intermediate sanctions should eventually enhance the deterrent effectiveness of the sentencing system as a whole. Future discussions about whether or not intensive supervision programs represent a promising direction for crime control policy might therefore move from micro-level issues, such as whether or not ISPs benefit offenders, to macro-level concerns about their contribution to improving sentencing policy.

Notes

1. The BJA is an agency within the U.S. Department of Justice. One of its functions is to provide financial support to local criminal justice agencies that wish to implement new practices. The BJA ISP Demonstration began in 1986, with five jurisdictions receiving funding to develop and implement ISPs for adult offenders, but not specifically for drug offenders. For a complete report, see Petersilia (1989) and Petersilia and Turner (1990).

2. Although ISPs were generally more intense than routine supervision, sometimes they were less intensive than originally planned.

3. For reviews of this evidence, see Petersilia and Turner (1990), and Byrne, Lurigio, and Baird (1989).

4. Georgia's program was one of the earliest ISPs implemented and had begun to serve as a model for similar programs throughout the nation. A complete description

of the program can be found in Erwin (1987). The training component was directed by Carol Shapiro and Todd Clear at Rutgers University, and the technical assistance was provided by Douglas Holien and Audrey Blake, formerly of the National Council on Crime and Delinquency.

5. Clients were identified as drug involved using two locally developed instruments, the Addiction Severity Index and the Drug Abuse Screening Instrument.

6. In Georgia participants were not selected on the basis of drug dependency, but only had to have prior alcohol or drug "involvement." Thus across sites the definition of *drug-involved offender* ranged from less serious use of drugs to heavy abuse of drugs with high drug treatment needs.

7. In five out of seven sites data collected on the background form allowed us to calculate the NIC risk score for each offender. However, since information was missing in the other two sites, a modified risk scale was constructed using only certain components of the standard NIC risk scale. The modified risk scale used here contains the following elements: age at first or current conviction, number of prior felony convictions, number of prior probation terms, number of prior probation and parole revocations, type of current offense, and drug treatment needs. These items were scored using the same point system as for the NIC scale. The correlation between the modified risk score and the NIC score (for the five sites) averaged .90.

8. This primarily reflects the fact that all offenders in Seattle were newly sentenced (front-end) offenders, whereas the other sites included substantial proportions of "back-end" offenders being reprocessed for probation or parole revocation, where the current offense was considered a "revocation."

9. This was expected, since the planned contact levels for the existing in-house ISP and enhanced ISPs were similar.

10. For this analysis, arrests were considered more serious than technical violations. Thus if an offender was arrested for a drug offense and also failed to report to his or her probation officer, he or she was classified as having a new arrest.

11. For ease of discussion, the control programs will be referred to as *routine supervision*, even though the Georgia sites used the existing ISP as the control program.

12. *Street time* is defined as the number of days under community supervision or in residential drug treatment and does not include time incarcerated.

13. The ISP offenders were usually known by local police and, in some instances, the police were asked to assist in making random home visits.

14. It is important to note, however, that most of the treatment programs utilized by the ISP staff were outpatient and usually entailed, at most, a couple of hours a week of counseling (usually group, not individual, counseling). In very few sites was inpatient residential treatment available.

15. There were some problems with the electronic monitoring equipment that may have affected this outcome.

References

Austin, J., & McVey, D. (1989). *The NCCD prison population forecast: The impact of the war on drugs.* San Francisco: National Council on Crime and Delinquency.

Byrne, J. M., Lurigio, A. J., & Baird, S. C. (1989). *The effectiveness of the* new *intensive supervision programs* (Research in Corrections, No. 5). Washington, DC: National Institute of Corrections.

Erwin, B. S. (1987, January). New dimensions in probation: Georgia's experience with intensive supervision probation (ISP). *Research in Brief.*

Office of Drug Control Policy. (1989). *National drug control strategy.* Washington, DC: Government Printing Office.

Petersilia, J. (1989). Implementing randomized experiments: Lessons from BJA's intensive supervision project. *Evaluation Review, 13,* 435-458.

Petersilia, J., & Turner, S. (1990). *Intensive supervision for high-risk probationers* (Publication No. R-3936-NIJ/BJA). Santa Monica, CA: RAND Corporation.

Wish, E., & O'Neil, J. (1989). *Drug use forecasting (DUF) research update.* Washington, DC: U.S. Department of Justice, National Institute of Justice.

PART II

Home Confinement and Electronic Monitoring

3. Home Confinement Programs: Development, Implementation, and Impact

Marc Renzema

In early 1986, only 95 offenders in the United States were participating in electronically monitored home confinement programs (Friel, Vaughn, & del Carmen, 1987, p. 16). By February 1990 the daily census was nearing 12,000 (Renzema & Skelton, 1990b).[1] This chapter describes how this exponential growth occurred, explains the goals of home confinement programs, and discusses the established and potential effects of such programs.

Key Terms

The terminology of electronic monitoring (EM) and home confinement (HC) programs continues to evolve rapidly. A few years ago, *house arrest* was the preferred term for what is now usually called *home confinement*. Both terms mislead the public. Most offenders under HC or house arrest are away from their homes for 50 or more hours per week working, attending treatment programs, performing community service, or doing other specifically authorized tasks. As generally practiced, HC is more similar to intensive supervision programs (ISPs) that impose strict curfews on probationers or parolees than it is to institutional confinement. However, there are differences. In 1987, Joan Petersilia found seven distinctions between ISPs and house arrest. Five years later, some of her distinctions have become clouded, but the following points are still useful in differentiating HC from an ISP:

- "House arrest is nearly always designed to ease prison crowding and serve a prison-bound population."

41

- "House arrest is usually a sentence imposed by a court" and is "virtually never" imposed by probation administrators.
- "In general, house arrest programs are designed to be much more punitive" than are ISPs.
- "Offenders sentenced to house arrest are increasingly being monitored by . . . electronic monitoring devices." (pp. 32-33)

The term *house arrest* has fallen into disuse, possibly because in some quarters it invokes imagery of totalitarian states suppressing political dissent by confining dissidents to their homes for long periods. A data-base search for the term *house arrest* in 1988 found more than five articles on foreign abuses for every article on judicially imposed domestic house arrest programs. The Florida Department of Corrections calls its HC program *community control*, a term that more accurately describes prevailing practice than does either *house arrest* or *home confinement*.

By whatever name, HC antedates EM by at least two millennia and lacks any inherent relation to it (Lilly & Ball, 1987). For example, as of August 1990 Florida's Community Control program had 10,549 offenders on HC, of whom only 873 were on EM (C. Lucas, personal communication, October 23, 1990). Whether used in HC or an ISP, EM currently is only a tool for increasing the accountability of offenders in the community.

Although the numbers of offenders being tracked using EM have been well documented for the last several years, its use does not always mean that an offender is under HC. A few agencies use EM to verify compliance with night-only curfews in ISPs. Other agencies that describe their function as "intensive supervision" employ EM and curfews just as restrictive as those used by self-identified HC programs. Conversely, in EM's absence HC can be monitored through random telephone calls and frequent random face-to-face visits. When dealing with an alleged HC or ISP, one cannot assume that the program name accurately describes its function: Program intent, the offender population served, and actual operations—including the amount of time the offender is restricted to the home—must all be considered. Because the line between "ISPs" and "HC without EM" is so finely—and likely unreliably—drawn, the present chapter focuses only on HC programs that employ EM.

History of Electronic Monitoring

THE HARVARD EXPERIMENTS

Although EM began its exponential growth in the mid-1980s, experiments begun at Harvard University in 1964 anticipated both the advantages and problems of EM. Those early experiments, reported in several articles by Ralph Schwitzgebel and his colleagues, used a two-pound belt-worn transceiver, a network of repeater stations in Cambridge and Boston, Massachusetts, and a central monitoring station (Gable, 1986). The body-worn pulsing transmitter (albeit greatly miniaturized and in a different radio frequency band) is a component of a majority of current monitoring systems; most also use central monitoring stations. A feature of the Harvard equipment that is only now becoming commercially available was its ability to track the offender over a range of several blocks. Most current EM equipment simply reports through telephone lines whether or not an offender is present at a single location.[2]

Some program goals for the Harvard equipment, described as "an electronic rehabilitation system," are very familiar to current EM, while others are largely forgotten. Schwitzgebel held out potential for three goals: reduction of criminal offenses, facilitation of therapy, and humanitarian advantages.

Reduction of criminal offenses was to be accomplished through both specific deterrence and the internalization of controls in ego-defective offenders. This was to be done by coupling the equipment's ability to assure accountability for behavior with a therapeutic relationship with a person (Schwitzgebel, 1969).

The potential for using EM as a tool to induce psychological development has been essentially forgotten in practice. A few jurisdictions gradually wean offenders from EM by switching from continuous monitoring to random phone calls of decreasing frequency. However, conscious use of EM in a therapeutic plan is exceedingly rare, and no programs have been found in which a primary focus is the use of the equipment to maintain a positive, therapeutic relationship 24 hours a day between the offender and a staff person (Schwitzgebel, 1969).

Facilitation of therapy was to be provided through the equipment's ability to provide communication from the central station to the offender through tone signals signifying warnings or praise. Current equipment lacks this capability, although at least two private monitoring services using random calling technology combine computer and human contact in each call.[3] The *humanitarian advantages* Schwitzgebel envisioned sprang from EM's ability to maintain offenders safely in the community without the necessity of subjecting them to the deprivations and degradations of prison.

After several years of experimentation at Harvard, EM was latent for more than a decade, only to resurface with different equipment and changing program goals.

THE GOSSlink

In March 1983, Judge Jack Love placed a probation violator on HC monitored by the "GOSSlink." A year earlier, Love had told Michael Goss, then a computer salesman, of the frustration he experienced in being obliged to commit people to jail and prison who did not really need incarceration but who also could not be managed on probation. The Santa Fe prison riot of 1980, which was caused in part by institutional crowding, crystallized Love's frustration. Goss's device received widespread publicity, but his company was undercapitalized and the equipment was plagued by technical problems that could not be solved immediately; trials ended after five offenders had experienced electronically monitored HC (M. Goss, personal communication, October 27, 1990).

Goss's equipment consisted of a small radio transmitter attached to the offender's ankle by a plastic strap and a field monitoring device (FMD) to detect the transmitter's signals. If the signals did not reach the FMD, it reported the offender's absence by telephone to a computer, which compared the absence report with a preprogrammed curfew schedule. If the absence had not been authorized, the computer printed a notice of suspected violation. This equipment used what is now called the *continuous signaling* (CS) approach to EM. Since then, over a dozen companies have entered the field. Their equipment varies in the frequency bands used, the means of encoding the transmitter's identity, the measures taken to reveal removal of the ankle transmitter or tampering with the field monitoring device, and the extent to which the FMD is programmable. CS equipment became the dominant form of EM and accounted for 54% of the offenders being monitored in February 1989 (Renzema & Skelton, 1990a, sec. 2, p. 11).

Despite Goss's early start, the first product to be used routinely as part of an ongoing program by a court or correctional agency was the CS system developed by Thomas Moody. In December 1983,

Judge Allison DeFoor placed Moody's equipment on a habitual unlicensed driver in Key Largo, Florida (T. Moody, personal communication, November 5, 1990). Judge DeFoor continued to use Moody's equipment on other probationers until electronically monitored home confinement became available in his county through a private service provider—PRIDE, Inc.—in 1985.

Another type of EM was initiated in April 1984 by the Florida Department of Corrections. Now called the *programmed contact* (PC) approach, the initial installation used the Telsol system manufactured by Digital Products Corporation.[4] This system used a telephone robot caller to place random calls to offenders. When an offender answered, he or she was told to say his or her name and to make other verbal responses, which were tape-recorded.

The common core of PC systems is a central station that places random calls to offenders and automatically records whether or not the offender has been identified successfully. The details of the systems vary considerably. Some are nonbiometric: They identify something that the offender *wears*. Others are biometric: They record a *biologically unique feature* of the offender, such as his or her face or voice. The multiple daily phone calls of the PC systems tend to be more intrusive than CS systems, and also have the disadvantage of not offering continuous surveillance. In the few programs that have experimented with both CS and PC systems, a majority of offenders have preferred the CS systems. Although 56% of the offenders monitored in February 1987 were monitored by PC devices, by 1989 the PC market share had declined to 37%, despite the generally lower costs of the PC systems (Renzema & Skelton, 1990a, sec. 2, p. 11). One variant of the PC approach that holds promise for increasing program effectiveness is the over-the-phone alcohol testing equipment sold by Guardian Technologies.

"Hybrid" monitoring equipment, which combines CS and PC technology, appeared in December 1987. In all cases, a wrist or ankle transmitter and a receiver/computer are used. Rather than, or in addition to, telephoning the monitoring center whenever the transmitter's signal is lost, a secondary means of determining the offender's presence is implemented automatically. Depending on which equipment is being used, secondary techniques include analysis of voice samples, transmission of a facial picture over a visual phone, and the insertion of a wrist-worn device into a verifying box. In addition to using the PC feature of hybrid equipment to back up CS failures, many users also require offenders to answer random calls. In February 1989, only a year after their introduction, hybrid systems were in use with 9% of the offenders being monitored. Despite (or perhaps because of) the nuisance of both wearing a transmitter and responding to phone calls, hybrid systems have grown proportionately faster than either CS or PC systems.

Implementation of HC Programs

EVOLUTION OF PROGRAM GOALS

Home confinement began in the United States in 1971 as an alternative to unnecessary, unjust, and costly juvenile detention (Lilly & Ball, 1987). Until the HC population explosion of the mid-1980s, stated program goals usually could be classified as humanitarian, rehabilitative/reintegrative, or cost reducing. For example, HC was offered as a means of avoiding the psychological destructiveness of incarceration, allowing the use of community treatment resources, avoiding the severing of family and community ties, and maintaining adequate control of offenders without the expense of incarceration.

Although these goals are reasonable and laudable, the rapid proliferation of HC from the mid-1980s to the present has been driven primarily by the need to manage jail and prison overcrowding. To make the use of HC as an alternative to incarceration acceptable to legislators and the public at large, many programs have declared punishment to be one of their purposes. Sometimes they do so forthrightly: Florida's Community Control law states that one of its purposes is to "punish criminal offenders" (Palm Beach County Sheriff's Department, 1987, p. 185). In other instances, punitive intent clearly can be inferred from the calling schedules used in PC and hybrid equipment monitoring programs. The preferences of staff members of some programs for large, heavy CS transmitters over smaller, more easily concealed models also are revealing.

In an April 1986 survey of the 10 HC programs using EM then operating, 7 listed "jail overcrowding" as a factor that precipitated the use of EM (Friel et al., 1987). In February 1990, I sent questionnaires to the 435 sites identified by equipment vendors as using EM. Preliminary analysis of the survey showed that the reduction of jail overcrowding was identified as a program goal—usually the primary program goal—by virtually all the 335 respondents. The next most frequent response, saving of money, also relates to crowding. Responses concerning the use of EM to diversify sentencing alternatives were a very distant third in the 1990 program goals question.

TABLE 3.1 Growth of Electronic Home Confinement, 1986–1990

Year	Number of States With Sites	Number of Monitorees in First Third of Each Year
1986	7	95
1987	21	826
1988	32	2,277
1989	37	6,490
1990	47	12,000 (est.)

SOURCES: April 1986 data, Friel et al. (1987, p. 16); February 1987 and February 1988 data, Schmidt (1988, p. 11); February 1989 data, Renzema and Skelton (1990a, sec. 2, p. 4); February 1990 data, author's preliminary estimates.

Thus, although born of practical problems and humane intent, HC has become primarily an emergency response to jail and prison overcrowding.

INCREASE IN HOME CONFINEMENT USE

Small, primarily experimental HC programs were administered throughout the 1970s; explosive growth in HC began in the mid-1980s, with the development of state-operated programs in Oklahoma, Florida, and Michigan. Petersilia (1987) estimates that by 1987 the number of home confinees "on any given day" was between 10,000 and 20,000. Although the number of HC programs that do not use EM remains elusive, the number of EM-based HC programs (or HC+EM programs) has been captured by a series of surveys, the results of which are shown in Table 3.1. By October 1990 all states, Puerto Rico, and the District of Columbia had HC+EM programs.

Impact of Home Confinement Programs

Over the last five years, published studies and internal agency evaluations have concluded that (a) most offenders placed in HC appear to be more similar to incarcerated offenders than to probationers and (b) HC does genuinely divert from incarceration at least half, and sometimes a much higher proportion, of those who receive it.[5] The claim is made that these true diversions lessen the strain on prison populations and government budgets. When HC is used in work-furlough or early-release programs, the case for its impact on crowding is even more compelling.

This apparent success of HC as a humane alternative to crowded prisons rests on at least three assumptions that may be partially false:

(1) that courts would not have restricted institutional populations if HC and other intermediate sanctions had not been available

(2) that without HC, governments would have continued to build cells, no matter how much such building detracted from other services or raised taxes

(3) that HC, especially HC+EM, provides significantly more public protection and punishment than cheaper intensive supervision programs

However, courts have responded to egregious overcrowding with caps on institutional populations, even when the consequences have been early releases from confinement or an inability to confine those deserving of incarceration. Although diverting offenders from incarceration to HC+EM is certainly more publicly palatable than diverting them to lesser sanctions or no sanctions at all, caps are still being enforced even where alternative sanctions are not available.

With respect to savings of construction costs, implementation of HC+EM cannot be proven to have averted institutional construction, even when correctional administrators and planners believe this to have occurred. For example, in 1989 program staff in one large state HC+EM program claimed that the state had avoided the construction of six small prisons through the use of an HC+EM/early-release program. Although they were certainly correct about program capacity, it cannot be proven that the state's legislature or voters would have funded the construction of six additional prisons.

Superiority of HC+EM to ISPs and lesser sanctions in the prevention of arrests and rules violations also is doubtful. Although no experimental research has been found directly comparing impact of the HC+EM with intensive supervision, the limited research on ISPs with and without EM has not demonstrated increased public protection by enhancing ISPs with EM (Erwin, 1990; Petersilia & Turner, 1990). The assumption of enhanced punishment has received research support (Baumer & Mendelsohn, 1990).

Because the doubtful assumptions about HC+EM are widely accepted, HC+EM (and other intermediate sanctions) are likely allowing the criminal justice system to provide more restriction and more punishment to greater numbers of offenders than it could otherwise. Such "net widening," if it can be shown to be occurring, is not necessarily bad social policy: The potential harm to individual offenders might be outweighed by increased system credibility (i.e., general deterrence) and public satisfaction with the quality of justice. Perhaps HC+EM could be superior (or is superior even now in certain places) to ISPs and other alternative sanctions, but there are reasons to doubt whether it is superior as commonly implemented.

PROBLEMS WITH HC+EM

Lack of Adequate Research

Other than the research described later in this chapter, all the published research on the impact on recidivism of HC+EM is uninterpretable because of shoddy or weak research designs. Randomized experiments are needed that compare HC+EM offenders with non-HC+EM offenders on recidivism, substance abuse, employment, and income.

Too Short and Too Superficial

Most HC+EM programs have three primary components: EM, frequent staff-offender contacts, and urine testing for substance abuse. In a random sample of 40 jurisdictions using EM, Renzema and Skelton (1990a) found the mean duration of monitoring to be 79 days; only 8% of the offenders in those jurisdictions were monitored for more than six months. Such short durations hardly seem adequate to help offenders build the habits needed for a noncriminal life-style, even if adjunctive services were made available.

Renzema and Skelton (1990a) found the modal category for reported office contacts between staff and offender to be four to eight per month, and the modal category for field contacts to be the same. Unfortunately, no information is available on the nature of contacts. Site visits suggest that most contacts may be surveillance oriented and perfunctory (Renzema & Skelton, 1990a). Substance abuse testing was an integral feature of most EM programs, with 63% of the programs routinely testing at least 50% of their offenders and another 15% testing between 10% and 50% of their offenders.

Failure to Modulate Sanctions for Rule Violations
or to Reward Progress

Schwitzgebel envisioned a system in which monitoring could be used to guide behavior: Positive behavior could be immediately reinforced, and deviant behavior could be averted or immediately sanctioned. In their 1989 survey, Renzema and Skelton (1990a) found that 10% of the reporting programs routinely incarcerated program rules violators. The most common violations involved positive substance abuse tests or breaking of curfew. Although useful for the maintenance of program credibility, such a policy ignores the realities of substance abuse. Only 43% reported using temporary detention, a technique potentially able to inhibit violations by removing their positively reinforcing consequences (Schwitzgebel, 1971).

Although curfews were tightened frequently to sanction violations (Renzema & Skelton, 1990a), it is rare for HC+EM programs to manipulate curfews systematically or frequently to reinforce positive behaviors. Combs (1990), a Michigan probation agent, has offered examples of his use of curfew changes as both rewards and sanctions. He extended curfews for catching up on restitution payments, reduced "social time" for positive drug tests, and extended curfews for special occasions to reward "significant positive behavior."

Whether EM changes offender behavior is not known. However, some definite changes are occurring in agencies' use of EM.

TOUGHENING OF THE CLIENTELE

In 1987, 6% of EM clients had committed violent offenses; in 1989, 12% had done so (Renzema & Skelton, 1990a; Schmidt, 1988). In 1987, 14% were drug offenders; in 1989, 22% were. Property offenders, mainly burglars, constituted 18% in 1987 but increased to 32% in 1989. Major traffic offenders, primarily those convicted of driving under the influence, declined from 33% in 1987 to 19% in 1989.

Part of the changes in offense distribution is caused by a disproportionate growth in HC+EM programs in agencies managing more serious offenders than typical probationers. In 1987, three of four EM clients were probationers; in 1989, only one in four was. By 1989 more than half of all EM clients were inmates serving time in HC, community confinees placed on HC directly by the courts, or parolees. Another area of growth was that of pretrial detention, which constituted a negligible proportion of offenders in 1987; by 1989, the proportion had climbed to 9%.

OTHER IMPACT ISSUES

Contrary to early expectations, use of EM has generally increased staff sizes when agencies have adopted it; these increases are often substantial.[6] Two-thirds of using agencies impose fees on offenders; when fees are imposed, they average $200 per month, which is often sufficient to cover the cost of monitoring, but not the total cost of supervision. Sliding scales are ordinarily used to avoid discrimination against impoverished offenders.

The legal challenges to the constitutionality of EM that were expected in its early days have not happened and now appear unlikely. The recurrent appellate court issues involving EM and HC have so far been whether HC should count as jail time and whether absconders can be convicted of escape (Renzema & Skelton, 1990a).

The Future of Home Confinement

The boom in HC has been driven by prison overcrowding. Regardless of research results, this boom seems destined to continue for at least several more years. Although the historic trend in prison population is upward, the present rate of incarceration is at an all-time high. However, changing demographics, economics, and cyclical changes in political climate are likely to result eventually in empty cells. What will and should then happen to HC under these circumstances?

Three conflicting scenarios are plausible: (a) HC will wither away because it was implemented to solve a problem that has abated. Favoring this is the position that EM equipment lasts only a few years, not the centuries that prisons endure. However, EM vendors and HC program employees will fight to save their jobs by redefining their missions. (b) HC will be implemented as a rehabilitative and reintegrative tool as envisioned in its early days by Schwitzgebel and others; it will be used both instead of and after incarceration. If this is to happen, serious evaluation and program development need to be done, beginning now. Perhaps HC+EM can become such a powerful tool that the era of the penitentiary can finally be brought to an end. (c) The civil libertarian's nightmares could come true: As prison space becomes available for more serious offenders, HC will be used ever more intrusively on decreasingly serious offenders. To prevent this from happening, groundwork should be laid now, through laws regulating the application of HC and EM as well as through aggressive litigation of any suspected abuses.

Notes

1. According to Jyoti Aggarawala, an analyst with Ladenburg, Thalman & Co., Inc., one monitoring equipment vendor estimates that by October 1990 the daily census of electronically monitored home confinees had reached nearly 20,000, and that a total of 28,000 monitoring units had been produced since 1984.

2. This limitation may be circumvented through use of cellular phone-based systems, through "drive-by" receivers, and through voice verification systems programmed to call two or more different telephone numbers; however, such systems are still very rare. The earliest commercial availability for real-time wide-area offender tracking systems is likely to be 1993. Whether such products would be attractive to correctional agencies is uncertain.

3. The Home Incarceration Program and ISEM companies, which operate in Kentucky and Cook County, Illinois, respectively, use equipment through which a human operator calls the offender and instructs him or her to insert a plug into a wrist-worn device to verify his or her identity. Program operators report that useful interactions occur, including the prevention of at least one suicide. PMI/McLaughlin, which operates services in Texas and Illinois, uses a variety of monitoring techniques, including a visual phone system. In that system a computer dials the calls, and when the offender answers, he or she is greeted by an operator who asks him or her to transmit a still picture, which is then compared with a file photograph. This system operator also reports averting a suicide.

4. Digital Products Corporation formed a subsidiary, Hitek Community Control Corporation, which enhanced the robot calling concept with a watchlike wristlet and a Verifier attachment to the offender's telephone. The enhanced equipment, named the ON GUARD system, required the offender to place the wristlet into the Verifier for electronic identity verification as well as merely giving a voice sample.

5. Claims of successful diversion of incarceration-bound offenders into HC+EM and other intermediate sanctions often are based on naive assumptions or primitive methodology. An example of an internal agency study that used conservative assumptions was one conducted by the Florida Department of Corrections (1987). A National Institute of Justice-sponsored study of Florida's Community Control program (Baird & Wagner, 1990), one of the most rigorous studies done to date, indicates that more than 50% of offenders participating in that program were bona fide diversions from incarceration.

6. An extended discussion of the issues mentioned in this section is contained in Renzema and Skelton (1990a).

References

Baird, S. C., & Wagner, D. (1990). Measuring diversion: The Florida Community Control Program. *Crime and Delinquency, 36,* 112-125.

Baumer, T. L., & Mendelsohn, R. I. (1990). *The electronic monitoring of nonviolent convicted felons: An experiment in home detention, final report* (Final report from NIJ Grant No. 86-IJ-CX-0041). Indianapolis: Indiana University, School of Public and Environmental Affairs.

Combs, T. (1990, October). *Tethering: Does it work?* Panel at the meeting of the Michigan Corrections Association, Grand Rapids.

Erwin, B. (1990). Old and new tools for the modern probation officer. *Crime and Delinquency, 36,* 61-74.

Florida Department of Corrections. (1987). *Community control "house arrest": A three year longitudinal report, 1983-1986.* Tallahassee: Florida Department of Corrections, Probation and Parole Services.

Friel, C. M., Vaughn, J. B., & del Carmen, R. (1987). *Electronic monitoring and correctional policy: The technology and its application.* Washington, DC: National Institute of Justice.

Gable, R. K. (1986). Application of personal telemonitoring to current problems in corrections. *Journal of Criminal Justice, 14,* 167-176.

Lilly, J. R., & Ball, R. A. (1987). A brief history of house arrest and electronic monitoring. *Northern Kentucky Law Review, 13,* 343-374.

Palm Beach County Sheriff's Department. (1987). Palm Beach County's in-house arrest work release program. In B. R. McCarthy (Ed.), *Intermediate punishments: Intensive supervision, home confinement, and electronic surveillance* (pp. 181-187). Monsey, NY: Criminal Justice Press.

Petersilia, J. (1987). *Expanding options for criminal sentencing* (Publication No. R-3544-EMC). Santa Monica, CA: RAND Corporation.

Petersilia, J., & Turner, S. (1990). Comparing intensive and regular supervision for high-risk probationers: Early results from an experiment in California. *Crime and Delinquency, 36,* 87-111.

Renzema, M., & Skelton, D. T. (1990a). *Final report: The use of electronic monitoring by criminal justice agencies, 1989: A description of extent, offender characteristics, program types, programmatic issues, and legal aspects* (Submitted to the National Institute of Justice under contract OJP-89-M-309). Kutztown, PA: Kutztown University Foundation.

Renzema, M., & Skelton, D. T. (1990b). Trends in the use of electronic monitoring: 1989. *Journal of Offender Monitoring, 3*(3), 12, 14-19.

Schmidt, A. K. (1988). *The use of electronic monitoring by criminal justice agencies, 1988.* Unpublished discussion paper, National Institute of Justice.

Schwitzgebel, R. K. (1969). Issues in the use of an electronic rehabilitation system with chronic recidivists. *Law and Society Review, 7,* 597-611.

Schwitzgebel, R. K. (1971). *Development and legal regulation of coercive behavior modification techniques with offenders* (Public Health Service Publication No. 2067). Washington, DC: Government Printing Office.

4. Electronically Monitored Home Confinement: Does It Work?

Terry L. Baumer

Robert I. Mendelsohn

For all practical purposes, electronic monitoring equipment first became commercially available early in 1985. Since that time, the number of programs, the number of offenders being monitored, and the variety of target populations have expanded rapidly and continuously (Renzema & Skelton, 1990; Schmidt, 1989). As Marc Renzema indicates in Chapter 3 of this volume, by February 1990, five years after the initial introduction, more than 12,000 individuals were being monitored by programs in every state in the union. Included in this count were programs that targeted offenders at virtually every level of the criminal and juvenile justice process (see Renzema & Skelton, 1990).

The reasons for the rapid adoption of this technology are largely unrelated to knowledge about the operation or impact of electronic monitoring. Pressure to "do something" about prison and jail overcrowding, aggressive marketing by vendors (Maxfield & Baumer, 1990), beliefs about technical infallibility (Blomberg, Waldo, & Burcroff, 1987), and a host of "technofallacies" (Corbett & Marx, 1991) all have contributed to the growth of these programs. Tonry (1990) has suggested that several latent functions, which probably apply to electronic monitoring programs, partially account for the similar popularity of

AUTHORS' NOTE: Preparation of this chapter was supported in part by Grant Number 88-IJ-CX-0052, and many of the cited data were collected with support from Grant Number 86-IJ-CX-0041, from the National Institute of Justice, U.S. Department of Justice. Points of view are those of the authors and do not necessarily represent the position of the U.S. Department of Justice.

intensive supervision. Electronically monitored home confinement promises to solve difficult problems; it is, in concept, politically palatable; and it breathes new life into beleaguered correctional professionals.

During this relatively short period, a body of literature about electronically monitored home confinement has developed. The early literature was, of necessity, descriptive, speculative, and focused on legal or ethical issues (Berry, 1985; del Carmen & Vaughn, 1986; Schmidt & Curtis, 1987). However, much of the more recent work in this area has been empirical. This chapter presents a review of the research on electronic monitoring conducted to date.

The Equipment

THE BASIC SYSTEMS

The two basic electronic monitoring technologies on the market are commonly referred to as radio frequency (RF) and programmed contact (PC) systems. Within these two basic approaches there are a variety of systems. For example, various programmed contact systems utilize the well-known wristlet, as well as audio and video technologies. In addition, there are now hybrid systems on the market that combine RF and PC technologies in an attempt to overcome some of the real or perceived disadvantages of either approach.

In RF systems a transmitter with a limited range is strapped to the offender, frequently on the leg. A receiver/dialer is then connected to the telephone system. This receiver/dialer periodically dials the central computer and reports the pattern of radio signals it has received. The central computer then matches these reports with a previously entered schedule and issues a status report. Technologically, RF systems may soon be capable of tracking an offender's movements regardless of location, much as biologists now track bears in the woods. The underlying principle of the system is to provide direct, real-time data about the offender's movements. Theoretically, this approach is often thought to be the most secure of the two (Petersilia, 1987). The relatively constant flow of information about offenders is designed to inform program officials immediately of unauthorized absences. From the offender's perspective, this same flow of information is supposed to deter unauthorized absences. The offender is not required to take an active part in providing the information. Indeed, in this system, action by the offender is thought of as negative—that is, as tampering with the equipment—and, where feasible, is to be guarded against with appropriate measures.

Programmed contact systems monitor the presence of the offender through the use of random telephone contacts—much like a manual system. For all systems of this type a central computer, using previously entered schedules, directs a dialing system to contact the offender's place of residence. When the telephone is answered, the equipment directs the offender to perform specific tasks. These tasks vary by system, but all are intended to obtain positive verification that the offender is present. The underlying principle in this approach is that the unpredictability of random contacts, combined with the threat of sanctions for violations, will control offender behavior and detect all but the shortest absences. PC systems are technically the simpler and less expensive of the two types of systems. This technology raises interesting questions about how much is gained or lost in conditioning the offender or in security by increasing or decreasing the number of contacts over a given period of time.

Both technologies are computer controlled and are intended to be less labor-intensive than manual monitoring systems. They also appear to be based on the assumption that the less conspicuous any equipment worn by the offender, the better. Not all systems using the programmed contact technology require the offender to wear equipment, which, under some circumstances, may have administrative or policy benefits (e.g., less cost involved in replacing lost equipment).

EQUIPMENT PERFORMANCE

Virtually all studies of electronic monitoring report technical problems with the equipment. Although early studies tended to attribute these problems to a young industry struggling to resolve unanticipated problems (Friel, Vaughn, & del Carmen, 1987), a recent national survey of program directors found that technical difficulties were still ranked as the most frequently mentioned problem (Renzema & Skelton, 1990). Equipment quality and reliability problems with both host computers and field units in offenders' homes have often been noted (Hatchett, 1987; Jolin, 1987; Kenosha County, 1990; Lilly, Ball, & Wright, 1987). While the failure rate of a host computer, as well as of individual units, may be controlled somewhat in the production process, hardware failures are inevitable in any computer-based system, and must be anticipated. Other authors have noted problems created by an unreliable power supply (Wahl, 1990) and, more frequently, incompatible or antiquated telephone systems (Hatchett, 1987; Jolin, 1987). Another recurrent hardware problem concerns the sensitivity of a tamper alarm added as an enhancement to some systems (Kenosha County, 1990).

Some technical problems are characteristic of radio frequency systems. Because the home unit searches for a signal from the transmitter attached to the offender, interference with this signal affects the reliability of messages generated by the host computer (Jolin, 1987; Kenosha County, 1990; Schmidt & Curtis, 1987). Any number of things have been known to cause this interference: sleep patterns, housing construction, cast-iron bathtubs, FM radio stations, and terrain. Although not discussed in the literature, one agency claimed to have discovered several relatively simple ways to compromise the security of their radio frequency system, prompting them to void their contract. While these systems are often thought to offer a higher level of security than the programmed contact systems, it is clear that there are technical problems. Indeed, the signal interference problem (in part) has prompted development of hybrid systems that switch to a programmed contact mode when the radio frequency system notes a possible violation.

The programmed contact systems also have demonstrated technical problems. At the present time there are three principal types of PC systems: the original wristlet device, voice verification, and visual verification. While each operates in a slightly different way, there are two very important problems connected with all currently distributed PC systems. First, because verification of compliance requires a telephone contact, a busy telephone line can effectively prevent the system from accomplishing its task. While most programs require offenders to agree to limit the number and length of telephone calls, this technical characteristic creates an opportunity for offenders to defeat the system, at least for short periods of time (Baumer & Mendelsohn, 1990). Second, in order to verify the offender's presence, a PC system must (a) successfully reach the correct telephone number, (b) obtain an appropriate response from the offender, and (c) correctly identify the response as coming from the offender. An error or failure at any of these three steps results in an unsuccessful attempted contact.

In addition to technical performance of electronic monitoring systems, there is also a conceptual issue related to the ability of the equipment to detect violations. In monitoring compliance with a home confinement order, it is helpful to distinguish between actual offender behavior (at home or absent) and electronic reports *about* offender behavior (at home or absent). If these two dimensions are crossed, two types of error can be identified: false negatives, in which the equipment reports the offender absent when he or she is actually at home; and false positives, in which the equipment reports that the offender is at home when he or she is actually gone. Because of the known technical problems and the programmatic necessity of responding to potential violations, most programs are aware of the possibility of false negatives and routinely attempt to follow offense reports with telephone calls or field visits. False positive reports, although seldom acknowledged or investigated, represent a potentially more serious problem for electronically monitored home confinement programs: They compromise program integrity, potentially threaten public safety, and offer alibis for offenders. The primary guard against this type of error is the periodic telephone or personal contact built into many electronic monitoring programs. It is clear that both types of error occur, and that false negatives are relatively common (Baumer & Mendelsohn, 1990). There is, as yet, little information about the relative frequency of false positives.

Viewed in its simplest form, electronic monitoring equipment automates manual verification. In this sense it appears to have clear advantages over manual methods of monitoring. In earlier work, we noted that the electronic equipment "provided considerably more intensive and consistent levels of attempted contacts" (Baumer & Mendelsohn, 1990, p. 37) than did a manual system of checks. Because manual monitoring methods are almost entirely personnel dependent, the level and quality of monitoring are affected by illness, turnover, and competence. If nothing else, electronic monitoring equipment is more persistent and consistent, and at least as reliable as underpaid, undertrained, and overworked employees.

Organizational Requirements

As with all computer-based technologies, the effective operation of electronic monitoring equipment requires training and expertise. At the most basic level, program personnel must possess, or obtain, the technical expertise required to operate and maintain what is essentially a microcomputer system with specialized peripheral equipment. This involves a basic knowledge of such systems that includes how to perform basic maintenance (e.g., routine backup of files) and an ability to make routine repairs (e.g., how to reboot after a power failure). In addition, someone must be on staff who understands the operation of the software in order to enter and remove clients, enter schedule modifications, and produce summaries of the electronic contact records. While these may seem like simple requirements, many criminal justice agencies have extremely limited experience with computer equipment. We have referred to the steep learning curve experienced by one agency as "technoshock" (Baumer & Mendelsohn, 1990). While this agency quickly mastered the most basic program operations (entering and removing clients), more refined maintenance and operational skills were slow to develop. It is likely that in small agencies the necessary expertise will be dependent on specific individuals, and program quality will vary with the turnover in personnel. In addition, the organizational learning curve will vary greatly depending upon prior computerization of the agency. Some agencies will attempt to acquire this expertise by contracting with one of the many available monitoring services.

While electronic monitoring equipment automates the basic monitoring process, it also creates a considerable amount of work. In addition to system maintenance and operation, program personnel must train and orient clients, in some cases connect equipment, update offender schedules, keep track of excused absences, review and interpret messages generated by the equipment, follow up suspected violations (both via telephone and in person), conduct independent field checks of the offenders and the equipment, and attend and/or conduct violation hearings. When the system is out of order for more than a brief period, offenders must be contacted manually. All of these tasks consume time and effectively limit caseload.

When compared with manual methods of monitoring offenders, electronic systems greatly extend the eyes and ears of the agency, producing information 24 hours per day, seven days per week. As a result, substantially more information must be reviewed and processed. Studies of electronic contact records have indicated that a substantial proportion of all messages are suggestive of possible violations and require some action by program personnel (Jolin, 1987; Baumer, Maxfield, & Mendelsohn, 1990). This constant flow of information implies that the agency should be prepared to respond to the data produced by its electronic monitoring system. Renzema and Skelton (1990) found that 63.1% of the responding programs reported provisions for around-the-clock response. The remainder operated within limited business hours.

The effective implementation of an electronic monitoring system involves considerably more than plugging it in, turning it on, and going home. For an agency to institute home confinement with electronic monitoring requires special skills and considerable organization, and is more labor-intensive than one might think. Even the best electronic equipment can be neutralized by ineffective or, worse, incompetent operation. We noted above that electronic monitoring automates the monitoring process, and in doing so provides more intensive and consistent monitoring than do manual methods. But, as Corbett and Marx (1991) have pointed out, there is no free lunch. In providing more intensive monitoring, the automated process produces its own configuration of tasks and duties, which may be more time-consuming and costly than manual methods of monitoring (Baumer & Mendelsohn, 1990, pp. 46-47).

Offender Reactions and Performance

REACTIONS

Offender reactions, based on exit interviews, clearly identify home confinement as an intermediate sanction (Baumer & Mendelsohn, 1990). When interviewed on exit from the program, offenders reported time on electronic monitoring to be moderately difficult and somewhat punitive, but, as they commonly put it, "better than jail." More specifically, when offenders were asked if staying home was easy or hard, less than half (46.2%) said it was very easy or easy. They were also asked to rate time on home confinement on a 10-point scale (1 = easy time, 10 = hard time); the mean rating for electronic monitoring was 5.63, or slightly in the direction of hard. However, in none of these cases were the responses significantly different for manually monitored offenders (Baumer & Mendelsohn, 1990). That is, electronic monitoring did not affect the offenders' assessment of the sanction.

There is some indication from qualitative reports that the reactions to home confinement may vary over the term of the sentence. Rather than growing increasingly difficult, there is some evidence that the most difficult times for offenders on home confinement are at the beginning and near the end of their sentences (Baumer & Mendelsohn, 1990). The offenders we interviewed tended to report that home confinement required changes in their lives, but, after a period of initial adjustment, the time at home was relatively easy to fill with television or other habitual domestic recreations. Then a period of boredom tended to appear, followed by a search for and development of new activity patterns (e.g., undertaking a long-delayed kitchen remodeling project). For some offenders the anticipation of release made "doing time" more difficult. Again, no particular difficulties were observed for the electronically monitored offenders (Baumer & Mendelsohn, 1990).

One of the few areas of documented differences resulting from electronic monitoring concerns the reactions of family members and cohabitants. We asked offenders if the people they lived with ever got upset or complained about home confinement, or any part of it. More than three-quarters (78.0%) of those on electronic monitoring responded yes to this question. This was significantly higher than the 49.1% of the manually monitored individuals who responded affirmatively. Many reported specific complaints about late or persistent calls, while others commented on the generally restrictive character of home confinement. Not being able to go out means that a housemate must take over a variety of common duties, such as going to the laundromat, getting the car repaired, and buying groceries. On a related topic, significantly fewer electronically monitored offenders reported that their family members or cohabitants thought that home confinement was a "good idea," or that they would recommend the sanction to an offender in their situation (Baumer & Mendelsohn, 1990). These data suggest that electronic monitoring may be significantly more demanding and stressful for family members than manual monitoring methods.

PERFORMANCE

The purpose of electronic monitoring equipment is to monitor compliance with a court-imposed home confinement order. Combined with the threat of sanctions for failure to comply with the home confinement order, most programs also assume that electronic monitoring equipment increases the probability that offenders will actually stay at home. There are two primary ways to measure compliance with a home confinement order: program records and self-reports. Each measure provides a different view of compliance.

Studies of programmed contact systems have found that the number of successful contacts ranges between one-half and two-thirds of all calls made by the electronic system (Baumer & Mendelsohn, 1990; Jolin, 1987; Maxfield & Baumer, 1990). One study of a radio frequency system found that around 28% of all messages received were "violation" notations (Jolin, 1987). When viewed at the individual level, very few offenders finish their sentences with more than 90% successful contacts (Maxfield & Baumer, 1990). In our study cited above, we found that 41.2% of the home confinement population were cited at least once for program violations (Baumer & Mendelsohn, 1990). While these figures are suggestive of unauthorized absences, it must be remembered that electronic contacts are a joint product of offender behavior, the electronic equipment, and the operation of the equipment (as well as of agency policies). However, at least from the "official record" it appears that unauthorized absences are not uncommon.

To date, our above-cited study is the only study that has employed self-reports of offender behavior while on home confinement (Baumer & Mendelsohn, 1990). In this study, we asked offenders, after program termination, "Did you ever go out when you weren't supposed to?" Of the 78 electronically monitored offenders, 40% responded that they had gone out at least once without authorization; 47% of the manually monitored offenders admitted such absences, but this difference was not statistically significant. Additional probes of these responses indicated that most of the admitted absences were for short household errands.

In a separate analysis, Baumer et al. (1990) have noted that the electronic records and official citations for violations were both significantly correlated with self-reports of absences. This partial triangulation further supports a conclusion that home confinement is something short of total. Given the life-styles, as well as the personal needs and obligations, of offenders, absences are to be expected in electronically monitored home confinement programs.

While technical compliance with the home confinement order is a concern, the implications of new arrests while being monitored are even more problematic for home confinement programs. Many programs attempt to sidestep this type of problem by accepting only offenders with minor criminal histories who have been convicted of or charged with nonviolent offenses (Petersilia, 1987; Renzema & Skelton, 1990). In recognition that criminal offenses can occur at home, there are often prohibitions against individuals charged with or convicted of "domestic crimes" such as incest, child abuse, and domestic violence. However, offenses do occur while offenders are in technical compliance with the home confinement order, and sometimes they are serious (see Gougis, 1990). Overall, the literature suggests that a new arrest while on home confinement is relatively uncommon. Renzema and Skelton (1990) report overall arrests at 3.7%; our study found that 3.3% of the offenders logged new arrests (Baumer & Mendelsohn, 1990). In a review of several programs, Petersilia (1987) reported in-program arrest rates for most programs around 5%, with one program reporting 16% arrested while being monitored.

One of the most intriguing aspects of electronically monitored home confinement programs is their virtually unexplored rehabilitative potential. For a variety of reasons, most electronically monitored home confinement programs emphasize punishment and incapacitation as the primary operational goals. Rehabilitation appears to be viewed as an afterthought, or possibly a nice side effect of the programs, but never an explicit goal. When reasonably well executed, a home confinement program externally encourages a change in the offender's life-style for the term of the sentence. For instance, a substantial number of the offenders we interviewed reported that home confinement allowed them to "dry out," review their lives, and get to know their families again (Baumer & Mendelsohn, 1990). Others obtained jobs, second jobs, or reported better job attendance and performance. Many of the offenders reported that their spouses were particularly attracted to home confinement because they knew the offenders would come home after work.

It appears that home confinement can help stabilize an offender's life-style, but the question of whether electronic monitoring can significantly enhance this possibility, either during the program or after release, remains open. In our study none of the above observations differed between the electronically monitored and manually monitored offenders (Baumer & Mendelsohn, 1990). Our finding that electronic monitoring is more intense and consistent than manual methods, and is perceived as such, suggests that electronic monitoring might contribute to positive change. The potential for rehabilitation rests in the ability to design and use electronic monitoring programs to encourage a noncriminal life-style, and to facilitate internalization of these changes by the offenders. Such a design would include the refined use of electronic monitoring equipment as well the extensive use of other program elements such as substance abuse treatment, drug/alcohol testing, graduated release, and extended, intensive aftercare.

POPULATION DIFFERENCES

The available evidence does suggest that there may be significant differences among populations in program performance. For example, we found that offenders charged with felony driving while intoxicated (DWI) performed significantly better in home confinement than offenders charged with other offenses (Baumer & Mendelsohn, 1990). In addition, the felony DWI offenders were significantly less likely to have any negative contacts with the criminal justice system within a year of release from the program. It is our belief that the DWI offenders were less committed to a criminal life-style, eager to avoid prison terms, and fairly low-rate offenders. In addition, home confinement, combined with a prohibition on alcohol consumption, helped control the behavior that produced their arrests.

There is also mounting evidence that there may be significant differences between pretrial and postconviction populations. Renzema and Skelton (1990) report that "programs dealing with the unconvicted did look particularly bleak" (sec. 3, p. 11). Baumer et al. (1990) found that pretrial clients were significantly more likely to abscond than were postconviction offenders. These differences were attributed to the perceived consequences of successfully completing the time on home confinement. In general, successful termination means more freedom for postconviction offenders, and therefore serves as an incentive to follow program rules. However, for a significant proportion of the pretrial population, successful completion of home confinement promises only a return to jail or prison. Faced with the alternative of incarceration, more pretrial offenders fail to complete their assigned time on home confinement.

It is important to note that the above are differences observed among populations, not differences produced by electronic monitoring. The DWI offenders performed better than the other offenders regardless of the method of monitoring (Baumer & Mendelsohn, 1990), and the electronically monitored pretrial clients were more likely to abscond than were the electronically monitored convicted offenders (Baumer et al., 1990). Given a decision to implement an electronic monitoring program, these findings suggest that the definition of the target population may be as important as program design and delivery. Many of the program characteristics will be reflective of the target population.

Summary Observations

In an area that is so new and developing so rapidly, conclusions would be premature. At this point we simply do not know much about electronically monitored home confinement, although agencies have accumulated several years of experience and some empirical studies have been completed. However, it appears that some general observations can be offered at this point.

The existing literature suggests that the incapacitative and public safety potential of this sanction have probably been considerably overstated. Home confinement, however monitored, is neither an electronic jail (Berry, 1985) nor home incarceration (Lilly et al., 1987). In the broadest sense, electronic monitoring provides technological assistance in monitoring compliance with a court-imposed order for the offender to stay at home during certain hours. At best, the electronic equipment can only identify the presence or absence of an offender and match this information with a schedule entered by program personnel. The incapacitation provided by home confinement programs is, thus, strictly voluntary, bolstered only by the threat of detection and sanctions for violations. This suggests that the primary target population for home confinement will continue to be "low-risk" offenders who are not thought to be a threat to public safety. In this sense, home confinement may be an acceptable sentencing alternative, but its application as an alternative to secure custody appears to be limited.

Similarly, in the rush to satisfy demands for punitive alternatives to incarceration, the rehabilitative potential of home confinement may have been seriously underestimated. Although the restrictive conditions create fairly high rates of technical violations, most studies have reported very low levels of arrest. Though some programs claim to accept only employed offenders, there is evidence that home confinement actually encourages offenders to work. In addition, the sanction appears to stabilize and structure the lives of many offenders while they are being supervised. The challenge is for programs to translate these temporary behavioral changes into more enduring personal habits.

To date, technical and operational problems have hindered the performance of electronic monitoring equipment in home confinement programs. Some of the technical problems are a result of poor quality control and/or overworked equipment, while others are inherent in the various types of equipment. The operational problems are related to the absence of technical expertise within criminal justice agencies as well as to failure to anticipate the extent and nature of the work generated by electronic monitoring equipment. It is likely that, as the industry matures, many of the current technical problems will be reduced significantly. Similarly, specific agencies will develop operational methods that they find acceptable. Because even the best equipment can be neutralized by incompetent operation, solution of operational problems is at least as critical as the elimination of technical flaws.

With the data currently available, there are few differences that can be attributed to electronic monitoring. Early evaluations demonstrated that electronic monitoring equipment can provide more intense and consistent monitoring than manual methods. However, as noted above, the quality of the information is highly dependent upon a variety of factors. Unfortunately, there is scant evidence that these differences have translated into better offender performance. There is some indication that electronic monitoring may be viewed more negatively by offenders and their families, but whether this is positive or negative is a matter of opinion. Some will interpret this as a measure of the intrusiveness of electronic monitoring; however, it is equally plausible to suggest that this is a measure of the extent to which electronic monitoring demands involvement from the offender and the family in the rehabilitative process.

In this age of electronics it is not surprising that some have hoped electronic monitoring would be a technological magic bullet, solving difficult problems with little effort or cost. To those who have seen other new and promising innovations, it comes as no surprise that there is no magic bullet. With only six years' experience with these systems, we know very little about either home confinement or electronic monitoring; there is still much to learn. The evidence to date indicates that home confinement may be a viable intermediate sanction, and electronically monitoring compliance with home confinement orders appears to work at least as well as manual methods of monitoring. It is important for the immediate future that correctional officials moderate their claims and expectations for electronically monitored home confinement—the American public deals a cruel fate to programs that disappoint. It is also important for experimentation to continue with various program delivery configurations, alternative goals, and identification of appropriate target populations.

References

Baumer, T. L., Maxfield, M. G., & Mendelsohn, R. I. (1990). *A comparative analysis of three electronically monitored home detention programs.* Paper presented at the annual meeting of the American Society of Criminology, Baltimore.

Baumer, T. L., & Mendelsohn, R. I. (1990). *The electronic monitoring of nonviolent convicted felons: An experiment in home detention, final report* (Final report from NIJ Grant No. 86-IJ-CX-0041). Indianapolis: Indiana University, School of Public and Environmental Affairs.

Berry, B. (1985). Electronic jails: A new criminal justice concern. *Justice Quarterly, 2,* 1-22.

Blomberg, T. G., Waldo, G. P., & Burcroff, L. C. (1987). Home confinement and electronic surveillance. In B. R. McCarthy (Ed.), *Intermediate punishments: Inten-*

sive supervision, home confinement, and electronic surveillance (pp. 169-179). Monsey, NY: Criminal Justice Press.

Corbett, R. P., Jr., & Marx, G. T. (1991). No soul in the new machines: Technofallacies in the electronic monitoring movement. *Justice Quarterly, 8,* 399-414.

del Carmen, R. V., & Vaughn, J. (1986, June). Legal issues in the use of electronic surveillance in probation. *Federal Probation,* pp. 60-69.

Friel, C. M., Vaughn, J. B., & del Carmen, R. (1987). *Electronic monitoring and correctional policy: The technology and its application.* Washington, DC: National Institute of Justice.

Gougis, M. (1990, December 1). House arrest didn't prevent killing and robbery. *Indianapolis Star,* p. 1.

Hatchett, P. (1987). *The Home Confinement Program: An appraisal of the electronic monitoring of offenders in Washtenaw County, Michigan.* Lansing: Michigan Department of Corrections, Program Bureau, Research Division, Community Programs Evaluation Unit.

Jolin, A. (1987). *Electronic Surveillance Program: Clackamas County Community Corrections Oregon evaluation.* Oregon City: Clackamas County.

Kenosha County, Wisconsin. (1990). Monitoring juvenile offenders: The Kenosha County Wisconsin experience. *Journal of Offender Monitoring, 3*(3), 1, 3-4, 6-7, 11.

Lilly, J. R., Ball, R. A., & Wright, J. (1987). Home incarceration with electronic monitoring in Kenton County, Kentucky: An evaluation. In B. R. McCarthy (Ed.), *Intermediate punishments: Intensive supervision, home confinement, and electronic surveillance* (pp. 189-203). Monsey, NY: Criminal Justice Press.

Maxfield, M., & Baumer, T. (1990). Home detention with electronic monitoring: Comparing pretrial and postconviction programs. *Crime and Delinquency, 36,* 521-536.

Petersilia, J. (1987). *Expanding options for criminal sentencing* (Publication No. R-3544-EMC). Santa Monica, CA: RAND Corporation.

Renzema, M., & Skelton, D. T. (1990). *Final report: The use of electronic monitoring by criminal justice agencies 1989: A description of extent, offender characteristics, program types, programmatic issues, and legal aspects* (Submitted to the National Institute of Justice under contract OJP-89-M-309). Kutztown, PA: Kutztown University Foundation.

Schmidt, A. K. (1989). Electronic monitoring of offenders increases. *NIJ Reports, 212,* 2-5.

Schmidt, A. K., & Curtis, C. (1987). Electronic monitors. In B. R. McCarthy (Ed.), *Intermediate punishments: Intensive supervision, home confinement, and electronic surveillance* (pp. 137-152). Monsey, NY: Criminal Justice Press.

Tonry, M. (1990). Stated and latent functions of ISP. *Crime and Delinquency, 36,* 174-191.

Wahl, R. H. (1990). Electronic monitoring decisions in Utah. *Journal of Offender Monitoring, 3*(4), 12-16, 18.

5. Electronic Monitoring of Drug Offenders in California

Ronald K. Watts

Daniel Glaser

Background

The last five years in the United States have witnessed rapid growth in the use of home confinement with electronic monitoring for the supervision of many types of offenders. This growth reflects the wider developing interest within the corrections and academic communities in use of "intermediate sanctions" as punishments midway between minimal justice system responses (such as restitution, fines, and community service with routine probation) and maximum system responses (such as jail or prison). This chapter focuses specifically on one type of intensive probation supervision, house arrest with electronic monitoring (HAEM), a rapidly growing alternative sanction developed principally as a means of relieving jail and prison overcrowding while presumably maintaining public safety.

The growth of HAEM in the state of California has paralleled its growth in the nation. In a National Institute of Justice (NIJ) survey, three states showed a monitored population on February 12, 1989 (designated as an electronic monitoring "census" day), of more than 500 individuals, as represented in Table 5.1. Of the three, California

AUTHORS' NOTE: Research reported in this chapter was supported under Award Number 90-IJ-CX-0005 from the National Institute of Justice, Office of Justice Programs, U.S. Department of Justice. Points of view in this document are those of the authors and do not necessarily represent the official position of the U.S. Department of Justice or the County of Los Angeles Probation Department.

TABLE 5.1 Use of Electronic Monitoring, 1989, for Those States With Most Use, and Total for All States

State	1989 Cases Monitored	1989 Percentage of State to Total
California	612	9.4
Florida	1,070	16.5
Michigan	1,138	17.5
Total (all states)	6,490	100

SOURCE: Renzema and Skelton (1990).

showed the largest percentage growth over the previous year, a 226% increase (see Renzema & Skelton, 1990).

In December 1987, only 2 California counties, San Diego and Orange, were operating monitoring programs. By March 1989 that number had jumped to 13, with 10 more counties either considering or in the process of establishing monitoring programs (State of California, Office of the Attorney General, 1987, 1989). Most common were programs monitoring offenders released from jails on work furloughs, while the next most common were for those released because of medical problems.

Although drug and alcohol testing have been frequent features in the programs of California counties for several years, only one such program has, to our knowledge, focused directly on drug offenders, specifically gang drug pushers (sellers).[1] The lack of attention paid specifically to drug offenders presented an opportunity to study the use of electronic monitoring under home confinement with this class of offenders on a larger and more systematic scale. It is to this project, with which we are currently occupied, that we now turn.

HAEM for Drug Offenders in L.A. County

BACKGROUND

Currently, half or more of those convicted in the criminal courts of our largest cities are found guilty of drug offenses, and many convicted on other charges have prior records of drug crimes or are known to be drug involved or drug addicted. Jails are overcrowded with these offenders, but most receive probation, with little supervision. With either of these penalties, jail or probation, they have high recidivism rates, higher than any other major offense group. Glaser and Gordon (1988, 1990) found that, of drug offense cases closed in the Los Angeles municipal courts in 1984 in which offenders received probation (with or without a jail term, financial penalties, or other specified conditions of probation), about half were rearrested and about 30% received new misdemeanor or felony sentences within two years after they were released into the community on probation.

The situation in Los Angeles County is at least as severe as it is in any other major metropolitan area. Of all adult felony arrests made in L.A. County in 1989, 56% were for drug law violations. Currently, approximately 7 out of every 10 people arrested in L.A. County, from traffic offenders to suspected murderers, have narcotics in their blood at the time (Freed, 1990). This avalanche of drug-involved crime clogs the courts, the jails, and the probation system. In order to comply with a federal court order restricting overcrowding in the L.A. County jails, sentences of fewer than 38 days in jail are actually served by less than 1 day of confinement. If pretrial jailing occurred, the time already served is credited toward the reduced penalty. Currently, three-fourths of drug law violators sentenced to probation in L.A. County (almost all those with prior criminal records who are convicted of possession or use of cocaine, heroin, or PCP) receive 30- or 60-day jail terms as a condition of probation. With 37 days canceled and 3 days off for good conduct, 30-day terms are served in 12 hours or less, the time devoted to being booked in and booked out; 60-day terms are served in about 20 days.

Not only is the situation difficult with respect to time served in the county jails, but there is ample evidence that going on probation in L.A. County means essentially being unsupervised by any law enforcement authority. In a recent speech, Barry Nidorf, the chief probation officer (CPO) for the County of Los Angeles Probation Department (CLAPD), noted the crisis conditions in probation supervision. In this largest of probation departments in the United States, there are more than 90,000 adult and more than 17,000 juvenile probationers, a severe caseload strain for the department's approximately 1,200 probation officers. According to Nidorf (1990), only 40% of the adult caseloads are actually supervised, with the remainder tracked on automated minimum services caseloads of 2,000 per team of two deputy probation officers (DPOs) and one computer operator. "It is critical that not only our overcrowded jails and prisons get relief through new programming, but that we also help our overburdened local probation and parole caseloads" (p. 3). This crisis in supervision is also reflected in the specialized work of the Narcotics Testing Units (NTUs) in the county. About 16,400 adults are, as of this writing, supposed to be tested for drugs regularly under the terms of their court-approved probations. Currently, only about 9,000 are in fact tested (Freed, 1990).[2]

As a response to the perceived need for good evaluative knowledge for case decision making of a program intended to provide relief of jail overcrowding by greater supervision of probationers, a research project focusing on drug offenders commenced operation in L.A. County in January of 1990. It was conceived by Professor Emeritus Daniel Glaser of the University of Southern California (USC) as a field experiment to test the usefulness of HAEM for this most common offender group. The experimental program and its evaluation were to be funded by a grant from NIJ to USC. The CLAPD provided a letter expressing approval of the design, suggested one of the design's features (the night response officer), and assured NIJ that more than enough cases would be recommended to the courts by the department and assigned by the courts to the experiment.

PROGRAM OBJECTIVES

The ultimate objectives of this program were several. First, the program was intended to give judges, as well as government officials making decisions on correctional budgets, much more valid knowledge than is now available on the relative effectiveness of HAEM for drug law violators who would otherwise be on probation without this restraint.

Second, the program was designed to investigate statistically how the effectiveness of HAEM varies for diverse types of drug offenders, differentiated by the two attributes found most predictive of recidivism in past research, prior criminal record and prior drug problems, and by the additional—presumably deterrent, but possibly criminalizing—sentence of jail confinement (both pretrial and as a condition of probation) immediately preceding release to the community on probation. The impacts of other differentiating factors such as age, gender, drug of choice, education, marital status, work record, racial/ethnic identity, and county area were also to be explored.

Third, the program was intended as a means of obtaining empirical grounds for recommending the most cost-effective methods of administering HAEM, based on explorations of how and why variations in its application affect recidivism rates. The principal variations or "experimental treatments" were to be tested by random assignment to one of four treatment cells or to a control group. Half the randomly selected participants were placed on active and half on passive equipment, and half of each of these two groups were randomly designated for "response" by the night response officer.

PROGRAM DESCRIPTION

Target Population

The target population for this experimental application of HAEM was defined as low- and mid-level drug users placed on probation in L.A. County. The only eligibility criteria established for participation in the program were that the offender (a) have an order for narcotic testing, (b) be considered "nonviolent," (c) have a permanent residence, (d) have a single telephone (with no call forwarding or other such services), and (e) live within one of the three supervisory areas under study.

Experimental Design

The project called for a rigorous experimental design with random assignment to treatment and control groups. It was to be conducted in the three county probation supervision districts with the highest crime rates, each differing somewhat from the others in the predominant ethnicity and drug-use patterns of its offenders: the San Gabriel Valley district (in the eastern part of L.A. County) is mostly Hispanic, with the county's highest heroin and PCP arrest rates; South Central is predominantly black, with the highest crack cocaine arrest rates; and the east San Fernando Valley is predominantly white, with the highest rates of arrests for amphetamines, concentrated especially in its "biker" population. However, all ethnic groups and all types of drug use are found in each district. Implementation in each of these sociographic areas would allow for a comparison of effectiveness with different types of drug usage and ethnicity.

Experimental cases were to be randomly assigned to two types of monitoring equipment, the intermittent ("passive") and the continuous ("active").[3] Also, a night response officer (NRO) was to be randomly assigned to half of the cases in each of these two monitoring equipment groups, yielding four treatment combinations for each of the three supervision districts under study. The NRO's duties would include responding to problems or alarms that occurred during evening hours or on weekends, when, in previous experience, they most often occurred.

Treatment groups were to differ from the control group in each of the three NTU supervision districts only in their assignment to house arrest with any of the combinations of monitoring/response for a 45-day period, after which they would be routinely supervised within the NTUs. The control groups (one for each district) were to receive routine probation with random drug testing, but with no house arrest or monitoring.

Figure 5.1 shows the expected directional "flow" of cases into the program. Cases eligible for the program were to be recommended for participation through two principal sources: (a) violation proceedings against a client already on probation for a narcotics offense, in which transfer to HAEM was ordered; and (b) initial adult investigations on new drug-related cases wherein the investigating officer recommended HAEM in the probation and sentencing report submitted to the court. Municipal and superior court judges in the three study districts would then order HAEM for whatever portion of these cases they deemed appropriate. Cases with the order would then be returned to the appropriate local NTU for supervision, including drug testing.

As the cases became available in the local NTUs, a case-flow randomization procedure was implemented (Glaser, 1988). Whenever an eligible drug offender was sentenced to HAEM and the judge's "minute order" was received by the NTU supervision unit, the NRO appointed for liaison with the project was to call the USC research office, which would instruct whether this house arrestee would be assigned to one of the four treatment cells or to a control group.

Both the experimental and control groups were to receive random drug testing with the same level of intensity (currently, a minimum of twice monthly). Routine supervising officer contact was planned for the control groups, while the experimental groups would receive one of the combinations of treatment.

The research was to be directed by a full-time research associate, a position to which the first author was appointed. Research activity was to include compilation of follow-up statistics on the postrelease criminal record, narcotics testing results, and other probation rule violations of all experimental group and comparison cases six months after their entry into the program or after their arrest for violations. Additionally, interviews were to be conducted with random subsamples of "successes" and "failures" in each of the four treatment and control group cells three months after program entry or after

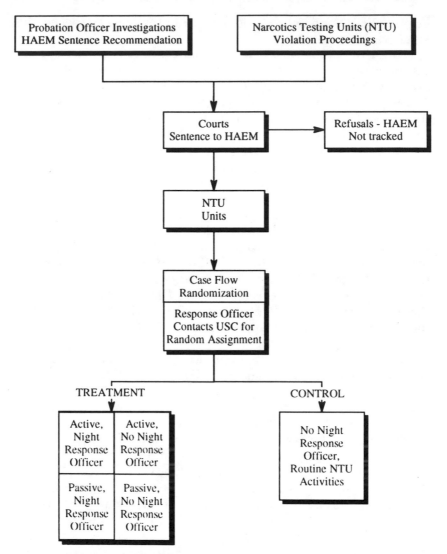

Figure 5.1. Electronic Monitoring of Adult Drug Offenders: Flowchart for Research Cases

NOTE: Both treatment and control groups receive routine NTU drug testing and deputy probation officer contact.

their arrest for violations. The interviews, for which the respondents would be paid and would be assured anonymity, were to focus on the impact of HAEM on their time schedules, legal and illegal activities, and social networks, and on the reactions of those monitored and their families to the monitoring experience, all to be related to their success or failure on probation.

Anticipated Case Flow

Based on the CLAPD estimate of 40 assigned cases per month in each of the three NTU supervision units, the program, when fully operational, would yield more than 700 cases within a six- to seven-month period. Attrition from offender noncooperation was not expected to be significant. In a letter to NIJ, and in a conference with the NIJ grant monitor before the project was funded, CLAPD had assured NIJ and USC that there would be no difficulty in carrying out the proposed experiment. Neither resistance on the part of DPOs to making recommendations for HAEM sentences nor that of the courts to issuing such sentences was expected to be a problem.

IMPLEMENTATION PROCESS

Project Start-Up

Having described the project as it was designed, we now turn to what has actually happened thus far in the real world. Our experience contrasts with that of a bureaucracy's own planned change, recently reported for the Massachusetts Probation Agency (Corbett, Cochran, & Byrne, 1987), in which a new agency head announced planning for an intensive supervision program one year in advance of its implementation. The L.A. HAEM program began after a number of months' delay in the funding decision, and with no formally announced policy of change. Although some preliminary groundwork was performed to apprise the director of the Narcotics Testing Unit (DNTU), the unit in which the program would be operating on a day-to-day basis, there was no systematic effort to solicit support for the project from all the potential organizational participants in advance of notification of funding. At USC this was due largely to uncertainty about whether the project would indeed be funded. At CLAPD it was due, in large part, to the department's preoccupation with trying to avoid budget cuts despite caseload increases.

The first organizational meeting between the USC researchers and both the director of Program Services (DPS) and the DNTU, along with a deputy probation officer staff member from each unit charged with working directly on the program, occurred on January 30, 1990.

At this meeting it was agreed that CLAPD would make all arrange-ments needed to apprise the judges and area probation offices of the objectives of the program, and to assure that the project would go forward as planned. The department was also charged with (a) organizing a series of demonstrations of equipment by various ven-dors, (b) securing bids for rental of electronic monitoring equipment, and (c) negotiating terms of contracts with sales representatives who also sought selection of their equipment for other current or expected programs with juvenile offenders and pretrial cases.

The probation personnel expressed confidence that the project would work as planned, and gave the researchers the impression that there would be no serious problems. A contract was to be drawn up between USC and CLAPD to pay for the electronic monitoring equipment rental, and for one year's employment of the night re-sponse officer, for which funds were allotted in the USC grant from NIJ. The department representatives advised that their agency could pay for these initially, then collect when we could prepare a contract and get it approved by both organizations.

As a fortunate coincidence, the NIJ held a seminar of funded researchers on electronic monitoring in San Diego on February 8-9, 1990. The USC project arranged for an invitation to be extended to CLAPD's director of Program Services and the newly appointed director of its NTUs. The plan for the USC project was presented at the San Diego seminar, and these CLAPD representatives expressed confidence that the project would receive at least 40 electronic mon-itoring cases per month from each of the three areas in which it was planned to conduct the experiment. We were pleased to hear a public expression of confidence on the feasibility of the project as designed.

IMPLEMENTATION PROBLEMS

Administrative Problems

The single most difficult problem thus far has been case acquisi-tion. The first two cases assigned to the program came in April, which by random chance were both assigned as experimental cases. Two cases were added in May and two more in June. Due to the low case flow, all were made experimental, as we anticipated that control cases could be selected when case flow increased. These six cases represented only a small fraction of those thought to be eligible within the affected NTUs alone, assuming 75 violations per month were being conducted within each of the three units, plus new cases that could be sentenced to HAEM.

Increasing concern expressed by the researchers about the slow case acquisition led to the issuance of moderately strong "grams," within-organization quasi-telegrams, by the DNTU ordering subordinates to make HAEM recommendations for all those clients qualified for it. When this did not evoke a faster case flow, a form was developed on which it was requested that the supervisors of each of the three district offices list monthly all cases recommended to the program, and all cases that could have been recommended for monitoring, with an accompanying explanation for any not being recommended. The information was supplied in varying ways, was delayed, and was not consistent across the three districts. The DNTU soon thought this request was too burdensome to the DPOs, and raised the issue of possible violation of union contract that called for consultation before increasing work load. DPO agreement to supply only listings of recommended cases was obtained.

It was then noted that all the cases received in the first few months were sentenced to monitoring as probation violators. It was learned that because the Program Services and Narcotics Testing units were in the same division of the staff hierarchy, while new case investigations were in another division, Program Services staff with whom we worked decided it would be simplest to recruit only cases referred to court by the testing unit as violators after positive drug test results, even though the packet of program literature had indicated cases would be solicited from adult investigations of new cases as well. It took several more months before the adult investigation units became involved in the recommendation process. By the end of June we had only 6 cases sentenced and installed on HAEM. Although reassured by the DPS that the case flow would increase, to ensure that CLAPD remained committed to the program, USC insisted the contract call for a minimum of 300 experimental cases to be assigned to monitoring.

As we continued to investigate the low case-flow problem, we came to realize that there were at least two features we had not originally considered that could account for some of the problems in getting cases. First, bureaucratic entrenchment and inertia have played, and continue to play, more of a role than we might ever have imagined. Because DPOs are highly routinized in their work activities and reasonably secure in their jobs, with relatively strong union support, they are reluctant to make changes to their routines even when directly ordered to do so. The method employed initially by supervisory personnel and the project liaison representative from

Program Services was one of "persuasion" to recruit support for the project within the three NTU district offices. Over time, persuasion turned to progressively more strongly worded grams that only slowly improved the responsiveness of the DPOs.

Second, just as there has been no "punishment" for not complying with the requirements of the program, there has been no incentive structure in place to encourage DPOs within the NTUs "positively" to make recommendations to the program. Recommending and successfully placing clients in the program meant no net reduction in the number of cases in the units. It merely meant that the case would return to the unit with "elevated" levels of supervision required because of the monitoring system.

DPO Professionalism and Autonomy

Related to bureaucratic inertia are the concepts of DPO professionalism and autonomy. We were repeatedly told that the DPOs were an independent group with considerable autonomy in case decisions and that it would not be easy to change their routines. No doubt, feeling that they were not consulted in advance on the procedures for this program, their professionalism and independence were invoked as tacit reasons for not making recommendations to the program. This resistance was probably felt even more strongly when it was realized that the program was initiated in Program Services but dropped into the lap of the NTUs.

Coordination and Communication, Intra- and Interorganizational Relationships

In addition to problems of bureaucratic inertia and DPO autonomy, the project faced problems of coordination between USC and CLAPD, and within CLAPD. Because the program was developed in Program Services and situated in the NTU, the inevitable question arose: Who is responsible for the project? The Program Services liaison was principally charged with the day-to-day development and promotion of the program. However, early on, the liaison obtained agreement from the NTU supervisors that the promotion of the program to the local courts would best be accomplished by the NTU supervisors, since they knew best the local court circumstances. Follow-up in these contacts was not fully achieved for months in all jurisdictions affected.

In the early months of the project, the USC-CLAPD contact was principally through the liaison, since it was he who was also charged with responsibility for obtaining monitoring equipment for the project, and it was he and the night response officer who were most intimately involved in the day-to-day efforts of the project. Unfortunately, while he and the NRO had the responsibility for establishing the program, they did not have sufficient authority to enter the domain of another organizational unit to obtain full compliance and cooperation from the NTUs, since personnel in those units had no reporting requirements to them. This "passive" resistance or inattention to the project extended to even higher levels. The DPS and the DNTU were of equal status in the organization, with the latter trying to "protect" the NTUs from too much additional work in an already overburdened setting, while the former was trying to justify and make work a program that was developed in his "shop."

Organizational factionalism was, in our view, expressed as inattention to the project. Related to this was the impression gained by the USC researchers that the two organizational units had quite different views of what their appropriate roles ought to be. Program Services representatives thought that it was their responsibility to develop the new program, place it in the units that were to operate it, and then withdraw and act only as consultants to the units running the project. It was the conception of the DNTU that Program Services would continue to take an active role in running the project.

In addition to intraorganizational issues of communication and coordination, there was also the issue of interorganization approval for certain aspects of the project. Although not initially involved in any important way when the focus was only on the NTUs as the source of cases, the union was formally consulted when the adult investigation units became affected, and agreed to the procedural requirements of this "pilot" project.[4]

Owing to increasing frustration with the department's lack of progress on this project, we contacted department representatives higher in the hierarchy, including the CPO, in order to express our concerns over the low case flow. This had the salutary effect of evoking a series of monthly meetings beginning in September 1990 and chaired by the superior of both the DPS and DNTU. This increased case flow, but still not at nearly the pace at which the project was originally planned.

Judicial Resistance

Meanwhile, both the low case flow and new circumstances in some of the courts forced a reconsideration of the experimental design. It was reported that some judges were angered by the idea that their authority would be weakened if probationers whom they sentenced to house arrest with electronic monitoring were instead, and without consulting them, assigned to the control group without this penalty. A highly influential judge expressed fear at a judges' meeting that such an occurrence would negate the credibility of their warnings to offenders. Therefore, USC informed probation officials that every probationer for whom HAEM was ordered by the court would indeed receive monitoring. Such assignment had already begun because of the low case flow, in the hope of being able to select more cases for the control group later when the case flow increased, or when funds for monitoring were used up.

Because getting a significant number of monitored cases to study required placing all in the four treatment groups, the control group would be replaced for statistical comparison of outcomes by three other sources of nonmonitored cases: (a) those who had been given a narcotics testing order and an order for electronic surveillance, but for whom no monitoring program was available (adjacent areas have some cases of this type); (b) those eligible cases whom probation officers recommended for participation in the program in one of the three target areas, but for whom, for whatever reasons, the judge declined to order monitoring; and (c) other cases with narcotics testing orders given probation without house arrest. Drug test and recidivism data are available on all these cases.

In addition, the interview schedule was designed to treat each monitored case as its own control by making comparisons on time utilization, social contacts, sources of income, drug use, and recreation in three periods: (a) the last premonitoring period of freedom in the community; (b) the monitoring period, and, for those not confined because of violations; (c) a postmonitoring period on probation, approximately 45 days after the end of monitoring. For initially monitored cases now incarcerated as probation violators, only the premonitoring and monitoring periods would be compared.

Thus the statistics compiled from the responses of interviewed individuals will indicate the average size, variation, and correlates of differences in activities and experiences from monitored to nonmonitored periods. The nonmonitored periods are the controls for all comparisons with the monitored period.

PRELIMINARY RESULTS

As of this writing there are approximately 125 cases assigned to monitoring. It is too early to provide useful information based on data collection efforts from case files or from the computerized data collection of the monitoring equipment. However, it is possible to provide some impressionistic comments from about 40 in-depth interviews that have been conducted thus far with participants in the project.

The interviews generally lasted about three hours, approximately 60% with subjects who have "succeeded" and 40% with those who have "failed" thus far on the program.[5] All were asked about their experiences in the two-month period before monitoring began, during the period of monitoring (averaging about 60 days), and the period of about 45 days after monitoring. Participants were asked about a variety of topics, including their housing circumstances while on monitoring (e.g., who was living with them while they were on monitoring); their number and type of contacts with their officers before, during, and after monitoring; drug testing experience; and a series of questions about the monitoring experience, particularly issues of social embarrassment. They were also asked about drug use history and about work and income, and were asked to evaluate monitoring time versus time in jail.

Most interviewees (even some of the violators in jail) said that they were glad that the HAEM option was available to them, and that they would choose HAEM again over jail. Results thus far support the argument that HAEM has a positive effect on participants' behavior. Most found that their lives were made more regular by the requirements of being in the home at specified times. Most found that they were interacting with family more, spending more time contemplating their circumstances, engaging in more constructive activities at home (e.g., nonregular work activities around the home, such as painting and fixing up things), and most found they saved money while on monitoring. Generally, their altered patterns under monitoring have persisted into the postmonitoring period (at least in the short run).

Nearly all of the respondents have experienced embarrassment over the monitoring experience in one form or another. Interviewees have experienced personal embarrassment, at times, with family, friends, and public, and have perceived embarrassment in others (family and friends). Many found HAEM difficult. Several expressed the view that when an individual is "behind bars," in a sense, in his or her own home, it is very difficult to "watch the world go by" outside and not be able to participate. In jail or prison, one knows that there is a "world out there," but it is not "seen" on a day-to-day basis. In sum, the interviews, thus far, show that successful arrestees, by being unable to go out with their cronies during their leisure hours, tend to become closer to their families, and are pleased thereafter to find that they have saved money.

Conclusion

Several lessons for both researchers and program managers may be drawn from our experience thus far with the HAEM project. First, appreciably more lead time than both researchers and managers may expect will be needed to move an entrenched bureaucracy to adopt new procedures that officials expect will change their routines while providing little or no benefit to them. As noted above, there has been no real incentive structure in place to reward supervision officers participating in the program. Informal questioning of the DPOs within the NTUs indicated that, on average, the officers felt that the work involved in supervising a client on HAEM was between 10% and 20% greater than that of a routine NTU case.

Second, resistance to change will be especially great if functionaries affected, who regard themselves as professionals with considerable autonomy in case decisions, are not consulted on the proposed change in advance by the higher officials who initiate it. This resentment will be particularly intense if these initiating officials (such as the DPS for the CLAPD and his staff charged with developing and implementing new programs) are not the normal supervisors of the functionaries expected to change their routines. The impression gained thus far has been that, due in part to the uncertainties of funding and the short lead time in developing the project, the NTU was not consulted very early on about project requirements and implementability within the unit.

Third, care must be taken to anticipate and mediate organizational factionalism and rivalry that may be expressed as noncooperation in, or inattention to, a project. These include both intraorganizational orders that one organizational entity (or unit) identifies as being imposed by another entity, and those posed by interorganizational relationships, such as between the bureaucracy and unions. On more than one occasion we were given the understanding that Program Services had no specific "authority" to enter the bailiwick of the NTU, for example, to make judgments about client eligibility for the program.[6]

Fourth, it is important to start a research project within a large bureaucracy only when it is understood and approved by the highest authorities there, and, if intra- or interorganizational relationship problems are encountered and cannot be mediated promptly on a lower level, to inform the higher officials soon and to recruit their assistance in resolving the problems. As previously noted, the CPO was fully aware of the project and even contributed to the development of the project design. However, this support alone has not been sufficient to overcome several problems encountered, chief of which has been "case getting."

In more general terms, typically one thinks of program evaluation research projects within criminal justice organizations, preferably with experimental or quasi-experimental designs, as assessing their achievement of *ultimate* goals, such as crime or drug-use reduction. This chapter shows that it is also important (a) to undertake process or other types of research to describe and interpret the organization's achievement of the project's *immediate* goal of providing the services to be evaluated, and (b) to assess and analyze its achievement of the *intermediate* goals of these services, such as closer supervision as a result of monitoring. Only if data are collected and interpreted on the achievement of both immediate and intermediate goals is the researcher in a position to interpret findings on the achievement or nonachievement of ultimate goals.[7]

Notes

1. This program began in 1987 when the County of Los Angeles Probation Department received a grant award from the Office of Criminal Justice Planning to add an electronic surveillance component to the existing Specialized Gang Supervision Program for a one-year period, which was renewed in 1988. A program evaluation has not yet been completed.

2. The shortage of resources to cover all narcotics testing orders led two years ago to the development of a five-tiered system that gives highest priority for testing to those considered a threat to public safety, such as burglars, child molesters, and people convicted of weapons charges, and lowest priority to nonviolent drug dealers and prostitutes, who are almost never tested (Freed, 1990).

3. With the cheaper passive type, the house arrestee wears an electronic wristlet, and whenever a computer-controlled monitoring center telephones the house, the arrestee must answer the phone and insert the wristlet into a device attached to the phone. The calls occur at random times when the arrestee is supposed to be at home, and more frequently if there is no response. With this equipment, the arrestee answers a recorded query on the phone and his or her response is tape-recorded. With the more expensive active type of equipment, the arrestee wears an anklet or wristlet that triggers an alarm if, when the arrestee is supposed to be at home, it is carried more than approximately 150 feet from the receiver/dialer attached to the house phone. Also, with the active type, an alarm is triggered if the wristlet or anklet is damaged or removed. The first response to any alarm is usually a staff phone call to the home.

4. Although USC initially objected to the use of the term *pilot* to describe the program in a gram from an official involved in implementing recommendation procedures for adult investigation units, it was explained that the term was a code word to indicate that the program was not a permanent one and that solicitation of union involvement and consent would be on a "meet and advise" basis rather than to consider permanent implementation of significant changes in work procedures.

5. *Failure* here is defined as either being rearrested or being found in violation by the supervising officer. One of the three failures has actually been reinstated on probation within the same NTU and may be considered, on the basis of his account as to "what happened," only a marginal failure. Another violated probation through apparent inability to respond to phone calls early in the morning and was awaiting a court finding at the time he was interviewed.

6. It is quite understandable that one organizational unit would resist the "invasion" of its organizational territory by another unit. In fairness, it must be said that there has also been much cooperation between the two units, particularly after the first seven months of the project, when a number of issues needed addressing.

7. For a fuller discussion of such distinctions among goals, and of the importance of measuring achievement of each goal, see Glaser (1988, pp. 18-19, 211-214).

References

Corbett, R. P., Jr., Cochran, D., & Byrne, J. M. (1987). Managing change in probation: Principles and practice in the implementation of an intensive probation supervision program. In B. R. McCarthy (Ed.), *Intermediate punishments: Intensive supervision, home confinement, and electronic surveillance*. Monsey, NY: Criminal Justice Press.

Freed, D. (1990, December 16-22). Justice in distress: The devaluation of crime in Los Angeles. *Los Angeles Times* (7-part series).

Glaser, D. (1988). *Evaluation research and decision guidance*. New Brunswick, NJ: Transaction.

Glaser, D., & Gordon, M. A. (1988). *Use and effectiveness of fines, jail, and probation in municipal courts* (Final report on NIJ Grant No. 86-IJ-CX-0028). Los Angeles: University of Southern California, Social Science Research Institute.

Glaser, D., & Gordon, M. A. (1990). Profitable penalties for lower level courts. *Judicature, 73*, 248-252.

Nidorf, B. J. (1990, September). *What do you do when you can't build your way out?* Paper presented at the National Institute of Justice Conference on Intermediate Sanctions, Washington, DC.

Renzema, M., & Skelton, D. T. (1990). *Final report: The use of electronic monitoring by criminal justice agencies 1989: A description of extent, offender characteristics, program types, programmatic issues, and legal aspects* (Submitted to the National Institute of Justice under contract OJP-89-M-309). Kutztown, PA: Kutztown University Foundation.

State of California, Office of the Attorney General. (1987, December). *The use and effectiveness of electronic monitoring programs*. Sacramento: State of California.

State of California, Office of the Attorney General. (1989, March). *The use and effectiveness of electronic monitoring programs: An update*. Sacramento: State of California.

6. Emerging Technofallacies in the Electronic Monitoring Movement

Ronald P. Corbett, Jr.

Gary T. Marx

> It's a remarkable piece of apparatus.
>
> FRANZ KAFKA,
> "In the Penal Colony"

Since its legendary inception in the mind of a New Mexico judge inspired by Spider-Man comics, the use of electronic monitoring as a correctional tool has grown in a manner most often described as "explosive" (U.S. Department of Justice, 1990). From very isolated use in 1984, the use of electronic monitoring (EM) has expanded to at least 33 states (American Correctional Association, 1989), with a threefold increase during 1988 alone (Schmidt, 1989).

Although hardly a mature industry, EM has attracted a growing number of manufacturers now totaling at least 14 (Tonry & Will, 1989). For the last several years, exhibition areas at the annual conference of the American Probation and Parole Association have been occupied almost entirely by vendors of new technology, most of it EM equipment.

Clearly, EM has arrived on the correctional scene and has drawn much attention. Significant research findings regarding its impact recently have begun to come in. These studies have intensified the debate about the proper place of EM in criminal justice. In this

AUTHORS' NOTE: An earlier version of this chapter was presented at the annual meeting of the American Society of Criminology, Baltimore, 1990. Another version appeared as "No Soul in the New Machine: Technofallacies in the Electronic Monitoring Movement," by Ronald P. Corbett, Jr. and Gary T. Marx, in *Justice Quarterly*, Vol. 8, No. 3, pp. 399-414. Copyright 1991 by the Academy of Criminal Justice Sciences. Reprinted with permission of the Academy of Criminal Justice Sciences.

chapter, we locate EM in the context of broader societal developments regarding surveillance, and we argue that unfortunately it has
fallen prey to a series of technofallacies that undermine practice.
Viewing the current electronic monitoring frenzy from the perspective of several decades of observing and participating in the correctional process, we have Yogi Berra's sense that "it's deja vu all over
again," as yet another panacea is offered to criminal justice without
adequate thought or preparation.

We address both academic and practitioner audiences. The former
will recognize the sociological perspectives of unintended consequences, irony, and paradox (e.g., Marx, 1981; Merton, 1957; Sieber,
1982) as applied to a new area. We hope that the latter—those who
develop and administer policy—will gain from this presentation by
seeing that innovations never stand alone and that avoidance of the
fallacies identified here can mean improved practice.

The New Surveillance

The development of EM in the 1980s not only is a response to
specific factors (to be discussed below), but also reflects broader
changes in surveillance. It must be viewed along with drug testing,
video and audio surveillance, computer monitoring and dossiers,
night vision technology, and a rich variety of other means that are
changing the nature of watching.

Although these extractive technologies have unique elements, they
also tend to share certain characteristics that set them apart from
many traditional means. Some of the ethos and the information-
gathering techniques found in the maximum-security prison are
diffusing into the broader society. We appear to be moving toward,
rather than away from, becoming a "maximum-security society." [1]

Such a society is transparent and porous. Information leakage is
rampant. Barriers and boundaries—distance, darkness, time, walls,
windows, and even skin—that have been fundamental to our con-
ceptions of privacy, liberty, and individuality give way. Actions, as
well as feelings, thoughts, pasts, and even futures, are increasingly
visible. The line between the public and the private is weakened;
observations seem constant; more and more information goes on a
permanent record, whether we will this or not, and even whether we
know about it or not. Data in many different forms, from widely
separated geographical areas, organizations, and time periods, can
easily be merged and analyzed.

Surveillance becomes capital- rather than labor-intensive. Technical developments drastically alter the economics of surveillance such that it becomes much less expensive per unit watched. Aided by technology, a few persons can monitor many people and factors. The situation contrasts with the traditional gumshoe or guard watching a few persons and the almost exclusive reliance on firsthand information from the unenhanced senses.

One aspect of this efficiency, and the ultimate in decentralized control, is self- or participatory monitoring. Persons watched become active "partners" in their own monitoring. Surveillance systems may be triggered directly when a person walks, talks on the telephone, turns on a TV set, takes a magnetically marked item through a checkpoint, or enters or leaves a controlled area.

There is an emphasis on the engineering of control, whether by weakening the object of surveillance (as in the case of EM) or by hardening potential victims (as with access codes or better locks). Themes of prevention, soft control, and the replacement of people with machines are present. Where it is not possible to prevent violations physically, or when that process is too expensive, the system may be engineered so that profit from a violation cannot be enjoyed, or so that the violator is identified immediately.

As the technology becomes ever more penetrating and more intrusive, it becomes possible to gather information with laserlike specificity and spongelike absorbency. If we consider the information-gathering net as analogous to a fishing net, then, as Stanley Cohen (1985) suggests, the mesh of the net has become finer and the net wider.

Like the discovery of the atom or the unconscious, new techniques bring to the surface bits of reality that previously were hidden or did not contain informational clues. People, in a sense, are turned inside out; what was previously invisible or meaningless is made visible and meaningful. Electronic monitoring and the forms that increasingly accompany it, such as video identification and drug/alcohol testing, are part of this qualitative change in monitoring. The home is opened up as never before. In focusing on the details, we must not forget that they are part of a much broader group of changes.

Ten Technofallacies of Electronic Salvation

New public policies are based partly on politics and interests, partly on empirical assessment, and partly on values. Unfortunately, wisdom too often plays only a modest role.

EM must be approached cautiously, or the stampeding herd may fall off the cliff. Before technical solutions such as monitoring are implemented, it is important to examine the broader cultural climate, the rationales for action, and the empirical and value assumptions on which they are based. Policy analysts must offer not only theories, concepts, methods, and data, but also—one hopes—wisdom. Part of this wisdom consists of being able to identify and question the structure of tacit assumptions that undergird action.

In the analysis of new surveillance technologies, Marx (1990, 1991) identifies a number of "tarnished silver bullet technofallacies" that characterize many recent efforts to use technology to deal with social issues. Some of these apply to the case at hand. In critiquing the EM movement, the following discussion draws on and expands this more general framework. We discuss 10 such fallacies:

(1) the fallacy of explicit agendas
(2) the fallacy of novelty
(3) the fallacy of intuitive appeal or surface plausibility
(4) the fallacy of the free lunch or painless dentistry
(5) the fallacy of quantification
(6) the fallacy of ignoring the recent past
(7) the fallacy of technical neutrality
(8) the fallacy of the 100% accurate or fail-safe system
(9) the fallacy of the sure shot
(10) the fallacy of assuming that if a critic questions the means, he or she must be opposed to the ends

THE FALLACY OF EXPLICIT AGENDAS

This entails assuming that new programs are developed for their declared purpose and/or that there *is* a clearly developed purpose. It also assumes that the ostensible reasons for policy decisions are the real reasons rather than a mask for a decision based on other considerations (e.g., fiscal or political). In the case of EM the goals are varied, contradictory, and shifting, and sometimes hide other goals.

An important theme in contemporary corrections is the emphasis placed on proportionality or symmetry in sentencing (Morris & Tonry, 1990; Petersilia, 1990). It is argued that, traditionally, few penal sanctions "between probation and prison" have been available. No appropriate sanctions exist for offenders who occupy the middle ground on a scale of severity of deserts. Liberals and conservatives alike have found appeal in this argument. A major rationale for EM is that it is an intermediate sanction that promises simultaneously to lighten onerous penalties and to increase lenient ones.

Nevertheless, EM has a number of other goals, sometimes acknowledged informally but rarely stated officially or in public. Policy disasters are more likely to occur when the declared purposes of a program are supplemented privately or eclipsed by additional, even contrary, objectives. With regard to EM, the foremost of these objectives is a powerful financial imperative.

In the late 1970s and early 1980s a "get tough" approach to sentencing offenders emerged from the presumed demise of the rehabilitative ideal. This was reflected first in the rhetoric of public officials and then in a spate of sentencing reform schemes, all pointing toward stricter and more certain punishment. Predictably enough, this approach put a tremendous strain on existing prison stock, and is an important cause of the decade-long prison overcrowding crisis.

Although building more prisons seemed the obvious solution, here again the agenda was by no means clear or uncomplicated. Prisons are very expensive institutions, averaging (in 1987 dollars) between $50,000 and $75,000 per new cell for construction and $14,000 for imprisoning one offender for a year (Petersilia, 1987). "Get tough" suddenly meant "Go broke"! The goal of sentencing severity gave way fairly quickly to the goal of fiscal stability. As Petersilia (1987) reports, this financial concern became "the bottom line in deciding what to do with lawbreakers" (p. xi).

Compounding the financial crisis was a nascent legal crisis of constitutional dimensions, brought on by overcrowded conditions in prisons. So serious was this situation that by 1987, 37 states were subject to judicial orders to address illegal conditions in their institutions (Petersilia, 1987).

The conservative trend in sentencing philosophy potentially was jeopardized by an emerging legal/fiscal crisis. If these multiple and conflicting goals were to be served, clearly it would be necessary to develop a program that would sound tough while also reducing and relieving overcrowding. Thus were born "sentencing alternatives," which in time would be renamed "intermediate sanctions" and, most recently, "intermediate punishments," of which EM is perhaps the leading example. Pressure was put on probation to remake itself. State correctional administrators looked to the lower-cost option to bail them out. Offenders who might be incarcerated under the prevailing philosophy would now, of necessity, face technologically enhanced home imprisonment, which was believed to cost only one-third as much as prison.

Another equally powerful (if less noted) agenda item—a desire to enhance the public image of probation—was also present; internally, the probation profession was feeling pressure to make itself more palatable in conservative times. Consequently, the field adopted rhetoric that was, in Clear and Hardyman's (1990) view, "unabashedly fierce," emphasizing qualities of toughness, strictness, and harshness (p. 46). In the face of a public relations crisis, wherein probation was depicted as pathetically soft, it became politically wise to put on a meaner face and develop a more punitive approach. Probation would seek to pack the same punch as prison, minus the expensive bricks and mortar, by launching programs involving intensive supervision, boot camps, shock incarceration, and home confinement with electronic monitoring.

If EM has not worked in an empirical sense to date, as the incoming evidence suggests, that failure might be traced, at least in part, to this melange of shifting and conflicting goals.

THE FALLACY OF NOVELTY

This fallacy entails the assumption that new means are invariably better than the old. Decisions are often based on newness rather than on data suggesting that the new will work or that the old has failed. The symbolism of wanting to appear up-to-date is important.

The fallacy of novelty is related to a "vanguard" fallacy: "If the big guys are doing it, it must be good." Smaller organizations copy the actions of the larger or more prestigious organizations in an effort to appear modern.

The field of corrections often has been accused of being in constant thrall to fads and panaceas (Finckenauer, 1982). Technofix attitudes unfortunately have become the knee-jerk response of our society to complex issues that arise from social, not technical, causes. In a theme with solid roots in U.S. history, newness is equated too quickly with goodness. New technology is inherently attractive to an industrial society. It is risky to be against new technology, however mysterious its operations or recondite its underlying engineering. Technical innovation becomes synonymous with progress. To be opposed to new technology is to be a heretic, to be old-fashioned, backward, resistant to change, regressive, out of step. As Reinecke (1982) observes sardonically, "To fall behind in the great technorace is to demonstrate a pathetic unwillingness to change with the times, to invite universal ridicule, and to write a recipe for economic disaster" (p. 13).

Agency administrators become fond of the new and the original as a matter of careerism and survival. Fast-track reputations are more likely to be built on introducing new programs than on maintaining the old; few professionals want to be regarded as caretakers. Invitations to speak at conferences, media coverage, job offers, and, most significantly, the availability of grant money depend on the implementation of novel approaches. Questions about the fit of innovation with the agency's mission and goals or about the existence of empirical support for the innovation will be considered mere details in the face of these forces. This point leads directly to our next fallacy.

THE FALLACY OF INTUITIVE APPEAL OR SURFACE PLAUSIBILITY

This entails the adoption of a policy because "it sure seems as if it would work." The emphasis is on commonsense "real-world" experience and a dash of wish fulfillment in approaching new programs. In this ahistorical and antiempirical world, evaluative research has little currency.

The models for rational policy development taught in schools of public administration advance the notion that in the domain of social policy, research and evaluation determine policy. Unfortunately, these models usually bear little resemblance to actual occurrences in corrections practice. Finckenauer (1982) refers to a tendency for agencies to ignore evidence of program failure if the ideological "spin" is right. Clear and Hardyman (1990) speak of a rush to embrace intensive probation supervision when the evidence supporting such adoption is "weak." Tonry and Will (1989) cite administrators who proliferate programs and believe in their efficacy, even in the absence of careful evaluations. They note that "in a field [community corrections] . . . in which few rigorous evaluations have been conducted, the persuasive force of conventional but untested wisdom is great" (p. 29).

Enthusiasm for EM programs runs high, even when data that call them into question are available. In her three-county random-assignment experiment involving EM in California, Petersilia (1990) found the following: "The highest technical violation and arrest rate occurred in the Electronic Monitoring Program in Los Angeles. About 35% of participants in the program had a technical violation, and 35% an arrest, after six months" (p. 105). Probation with EM was found to result in rearrest rates identical to those of offenders under regular supervision.

An Indianapolis study released in 1990 compared the effectiveness of EM with that of human monitoring. No significant differences were found between the two methods. The study revealed, however, that nearly 44% of all participants "sneaked out" on the monitoring (Baumer & Mendelsohn, 1990).

In her report on the use of EM in the Georgia intensive probation supervision program, Irwin (1990) concludes that it was a failure and that it seemed to exacerbate recidivism rates. Palumbo, Clifford, and Snyder-Joy (1990) report that in an Arizona EM study concentrating on cost-effectiveness, the evidence suggests that EM did not reduce and might very well have increased overall correctional costs due to net widening.

Just as innovations are promoted without regard to supporting data, so can traditional approaches be abandoned casually with a lack of evidence. In the late 1970s and early 1980s it became the conventional wisdom that rehabilitation was a failure and that programs aimed at reforming offenders were bankrupt. EM and other "get tough" approaches to community corrections flourished in this environment, as the emphasis shifted toward punishment and deterrence.

Again, it is remarkable how little this conventional wisdom was supported by the available research. Byrne (1990), in an overview of intensive supervision programming, inveighs against systems that blindly negate or minimize the importance of treatment interventions and overestimate the impact of control-oriented interventions such as EM. Petersilia's (1990) methodologically rigorous study reports, as its only *positive* finding, that lower recidivism rates were found "among those ISP offenders who were fortunate enough to receive some rehabilitative programming" (p. 3). In a major study of the effects of a sanctioning approach versus a treatment approach in reducing recidivism, Andrews and his colleagues (1990) found that, across 80 different studies, criminal sanctioning without the provision of rehabilitative services did not work, and only programs incorporating principles of rehabilitation reduced recidivism significantly. They conclude, "There is a reasonably solid clinical and research basis for the political reaffirmation of rehabilitation" (p. 384).

THE FALLACY OF THE FREE LUNCH OR PAINLESS DENTISTRY

This fallacy involves the belief that there are programs that will return only good results, without any offsetting losses. It ignores the existence of low-visibility or longer-range collateral costs, and fails to recognize that any format or structure both channels and excludes.

In the making of public policy, new ideas all too often drive out old ideas, irrespective of their merit. New programs draw attention and resources away from traditional efforts. This situation can entail significant opportunity costs. Personnel and other resources are allocated to the innovation, often starving (or undernourishing) existing programs. Over time, the conventional ways of doing business may suffer from choked-off budgets and the retention of less competent staff members who have been excluded from the new, high-priority program. Such persons also may be angry about not being included in the new programs.

Eventually this Gresham-style effect may develop a self-fulfilling quality. Whatever the merits of conventional programs, they become defenseless against the drain of resources into the innovation. Conversely, the innovation, whatever its merits, is provided with an introduction under the most favorable circumstances (ample start-up funds, generous publicity, an elite, handpicked staff). This makes for an unrealistic test of its potential under normal, non-"halo" conditions.

The EM movement illustrates these dynamics nicely. Clear, Flynn, and Shapiro (1987), in their review of three intensive supervision projects, discuss the "secondary place" taken by treatment efforts when control is emphasized. Irwin (1990), in discussing the use of EM in Georgia, observes that although the technology makes the control function easier, "at the same time [it] may make more difficult the part of the job that involves the motivation of offenders and gaining their cooperation" (p. 73). Palumbo et al. (1990) conclude that because the program is sold on the basis of its capacity to control offenders, treatment becomes at best an "add-on": "Under these conditions, there is likely to be little if any real treatment provided" (p. 16).

THE FALLACY OF QUANTIFICATION

When this fallacy is operating, costs and benefits and the values of goods and services are defined in a manner that gives priority to things that can be measured easily. In a related fallacy, seemingly attractive means can serve to determine the end, rather than the reverse.

One potentially attractive feature of EM systems for administrators and line officers alike is its seeming operational simplicity. EM is a comparatively straightforward process, easy to learn, implement, and monitor. In this respect it stands in sharp contrast to the traditional "casework" approach to probation.

Traditional probation supervision might be characterized as counseling with an edge. It resembles social work plus the complications of coercion and involuntariness. Although offenders clearly prefer probation to prison, they could hardly be said to embrace the experience in the same way, for instance, as mental health "clients" may embrace therapy. Probation officers work in the shadow of the prison cell and can arrange for the imprisonment of intractable offenders. Simultaneously, they are expected to remediate a range of profound personal difficulties (e.g., drug abuse, illiteracy, mental illness, joblessness) that are pushing the offender toward crime. Therefore, they are charged with hating the sin and loving the sinner. They have a dual role—cop and counselor—that is often misunderstood, if not resented, by offenders, who correctly sense the mixed message.

The complexity and the contradictory nature of the job are compounded by the "technical uncertainty" (Thompson, 1967) inherent in the role. Traditional casework is assumed to be an imprecise science at best, even though a line of research by Andrews and colleagues has established a strong empirical foundation for effective supervision (see Andrews & Kiessling, 1980; Andrews, Kiessling, Robinson, & Mickus, 1986; Andrews et al., 1990). Clear and Gallagher (1985) suggest that in the face of this technical uncertainty, "officers will tend to select conservative practices in offender management" (p. 426).

The EM movement reconceptualizes the task before the probation officer as more mechanical and more concrete: Install equipment, test, monitor, record, and respond. Redefining the goal as offender surveillance through technology eliminates the professional anxiety and guesswork endemic to the casework approach. EM minimizes, if it does not eliminate, the discretionary judgment and complex analysis required of the treatment model and replaces it with responsibilities akin to those of a clerk/technician.

EM also makes the manager's job less taxing. The traditional approach requires considerable investment in staff training in a variety of higher-order skills (interpersonal communications, personality assessment, diagnostic protocols, crisis intervention, substance abuse assessment and referral). Supervising staff members with these responsibilities is difficult, as is the related task of setting performance criteria and organizational goals.

Small wonder, then, that organizations will find the relatively uncomplicated world of EM attractive. What had been nebulous and "soft" in casework systems becomes quantifiable and concrete with EM. If only it worked! A major change in the probation officer's job is being introduced without broad discussion, simply as an artifact of a seemingly simple technology.

THE FALLACY OF IGNORING THE RECENT PAST

For the case at hand, this fallacy involves denying the possibility that EM might be just another corrections fad. Of course, this characterizes nontechnical reforms as well. Yet, whether from genuine enthusiasm or as a political strategy, those caught up in the excitement and the high stakes of promoting a reform often wear historical blinders. They do so at their peril.

The intense interest in EM has all the earmarks of a fad—broad media attention, quick, widespread adoption, rapid expansion and diversification of the product. Even a superficial familiarity with the recent history of community corrections should encourage a skeptical or, at least, a go-slow approach.

The history of the last 20 years of community corrections is punctuated at about 5-year intervals by the appearance of new "panaceas," typically arriving suddenly and attracting enormous attention. The bad news is that they tend to disappear just as quickly. Examples include pretrial diversion in the late 1960s, mandatory sentencing in the mid-1970s, and intensive probation supervision in the early 1980s. Their trajectories have been roughly similar: great early enthusiasm, widespread adoption, less-than-positive evaluations followed by disillusionment, and finally downscaling or elimination and receptiveness to the next panacea.

THE FALLACY OF TECHNICAL NEUTRALITY

This involves the assumption that technology per se is morally and ethically neutral; that any piece of machinery can have both good and bad implications, *depending on how it is used.* This fallacy can stop critical thought. It ignores the fact that the technology is always developed and applied in a social context that is never neutral.

EM technology is morally distinguishable from a microchip, for example. It is meant as a form of human restraint and tracking; with few exceptions, it has been used to incarcerate people in their own homes. Thus the moral rub.

In a democracy, the concept of "home" is a near-national icon; home represents a refuge, a sanctuary, the last bastion of privacy. The walls of a home have been thought to serve as an impermeable barrier, inviolate in defining the line between public and private domains. The

Fourth Amendment incorporates this understanding into law: it admonishes the state that in a free society, it is to have little dominion over and very limited intrusion into the activities within a home.

With EM the home becomes deprivatized. The intrusion is telemetric and nearly invisible, and, as such, perhaps more insidious (Marx, 1989). We have progressed from first-generation equipment that simply monitored physical presence, through emissions transmitted over telephone lines, to more recently manufactured equipment that allows for visual inspection and telemetric alcohol tests. Tonry and Will (1989) report that two-way video transmission soon will be cost-effective for use in home confinement programs.

The use of EM typifies trends toward decentralization of social control. Figuratively, prisons have been dismantled, and each individual cell has been reassembled in private homes. Once homes start to serve as modular prisons and bedrooms as cells, what will become of our cherished notion of "home"? If privacy is obliterated *legally* in prison and if EM provides the functional equivalent of prison at home, privacy rights for home confinees and family members are potentially jeopardized.

What price intermediate sanctions? In finding feasible alternatives to traditional incarceration, we might wish to preserve rather than dilute or corrode the time-honored distinctions between private and public realms. In Robert Frost's poem "The Death of the Hired Man," we read:

> Home is the place where, when you have to go there,
> They have to take you in.

The proliferation of EM programs may require that we update the poet as follows:

> In the late twentieth century, home is the place where, when you
> want to leave there,
> They have to keep you in.

THE FALLACY OF THE 100% ACCURATE OR FAIL-SAFE SYSTEM

The glamour surrounding sophisticated electronic technology may lead the uncritical to assume that its results are invariably reliable. In their enthusiasm, vendors and program entrepreneurs may fail to acknowledge the technology's weaknesses. As an assessment of EM in Florida put it, "The technology has proven both reliable and unreliable" (Papy & Nimer, 1991). It may break or fail to work under certain conditions. The technology is also applied and interpreted by humans, which introduces the possibility for errors and corruption.

There are many examples of technical failures: Transmissions can be blocked or distorted by environmental conditions such as lightning, proximity to an FM radio station, the metal in mylar wallpaper and trailer walls, some housing construction materials, and water in waterbeds or bathtubs (with some early versions, participants even got electrical shocks while bathing). Poor telephone lines, wiring, and equipment may transmit signals that cannot be read accurately. Power, telephone, and computer failures may make it appear that a violation has occurred when it has not, or the reverse. The quality of telephone service required for confidence in the voice verification system is not available in many places. Those monitoring the system to report violations can be compromised, and with private contractors there may be less accountability than in the public sector. Of course, in the adversarial context many participants will seek ways to neutralize the system and to exploit its ambiguities (at least 4 in 10 do so, according to research by Baumer & Mendelsohn, 1990).

THE FALLACY OF THE SURE SHOT

This fallacy assumes that technically based social interventions will reach their intended targets with laserlike precision—the public policy equivalent of a surgical strike. There will be no impact on adjacent or unintended targets. Key participants are seen to be cooperative and of good will and to agree on the goal—rather than passively resisting or adhering to established customs and business as usual.

This fallacy encompasses "net widening" in the sense that programs may reach their intended target groups and beyond. But it also includes the many criminal justice programs in which displacement occurs instead. Research on intermediate sanctions has frequently found that the intended target group is bypassed.

Highly independent judges may apply intermediate sanctions to an offender pool not envisioned by program planners. Judges may reduce their own vulnerability by sentencing less risky clients to EM, even when the program is intended as an alternative to incarceration for more serious offenders. Morris and Tonry (1990), in a study of intermediate sanctions, report that "when an intermediate choice is offered, it will tend to be filled more by those previously treated more leniently than by those previously treated more severely."

It is possible that the announced target is not the intended target. Intensive supervision programs such as EM are anxious to present themselves as directed at high-risk, prison-bound offenders, since the expected savings of prison bed space and related expenses would otherwise not ensue. Hence the publicized target group is variously described as "serious," "dangerous," and "recidivist."

However, the fine print of selection criteria for program participants often incorporates exceptions and exclusions that minimize the possibility that truly serious offenders will participate. This lessens the stakes for administrators, who naturally wish to decrease their exposure. Clear and Hardyman (1990) offer examples of the recruitment of comparatively low-risk offenders for what was promoted as an intensive program aimed at high-risk offenders.

Implementing the program with the original target group may come to be seen as practically or politically too difficult. Palumbo et al. (1990) report that in Arizona, where the legislature set definite criteria for participation in the EM program, the Board of Pardons and Parole (BPP) was reluctant to utilize them, waiting five months to place the first inmate in the program. The BPP eventually came to substitute its own criteria—applying EM only to low-risk offenders who would ordinarily have received regular supervision, thereby undermining the intended cost savings. Clear and Hardyman (1990) report on sites that repeatedly had to alter their eligibility requirements when insufficient referrals threatened the visibility of the programs.

Rather than the ready-aim-fire model of the traditional bureaucracy, some of the initial experience with EM suggests that Peter Drucker's ready-fire-aim model may be more appropriate. One fires first and whatever is hit becomes the target.

THE FALLACY OF ASSUMING THAT IF A CRITIC QUESTIONS THE MEANS, HE OR SHE MUST BE OPPOSED TO THE ENDS

This fallacy involves an attempt by technology's cheerleaders to meet any criticism of their means with the claim that the critics are really soft on, or opposed to, the ends—in this case, alternatives to incarceration or enhanced forms of probation. This insinuation of bad faith is often a cheap shot. Nevertheless, critics have an obligation to acknowledge the decent intentions and real problems often associated with attempts at innovation.

And we do. To understand that policy experiments are often riddled with hidden, contradictory, ironic, and sometimes perverse consequences is not to suggest that they are inevitably doomed or necessarily directed toward the wrong goals. Awareness of technofallacies can sensitize policymakers to potential pitfalls, but it need not paralyze them. What we distort through our eagerness to innovate and our infatuation with technical progress we can correct in part through a growing policy "wisdom," sound program design, and sensitive and intelligent management.

We approach this topic not as Luddites who want to ban new technology, but in a spirit of responsible conservatism, which asks us to pause in the face of any proposed change and to consider its fit within the agency, the appropriateness of its possible latent agenda, alternative development scenarios, the costs of doing nothing, and its likely short- and long-range unintended consequences.

In Kafka's story "In the Penal Colony," a correctional officer and his superior develop a complicated new machine capable of inflicting horrible mortal punishment on inmates. In the end, the officer who argued so proudly for the new technology is horrifically consumed by it. We do not suggest that anything like this will necessarily happen in corrections, but it is clear that innovations that are not thought out carefully and offered honestly and modestly run the risk of doing great damage. So far, we have seen little theoretical or empirical support to justify the rush to EM.

Note

1. This section draws from Marx (1988, chaps. 1, 10).

References

Andrews, D. A., & Kiessling, J. J. (1980). Program structure and effective correctional practice: A summary of the CaVIC research. In R. R. Ross & P. Gendreau (Eds.), *Effective correctional treatment*. Toronto: Butterworth.

Andrews, D. A., Kiessling, J. J., Robinson, D., & Mickus, S. (1986). The risk principle of case classification: An outcome evaluation with adult probationers. *Canadian Journal of Criminology, 28,* 377-396.

Andrews, D. A., Zinger, I., Hoge, R. D., Bonta, J., Gendreau, P., & Cullen, F. T. (1990). A clinically relevant and psychologically informed meta-analysis. *Criminology, 28,* 369-397.

American Correctional Association. (1989). *Emerging technologies and community corrections.* Laurel, MD: Author.

Baumer, T. L., & Mendelsohn, R. I. (1990). *The electronic monitoring of nonviolent convicted felons: An experiment in home detention, final report* (Final report from NIJ Grant No. 86-IJ-CX-0041). Indianapolis: Indiana University, School of Public and Environmental Affairs.

Byrne, J. M. (1990). The future of probation supervision and new intermediate sanctions. *Crime and Delinquency, 36,* 6-14.

Clear, T. R., Flynn, S., & Shapiro, C. (1987). Intensive supervision in probation: A comparison of three projects. In B. R. McCarthy (Ed.), *Intermediate punishments: Intensive supervision, home confinement, and electronic surveillance.* Monsey, NY: Criminal Justice Press.

Clear, T. R., & Gallagher, K. W. (1985). Probation and parole supervision: A review of current classification practices. *Crime and Delinquency, 31,* 423-444.

Clear, T. R., & Hardyman, P. (1990). The new intensive supervision movement. *Crime and Delinquency, 36,* 42-60.

Cohen, S. (1985). *Visions of social control.* Cambridge: Polity.

Finckenauer, J. O. (1982). *Sacred Straight! and the panacea phenomenon.* Englewood Cliffs, NJ: Prentice-Hall.

Irwin, B. (1990). Old and new tools for the modern probation officer. *Crime and Delinquency, 36,* 61-74.

Lempert, R. D., & Visher, C. A. (Eds.). (1987). *Randomized field experiments in criminal justice agencies: A summary of workshop proceedings.* Washington, DC: Commission on Research on Law Enforcement and the Administration of Justice, National Research Council.

Marx, G. T. (1981). Ironies of social control: Authorities as contributors to deviance through escalation, nonenforcement and covert facilitation. *Social Problems, 28,* 222-246.

Marx, G. T. (1988). *Undercover: Police surveillance in America.* Berkeley: University of California Press.

Marx, G. T. (1989). Privacy and the home: The king doesn't have to enter your cottage to invade your privacy. *Impact Assessment Bulletin, 7*(1), 31-59.

Marx, G. T. (1990). Privacy and technology. *World & I, 3,* 523-541.

Marx, G. T. (1991). *Windows into the soul: Surveillance and society in an age of high technology.* Unpublished manuscript.

Merton, R. (1957). *Social theory and social structure.* Glencoe, IL: Free Press.

Morris, N., & Tonry, M. (1990). *Between prison and probation: Intermediate punishments in a rational sentencing system.* New York: Oxford University Press.

Palumbo, D. J., Clifford, M., & Snyder-Joy, Z. (1990). *From net widening to intermediate sanctions: The transformation of alternatives to incarceration from malevolence to benevolence.* Paper prepared the annual meeting of the American Criminological Association, Baltimore.

Papy, J., & Nimer, R. (1991). Electronic monitoring in Florida. *Federal Probation,* pp. 31-33.

Petersilia, J. (1987). *Expanding options for criminal sentencing* (Publication No. R-3544-EMC). Santa Monica, CA: RAND Corporation.

Petersilia, J. (1990, September 17). Officials aim to fill the gap between probation and parole. *Criminal Justice Newsletter.*

Petersilia, J., & Turner, S. (1990). Comparing intensive and regular supervision for high-risk probationers: Early results from an experiment in California. *Crime and Delinquency, 36,* 87-111.

Reinecke, I. (1982). *Electronic illusions.* New York: Penguin.

Schmidt, A. K. (1989). Electronic monitoring of offenders increases. *NIJ Reports, 212,* 2-5.

Sieber, S. (1982). *Fatal remedies.* New York: Plenum.

Thompson, J. D. (1967). *Organizations in action.* New York: McGraw-Hill.

Tonry, M., & Will, R. (1989). *Intermediate sanctions.* Report to the National Institute of Justice, Washington, DC.

U.S. Department of Justice. (1990). *Survey of intermediate sanctions.* Washington, DC: Government Printing Office.

PART III

Shock Incarceration

7. Boot Camp Prisons
for Young Offenders

Doris Layton MacKenzie

Dale G. Parent

Shock incarceration, or "boot camp" prison, programs are a rapidly growing phenomenon in U.S. corrections. Correctional boot camps are patterned after military basic training. Offenders, usually young adults serving their first prison terms, spend 90 to 180 days in a boot camp atmosphere. There is a demanding daily schedule of activities characterized by strict rules and discipline. If offenders succeed in completing the program, they are released to community supervision. Those who leave the program, either as disciplinary cases or by voluntarily dropping out, must serve longer terms in traditional prisons or go before judges for resentencing.

On a typical day in a boot camp, participants arise before dawn, dress quickly and quietly, march in cadence to an exercise area, spend an hour or more doing calisthenics and running, and march back to their quarters. Following this, they march to breakfast, where they stand at parade rest when the serving line is not moving, and execute crisp military movements and turns when the line does move. Inmates are required to approach the table, stand at attention until commanded to sit, and eat without conversation. After breakfast, they practice drill and ceremony. They then march to (or are transported to) a work site, where they perform six to eight hours of labor selected specifically to exact maximum physical effort from them. Upon completing the workday, they return to their living compound, where they face more exercises, and drill and ceremony. After a quick evening meal, inmates may spend four to five hours in treatment or educational programs before lights out. During their stay in the boot camp, they have no direct contact with regular prison inmates, strict rules govern all facets of their comportment and behavior, and punishments for rule violations are summary, certain, and often physical in nature (push-ups, running, and so on).

Rapid Growth of
Shock Incarceration Programs

The first shock incarceration programs began in 1983 in Georgia and Oklahoma (Parent, 1989). By early 1990, there were more than 21 programs for adults in 14 state correctional systems (MacKenzie, 1990; MacKenzie & Ballow, 1989) and 10 more states were considering opening programs. Several city and county jurisdictions had opened boot camp prisons for adults and a number were also considering boot camp prisons for juveniles.

Several factors account for this rapid growth. Boot camps clearly were in tune with the conservative political climate of the 1980s. Politicians who failed to appear tough on crime did so at extreme peril (remember Willie Horton?). Likewise, sanctions such as probation that seemed "soft" on criminals had trouble attracting political support and adequate funding. Boot camps appealed directly to the "gut instincts" of a public that wanted criminals punished swiftly and harshly, in austere, no-frills settings, where they learned to respect authority and to obey rules (see White House, 1989, p. 25).

Journalists publicized shock incarceration widely. Boot camps and electronic journalism, in particular, are a perfect match. Television needs powerful visual images, and boot camps provide them: young criminals snapping to attention when a staff member approaches; a swaggering street thug entering a boot camp whose bravado quickly cracks under a barrage of verbal abuse (delivered in high decibels at extremely close range) by a tough-as-nails drill sergeant; an inmate work crew digging ditches under the scorching sun. The electronic media also need to portray stories quickly; television news programs rarely have the time to give viewers lengthy explanations or detailed background. Millions of Americans have experienced military basic training, and those who have not usually know someone who has, or have seen a score of movies portraying basic training. Boot camps have a "face validity" (Gauthier & Reichel, 1989) that is absent in most corrections programs. Hence they make great 60-second features in the evening news. Americans' wide exposure to military basic training promotes immediate, widespread, and uncritical public and political support for boot camp prisons.

Boot camps are linked to strong traditions in American culture. The basic training model typifies police recruit training in the United States, and tends to reinforce law enforcement support for boot camp prisons. Middle- and upper-income families have long placed unruly male offspring whose behavior borders on the deviant in military boarding schools. In the past, courts sometimes gave these boys' older and less affluent counterparts the choice of going to jail or joining the army, which, it was believed, would "make a man" out of a troublesome boy.

Boot camps also have strong links to U.S. correctional history. Prisons have long been organized around a military-style command structure, even down to custodial job titles—captains, lieutenants, sergeants, and so on. Hard labor, strict rules, rigid discipline, and enforced silence existed in early penitentiaries. More than a hundred years ago, New York's Elmira Reformatory incorporated many elements of today's shock incarceration programs, including drill and ceremony (during which the inmates carried dummy rifles). Inmate movement in lockstep and use of chain gangs are features of prison life many current correctional employees recall. Until the 1960s, summary punishment, unencumbered by written charges and disciplinary hearings, was the rule. In a real sense, boot camps involve returning to familiar themes in American corrections.

Boot camps also are consistent with several current correctional needs and trends. Boot camps let prison officials use the media to spread "good news" about corrections for a change. Severe crowding during the 1980s led to a search for new sanctions that were both tough and affordable, and that plausibly could reduce commitments or inmate populations. Boot camps fit the bill. Crowding also heightened administrators' need to control prisoners via more stringent regulations and stricter discipline.

The Controversy

Opposition to boot camp prisons has been muted, especially from correctional practitioners, but opponents have cited varied reasons for their anti-boot camp positions (see, e.g., Meachum, 1990; Morash & Rucker, 1990). Some question the relevance of the military basic training model for corrections. Obviously, the ultimate mission of military training—teaching killing skills and eliminating soldiers' reluctance to employ them—is not relevant. Although real-world employment requires individuals to be able to exercise self-discipline and, to an extent, suppress their individuality to accommodate organizational needs, the military requires immediate obedience to command and unquestioning acceptance of authority.

More thoughtful critics have argued that basic training prepares soldiers for three to four years of military life, during which they are fed, clothed, sheltered, and given medical care, a job with chances of promotion and pay increases, and opportunities for continued education and training. If the experience changes soldiers' attitudes, behaviors, and postmilitary adjustment for the better, it probably is due more to the period of extended support and structure than to six or eight weeks of basic training. By contrast, under current practice, most prison boot camp graduates return from whence they came, usually no better off in terms of education, jobs, and living conditions or prospects for the future. They daily face the same problems and temptations that got them into trouble before. Critics argue that if a military model has correctional relevance, we must provide a parallel extended period of support, services, and opportunities. They maintain that when we expect 90 days of verbal abuse, push-ups, and marching to cure addiction and reduce recidivism, we not only deceive ourselves, we also sidetrack chances for really effective reforms in the vain search for cheap and quick panaceas.

Critics raise concerns that boot camp prisons expose inmates to increased likelihood of abuse by staff, and injury or even death during physical exercises or hard labor. (To date, two inmates have died during boot camp physical training sessions—both had serious preexisting medical problems that were not detected during routine prison medical examinations.) They argue that boot camp prisons tend to attract the wrong kind of staff—those who are on a "power trip," or who would use enhanced control and discipline to "get even" with inmates. They note that staff burnout and turnover rates are higher in boot camps than in regular prisons, making it especially difficult to recruit and retain qualified staff. Finally, they note that many facets of boot camp prisons (summary punishment, humiliation of inmates, and the like) conflict with standards of accepted professional practice promulgated by the American Correctional Association.

Advocates respond that inmates are abused and injured in regular prisons as well, and that some die there. The key to preventing such incidents lies in effective program design and proper control of staff recruitment, training, and supervision. They argue that, by comparison with regular prisons, boot camps are remarkably free of inmate-on-inmate violence. Properly detailed medical assessments can screen out inmates whose health problems make their participation dangerous. Standards were promulgated before the concept of boot camp prisons appeared, and may need revision. In boot camps, summary physical punishments (push-ups, running, and the like) and verbal humiliation are not intended to degrade inmates (which is what standards try to prevent), but are part of a treatment model designed ultimately to improve inmates' self-esteem, self-control, and respect for authority.

Finally, opponents argue that, as most boot camps are currently used, they cannot help but "widen the net" of correctional control and increase prison populations. Supporters counter that if eligibility and selection are properly structured, boot camps can cut prison populations.

Different Models of Shock Incarceration

In all shock incarceration programs, offenders serve a short period of time in a military boot camp prison (MacKenzie, 1990). They are separated from other prison inmates and are required to participate in military drills, physical training, and hard labor. Beyond this core of similarities, shock incarceration programs differ in purposes, the numbers and sizes of programs provided, the locations of those programs, the types of offenders eligible to participate, selection and screening procedures, program content, release mechanisms, and types of postrelease community supervision. The following sections highlight these differences.

NUMBER AND SIZE OF PROGRAMS

In January 1990, the number of participants in boot camp programs varied from a low of 42 offenders in the Tennessee program to more than 1,600 in New York's programs, with most states having between 100 and 250 boot camp participants (MacKenzie, 1990). Most states operate only one or two programs, although New York now operates five. Other than in New York, the participants make up a very small proportion of the total inmate population.

The size of a program is determined in part by the number of offenders who are eligible and the number who are permitted to drop out or are dismissed for disciplinary reasons. Programs differ in these respects. Some programs have high dropout rates. For example, in the early years of the shock program in Louisiana, 30-40% of the offenders left the program before completion, and in Florida 50% were dismissed. In contrast, almost all who begin the Oklahoma program complete the full program, in part because participants are sent to a "motivational squad" if they are not performing up to expectations. In eight programs the offender must volunteer in order to be eligible to enter the program, and in seven programs offenders can voluntarily drop out.

The average number of days offenders spend in a boot camp prison varies from 90 to 120 in all programs except the New York model, which lasts 180 days. Because program durations are relatively short, their annual capacity is substantially greater than the number of beds they provide. In a 90-day program, each boot camp bed turns over more than four times a year, when dropout and in-program failures are considered. Thus more than 800 inmates can be processed annually through a 200 bed, three-month boot camp program.

PROGRAM LOCATION

Most correctional boot camps are housed in units at larger medium- or maximum-security prisons that serve general inmate populations. This gives participants a more accurate (if distant) vision of what "real" prison is like. It also lets general-population inmates direct taunts and catcalls (often of a threatening sexual nature) at participants when they pass within earshot. Some advocates think locating boot camps at regular prisons improves deterrent effects. It also lets boot camps use resources and services (such as treatment, education, and vocational programs) that might not be available in a small separate institution, or that would be costly to provide separately. Staff recruitment and replacement also are easier when the boot camp is located within a larger general-population prison.

In early 1990, New York was the only state that operated "stand-alone" correctional boot camps. In New York, existing minimum-security forestry camps were converted to house only boot camp inmates. Many staff previously employed at the forestry camps continued to work at the facilities when they were converted to boot camps. The department of corrections developed an elaborate training program for all individuals (including teachers and kitchen staff) working at the shock facilities. Such training may be particularly important when programs are located at separate facilities and staff cannot be rotated in and out of the program.

Advocates of separate facilities note that boot camp inmates do not require expensive high-security facilities. Hence, even if enhanced support programs and services are needed, separate minimum-security boot camps may be a more economical use of existing bed space.

ELIGIBILITY

The majority of the offenders admitted to shock programs are young, convicted of nonviolent crimes, and have not served time in prison on previous felony convictions. There is some variance in programs regarding these characteristics. Of the 14 states with programs in January 1990, half permitted offenders convicted of violent crimes to enter the program. However, all states except Michigan report that most participants were convicted of nonviolent crimes.

Most programs are also designed for first offenders, but the definition of *first offender* varies among states. *First felony offender* means first state felony incarceration in five states, first state felony in one state, and first felony conviction ever in the remaining states. Participating offenders in many of the programs could have served time in jail for felonies or misdemeanors. Only Idaho and Michigan do not necessarily have first felony offenders (by any definition) in their programs.

Most programs were open to males only; however, Louisiana, Mississippi, and New York have programs that include males and females, and South Carolina has a separate program for females. There are also wide differences among programs in age limits for participants. The majority of the states limit participation to those under 25 years old, some have no age limits, and in a few states the offender must be less than 30 or 40. Although the maximum age limit varies, the majority of the participants are young.

SELECTION PROCESSES

Of the 14 state jurisdictions that had programs operating in 1990, judges selected participants in 8, judges and corrections departments shared selection responsibility in 2, the parole commission selected participants in 1, and corrections departments selected participants in 3.

PROGRAM CONTENT

Programs differ greatly in the number of hours devoted to physical training, work, and education or counseling. If the time allotted to rehabilitation-type activities (including such activities as counseling, any type of treatment, education, and vocational training activities) is compared with time spent working, the wide differences among programs become obvious. In some states, offenders spend an amount of time in rehabilitation activities equal to or greater than the amount of time they spend working (e.g., in Alabama, Arizona, Mississippi, New York). For example, Louisiana offenders spend approximately 4.5 hours each day in rehabilitation activities, 4.5 hours working, and 4.5 hours in physical training or drill.

In other states, offenders spend one-half to one-quarter less time in rehabilitation (e.g., in Michigan offenders spend approximately 6 hours per day working, 2.5 hours in rehabilitation activities, and 1.5 hours in physical training and drill). In comparison with offenders in other programs, the Georgia participants spend the least time in rehabilitation activities. They spend less than half an hour per day in rehabilitation. Despite the fact that there is a wide variance in the amount of time devoted to rehabilitation in shock incarceration programs, it appears that most of these offenders spend more time in rehabilitation-type activities in shock programs than they might in traditional prisons.

Several programs are being designed to focus on treatment for drug offenders. Texas, New York, Oklahoma, and Illinois have received federal funding to develop innovative programs addressing the needs of these offenders.

RELEASE AND SUPERVISION

Programs vary greatly in regard to release decision making, and this depends, in part, on the placement authority and the state release mechanism. There are also differences in release supervision. In some cases the offender returns to regular supervision, in eight states the supervision varies as a function of risk level, and in Louisiana, Michigan, and New York offenders are intensively supervised upon release from shock programs.

Only New York has developed an enhanced aftercare program for releasees. While intensive supervision increases the surveillance of offenders in the community, the aftercare program increases their opportunities. In New York City the shock releasees are given work, drug treatment, and counseling opportunities. They are also given the opportunity to meet with other shock offenders in a supervised setting in order to share their experiences and difficulties during transition from shock to the community.

Do Boot Camps Work?

In order to determine whether or not boot camps "work," officials must define, in clear, operational terms, what boot camps are supposed to achieve. The differences noted above in structure and design suggest differences among programs in goals and in what goals can be achieved.

Data are currently being collected from a study of seven different shock incarceration programs (MacKenzie, 1990). The sites were selected specifically because they varied in characteristics that are expected to have a major impact on whether specific goals can be achieved by the shock programs. Although the multisite study of shock incarceration is still in progress, some research has been completed examining specific programs.

REDUCING PRISON CROWDING

Officials in virtually all shock incarceration programs say one of their major goals is to reduce prison crowding. That could occur in two ways. The first, or direct, way is to shorten the period of time offenders spend in prison. The second, or indirect, way is to change the postrelease behavior of boot camp graduates so that fewer return to prison for new convictions or violations of conditions of supervision. This section deals with the direct method; changing offenders' postrelease behavior is considered below.

Boot camps' impact on prison bed space will vary with five factors:

(1) the size of the pool of eligible offenders
(2) the probability that those offenders would be imprisoned if placement in the boot camp program were not available
(3) the rate at which those admitted to boot camps complete the program
(4) the difference between the offenders' regular prison terms and the duration of the boot camp program
(5) the rate at which boot camp graduates return to prison, either for violations of release conditions or for new criminal convictions

Using these characteristics, a model was developed for one jurisdiction, Louisiana, to examine changes in bed space needs as a function of the shock program. The model indicated that a program such as shock incarceration could be used to reduce prison crowding (MacKenzie & Parent, 1991). However, the results of this analysis were dependent upon unique features of the Louisiana program that might differ from other jurisdictions.

One of the estimates necessary for a bed space model is the probability that an offender would have been imprisoned if the program had not been operational. That is, the effectiveness of the program in reducing crowding would depend upon the selection of offenders for the program who would, under other circumstances, be serving time in prison. A frequently encountered problem with intermediate punishments is that they actually *widen* the net of control. According to this thesis, as options are developed that are less restrictive, those who have been treated more leniently in the past will be placed in the program instead of those who previously have been treated more severely (Austin & Krisberg, 1982; Morris & Tonry, 1990).

It was hypothesized that an important distinguishing factor among programs in the degree of net widening would be whether the judge or the department of corrections selected offenders. If the judge made the decisions, net widening was expected to be more apt to occur. The rationale for this hypothesis was that judges appear to be searching for options for offenders who would normally be given probation, and this is why net widening occurs when intermediate punishments are introduced into the system. On the other hand, if selection decisions were made by the department of corrections, offenders would already be prison bound and, theoretically, their time in prison would be reduced if they completed the shock program. As noted above, the authority for selecting offenders differs among jurisdictions.

There are other differences among programs that would be expected to have an impact on prison crowding as well. For instance, there must be a sufficient number of offenders who are eligible and who complete the program. The voluntary nature of a program might limit the number of participants. Shock programs differ in this respect. In eight programs the offender must volunteer in order to be eligible to enter the program, and in seven programs the offenders can voluntarily drop out of the program.

COST OF BOOT CAMP PRISONS

Many policymakers seem to accept, uncritically, a belief that boot camps are less costly than regular prison. However, studies show that prison boot camps cost as much as or more than regular prisons on a per inmate per day basis (Aziz, 1988; MacKenzie, Shaw, & Gowdy, 1990). Boot camps that offer minimal programming and focus mostly on the military regime, exercise, and hard work cost about the same as regular prison on a per inmate per day basis. Boot camps that offer an array of treatment programs and services cost more than regular prisons on a per inmate per day basis. Stand-alone boot camps cost somewhat more than those co-located in regular prisons, because administrative and support costs are not shared among several housing units (Parent, 1989).

Thus boot camps are less costly than regular prisons only if they shorten the duration of confinement for persons who otherwise would be imprisoned. Because boot camps cost much more than probation (even in its most intensive forms), if a large percentage of participants would have been on probation if boot camps had not been available, then boot camps increase total correctional costs. If prison durations are shortened only slightly, boot camps are unlikely to cost less.

Studies of shock incarceration programs in New York and Louisiana found that boot camps reduced correctional costs (Aziz, 1988; MacKenzie et al., 1990). In both of these states prison officials select participants from regular prison admissions.

CHANGING THE OFFENDER

Of course, not everyone expects a short-term program such as shock incarceration to reduce prison crowding. Some advocates of shock may support the programs as an option for those who would previously have served their sentences on probation. They might believe that offenders who complete these programs may be rehabilitated or deterred from future criminal activities. This might secondarily have an impact on prison crowding because these offenders would not return to prison.

Prison populations could be reduced if the criminal activities of shock offenders were reduced upon release. This would be an indirect effect on prison crowding, and would take some time to have an impact. The assumption is that offenders would be rehabilitated or deterred by the experience of the shock incarceration program and would be less apt to be involved in crime in the future. As a result, there would be fewer criminals, fewer convictions, and, hence, fewer offenders sentenced to prison.

Some early research has examined the performance of offenders during community supervision after release from shock incarceration programs. Studies have been completed in Georgia (Georgia Department of Corrections, 1989), Florida (Florida Department of

Corrections, 1989), New York (New York Department of Correctional Services, 1989; New York State Division of Parole, 1989), and Louisiana (MacKenzie, 1991) comparing the recidivism of shock offenders with similar offenders released on parole after spending a longer period of time in a traditional prison and, in Louisiana, with offenders entering a term of probation. No differences were found between the shock offenders and others in either rearrests or reincarcerations.

The groups in the studies cited above were not randomly assigned to treatment conditions. It is hoped that in the future true experimental designs will give more conclusive results. However, to date no research we have seen suggests that the offenders who complete shock programs will have lower recidivism rates in comparison with other offenders. Thus there is no support for the idea that prison crowding will be reduced by shock programs by decreasing the recidivism of offenders.

Deterrence and rehabilitation are two sentencing goals that would result in changing offenders; both methods would be expected to reduce criminal activities. The failure to find that offenders who complete shock programs have lower recidivism than others suggests that these programs may neither deter nor rehabilitate offenders.

It is possible that the measures of recidivism used are not sensitive enough to reflect differences among offender groups, or that the length of follow-up has not been sufficiently long to show the differences in behavior. The New York State Department of Correctional Services (1989) argues that the programs represent a cost savings and that, at the least, the offenders who complete the shock programs do no worse than offenders who spent longer periods in prison. In the end, however, the possibility that these programs do not have a rehabilitative effect cannot be ruled out.

CONSTRUCTIVE PUNISHMENT

One question is whether the punishment aspect of boot camp prisons could have a constructive effect on offenders (MacKenzie, 1991). Physical training, drill, hard labor, and the difficult daily regime may have advantages that should be examined in the future. For example, the physical exercise may free offenders of drugs and make them physically fit. Offenders interviewed near the ends of their sentences in shock report that, in their view, these are benefits of the program (MacKenzie et al., 1990). Another advantage, in the opinion of inmates, is that they have learned to get up in the morning and be active all day.

There may also be an advantage in the fact that boot camp prisons create radical changes in the everyday living patterns of these offenders. Zamble and Porporino (1988) believe that a period of radical change that creates reasonable stress may be a time when people are particularly susceptible to outside influences. In their opinion this may be an excellent time to have an impact on offenders, making them reconsider their past choices. If the program makes an attempt to change the thinking of offenders, the boot camp prison atmosphere may help facilitate this change.

Programs that are not rigorous, that do not allow dropouts, or that do not kick offenders out may have problems with troublemakers in the program; also, such programs provide little test of an individual's commitment to change (MacKenzie & Shaw, 1990). Such programs would also lose some of their challenge; consequently, graduates may not feel that they have succeeded at accomplishing a difficult task. The importance of this aspect of programs is still unknown.

If shock programs were changed to focus on therapy but the boot camp atmosphere was eliminated, perhaps the most important change would be in the attitudes of the public and policymakers. If they are willing to trade a longer term in prison for a program such as this because the program involves hard work and strict discipline, it might be possible to combine the punishment aspects with other components that bring about constructive change in offenders.

RETRIBUTION

Few people mention retribution or punishment as a goal of shock incarceration programs. However, this may be one of the most desirable features of these programs from the perspective of the public and policymakers.

To some extent, shock incarceration programs may be a marketing ploy designed to sell today's policymakers treatment when what they really want to buy is retribution. Correctional administrators are more likely to receive support and funding for programs in which treatment interventions have a punitive aura, which, with some embellishment and clever packaging, enable a legislator to portray it to his or her constituents as punishment.

There are several questions related to the retributive aspects of shock programs that remain unanswered. Retribution has been a generally acknowledged sentencing goal. The degree of punishment of a sentence is usually measured by the sentence length: A longer prison sentence is considered to be more punishment than a shorter sentence; similarly, a longer term of probation is thought to be more punishment than a shorter sentence. The question that arises with regard to shock incarceration is whether the shorter but harsher shock programs are sufficiently retributive and can be exchanged for longer but possibly less harsh terms in traditional prisons. In a sense, this might be considered an issue of quality versus quantity of punishment—shock, with its more intense delivery of punishment, gives "quality" retribution, whereas a longer but less harsh sentence in prison gives "quantity" punishment.

From this perspective, shock programs involving hard work, strict rules, and discipline are punishing environments. Opponents of shock incarceration point out that this is a major change for corrections (Meachum, 1990). According to them, prisons (traditional corrections) have been used *for* punishment, not, as in the shock programs, *as* punishment.

IMPACT OF BOOT CAMPS ON STAFF

Prisons officials note that boot camps have immediate rejuvenating effects on staff who work in them, by giving them a renewed sense of mission (rehabilitation) and by letting them work with a population of inmates (young, never in prison before) who develop positive rather than negative attitudes toward staff.[1] However, these effects seem transitory. As shock programs mature, particularly intense staffing problems emerge. The programs are high-stress environments for both inmates and staff. Staff burnout rates reportedly are much higher than in regular prison assignments. Given the high potential for staff to abuse inmates physically, administrators must be especially vigilant, monitoring staff performance and intervening before it degrades seriously. One state routinely rotates boot camp staff back into regular prison assignments every six months in order to prevent burnout.

Because boot camps have higher staff turnover rates than do regular prisons, recruitment of suitable replacement staff is a continuing problem, particularly if the boot camp is attached to a small general-population prison located in a remote area. In states with small boot camp programs, training for new and replacement staff is minimal and generally done on the job. (With its large-scale boot camp operation, New York has the most elaborate training program for new and replacement boot camp staff.)

LEGAL ISSUES

Prison boot camps pose important legal issues. The potential for injury and staff abuse increases the risk of liability for both the state and individual employees. Appropriate shields against liability, including setting forth written policy and procedures, would minimize chances of inmate injury or death, and stringent program administration would ensure that those policies and procedures are, in fact, followed. For example, routine prison medical assessments may need to be supplemented with additional tests to discover conditions such as endocarditis, which could be life threatening to an inmate doing heavy physical exercise. During hard labor in hot weather, inmates' attire, water intake, and number of breaks must be clearly prescribed in regulations and rigorously observed in practice.

Summary punishments—those inflicted on the spot by officials who have observed infractions, without benefit of written charges or hearings—are the rule in many boot camp prisons. There is a need to develop written policy to guide the use of such punishments. They might be restricted to minor violations, while major violations— those that could adversely affect inmates' liberty interests—could continue to receive due-process guarantees.

There are also legal issues related to those who are not given the opportunity to shorten their sentences through participation in boot camp prisons. Equal-protection requirements imply that if young, physically able male inmates can shorten their prison terms by completing boot camp programs, female inmates and physically handicapped inmates should be eligible for the same reductions. Programs differ on whether or not participation by these groups is possible.

Conclusion

Shock incarceration as a correctional approach is relatively new, but there are precedents in U.S. society in general and in corrections in particular that make these programs not an entirely new method of handling young men. This fact, along with several trends (conservative philosophy, prison crowding), has probably led to the rapid growth of these programs in the United States.

This growth has not, however, been without controversy. Some people strongly oppose these programs and they have numerous reasons for their position. On the other hand, there are many who believe strongly in the worth of these programs. In this chapter we have tried to present both sides of this issue and to examine the available research to support or refute the two positions. Part of the difficulty in examining the research is the need to identify the goals of the programs. Two of the major goals of most programs appear to be to reduce prison crowding and to reduce recidivism. Debate continues about the role of the tough boot camp atmosphere and whether it is a framework for positive change or a method of punishment.

There are other aspects of shock incarceration programs that are of concern to opponents and advocates of the programs. Protecting inmates' rights, screening for medical problems, equal opportunities for women and handicapped offenders, and standards and guidelines are just a few of these issues.

Note

1. During interviews with one of the authors, a drill instructor emotionally described getting a "thank you" letter from a recent boot camp graduate—a first during his 15 years as a prison guard. Also, a probationer who graduated from boot camp two years earlier noted he frequently corresponded with his favorite drill instructor.

References

Austin, J., & Krisberg, B. (1982). The unmet promise of alternatives to incarceration. *Crime and Delinquency, 28,* 374-409.

Aziz, D. (1988). *Shock incarceration evaluation: Preliminary data.* Unpublished report to the New York Department of Correctional Services, Shock Incarceration Legislative Report.

Florida Department of Corrections. (1989). *Boot camp evaluation* and *boot camp commitment rate.* Unpublished report by the Bureau of Planning, Research and Statistics.

Gauthier, A. K., & Reichel, P. L. (1989). *Boot camp corrections: A public reaction.* Paper presented at the annual meeting of the Academy of Criminal Justice Sciences, Washington, DC.

Georgia Department of Corrections. (1989). *Georgia's special alternative incarceration.* Unpublished report to the Shock Incarceration Conference, Washington, DC.

MacKenzie, D. L. (1990). Boot camp prisons: Components, evaluations, and empirical issues. *Federal Probation, 54*(3), 44-52.

MacKenzie, D. L. (1991). The parole performance of offenders released from shock incarceration (boot camp prison): A survival analysis. *Journal of Quantitative Criminology, 7,* 213-236.

MacKenzie, D. L., & Ballow, D. B. (1989). Shock incarceration programs in state correctional jurisdictions: An update. *NIJ Reports, 214,* 9-10.

MacKenzie, D. L., & Parent, D. G. (1991). Shock incarceration and prison crowding in Louisiana. *Journal of Criminal Justice, 19,* 225-237.

MacKenzie, D. L., & Shaw, J. W. (1990). Inmate adjustment and change during shock incarceration: The impact of correctional boot camp programs. *Justice Quarterly 7*(1), 125-150.

MacKenzie, D. L., Shaw, J. W., & Gowdy, V. B. (1990). *An evaluation of shock incarceration in Louisiana.* Unpublished report to the Louisiana Department of Public Safety and Corrections.

Meachum, M. (1990). *Boot camp prisons: Pros and cons.* Paper presented at the annual meeting of the American Society of Criminology, Baltimore.

Morash, M., & Rucker, L. (1990). A critical look at the ideal of boot camp as a correctional reform. *Crime and Delinquency, 36,* 204-222.

Morris, N., & Tonry, M. (1990). *Between prison and probation: Intermediate punishments in a rational sentencing system.* New York: Oxford University Press.

New York State Department of Correctional Services. (1989). *Initial follow-up study of shock graduates.* Unpublished report by the New York State Department of Correctional Services, Division of Program Planning, Research and Evaluation.

New York State Division of Parole. (1989). *Shock incarceration: One year out.* Unpublished report.

Parent, D. (1989). *Shock incarceration: An overview of existing programs.* Washington, DC: National Institute of Justice.

White House. (1989). *National drug control strategy.* Washington, DC: Government Printing Office.

Zamble, E., & Porporino, F. J. (1988). *Coping, behavior, and adaptation in prison inmates.* New York: Springer-Verlag.

PART IV

Other Intermediate Sanctions

8. The Use of Fines as an Intermediate Sanction

Sally T. Hillsman

Judith A. Greene

Intermediate sanctions are not new in American sentencing, and fines in particular are a very ancient and widely used penalty in our courts. What *is* new is the surge of enthusiasm for systematically incorporating nonincarcerative sanctions into emerging sentencing systems. This development is a direct response to the pressing fiscal and justice concerns that have arisen from the uniquely American reliance on imprisonment as the primary means of punishing criminal behavior.

Despite more than a decade of unprecedented jail and prison building across the United States, few inroads have been made in alleviating conditions in our crowded and deteriorating correctional institutions. Although prison expansion has been accompanied by an explosion of experimental alternative sanctions—community service orders, house arrest, electronic monitoring, intensive probation, boot camps, and more—the intermediate penalties movement has yet to engage in any significant way the problems raised by our broad use of imprisonment. This is partly because the new sanctions have been developed piecemeal, and partly because they are typically used in combination with imprisonment and probation rather than imposed as stand-alone sentences.

Yet continued concern about our financial capacity to use incarceration to deliver fair and just punishment has compelled a focus on creating a graduated progression of intermediate penalties that would permit imprisonment to be reserved for violent, predatory crimes. What has emerged over the last decade is a range of nonincarcerative sentencing options that have the potential to be applied broadly and scaled systematically to provide appropriate levels of punishment across offenses of varying severity. This development has now begun to foster efforts to integrate intermediate penalties into existing or reconfigured sentencing schemes (Knapp, 1988; Morris, 1987; Morris & Tonry, 1990; Tonry, 1988; von Hirsch, Wasik, & Greene, 1989).

The design of systems of graduated sanctions can be encouraged by emphasizing nonincarcerative penalties that meet the long-standing requirements of American jurisprudence: clear purposes, proportionate punishment calibrated in relation to the gravity of the offense, wide applicability across the spectrum of criminal behavior, effective enforcement, and relatively simple, inexpensive administration. In this context, among the nonincarcerative sanctions already in place in most jurisdictions, the criminal fine is a particularly attractive option.

The Fine as a Criminal Penalty

Fines have many characteristics that lead them to be used more widely as a criminal penalty in American courts, as well as in Europe and elsewhere, than is commonly recognized (Hillsman, 1990). These same characteristics make fines especially well suited to systematic application as an intermediate penalty.

The fine is unmistakably punitive and deterrent in its aim, fitting well into current trends toward retribution and deterrence in sentencing philosophy.[1] It stresses offender accountability by demanding the offender pay his or her debt to society, and permits the size of that debt to be scaled to reflect the severity of a particular offense across an almost unlimited range of criminal behavior.[2] This flexibility also extends to adjusting the size of the offender's fine to his or her income so that equal punishment can be administered across offenders with vastly different financial circumstances who are convicted of the same crime. Fines can also be enforced relatively easily and inexpensively even though the offender is in the community. Despite the widespread belief in American courts that fines cannot be collected (Cole, Mahoney, Thornton, & Hanson, 1987), research on courts' actual track records provides significant support for viewing the criminal fine as enforceable (Hillsman & Mahoney, 1988; Tait, 1988; Wick, 1988).

Finally, the fine is already part of the sentencing repertoire of most American courts, large and small, urban and rural, and the structures to administer it effectively are generally in place (Hillsman, 1988). In addition, unlike other intermediate penalties, fines generate revenue. They can, therefore, be financially self-sustaining and possibly even provide revenue for other related purposes, such as victim compensation.

Despite these obvious advantages, the fine has not yet been systematically developed as an intermediate penalty in the United States, although this situation is rapidly changing, as we indicate below. Research on the use of fines across courts of limited and general jurisdiction in this country indicates that fine use is highly variable (Hillsman, Sichel, & Mahoney, 1984) and that fines, like newer intermediate penalties, are often combined with other sanctions rather than allowed to stand on their own as the sole punishment (Cole et al., 1987, p. 8).[3]

This American pattern is in stark contrast to the use of fines in much of Western Europe, where they are imposed, as sole sanctions, as the sentence of choice in most criminal cases (Casale, 1981). In West Germany, for example, 81% of all adult crimes and 73% of all crimes of violence are punished by fines as the sole penalty (*Strafverfolgungsstatistik*, 1986). In England, 38% of all offenses equivalent to our felonies and 39% of all violent offenses result in fines (Home Office, 1988). The use of the fine as the primary sanctioning device in Western Europe is not recent. It stems from a long-standing tradition of jurisprudence committed to retribution and deterrence as the primary purposes of sentencing that was never weakened by the treatment/rehabilitation model of imprisonment embraced by Americans in the nineteenth century (Hillsman, 1990, pp. 52ff.).

Setting Fine Amounts:
The Key to Their Usefulness
as an Intermediate Sanction

Why has the fine not come into similar prominence in the United States as we have moved toward greater emphasis on punishment and deterrence in sentencing? Among American criminal justice practitioners, there lingers a deep skepticism about the usefulness of fine sentences that focuses on the *absolute* size of the fine: Don't fines need to be large in order to be punitive and to deter? This emphasis on large fines leads to further issues about the fairness of fine sentences: If fines are large enough to punish and deter, how can they be collected from the majority of offenders who come before American courts? And if only those who can pay sizable amounts are fined, are not these more affluent offenders buying their way out of the more punitive sentences to imprisonment?[4]

These concerns are voiced often in the United States. They help explain why criminal justice practitioners, in a country that relies heavily on financial incentives and disincentives in many areas of social and economic life, are cautious about the effectiveness of fines to punish and deter criminal behavior.

By contrast, European discussions of the fine's usefulness emphasize the *variability* of fine amounts and thus the flexibility of this sanction to deliver punishment and deterrence in a manner both fair and effective (Albrecht, 1980; Morgan & Bowles, 1981; Thornstedt, 1975). Because the fine is numerical, Europeans note, its size (and therefore its punitiveness) can be varied to reflect simultaneously the severity of the offense and the affluence of the offender. Fines of variable amounts, therefore, if they are systematically set, are regarded as imposing a fair and equitable level of punishment as well as being collectible. Since a collected fine delivers the intended punishment, it is viewed as an effective deterrent.[5]

FIXED-FINE TARIFF SYSTEMS

Research on fining practices in the United States helps explain American judges' focus on the absolute size of the fine and its troubling justice consequences. Despite their broad discretion in setting fine amounts, American judges generally impose fines well below statutory limits even though legislatures have recently begun to expand the fine's potential punitive range by raising fine ceilings (Hillsman et al., 1984). This pattern occurs because, in determining what penalty to impose in a particular case, the retributive trend in sentencing leads judges to emphasize the severity of the offense. When considering whether a fine would be an appropriate punishment, however, American judges generally have only "tariff" or fixed-fine systems to guide their decisions as to what constitutes an appropriate amount.

As in setting the "size" of other sentences (days of imprisonment, hours of community service, years of probation supervision), American judges tend to apply "going rates" for fines that are based upon (usually informal) understandings that the same or similar amounts will be imposed on *all* defendants coming before the court convicted of a particular offense. These tariff systems have evolved in courts to meet judicial concerns about equity and consistency in sentencing.[6] It is the extension of these traditional tariff or going-rate systems of sentencing to setting *fine* amounts, however, that has limited the usefulness of fines as an intermediate sanction in the United States.

In developing tariffs for fines, American courts tend to set the going rates with an eye to the lowest common economic denominator of offenders coming before the court. This is in order to address another central judicial concern, namely, that sentences be credible (i.e., that the fines they impose be collectible). As a result, fixed-fine tariff systems tend to depress fine amounts, causing them to cluster near the bottom of the statutorily permissible range. This outcome constricts the range of offenses for which judges will view a fine as an appropriate sole sanction to those at the lower end of the severity spectrum, thus restricting the fine's usefulness as a penalty.

In addition, insofar as the tariff systems common to American courts encourage judges to define consistency in sentencing as requiring the same fine *amount* for all offenders sentenced for the same crime, the punitive impact of fine sentences will be comparatively less for more affluent offenders. This clear lack of fairness distorts the principles of equity and proportionality and contributes to American judges' "ambivalence and confusion about fining" (Cole et al., 1987, p. 19).

VARIABLE FINE SYSTEMS

Research on fining practices in several Northern European countries reveals a quite different process for determining the amount of a fine (Albrecht & Johnson, 1980; Casale, 1981; Hillsman, 1990). Fining systems in West Germany, Sweden, Finland, Denmark, France, Portugal, and Greece (and, more recently, in Austria, Hungary, and, on an experimental basis, England) initially separate the judge's assessment about the gravity of the offense entirely from any examination of the offender's ability to pay a fine.[7] Although both factors are crucial in setting a fine amount that is just and collectible, as well as appropriate, they are assessed independently and linked only at the very end of the sentencing process. Then, taken together, these factors permit the judge to set a financial penalty that is proportionate to the severity of the crime *and* that produces an equal economic burden on offenders with unequal means.

In practice, judges in these countries first determine the number of fine *units* to which an offender will be sentenced by selecting a number that reflects the degree of punishment appropriate for the specific criminal behavior. These units of punishment are expressed numerically (e.g., 10, 50, 125), without reference to any monetary value. To ensure uniformity in setting the number of fine units, courts have developed (often informal) guidelines or benchmarks that indicate what range of units is appropriate for crimes of differing severity.

After determining the number of fine units, the judge then reviews the offender's financial circumstances in order to set a *monetary value* for these fine units. Again, European courts have typically developed rough but standardized methods for calculating these values. Generally, unit values are based on some proportion of a defendant's daily income that is considered a "fair share" for the purposes of fining. It is this use of daily income for valuing the fine units that has led the resulting fine sentences to be called *day fines* everywhere except England, where they are called *unit fines*.

Using information routinely available from police or probation departments, or, more often, directly from the defendant and his or her counsel, the judge using a day-fine system estimates the defendant's daily income, calculates the unit value at some proportion of that amount, and multiplies it by the number of units to which the offender has been sentenced. The resulting "day fine," therefore, is an amount that is in direct proportion to the seriousness of the specific criminal behavior but should also impose an equivalent economic burden on offenders convicted of the same crime who have vastly different financial circumstances.[8]

THE POTENTIAL OF THE DAY FINE FOR AMERICAN PRACTICE

While fines currently play a less central role in sentencing in the United States than in Western Europe, this outcome appears to flow more from the "ambivalence and confusion about fining" that characterizes judicial attitudes than from explicit sentencing preferences. Indeed, the enormous variability in fine use revealed by research on American courts over the last decade suggests there is room for expanding the usefulness of this sentencing tool in the United States *if* the rigidities and resulting inequities of the tariff system can be overcome.

In many American courts, individual judges are already struggling to free themselves from the limitations of fixed-fine systems. Sometimes they adjust the "going rate" by reviewing whatever they can learn about an individual's circumstances at sentencing (Hillsman et al., 1984, pp. 64-65, 182). At other times, judges modify the amounts originally imposed, either by formally excusing the outstanding balance at some point postsentence, or by letting court supervision expire without enforcing the fine order. Judges acknowledge, however, that such case-by-case decisions may not always conform to the requirements of due process or be demonstrably fair (Casale & Hillsman, 1986; Hillsman et al., 1984, p. 60).

When asked about the desirability and feasibility of experimenting with the systematic imposition of variable-amount fines, such as the European day fine, more than half of a national sample of American trial judges interviewed in 1985 said such a system could work in their courts (Mahoney & Thornton, 1988, pp. 59ff.). And, as we have found since then, the judges are right; it can work. In August 1988, the first day fine in the United States was imposed by a judge of the Richmond County Criminal Court in Staten Island, New York, a borough of New York City. This experiment was part of a pilot project run jointly by the court and the Vera Institute, and funded by the National Institute of Justice and the City of New York.

Day Fines in New York: The Staten Island Economic Sanctions Project

The first effort to substitute systematically day fines for fixed fines in an American court was the product of an 18-month planning process. It involved the Staten Island Criminal Court bench, prosecutors, public and private defense attorneys, court administrators, and planners and researchers from the Vera Institute of Justice in New York City (Hillsman & Greene, 1987).

During the previous decade, Vera researchers and colleagues from the Institute for Court Management of the National Center for State Courts had been studying American and European courts' use and administration of fines.[9] From this investigation of courts' actual experiences with fines, there emerged a belief that the European day-fine technique could provide the flexible tool needed by American courts to make the criminal fine a more useful intermediate penalty in the United States.[10] The initial obstacle that needed to be overcome, however, was to demonstrate that this concept could be adapted to an American context and successfully implemented in a fairly typical American court.[11]

Since its inception, the Staten Island pilot project has demonstrated that the day fine is a workable sentencing option: A scale of benchmarks for fine units can be informally agreed upon and implemented by all the major actors in the sentencing process; a system for valuing those units can be developed and the necessary means information secured in a busy court without disrupting the flow of cases or burdening court staff; collection procedures can be streamlined and result in high levels of compliance without significant jailing for default; and revenues can rise as a result.

COMPONENTS OF THE STATEN ISLAND DAY-FINE SENTENCE

The court-based planning group began the process of replacing the traditional "going fine rates" by creating sentencing benchmarks that Staten Island judges could use as a guide to impose an appropriate number of day-fine units. Aided by data from samples of recent cases, the planning group classified common criminal behaviors coming before the court according to their seriousness. They then distributed a range of fine units across these offenses.[12] "Discount" and "premium" numbers of units were established on either side of the presumptive number for each offense, to provide the judge with flexibility in individual cases. The benchmarks were then distributed in workbook form to the Staten Island bench and bar (see Table 8.1).

Similarly, the planning group crafted a systematic method for giving a dollar value to the fine units, taking into consideration both what information was readily available to the court and the defendant's privacy rights. The court's pretrial services agency was already providing the bench with a significant amount of relevant information (often verified) for the purposes of setting release conditions. This included employment, other sources of income (parents, welfare, unemployment), school enrollment, residence, and dependents.[13]

The Staten Island planning group decided to begin with the offender's daily income net of taxes, discounting that amount according to the number of dependents supported by the offender. (The formula used was based on common approaches to setting child support payments for noncustodial parents.) The initial valuation method was then tested out on a set of real cases sentenced previously by the court to see what day-fine amounts would result. In response to the findings, a second discount was added by the planning group to bring the day-fine amounts into closer conformity with the tariff levels prevailing before the reform. However, the planning group wanted to make this adjustment primarily at the lower end of the income spectrum, rather than at the higher end, which the group felt had been underfined previously as a result of the "lowest common economic denominator" character of the tariffs. Thus, in the Staten Island day-fine system, net daily income is discounted for dependents

TABLE 8.1 Broad Classification of Penal Law Offenses Into Staten Island Day-Fine Benchmark Severity Levels (partial list)

Severity Level/Penal Law Number		Behavior	Offense and Degree	Day-Fine Units	
Level 1 (95-120 day-fine units)					
130.20	AM	harm persons	sexual misconduct	90-120	DF
120.00	AM	harm persons	assault 3	20-95	DF
Level 2 (65-90 day-fine units)					
260.10	AM	harm persons	endangerment of child welfare	20-90	DF
215.50	AM	obstruction of justice	criminal contempt 2	75	DF
120.20	AM	harm persons	reckless endangerment 2	65	DF
110-155.30	AM	property	attempted grand larceny 4	20-65	DF
Level 3 (45-60 day-fine units)					
265.01	AM	weapons	possession of weapon 4	35-60	DF
155.25	AM	property	petit larceny	5-60	DF
165.40	AM	property	possession of stolen property 5	5-60	DF
165.05	AM	property	unauthorized use of a vehicle	5-60	DF
221.40	AM	drugs	sale of marijuana 4	50	DF
225.05	AM	misconduct	promotion of gambling 2	50	DF
220.03	AM	drugs	possession of contraband substance 7	35-50	DF
110-120.00	BM	harm persons	attempted assault 3	10-45	DF
Level 4 (30-40 day-fine units)					
170.05	AM	theft	forgery 3	40	DF
221.15	AM	drugs	possession of marijuana 4	35	DF
110-140.15	BM	property	attempted criminal trespass 2	30	DF
245.00	BM	sex crime	public lewdness	30	DF
110-155.25	BM	property	attempted petit larceny	5-30	DF
110-165.40	BM	property	attempted possession of stolen property 5	5-30	DF

continued

TABLE 8.1 Continued

Severity Level/Penal Law Number		Behavior	Offense and Degree	Day-Fine Units	
Level 5 (15-25 day-fine units)					
240.37	AM	sex crime	loitering/prostitution	25	DF
205.30	AM	obstruction of justice	resisting arrest	25	DF
110-221.40	BM	drugs	attempted sale of marijuana 4	25	DF
110-265.05	BM	weapons	attempted possession of weapon 4	5-25	DF
110-120.20	BM	harm persons	attempted reckless endangerment 2	20	DF
140.10	BM	property	criminal trespass 3	20	DF
240.25	VIO	misconduct	harassment	15	DF
Level 6 (5-10 day-fine units)					
165.09	AM	property	auto stripping 2	10	DF
221.10	BM	drugs	possession of marijuana 5	5	DF
230.00	BM	sex crime	prostitution	5	DF
190.05	BM	theft	issuing bad check	5	DF
240.36	BM	misconduct	loitering 1	5	DF
140.05	VIO	property	trespass	5	DF
240.20	VIO	misconduct	disorderly conduct	5	DF

SOURCE: From S. T. Hillsman, "Fines and Day Fines," in M. Tonry & N. Morris (Eds.), *Crime and Justice: A Review of Research* (Vol. 12), pp. 86-87. Copyright 1990 by the University of Chicago Press. Reprinted by permission.
NOTE: AM = A-misdemeanor; BM = B-misdemeanor; VIO = violation.

and then by one-half if the offender is below the federal poverty line; if the offender's income is above the poverty line, however, it is discounted by one-third.[14]

The resulting "finable shares" of offenders' net incomes were viewed by the Staten Island planning group as appropriate and equitable. A chart similar to a tax table was constructed, with net daily income down the vertical axis and number of dependents across the horizontal axis. Using this table, the judge on the bench can quickly locate a specific offender at the intersection of these two dimensions and select the appropriate day-fine unit value from the table. Multiplying this value by the number of fine units the judge has already selected from the benchmark scales, the calculation of the day-fine amount due is simple and routine for the sentencing judge, and predictable for the defendant.[15]

RESULTS OF THE PILOT

In practice, day fines are not as complicated as they may appear. Indeed, a participant in the Staten Island planning process tends to quip: "There's less here than meets the eye." Once the planning group confronted and discussed the conceptual issues underlying construction of the first American day-fine benchmarks and valuation scheme, its members recognized that they were already handling the same issues on a case-by-case basis in their courts every day. Crafting the mechanics of the day-fine system, therefore, became a matter of thoughtfully standardizing and systematizing their collective best judgments and making them visible to all participants in the sentencing process.[16]

It is not surprising, therefore, that implementation of the day-fine system in the Staten Island court was relatively smooth and, as we shall discuss below, that the model is currently being adapted for use in other limited and general jurisdiction courts across the country. Although use of the day-fine system was not mandatory for the Staten Island judges, they virtually substituted day fines for all fixed fines in penal law cases.[17] Fine use also appears to have remained stable during the pilot year. Thus, while the process of reforming the fining process was not a disincentive to imposing fine sentences, introducing the day fine does not appear to have either encouraged the court to use fines more often or changed the court's pattern of fine use, at least during the initial trial period.[18]

The impact of the day fine is clearest in the increased variability of fine amounts and in their overall size. Under the traditional fixed-fine system, fines clustered at the court's different tariff points; under the day fine, they scattered across the statutorily permissible range (and would have scattered further if state statutes had not limited that range). Furthermore, fine amounts rose, reflecting the larger day-fine amounts levied on more affluent offenders. The total dollar amount of fines imposed using the day-fine method during the pilot year rose 14% over the previous year, according to the project evaluation.

However, the real impact of day fines on fine amounts is actually greater than the pilot data suggest. This is because the Staten Island day-fine pilot had to operate within low statutory fine maxima that the state legislature has not increased since 1965. These statutes effectively "capped" about a quarter of the higher fine amounts arrived at by the Staten Island judges through application of the day-fine system. Without these statutory fine limits ($1,000, $500, and $250 for different levels of misdemeanors), the mean day-fine amount in the first year of the pilot would have been more than twice the mean under the tariff system in the previous year ($441 compared with $206). With the caps, however, the mean day fine actually imposed was still higher than before ($258), but only by 25%.

Despite the higher fine amounts imposed during the pilot, the court's already good record of collection remained good. Project data indicate that, to date, 70% of the offenders sentenced to day fines during the pilot year have paid the full amount, and another 1.3% paid a substantial proportion of the amount originally set before the court remitted the balance. An additional 13% of the offenders originally sentenced to day fines have been returned to court for resentencing (generally to community service, "time served," or to jail terms averaging 11 days); 2% are still paying or have their cases under appeal (Greene, 1980).

In all, therefore, 84% of the offenders sentenced to day fines in Staten Island have had their sentences enforced by the court, most through payment of the original day fine and a few through revocation of the fine and a resentence; enforcement has failed with the remaining 14%, for whom arrest warrants are currently outstanding. This is a significant record of compliance with an intermediate penalty. Furthermore, to achieve this level of compliance, the court needed to resort to the most coercive enforcement device, a brief period of imprisonment for default, in relatively few cases (10% of the completed cases).

Given the successful implementation of the day-fine pilot, and the justice as well as revenue implications of these program results, the

New York State Legislature will soon consider a bill to raise the fine maxima as well as to formalize the day fine for application in other jurisdictions within the state.[19]

The Future of the Day Fine as an Intermediate Penalty

Continued adaptation of the day-fine concept to the U.S. context, based upon the model developed in Staten Island, is occurring beyond the state of New York. The Maricopa County Superior Court (Phoenix, Arizona) and its Adult Probation Department launched a pilot in 1991, with support from the State Justice Institute, that extended day fines into the felony range. The work of this court is significant for other reasons as well.

First, the superior court is testing whether day fines can be used as an alternative to supervised probation for individuals now sentenced to probation for felony convictions but who do not require the full range of supervision and services typically provided by the Probation Department. The goal is to provide appropriate punishment for a significant number of felony offenders while at the same time conserving the scarce resources of the department so it can expand the efforts of its active Community Programs Division to provide different types of supervised intermediate penalties for cases now being incarcerated. The Probation Department is monitoring those sentenced to day fines, but only with regard to their payments, until they have fulfilled the monetary obligation established by the court using the day-fine system.

The second significant dimension of the Maricopa County day-fine pilot stems from the fact that, by Arizona statute, the judges must impose a full array of mandatory monetary penalties (including several that are fixed amounts as well as full, maximum restitution) on all offenders regardless of their sentences. Planners from the court, the Probation Department, and the Vera Institute have addressed this issue, increasingly common around the country, by using the day-fine system to set a total dollar amount available for sentencing that is proportionate to the offense and reflective of the offender's means. This amount is distributed by the judge to the various monetary penalties required by law and selected by the judge. As indicated above, the offender then remains under court control on the special fine-monitoring caseload of the Probation Department only so long as it takes to collect the total day-fine amount; if additional mandatory amounts are still owed (i.e., drug fines), civil enforcement remains available.[20]

While Phoenix and New York State pursue these new agendas to improve existing day-fine models and extend their application, the Bureau of Justice Assistance has also initiated a national day-fine demonstration involving additional sites in Oregon, Connecticut, and Iowa (see Bureau of Justice Assistance, 1991). This effort is being evaluated by the Rand Corporation under a grant from the NIJ. It will provide an important test of the capacity of American courts to develop day-fine sentences and to locate them within an array of intermediate penalties that provide an alternative to imprisonment.

Finally, two states that have already moved significantly to develop structured sentencing schemes (Minnesota and Oregon) are attempting to integrate nonincarcerative penalties into a graded progression of sanctions. In 1990 the Minnesota legislature directed its sentencing guidelines commission to establish a system of day fines as part of this effort, and in Oregon the sentencing guidelines council is moving forward on a parallel path.

It remains to be seen, however, whether these or other American jurisdictions will move in the direction suggested by Morris and Tonry (1990), in their pathbreaking book on intermediate punishments, to make "the fine the basic coin of punishment, . . . the preferred sanction in all cases where a prison sentence of two years or less is to be imposed" (pp. 123-124). The preconditions for the fine to be such a building block in a rational system of sentencing, according to Morris and Tonry, are "a principled means for adjusting the amount of the fine both to the offender's culpability and to his resources, and . . . efficient and reliable systems of enforcement and collection to assure that fines imposed will in fact be paid." In the last decade, American courts have come a long way toward meeting this challenge.

Notes

1. "It is not difficult to find reasons for the attractiveness of fines for sentencers. . . . Fines are unequivocally punitive, designed to deter, a significant attraction now that the treatment/rehabilitative ideal has fallen from grace. The meaning of fines is clear. Unlike community service, probation, or even custody, it is doubtful whether sentencers, defendants, victims, and public at large disagree about what a fine represents though . . . different sentencing purposes may result in considerable disagreement as to the appropriate size of a fine in any particular case" (Morgan & Bowles, 1981, p. 203).

2. This is not to say that some offenses might be inappropriate for a fine, although Morris and Tony (1990) suggest that "there can in principle be no reason why the fine cannot serve as a credible punishment for nontrivial, indeed serious crimes. And no one can doubt that financial penalties can be devised that are draconic to a point where they ultimately constitute financial capital punishment" (p. 112; see also pp. 119-122).

3. Fines do not, however, tend to be combined with imprisonment in the United States (unless the term is suspended); rather, they are combined most often with other monetary penalties (such as court costs, restitution, and fees of various types) and with probation. When combined with probation, it is not always clear whether probation was intended to be the primary sanction, with the fine an added punishment, or whether the fine is the primary punishment, with probation imposed as the vehicle for its collection (Hillsman, 1990, pp. 61ff.).

4. There is some irony that this skepticism has not discouraged American legislators and judges from imposing large restitution payments and multiple, often mandatory, reimbursements and fees on many offenders *in addition to* their primary sentences. As a sentencing policy, this proliferation of fees and "taxes" has been viewed less in terms of sentencing jurisprudence than as a way of transferring the social costs of crime to the offender population. A 1987 National Institute of Corrections monograph, for example, lists 23 different types of service fees and five special assessments that are being imposed in courts around the country in addition to fines, court costs, restitution, and reparations (Mullaney, 1987). Even this list is not exhaustive; New York State's penalty assessment and Arizona's antiracketeering assessment are not included.

5. The research literature from both sides of the Atlantic is not discouraging with regard to the deterrent value of fines, although most deterrence research is methodologically weak. Comparative reoffense rates for German offenders sentenced to imprisonment and to fines, for example, controlling for offense type and severity, prior record, age, and social class, suggest an advantage for fines (Albrecht & Johnson, 1980). Similar findings for the United States have been reported for Los Angeles by Glaser and Gordon (1988) and for England by McCord (1985), Softley (1977), Davies (1970), and McClintock (1963).

6. Indeed, the tariff systems operating in particular courts are one of the reasons research tends to find greater consistency in sentencing patterns within jurisdictions than across them. While tariff systems do not eliminate disparity, they do tend to reduce it.

7. Similar variable fine systems are also found in the penal laws of Cuba, Peru, Brazil, Costa Rica, and Bolivia, and efforts to establish such systems are progressing in Spain and Switzerland.

8. For a more detailed discussion of the most prominent of these day-fine systems, those in West Germany and Sweden, see Hillsman (1990).

9. Prior to the 1980s, little was known about the use of criminal fines in the United States, or their collection and enforcement. The National Institute of Justice wanted to fill this gap with policy-relevant empirical research; therefore, it funded four studies between 1980 and 1988 (Casale & Hillsman, 1986; Cole et al., 1987; Glaser & Gordon, 1988; Hillsman et al., 1984). NIJ also funded the Staten Island day-fine demonstration project (Greene, 1990; Hillsman & Greene, 1987; Winterfield & Hillsman, 1991), and is currently working with the Bureau of Justice Assistance on a national day-fine demonstration.

10. West Germany's experience in using day fines to replace fixed fines was particularly instructive. The well-documented results of this major sentencing reform were strong evidence that the day-fine approach to ensuring greater equity and efficiency could facilitate the expansion of fines as a nonincarcerative option. While

the policy shift was more dramatic in West Germany than would ever occur in the United States, it was nonetheless encouraging.

In response to exceedingly overcrowded conditions in West German prisons and to a high court decision that triple-celling was unconstitutional, the legislature revised the Federal Republic's penal code in 1969. The principle established by the legislature was that short terms of imprisonment (six months or less) should be replaced by fines in all but exceptional cases. To facilitate this transition, the reform statutes required the introduction of a day-fine system (based on the Scandinavian model) to ensure fines would be set at levels that were proportionate and equitable, and therefore collectible (Friedman, 1983).

Researchers from the Max Planck Institute studied the reform and concluded: "Ten years after the introduction of the fine on a large scale, our data support the view that the policy has been found politically acceptable, administratively practical and penologically sound" (Albrecht & Johnson, 1980, p. 13). This highly positive but somewhat dry assessment fails to convey the stunning impact of these changes on West Germany's use of imprisonment: Prior to the reform, more than 110,000 prison sentences of less than six months were imposed each year in West Germany (20% of all convictions); the number declined to just over 10,000 (1.8%) by 1976, with a corresponding increase in the number of stand-alone fines (Gillespie, 1980).

11. The criminal court in Staten Island is like many other American lower courts, which have long been the major users of fine sentences in this country. This court sentences a broad range of criminal offenses, including many felonies disposed as misdemeanors. Its repertoire of sentencing options includes jail sentences of less than one year, supervised probation, restitution, and community service as well as fines. Fines were already in heavy use in this court; however, the judges wanted to impose fines that were more "meaningfully tailored to the individual, so that the offender understands that crime does not pay, rather it is the criminal who pays" (McBrien, 1988, p. 42). Similarly, prosecutors wanted to make these sentences more viable: "One of the functions of criminal fines is to make it hurt a little bit. By having some idea of the economic effect, you have an idea whether it's just a slap on the wrist or for real. The way it is now, fines are basically just imposed 'off the hip' " (Berliner, quoted in Hurley, 1988).

12. Modeling some aspects of the Staten Island day-fine system on the West German system, an initial 120-unit range was selected for the Staten Island benchmark scales. This was the bottom third of the 360-unit range used in West Germany to link (at least roughly) day-fine sentences to the number of days of imprisonment they were meant to replace. Because the Staten Island court caseload does not include the full felony range of criminal offenses under New York State statutes, the misdemeanor benchmarks for this court were restricted, leaving the upper two-thirds of the 360-unit range for felonies, should day fines be expanded to offenses sentenced in the upper court.

13. A survey of judges across the country about their fining practices indicates that judges in many courts view the lack of financial information as a major problem (Cole et al., 1987). It is possible, however, that judges in some American courts could have far more information, without major structural reforms, if they asked for it.

European judges using day fines, as well as American judges setting bail, typically ask defendants and their counsel for relevant information. European judges report a high degree of confidence in the self-reported information they receive from typical offenders, and verification efforts in the Staten Island court support the parallel view of its judges. However, European judges are somewhat less confident about the accuracy of reports from higher-income offenders. As a result, when such offenders are reluctant to provide verification, judges tend to use the "best guess" method, based upon what they do know about the offender or can extract from him or her, including information about occupation, residence, make of car, and the like. Since there are few appeals of these sentences, it would appear this informal process works relatively well.

In the United States, similar processes at the bench are common at sentencing. Most state statutes, in fact, permit extensive, virtually unlimited, presentence investigations; this provides judges with a statutory basis for requesting detailed information, *and documentation* when necessary, from individuals about their financial circumstances. The only significant legal limitation to this inquiry is the inability of American courts to get tax or financial information directly from the IRS or financial institutions. In most routine criminal cases, however, this is not much of an impediment to the sentencing judge, including those imposing day fines in Staten Island (Greene, 1990).

14. Even with means-based fines, poverty and wealth remain difficult issues in the use of monetary penalties. Presumably a totally destitute person should not be sentenced to such a penalty; however, a person with a steady source of income, even if it is very low—welfare or other fixed incomes—can be fined using a means-based system (and are in Staten Island), so long as reasonable installment payments are set as required by both common sense and the U.S. Constitution (*Tate v. Short*, 401 U.S. 395 [1971]). This logic extends to those "indigent by virtue of age"—unemployed or in-school youth—or, for that matter, unemployed but employable adults in a household who may be fined, as they are in Staten Island, based on the assumption that they can get minimum-wage jobs in fast-food restaurants or similar establishments.

For the very wealthy, inequities may also remain with a means-based system, although they will be significantly smaller than under a fixed-fine system, at least for the routine criminal cases found in most state courts. For more specialized and less frequent cases, however, further consideration of ways to take account of very high incomes and capital assets would be useful.

15. Samples of the benchmarks and valuation tables from the Staten Island workbook can be found, along with illustrations of their use in specific cases, in Hillsman (1990) and in Greene (1990).

16. One of the key elements in the German day-fine legislative reform was to ensure "truth in sentencing," that is, full disclosure to the defendant and the public of the method by which the amount of the criminal penalty was being determined. In Staten Island, the *Day-Fine Workbook* was widely circulated to the defense bar, public and private, many of whom participated in the court's pilot project, and the court's pilot activities also received positive attention from the local press as well as from the *New York Times* (see, e.g., Brozan, 1988; "Criminal Fines," 1988; Gerstel, 1988; Hurley, 1988).

17. The day fines were imposed in 67% of all penal law fine sentences imposed during the pilot year; the remaining fixed-fine sentences involved cases handled by judges temporarily sitting as substitutes in the court who had not been trained to use the *Day-Fine Workbook*, or uncommon offenses that had not yet been incorporated into the benchmark scales. The Staten Island pilot also did not include criminal cases stemming from traffic violations (most driving under the influence). This exclusion was necessary because New York State statutes require fixed fines in these specific cases and planners did not want to deal with this legislative issue during the pilot.

18. A detailed analysis of these issues is found in an evaluation of the pilot conducted by the Vera Institute Research Department under a grant from the NIJ (Winterfield & Hillsman, 1991). Researchers are modeling the sentencing process in Staten Island before and after introduction of the day fine to see if there are any

changes in sentencing patterns; if so, the analysis will address what nonfine sentencing categories (e.g., probation, imprisonment, or an unconditional discharge) day fines displaced, and whether day fines were imposed for offenses of more or less severity than were fixed fines.

19. To date, 77% of the day-fine dollars levied by the Staten Island court have been collected. The project estimates, however, that the actual dollar value of fine revenues would have been approximately 79% *higher* if the statutory fine maxima had not capped the fines for the most affluent offenders sentenced by the court (Greene, 1990).

20. By projecting hypothetical day-fine amounts using actual superior court cases, planners estimate that the day fine will cover all mandatory monetary penalties in more than 80% of the target cases. In most of these cases, the day fine will also include a nonmandatory amount imposed to cover the monitoring activities of the Probation Department. However, because of the mandatory full damage standard for restitution required by the Arizona statutes, a small proportion of target cases will be excluded from the day-fine experiment because their restitution obligation will exceed the amount calculated under the day-fine system.

References

Albrecht, H.-J. (1980). *Strafzumessung und Vollstreckung bei Geldstrafen.* Berlin: Duncker & Humbolt.

Albrecht, H.-J., & Johnson, E. H. (1980). Fines and justice administration: The experience of the Federal Republic of Germany. *International Journal of Comparative and Applied Criminal Justice, 4,* 3-14.

Brozan, N. (1988, September 17). In S.I. court, each is fined to fit means. *New York Times.*

Bureau of Justice Assistance, Office of Justice Programs. (1991). *Structured fines: Edward Byrne Memorial State and Local Law Enforcement Assistance Program.* Washington, DC: U.S. Department of Justice.

Casale, S. S. G. (1981). *Fines in Europe: A study of the use of fines in selected European countries with empirical research on the problems of fine enforcement* (Fines in Sentencing Working Paper No. 10). New York: Vera Institute of Justice.

Casale, S. S. G., & Hillsman, S. T. (1986). *The enforcement of fines as criminal sanctions: The English experience and its relevance to American practice* (Executive Summary). Washington, DC: National Institute of Justice.

Cole, G. F., Mahoney, B., Thornton, M., & Hanson, R. A. (1987). *The practices and attitudes of trial court judges regarding fines as a criminal sanction.* Washington, DC: National Institute of Justice.

Criminal fines, by the day [editorial]. (1988, August 29). *New York Times.*

Davies, M. (1970). *Financial penalties and probation* (Home Office Research Study No. 5). London: Her Majesty's Stationery Office.

Friedman, G. M. (1983). The West German day-fine system: A possibility for the United States? *University of Chicago Law Review, 50,* 281-304.

Gerstel, J. (1988, September 15). Experimental island program fines rich more. *Staten Island Register.*

Gillespie, R. W. (1980). Fines as an alternative to incarceration: The German experience. *Federal Probation, 44*(4), 20-26.

Glaser, D., & Gordon, M. A. (1988). *Use and effectiveness of fines, jail, and probation.* Los Angeles: University of Southern California, Social Science Research Institute.

Greene, J. A. (1990). *The Staten Island day fine experiment.* New York: Vera Institute of Justice.

Hillsman, S. T. (1988). The growing challenge of fine administration to court managers. *Justice System Journal, 13,* 5-16.

Hillsman, S. T. (1990). Fines and day fines. In M. Tonry & N. Morris (Eds.), *Crime and justice: A review of research* (Vol. 12). Chicago: University of Chicago Press.

Hillsman, S. T., & Greene, J. A. (1987). *Improving the use and administration of criminal fines: A report of the Richmond County, New York, Criminal Court Day-Fine Planning Project.* New York: Vera Institute of Justice.

Hillsman, S. T., & Mahoney, B. (1988). Collecting and enforcing criminal fines: A review of court processes, practices and problems. *Justice System Journal, 13,* 17-36.

Hillsman, S. T., Sichel, J. L., & Mahoney, B. (1984). *Fines in sentencing: A study of the use of the fine as a criminal sanction.* Washington, DC: National Institute of Justice.

Home Office. (1988). *Criminal statistics, England and Wales, 1987.* London: Her Majesty's Stationery Office.

Hurley, J. E. (1988, September 11). Island court refining criminal fine system. *Staten Island Sunday Advance,* p. A-1.

Knapp, K. (1988). Structured sentencing: Building on experience. *Judicature, 72,* 46.

McBrien, R. (1988). Tailoring criminal fines to the financial means of the offender: A Richmond County judge's view. *Judicature, 72,* 42-43.

McClintock, F. H. (1963). *Crimes of violence.* London: Heinemann.

McCord, J. (1985). Deterrence and the light touch of the law. In J. McCord, *Reactions to crime: The public, the police, courts, and prisons.* New York: John Wiley.

Mahoney, B., & Thornton, M. (1988). Means-based fining: Views of American trial court judges. *Justice System Journal, 13,* 51-63.

Morgan, R., & Bowles, R. (1981, April). Fines: The case for review. *Criminal Law Review,* pp. 203-14.

Morris, N. (1987). Alternatives to imprisonment: Failures and prospects. *Criminal Justice Research Bulletin, 3(7).*

Morris, N., & Tonry, M. (1990). *Between prison and probation: Intermediate punishments in a rational sentencing system.* New York: Oxford University Press.

Mullaney, F. G. (1987). *Economic sanctions in community corrections.* Washington, DC: National Institute of Corrections.

Softley, P. (1977). *Fines in magistrates' courts* (Home Office Research Study No. 43). London: Her Majesty's Stationery Office.

Strafverfolgungsstatistik 1985. (1986). Wiesbaden: Statistisches Bundesamt.

Tait, J. (1988). A court-based defendant notification system for traffic defendants. *Justice System Journal, 13,* 73-79.

Thornstedt, H. (1975, June). The day fine system in Sweden. *Criminal Law Review,* pp. 307-312.

Tonry, M. (1988). Structured sentencing. In M. Tonry & N. Morris (Eds.), *Crime and justice: A review of research* (Vol. 10). Chicago: University of Chicago Press.

von Hirsch, A., Wasik, M., & Greene, J. A. (1989). Punishments in the community and the principles of desert. *Rutgers Law Journal, 20,* 595-618.

Wick, K. A. (1988). Evaluating three notification strategies for collecting delinquent traffic fines. *Justice System Journal, 13,* 64-71.

Winterfield, L. A., & Hillsman, S. T. (1991). *The effects of instituting means-based fines in a criminal court: The Staten Island day-fine experiment.* New York: Vera Institute of Justice.

9. Monetary Sanctions: The Problem of Compliance

George F. Cole

Fines and court costs have long been part of the sentencing repertoire of judges. Many states now also require that such additional monetary penalties as victim restitution, probation supervision fees, and assessments to special-purpose funds be made by offenders. With prison overcrowding and overloaded probation caseloads a fact in most jurisdictions, and the new interest in the development of intermediate punishments, monetary sanctions have taken on increased importance. Offender compliance with monetary sanctions is, however, a national problem. This chapter addresses many of the issues surrounding the problem.

As with other criminal punishments, monetary sanctions must be enforced if they are going to serve the goals of justice (Morris & Tonry, 1990, p. 10). A monetary sanction is a court order. If it is not paid, the integrity and credibility of the criminal justice system is called into question. An uncollected fine or fee has an impact on the offender, the judiciary, and the community. Without compliance, the offender may believe that he or she has successfully "beaten the system" and can continue in criminal ways. Judges who observe that the punishments they have imposed are not being enforced may be less willing to use monetary sanctions in the future. The community may view low levels of collection as an indication that the criminal justice system is inefficient and may call for tougher ways to deal with offenders.

Use of Monetary Sanctions

Two factors concerning the utilization of monetary sanctions in the United States should be noted. First, research has shown that fines are widely used by both limited- and general-jurisdiction courts, yet they are seldom employed as the sole sanction for any but minor offenses (Cole, Mahoney, Thornton, & Hanson, 1987). Most often, fines are imposed as an "add-on" to the "real" punishment, such as probation or incarceration. Judges have expressed reluctance to use monetary sanctions as sole punishment because they believe that at the levels necessary to achieve justice, they cannot be collected.

Second, although we tend to think of fines and court costs as the prototypes of monetary punishments, legislatures have recently added a range of financial penalties. This thrust seems to be derived from the popular belief that offenders should pay for the correctional services provided them by the state. Many legislatures have stipulated that these penalties are mandatory and that judges shall impose them in specific types of cases. As a result, it is now quite common for an offender to be required to pay a fine, court costs, victim restitution, and a probation supervision fee. Some states have carried this to extremes; for instance, in Harris County, Texas, drunk drivers are even assessed the cost of the videotape used to record their behavior. The expansion of the number of monetary sanctions and their mandatory character often results in a total assessment being imposed on an offender that is unrealistically high, given the individual's means, and thus uncollectible.

Extent of the Collection Problem

In a national survey of trial court judges, 47% of the general-jurisdiction judges and 62% of the limited-jurisdiction judges said their courts had a moderate or major problem collecting fines (Cole, 1989, p. 4). However, there also appears to be considerable diversity in success rates among similar types of courts. A 1984 survey of 126 administrators of limited-jurisdiction courts found that 3 in 10 estimated that 80% of fined offenders paid on the day of sentence and another 4 out of 10 reported that between 50% and 80% of those given additional time ultimately paid in full (Hillsman, Sichel, & Mahoney, 1984, pp. 83-85). Clearly, there are some courts that are successful with respect to the administration of their collection programs.

We have very little empirical data about the amount of monetary sanctions that are unpaid. Most courts maintain records on the levels of fines and fees imposed, but not on the amounts uncollected. An exception is a survey of a sample of courts in Virginia. That study showed that 21% of the fines and costs imposed by district (lower) court judges were unpaid ($16.5 million) and 60% of those imposed by circuit (upper) court judges ($5.5 million) were uncollected (Virginia Department of Planning and Budget, 1987). In the state of Washington an estimated $17 million is uncollected annually by the courts of limited jurisdiction. It has been estimated that nationally, noncompliance with court orders equals more than $2 billion per year (Hillsman et al., 1984, p. 76).

In many jurisdictions a variety of collection techniques—including allowing use of credit cards and installment payments, automatic noticing, computerized record keeping, civil remedies, and private collection agencies—are now being used effectively (Cole, 1989, p. 9). In other jurisdictions, such nonjudicial agencies as those supervising probation and those offering victim assistance have become actively involved in enforcement (Smith, Davis, & Hillenbrand, 1989; Wheeler & Rudolph, 1990). Administrators have learned that they can utilize many of the techniques successfully employed by private creditors to encourage payment.

Although successful collection techniques are now widely available, huge sums are still unpaid. Why have most courts not forcefully attacked the problem? Is it that they are unaware of the approaches that have proved successful, or are there more basic factors related to the incentive structures and organizational context of courts that account for low enforcement rates?

The Judiciary and
the Problem of Compliance

Among the forms of punishment, monetary sanctions are the only ones that are implemented mainly by the judiciary. For each of the other sanctions, the sentencing judge knows that another agency of government, usually in the executive branch, has the responsibility for seeing that the terms are carried out. By contrast, the collection of monetary sanctions is primarily a judicial responsibility and is administered mainly in the court clerk's office.

Despite the importance of implementing monetary sanctions, judicial attention has tended to be narrow, focusing on accounting and record keeping rather than on enforcement. If monetary sanctions are to become a major part of the intermediate sentencing menu, the collection problem must be addressed. Successful use of monetary sanctions requires that judges and court administrators be attuned to the problem of compliance. Just as courts are concerned that their orders stipulating probation and incarceration be carried out, so too must they be resolved that sentences with monetary stipulations result in compliance.

The Role of Sentencing

Efforts to ensure compliance with monetary orders begin at the time of sentencing. Sentencing may be viewed as a process of communicating to the offender the terms of his or her punishment. The court must clearly impress upon the offender its expectation that the offender will comply with the order and that failure to pay the amount will result in harsher action. Relatively few judges appear to follow sentencing practices that have been shown to enhance the likelihood of collecting fines. For example, research in the United States and England has pointed to several aspects of the initial sentencing process that appear to be associated with effectiveness in collecting monetary sanctions: setting the total amount of fine, costs, and fees at a level that is within the ability of the offender to pay, even though it might involve some hardship; making only limited use of installment payment plans; and allowing relatively short periods of time for payment (Casale & Hillsman, 1986, pp. 155-172, 248-257; Hillsman et al., 1984, pp. 37-38, 204-210).

First, although fine amounts tend to be relatively low, fines are often combined with other monetary sanctions that significantly increase the amount of the total bill. As discussed above, legislatures have added various fees to the criminal code. In addition, legislatures in many states have reduced the sentencing discretion of judges by stipulating that these fees be mandatory. For example, New Jersey requires mandatory penalties of between $25 and $10,000 to the Violent Crime Compensation Board for convictions for crimes involving disorderly conduct or violence, and a Drug Enforcement Demand Reduction Penalty of between $500 and $3,000 for convictions for crimes involving controlled substances and drug paraphernalia.

When judges do have discretion, they generally have little or no information about the offender's economic circumstances. To the extent that this is the case, it obviously reduces the likelihood that the amount will be within the ability of the offender to pay. Alternatively, without means information, many judges impose fines that are lower than appropriate given the severity of the offenses, thus losing the retributive and deterrent value of the sanction.

Second, installment payment arrangements seem to be widely and indiscriminately useful. Judges rarely require the full amount of a fine to be paid on the day of sentencing, and when they allow delayed payment it is very common to permit installments over a long period of time. Experience in the private sector suggests that successful completion of a payment schedule depends upon a significant amount being paid "up front," with the remainder being scheduled over a limited number of payment periods.

Compliance with the terms of a sentence is also related, in part, to effective communication. The offender must know the amount of the payment, where to make the payment, the form of the payment, and the method of payment. As noted above, the expectation of compliance and the seriousness of the order must be impressed upon the offender.

The Enforcement Environment

To gain a better understanding of the lack of interest and effort on the part of the judiciary, it is necessary to look at the organizational context within which monetary sanctions are enforced. Theorists and policy analysts have identified the culture and incentive structures of public organizations, including courts, thought necessary for goal achievement. This approach, pioneered by Barnard (1938), defines a formal organization as a "system of consciously coordinated activities or forces" and emphasizes that incentives are necessary to get individuals to contribute to work toward those goals. As stressed by Clark and Wilson (1961), "The incentive system is the principal variable affecting organizational behavior" (p. 129). A problem for public organizations is addressed by Lipsky (1980, p. 44), who argues that participants see their responsibilities almost solely in terms of their immediate work environment rather than the policy goals or standards imposed by the management.

Incentive theory has been applied to the courts. Church and Heumann (1987) looked at the use of monetary incentives to induce desired delay reduction behavior in the offices of prosecutors. Caldeira (1977) and Sarat (1977) have identified job satisfaction as an incentive for trial court judges who are attracted by problem solving and work on substantive issues. In a study of delay reduction in three appellate courts, Chapper and Hanson (1987) found the "program incentive" to be a major factor. Citing the English experience, Hillsman (1988) argues that "the key incentive for good fine administration in a court is its judges' concern about whether fines are paid" (p. 12). These examples from the literature point to the importance of incentives and raise questions about the extent to which the court environment encourages judges and administrators to pursue actively the enforcement of monetary sanctions.

Evidence from a number of jurisdictions where collection has been given a high priority underscores the importance of incentives. For example, approximately 50% of the operating budget of the Harris County (Texas) Department of Adult Probation is derived from probation supervision fees. Probation officers understand that collection is directly related to the agency's mission, and this has resulted in a success rate of collection of approximately 80% of fees imposed (Wheeler, Hissong, Slusher, & Macan, 1990, p. 18). In Maricopa County, Arizona, and in Washington State, budget shortfalls have been credited with encouraging fine collection activities (Cole, 1989). In jurisdictions with victim support agencies, client pressures have been an incentive to press for the payment of court-ordered restitution (Smith et al., 1989).

There are aspects of the judicial environment that seem to lie at the root of the compliance problem. The role orientation of judges and administrators, the dispersion of responsibility, budgetary disincentives, multiple tasks, and enforcement dependence are all factors that seem to militate against active programs for the collection of monetary sanctions.

ROLE ORIENTATION

Many courts do not consider fines collection a major or legitimate responsibility of the judicial system. Judges seem to have the attitude that they are dispensers of justice (their work is to evaluate cases) and that they should not be actively involved in collection efforts. Likewise, court administrators and related staff have expressed resentment that they should serve as "collection agents" (Cole, 1989). On the other hand, Standard 3.5, "Responsibility for Enforcement," of the *Trial Court Performance Standards,* states, "The trial court takes responsibility for the enforcement of its orders," and the commentary makes clear that collection of financial levies is an explicit part of this responsibility. Some judges and administrators seem to see their involvement more as a favor to the executive than as an integral judicial function and responsibility.

DISPERSION OF RESPONSIBILITY

In some jurisdictions there is confusion as to who is actually responsible for compliance. Is it the judge who imposed the sentence, the clerk who has a duty to receive moneys owed the court, the probation officer who supervises the offender, the police who are to implement arrest warrants for nonpayment, or the prosecuting attorney whose role it is to prosecute those not paying? This dispersion of responsibility is such that no one is really in charge, with the result that compliance efforts are fragmented and given a very low priority.

DISINCENTIVES

Many courts see no link between expenditure of their administrative resources to enforce monetary orders and their budgetary allocations. Typically, money received by the courts from offenders is earmarked for other state or local agencies. For example, in Virginia, fines assessed for offenses against the state are deposited in the Literary Fund to provide support for the construction and renovation of public school buildings. Indiana requires that fines collected by general-jurisdiction courts go into a nonreverting school fund; in Michigan, they go to support county libraries; in Connecticut, they go to the state general fund. Limited-jurisdiction courts normally send amounts received to the county or municipal revenue agency.

Funding for judicial operations is allocated by legislative and executive bodies that tend not to provide direct incentives for courts to pursue enforcement forcefully. It is only through the politics of the budgetary process that some courts have been able to argue for increased resources to compensate for the costs of collection.

MULTIPLE TASKS

Increasingly, trial courts have been given tasks that are quasi-correctional, in that judges and administrators must oversee enforcement of a variety of monetary and community service orders (Hillsman, 1988, p. 7). The recent proliferation of fees and assessments means that courts not only collect monetary sanctions but also disburse them to a variety of executive branch accounts.

The distribution of monetary sanctions by the court depends upon such factors as the nature of the offense, the jurisdiction of the arresting officer, the funding of probation supervision, and whether or not restitution is owed the victim. One result is that courts have been assigned multiple financial tasks that involve multiple agencies.

One of the most complicated states with regard to the distribution of court-collected monies is Illinois, where, although the law designates the state's attorneys as the collectors of fines, the function is performed by circuit court clerks who must follow a set of criteria to decide how much of each fine judgment has to be sent to the state, county, or municipal treasury (Tobin, Gainey, & Steelman, 1988). The factors used to make this determination depend upon whether the fine was for a misdemeanor or felony, which law enforcement agency was involved, and, in some cases, such as those involving drugs, the type of offense. Given the complicated nature of many cases, clerks exercise considerable discretion in making these decisions.

ENFORCEMENT DEPENDENCE

To enforce monetary orders successfully, courts depend on the services of a variety of agencies, including probation, prosecution, police, marshals, and city attorneys. Given the crime control priorities of police agencies, a warrant for the arrest of an offender who has not paid a monetary sanction generally receives little attention. Court administrators are seemingly powerless to "force" the sheriff to enforce this judicial order. Probation officers are often reluctant to request that revocation be undertaken for nonpayment if they believe that the process will have little impact, given crowding in the local jail. Prosecution for willful failure to pay a fine is viewed by many district attorneys as complicated and less important than the criminal cases awaiting trial. Thus, even when courts take responsibility for their collection mission, they have little formal power to demand that nonjudicial agencies perform enforcement functions.

Discussion

Advocates of increased use of monetary sanctions point to a number of advantages, such as the fact that they can be set at levels that comport with the severity of the offense and the means of the offender. They also argue that fines, costs, and fees can serve retributive, deterrent, and even rehabilitative goals without great additional costs to the criminal justice system. In fact, monetary sanctions provide additional revenues to government. However, if monetary sanctions are to become meaningful intermediate punishments, they must be collected.

Much of the folklore of the courthouse points to offenders of limited means as the reason fines and costs are not collected. However, evidence from Europe and the experience of many courts in the United States show that compliance can be achieved. As discussed above, however, there are impediments in many courts that make it difficult to gain compliance. Judges do not have means information on offenders at the time of sentencing, legislatures have instituted required fees that are beyond the resources of most offenders, and there is dispersion of responsibility for collection and disagreement as to which agencies of government are charged with gaining compliance.

To address the problem of compliance with judicial orders, courts and legislators must work to overcome the organizational and political barriers to the effective collection of monetary sanctions. One approach would be to install incentive structures that would encourage judges and court administrators to give a high priority to gaining compliance. Another step would be to encourage courts to adopt the technology and practices used in the business world to collect money due. Gaining compliance with monetary sentences is being achieved in many courts. Active judicial leadership could bring about changes in the majority of criminal courts, where compliance is viewed as a problem.

References

Barnard, C. (1938). *The functions of the executive.* Cambridge, MA: Harvard University Press.

Caldeira, G. A. (1977). The incentives of trial court judges and the administration of justice. *Justice System Journal, 3,* 163-170.

Casale, S. S. G., & Hillsman, S. T. (1986). *The enforcement of fines as criminal sanctions: The English experience and its relevance in American practice.* Washington, DC: National Institute of Justice.

Chapper, J., & Hanson, R. A. (1987). *Managing the criminal appeals process.* Washington, DC: National Institute of Justice.

Church, T. W., & Heumann, M. (1987). *Monetary incentives and policy reform: Notes toward a theory.* Paper presented at the annual meeting of the Association of Management and Policy.

Clark, P. B., & Wilson, J. Q. (1961). Incentive systems: A theory of organizations. *Administrative Science Quarterly, 6,* 125ff.

Cole, G. F. (1989). Fines can be fine—and collected. *Judges' Journal, 28,* 2-6.

Cole, G. F., Mahoney, B., Thornton, M., & Hanson, R. A. (1987). *The practices and attitudes of trial court judges regarding fines as a criminal sanction: Executive summary.* Washington, DC: National Institute of Justice.

Hillsman, S. T. (1988). The growing challenge of fine administration to court managers. *Justice System Journal, 13,* 5-16.

Hillsman, S. T., Sichel, J. L., & Mahoney, B. (1984). *Fines in sentencing: A study of the use of the fine as a criminal sanction.* Washington, DC: National Institute of Justice.

Lipsky, M. (1980). *Street level bureaucracy.* New York: Russell Sage Foundation.

Morris, N., & Tonry, M. (1990). *Between prison and probation: Intermediate punishments in a rational sentencing system.* New York: Oxford University Press.

Sarat, A. (1977). Judging in trial courts: An exploratory study. *Journal of Politics, 39,* 368-374.

Smith, B. E., Davis, R. C., & Hillenbrand, S. W. (1989). *Improving enforcement of court-ordered restitution.* Washington, DC: American Bar Association.

Tobin, R. W., Gainey, J. A., & Steelman, D. C. (1988) *Illinois court finance study: Legal analysis of Illinois court finances.* North Andover, MA: National Center for State Courts.

Virginia Department of Planning and Budget. (1987). *Unpaid fines, court costs, and restitution in district and circuit courts of the commonwealth.* Richmond: Author.

Wheeler, G. R., Hissong, R. V., Slusher, M. P., & Macan, T. M. (1990). Economic sanctions in criminal justice: Dilemma for human service? *Justice System Journal, 14,* 63-77.

Wheeler, G. R., & Rudolph, A. S. (1990). New strategies to improve probation officers' fee collection rates: A field study in performance feedback. *Justice System Journal, 14,* 78-94.

10. Day Reporting Centers: An Innovative Concept in Intermediate Sanctions

Jack McDevitt

Robyn Miliano

The use of day reporting centers as an intermediate sanction is a relatively new concept in the field of corrections. In fact, in a recent study funded by the National Institute of Justice, it was found that only a handful of states (six) use day reporting centers as a correctional alternative (Parent, 1990). However, many states are currently considering the development of day reporting-type programs.

The impetus for the development of day reporting centers (DRCs) in Massachusetts, where the first day reporting center in the United States was developed, was to help relieve the overcrowded conditions throughout correctional facilities in the state. Specifically, the governor convened a committee to study alternative intermediate sanctions, and in conducting its research, the committee discovered the day reporting concept already in place in Great Britain. With modifications to the British system, a model program was implemented in Springfield, Massachusetts.

In Massachusetts, DRCs were originally designed to reduce prison overcrowding by providing an early-release mechanism for sentenced offenders who were relatively close to their parole eligibility dates or to the completion of their sentences. Day reporting centers were not conceived as an alternative sentencing option. While all Massachusetts DRCs accept offenders already in county jails, some are now also accepting pretrial detainees and inmates with state prison sentences.

Although all centers have similar program elements, such as frequent client contact, formalized scheduling, and drug testing, the

152

operations of different DRCs are quite varied. Therefore, it is difficult to define specifically what a day reporting center is; each center is unique. The philosophy of DRCs, as Elizabeth Curtin (1990) from the Crime and Justice Foundation states, "is better described as a concept rather than as a 'model' program. As a concept, it can be adapted to the particular needs and goals of a variety of situations, with a variety of populations" (p. 8).

In this chapter, we discuss day reporting programs as they currently exist in Massachusetts. This overview examines the characteristics of DRCs in Massachusetts and the clientele serviced by these programs. The data presented here were gathered from MIS forms of four DRCs currently in operation in Massachusetts. We will also discuss how this new day reporting concept relates to other types of intermediate sanctions, such as intensive probation supervision (IPS) and electronic monitoring. Finally, we will discuss the implications of the use of day reporting centers as an alternative community corrections program.

Massachusetts Programs

As the result of a year-long planning process involving the Hampden County Sheriff's Department and the Crime and Justice Foundation, the first day reporting center in the United States was established in 1986 in Springfield, Massachusetts (located in Hampden County). This particular site was chosen for the first day reporting center because it met four primary criteria:

(1) political and organizational stability
(2) demonstrated management abilities, including successful implementation of innovative programs
(3) potential willingness to participate
(4) urban setting

The sheriff and his administration had been in office for more than 12 years, during which time he had gained much respect for his management capabilities. He was willing to participate in this program because, at the time of implementation, the county jail and house of correction was at 200% its capacity (Warwick & McCarthy, 1990). Additionally, the program—as a community corrections alternative to incarceration—was philosophically consistent with past and present initiatives, as well as future goals of the sheriff and his administration. Springfield is the second-largest city in Massachusetts, with a population of more than 156,000. Within this urban setting, there was access to an already-existing network of community services (e.g., vocational/educational training, substance abuse counseling, family counseling).

PROGRAM CHARACTERISTICS

Currently, there are six DRCs operating in Massachusetts, and these cover 7 of the 11 counties in the state. Table 10.1 summarizes the characteristics of four of six day reporting centers currently operating in Massachusetts. We chose these four because they were the first four DRCs and are currently the four largest in the state. They include the Hampden County Day Reporting Center, the Metropolitan Day Reporting Center, the Norfolk County Day Reporting Center, and the Worcester County Day Reporting Center. Each center, except the Metropolitan DRC, is administered by the Sheriff's Department in the respective county.[1] The Metropolitan DRC is run by a private organization, the Crime and Justice Foundation. This DRC serves clients from two adjoining counties, Middlesex and Suffolk (which includes Boston).

The eligible population for each center comprises offenders from the various county houses of correction (HOCs) and jails. In the Hampden County DRC, offenders are also included from the Western Massachusetts Correctional Alcohol Center (WMCAC), a local inpatient alcohol treatment facility. All programs accept women from the respective counties who are sentenced to MCI-Framingham, the major correctional institution for women in Massachusetts.

One eligibility criterion for an individual to be accepted to any DRC is the amount of time remaining to release, whether through parole or through completion of an original sentence. The DRCs vary in the required time to release: from 60 days at the Metropolitan DRC to six months at the Worcester DRC. This variation reflects the differing philosophies of the various programs. For example, the Metropolitan DRC has developed a program that is geared for 60-90 days, whereas the Worcester DRC program has no time limit.

A second eligibility criterion for any DRC is that the offender not have any recent disciplinary reports on file. This is fairly consistent across all programs. Using disciplinary reports as a measure of eligibility allows DRC staff a certain amount of discretion in the selection of clients. The statewide standards for eligibility, set forth by the Executive Office of Human Services, call for no recent major

TABLE 10.1 Characteristics of Massachusetts Day Reporting Centers

Characteristic	Hampden DRC	Metropolitan DRC	Norfolk DRC	Worcester DRC
Administration	public	private	public	public
Eligible population	HOC; WMCAC within 4 mos. of parole eligibility or wrap; pretrial	HOC within 90 days of parole eligibility or wrap	HOC within 60 days	HOC; jail within 6 mos. of confirmed parole wrap
Institutional history	no recent major disciplinary reports	no recent major disciplinary reports	2 mos. stability after disciplinary report	no recent major disciplinary reports
Average daily census	110 [a]	30	70	65
Contacts/week	50-80	42	3 face-to-face; active monitor	24-30
Average length of stay (days)	85	42	47	45
Electronic monitoring	yes (passive)	no	yes (active)	yes (passive)
Mandated treatment	21-day substance abuse program	substance abuse program, community service, transition group	none	4 NA/AA meetings per week
Drug testing	yes	yes	yes	yes
Curfews	yes	yes	yes	yes

NOTE: Information gathered from four of six DRCs currently in operation in Massachusetts.
a. Of these, 25-30 are sentenced population; remainder are pretrial.

discipline reports. The ambiguous language offers a great deal of latitude in the definition of a discipline problem. The judgment inherent in defining whether a disciplinary report is recent or major allows the DRC staff leeway to disqualify clients they feel are potential problems or to take potentially good clients even if they have had some trouble during their incarceration.

The average daily census indicates a broad range of program size across the Massachusetts centers. Programs range from an average of 30 clients in the Metropolitan DRC to an average of 110 clients in Hampden County's DRC. There appear to be large differences in the numbers of offenders accepted from program to program. One source of this variation is the fact that many of Hampden County's clients are pretrial detainees.

One pattern that has emerged as we have reviewed census figures over time from each of the Massachusetts programs is that it appears each program has trouble obtaining clients during its first 12 to 18 months of operation. All programs remained at an average daily census of 20 or fewer throughout their first year of operation. After the first 12 to 18 months, all programs began to grow, and the census quickly doubled or tripled during the program's second year. According to interviews with program staff, this may be due to reluctance on the part of clients to apply to a "new" program as well as reluctance on the part of institutional staff to refer clients to a "new" program until the program has proved itself.

As Table 10.1 indicates, the numbers of contacts between program staff and clients are quite varied, but are substantial in all cases. Hampden County requires the most intense contact, with 50-80 contacts per week. As the offender moves through the 90-day program period, the contacts become less frequent. By comparison, Norfolk County requires only 3 face-to-face contacts, but this is the only DRC that uses an active electronic monitoring system.[2] These figures indicate the extensive level of supervision inherent in the DRC concept. With up to 10 contacts per day in one case, these programs keep unusually close contact with clients as they make their transition from incarceration to life back in society.

Most DRC clients remain in the program for approximately 6-8 weeks. The average length of stay for clients in the program is between 40 and 50 days. However, these figures include those who have been terminated for technical or criminal violations and returned to the institution. Hampden County clients average longer stays in the program than do those in any other county. Each of the three remaining DRCs have about equal lengths of stay for their clients. One reason for the longer length of stay in Hampden County is, again, the number of pretrial clients in the program. These clients cannot be moved out of the program once they have completed a set of obligations (e.g., community service); they must remain in the program until their cases come to trial.

Norfolk County DRC is the only program that does not have mandated treatment for participants. Hampden County, Metropolitan, and Worcester all require those offenders with substance abuse problems to attend some form of substance abuse treatment. Additionally, the Metropolitan DRC requires clients to participate in community service (e.g., helping in soup kitchens or painting over graffiti at local schools). Staff at the Metropolitan DRC believe this is an important element in their philosophy of helping offenders make the transition out of crime. Although other programs utilize community service for specific program participants on a case-by-case basis, only the Metropolitan DRC mandates community service as part of its overall treatment program.

All DRCs employ some form of drug testing, both scheduled and random. In this way, they are able to determine which clients are not complying with program contracts and administratively terminate them from the program. Day reporting staff interviewed believe that drug testing is their most effective behavior control program element, more effective than electronic monitoring. The staff believe that frequent, random drug testing forces clients to alter their behavior in a profound and systematic way. In many cases, this leads to a reevaluation of many daily life choices, such as whether to use alcohol or drugs. In addition, most DRC staff feel that their clients who fail the program do so primarily because of alcohol or other drug usage. Drug testing, therefore, seems to keep clients away from behaviors that could get them into trouble and seems to force them to change their life-style in substantial ways by eliminating the decision to drink or use drugs. Curfew checks represent another method through which participants are supervised to make sure they are in compliance with program rules and regulations.

TYPICAL OFFENDER CHARACTERISTICS

Overall, day reporting centers are serving a broad cross section of the Massachusetts corrections population. Table 10.2 provides information on typical offender characteristics for the same four DRCs as shown in Table 10.1. This information was gathered from the quarterly reports that are submitted every three months to the Executive Office of Human Services—the state office that oversees DRCs in Massachusetts. We collected these data for a one-year period, ending June 1990. The Hampden County figures do not include pretrial population, and Norfolk County provided information for only one quarter (April-June 1990). As a secondary source of data, we were able to interview staff from all day reporting centers that were in operation during the summer of 1990. These interviews took place in conjunction with a series of task force meetings that were held for practitioners of DRCs in Massachusetts.

The racial and ethnic composition of the client populations of the DRCs closely reflects the racial and ethnic makeup of those Massachusetts houses of corrections with participating DRCs. Overall, almost three-fourths of the DRC clients are white, 14% are black, and 14% are Hispanic.

TABLE 10.2 Offender Characteristics of Massachusetts Day Reporting Centers (in percentages)

Characteristic	Hampden DRC	Metropolitan DRC	Norfolk DRC[a]	Worcester DRC	Total
Race					
Caucasian	46	58	86	83	72
black	17	27	8	5	14
Hispanic	37	12	3	11	14
Asian	0	0	3	0	0.1
other	0	1	0	0	0.1
Sex					
male	90	94	100	97	95
female	10	6	0	3	5
Offense					
against the person	7	4	6	10	8
drug related	46	36	20	22	29
property crime	19	29	31	20	23
violation of parole /probation	5	5	0	13	9
DUI	15	10	37	21	18
other	8	15	6	39	27
pretrial	0	1	0	0	0.1
Primary substance abuse					
marijuana	3	10	3	31	19
cocaine	14	29	26	24	25
heroin	10	12	9	10	10
hallucinogenics	0	0	0	1	0.5
tranquilizers	0	0	0	1	0.4
alcohol	29	27	48	63	47
no use	17	22	14	11	15
Counseling					
individual substance abuse	97	0	0	0.4	11
substance abuse treatment	97	1	0	0	11
residential	97	1	0	0	11
group substance abuse	97	83	0	62	68
family counseling	97	2	0	0	11
NA/AA program	46	71	43	73	67
n	59	168	35	284	546
Terminations					
successful	88	72	77	82	79
administrative	12	25	20	8	16
failure	0	4	3	10	5
n	60	158	35	182	435

NOTE: Information gathered from quarterly reports for four of six DRCs currently in operation in Massachusetts.
a. Information provided for one quarter only.

Most (95%) of the clients in day reporting centers are male. Including more female offenders is one area on which Massachusetts DRCs have focused more attention over the last year. Day reporting centers can effectively serve female clients because of the emphasis on community involvement and because they are able to be at home, which, in the case of convicted mothers, is a very important aspect of the program. However, in Massachusetts, getting women into DRC programs has been difficult. The fact that most women are incarcerated in one institution in Framingham provides logistical problems for DRC staff from other counties. Locating and performing screening interviews with the women from their counties is difficult. Additionally, the women in Framingham who meet the program eligibility criteria are frequently serving relatively short sentences. By the time these women are located by DRC staff and have had a client screening interview, often their sentences are almost complete.

The types of offenses for which DRC clients have been incarcerated are primarily drug and alcohol related or property offenses. Specifically, in our sample of DRC participants, 29% were incarcerated for drug-related offenses, 23% were incarcerated for committing property offenses, and 18% were incarcerated for operating under the influence of liquor. Only 8% were incarcerated for having committed violent acts against persons. An explanation for this low number is that Massachusetts General Law, Chapter 127, prohibits most violent offenders from participating in day reporting center programs. However, under unusual circumstances, a violent offender may be admitted to the program if he or she is not regarded as a risk to the community.

As with the incarcerated population in the county houses of correction, most DRC clients have substance abuse problems and need counseling and/or treatment. More than 80% of the DRC clients self-report having had some form of substance abuse problem (alcohol and cocaine being the most prevalent) prior to their present incarceration. As indicated in Table 10.2, only a small percentage of DRC clients receive individual substance abuse counseling or substance abuse treatment. However, more than two-thirds of the clients do attend group substance abuse counseling and/or Narcotics/Alcoholics Anonymous meetings.

Perhaps most important, however, is the percentage of clients who successfully complete the program. Successful completions can be the result of an expiration of the original sentence, parole, having the case dismissed, or being sentenced (if pretrial). As can be seen in Table 10.2, 79% of our sample successfully terminated the program.

A total of 16% were administratively terminated from the program and returned to higher custody due to program violations such as drug use, contract violations, or unexcused absence. Only 5% were returned to higher custody because they committed new crimes or had escaped. These preliminary results suggest that day reporting centers can work and that, in Massachusetts, they have been of limited risk to the community.

Day Reporting and
Other Intermediate Sanctions

Day reporting centers are unique among intermediate sanctions currently used throughout the United States. As Parent (1990) suggests:

> In many ways, the DRCs repackage elements of other, more familiar correctional programs. Some DRCs provide a treatment regimen comparable to a halfway house, but without a residential facility's siting problems. Some provide contact levels equal to or greater than intensive supervision programs (ISP), in effect, creating a community equivalent of confinement. (p. 1)

As an example of just how stringent supervision can be, the Hampden County Day Reporting Center begins each client on a schedule of at least 50 contacts per week for the first, most intense, stage of supervision. These include phone contacts, on-site checks at the client's home or place of employment, and at least one face-to-face contact at the DRC each day. Although this level of contact may decrease as a client continues through the program, overall the level of supervision utilized in DRCs is more intense than any other correctional alternative currently being used.

DRCs are often compared with intensive probation supervision programs because of the level of supervision DRC clients must endure (Byrne & Kelly, 1989). However, as indicated in Table 10.1, most Massachusetts day reporting centers require more daily contacts than the general level of contact required by IPS programs. Also somewhat unique to the concept of DRCs is that the staff have the authority to reincarcerate individuals who do not comply with program requirements. The Sheriff's Department in each county has legal authority to release inmates to community programs. Technically, however, these inmates are still considered to be incarcerated. If a participant is terminated from the DRC program for failure to comply with program requirements (e.g., using alcohol or drugs), the sheriff has the legal authority to reincarcerate the individual.

Generally, the DRCs in Massachusetts police themselves effectively, in that they are able to return to custody those clients who do not fulfill program requirements. This can be done through itineraries as well as through urine testing.[3] When a client fails to follow the itinerary set forth, for example, he or she can be administratively terminated from the program. In this way, the DRC can immediately return the offender to higher custody.

Electronic monitoring is another means of policing participants in DRCs. As with the other components of day reporting center programs, electronic monitoring can be used within a day reporting framework. In Massachusetts, programs range from no use of electronic monitoring, to the use of a passive system, to the use of an active, 24-hour system in one program (see Table 10.1). The Massachusetts experience, to date, indicates that the existence of an electronic monitoring system in a given program appears to have little to do with how successfully the program functions.

The experience of day reporting programs with electronic monitoring seems to be similar to the experiences documented in national evaluations of electronic monitoring (Schmidt, 1989); that is, the use of electronics in a program does not guarantee a successful program. In Massachusetts, interviews with DRC staff indicate that, initially, the monitors are seen as an integral part of the security portion of the program. In the first phase of the program, most staff believe that the monitors provide some protection from escape by clients. However, shortly after electronic monitors are implemented, the limitations of the monitors and the technical problems inherent in such systems are realized (Renzema & Skelton, 1990). After some experience with electronic monitors, program staff seem to come to the conclusion that these monitoring systems are only an aid to program security and are less reliable than more traditional forms of security—careful screening, agreed-upon contracts of expectations, and personal commitment between program staff and clients.

The use of monitors does seem to have some positive impacts on day reporting centers, however. First, it is a new technology and, for most clients, something they have never experienced before. This reinforces the message that this program is different from programs they have been associated with in the past. For most offenders, this use of technology indicates at the outset that this program is "tough" and that violations will not be tolerated. Although this message may be diluted over time, some program staff believe the use of electronic monitoring helps send a positive message regarding the expectations and responsibilities of the client.

A second positive impact of the existence of electronic monitoring in these programs appears to be its role in facilitating program siting. For example, in the original decision to site the Hampden County program, local community resistance was a problem. The community of Springfield (as has occurred elsewhere across the country in attempts to establish community corrections programs) cited general safety as a major reason citizens did not want the program located in their area. Once it was disclosed that the program would involve the use of monitors, much of this resistance was reduced. This may be a role electronic monitoring can play in the area of community corrections—it may reduce the fears of local residents about the safety of programs located in their communities.

DISCUSSION: DRCs AS AN INTERMEDIATE SANCTION

Currently in the United States, the term *intermediate sanction* describes an extremely broad range of correctional programs. The term is used to describe programs as diverse as probation, halfway houses, electronic monitoring, house arrest, and day reporting. In a discussion of day reporting, it would be instructive to see how day reporting compares with other intermediate sanctions.

One way to address this question would be to arrange the various intermediate sanctions on a continuum ranging from least intrusive (e.g., unsupervised probation) to most intrusive (e.g., 24-hour house arrest with electronic monitoring). Within this framework, most day reporting programs would fall somewhere on the more restrictive side of the continuum. The reason for this is twofold: (a) the structure inherent in day reporting programs and (b) the frequency and type of client contact.

As indicated above, structure is a major element of day reporting centers in Massachusetts. Each client files in advance a daily itinerary that lists his or her activities on a moment-to-moment basis. These itineraries, which began as a security measure to keep track of clients' whereabouts, have become an important therapeutic tool: They force clients to plan their daily activities, something many have never done before in their lives.

The second major restrictive component of day reporting is the number of client contacts. With multiple daily client contacts, these programs keep close track of all clients (with some clients being contacted up to 10 times a day). In addition, all programs have regular urinalysis testing, which also serves as a control on clients' behavior.

Conclusions and Recommendations

Day reporting is more of a concept than a program. A day reporting program can include a variety of components commonly associated with community correctional programs. What makes day reporting different is the focus on a single site for a community-based program and a team approach to providing support for clients. The fact that day reporting is so flexible is both its greatest strength and its greatest weakness.

The strength of the day reporting concept is that a program can be developed that can take advantage of the most recent and promising strategies available in the field of community corrections. For example, day reporting programs can include extremely close supervision, with daily face-to-face contacts, drug testing, electronic monitoring, substance abuse counseling, employment opportunity programs, literacy programs, day-care support, and community service. Since day reporting is community based, these programs can be offered without an expert on staff by utilizing existing programs in the local community, or they can be offered on-site to a larger group of clients.

Although this flexibility makes day reporting programs appealing to local program developers, it is also a source of concern. The experience, to date, across the country with day reporting seems to be positive; few programs have closed and many have expanded. However, it is this expansion that seems to be the area of chief concern to practitioners.

As mentioned above, day reporting can be designed to service the needs of a number of different clientele, from first-time DUI offenders to felons with long prison records. As programs begin to develop and are deemed successful, local criminal justice authorities become aware of the programs and the fact that the concept can serve additional populations. Pressure then increases for programs to take on additional clients, some of whom may not fit the original intent of the programs. This not only puts a strain on the resources of the programs, but can force programs to deal with clientele with different legal statuses and different levels of need.

Specifically, in Massachusetts, programs originally intended as early release for county inmates were expanded to include pretrial detainees. This change forced the programs to deal with clients who were not convicted, and over whom they had less legal authority. Additionally, these clients put an added strain on the administration of day reporting programs. Since they have not yet been convicted, their classification files are much less complete. The program staff generally rely on these files for screening and for developing treatment programs for their clients. Thus alternative sources of information must be located.

The problem with this expansion is not that it cannot be accommodated, but that programs designed to service one clientele may not be able to serve other clientele adequately. Day reporting programs should be constructed with this in mind, and, possibly through legislation, be limited to one or two specific kinds of populations.

The day reporting concept, at least at this embryonic stage, appears to be applicable to a broad range of correctional settings and correctional clientele. Existing programs seem to be flexible enough to allow tailoring to the needs of individual clients, but the elements of programs must allow the structure and support necessary to help offenders make the transition out of crime. Further evaluative research needs to be conducted to determine if this concept is actually a viable correctional alternative for relieving crowding conditions while at the same time placing the community at limited risk. In addition, future research must focus on the long-term impacts of participation in these programs.

Notes

1. In Massachusetts, the sheriffs' departments oversee the county-level houses of correction.
2. The fact that Norfolk County DRC clients are on an active electronic monitoring system indicates that they are virtually under 24-hour surveillance. The minimal face-to-face contacts are supplemented by this component.
3. Itineraries are daily schedules that DRC participants are required to fill out and submit, generally two days in advance. They include information on the dates, times, and places the client is expected to be on any given day. A typical itinerary might read as follows: The client will be at work from 7:30 a.m. until 5:00 p.m., at home from 5:30 p.m. until 7:00 p.m., at NA/AA counseling from 7:30 p.m. until 9:30 p.m., and at home from 10:00 p.m. until 7:00 a.m. At any time during this 24-hour period, the client may be subjected to random urine checks, random phone checks, or in-person visits from a DRC staff member.

References

Byrne, J. M., & Kelly, L. (1989). *Restructuring probation as an intermediate sanction: An evaluation of the Massachusetts Intensive Probation Supervision Program.* Washington, DC: National Institute of Justice.
Curtin, E. L. (1990). Day reporting centers: A promising alternative. *International Association of Residential and Community Alternatives, 1,* p. 8.

Parent, D. G. (1990). *Day reporting centers for criminal offenders: A descriptive analysis of existing programs.* Washington, DC: National Institute of Justice.

Renzema, M., & Skelton, D. T. (1990, November-December). Use of electronic monitoring in the United States: 1989 update. *NIJ Reports,* pp. 9-13.

Schmidt, A. K. (1990, January-February). Electronic monitoring of offenders increases. *NIJ Reports,* p. 212.

Warwick, K., & McCarthy, R. (1990). The Hampden County Day Reporting Center: The final phase in a continuum of community reintegration of inmates. *International Association of Residential and Community Alternatives, 1,* 18-19.

11. Residential Community Correctional Programs

Edward J. Latessa

Lawrence F. Travis III

Community residential programs for criminal offenders have a long history in the United States (Allen, Carlson, Parks, & Seiter, 1978; Latessa & Travis, 1986). In the past, the typical use of community residential facilities was as "halfway houses." These programs were designed as transitional placements for offenders to ease the movement from incarceration to life in the free society. In time, some programs developed as alternatives to incarceration, so that the "halfway" aspect could mean either halfway *into* prison, or halfway *out of* prison.

Between 1950 and 1980, the number and use of such halfway houses grew considerably. In the last 10 to 15 years, residential placements for criminal offenders have also undergone considerable role expansion. Increasingly, the population served by these programs has come to include large numbers of probationers and persons awaiting trial. In many jurisdictions, placement in a residential facility is available as a direct sentencing option to the judge. These changes in the role and population of residential programs supported the replacement of the traditional halfway house notion with the broader title of *community corrections residential facility*.

This chapter reviews the history, purposes, and structure of residential community corrections programs. It includes an assessment of the types and effectiveness of programs, and concludes by describing emerging trends and future directions for residential programs.

What's in a Name?

Until recently, community corrections residential programs were subsumed under the general title of halfway houses. This label, however, has proven to be inadequate as a description of the variety of residential programs used with correctional populations today. The International Halfway House Association, founded in 1964, has itself changed its name to reflect more accurately the variety of purposes and persons served by residential programs.

The contemporary name given to such programs, community corrections residential facilities, is a broader title that reflects the role expansion of the traditional halfway house that has occurred in recent years. Rush (1991) defines a residential facility as "a correctional facility from which residents are regularly permitted to depart, unaccompanied by any official, for the purposes of using community resources, such as schools or treatment programs, and seeking or holding employment" (p. 265).

This definition is free of any reference to incarceration that was implicit in the term *halfway*. Further, it does not necessitate the direct provision of any services to residents within the facility, and clearly identifies the program with a correctional mission. Thus, unlike the traditional halfway house, the community residential facility serves a more diverse population and plays a broader correctional role. Traditional halfway houses are included within the category of residential facilities, but their ranks are swelled by newer adaptations, such as community corrections centers, prerelease centers, and restitution centers.

The Development of Community Residential Programs

Halfway houses as transitional programming for inmates released from prisons are not a new phenomenon (Latessa & Allen, 1982). Their origins can be traced at least as far back as the early nineteenth century in England and Ireland (Keller & Alper, 1970). In the United States, the exact origin of halfway houses is not clear, but one such program was started in New York City in 1845, the Isaac T. Hooper Home (Rush, 1991, p. 143). A halfway house for released female prisoners was opened in Boston, Massachusetts, in 1864. For nearly 100 years, halfway houses tended to be operated by charitable organizations for the benefit of released inmates. Halfway house programs did not begin a period of expansion until after World War II (Beha, 1977).

In the 1950s, specialized residential programs designed to deal with substance-abusing offenders were added to the traditional halfway house programs. Residential programs for alcoholic or drug-addicted offenders opened and spread throughout this period, and into the 1960s. For typical criminal offenders, however, halfway house placements were rare.

In the middle 1960s, the President's Commission on Crime and Administration of Justice (1967) signaled a change in correctional philosophy toward the goal of reintegration. Reintegration placed increased emphasis on the role of the community in corrections, and on the value of keeping offenders in the community, rather than in prison, whenever possible. This ideology of community corrections supported the notion of residential placements for convicted offenders, and halfway houses began a period of unprecedented expansion, supported by federal funds from programs as diverse as the Office of Economic Opportunity and the Law Enforcement Assistance Administration (Hicks, 1987, p. 6).

During the early 1980s, however, support for halfway house programs dwindled. The effects of recession, demise of LEAA, and a general hardening of public attitudes toward offenders worked against the continued growth and development of halfway houses or other residential programs. This period of retrenchment was, however, short-lived. The same forces that temporarily halted the growth of residential programs soon added their weight to continued development.

In the last decade, community corrections residential facilities have grown in response to the crisis of prison crowding. Allen et al. (1978, p. 1) attribute an increased use of halfway houses with parole populations to three factors: the philosophy of reintegration, success with such programs in the mental health field, and the lower costs of halfway houses compared with prisons. To these was added the need to respond to prison crowding in the 1980s.

The lack of prison capacity, coupled with an increasing emphasis on risk control and retributive sentencing, spurred a search for intermediate sanctions. Over the last several years, a number of observers have called for the creation of penal sanctions that range in severity between incarceration and traditional probation supervision (McCarthy, 1987). They suggest that such sanctions will allow the correctional system to meet the punitive and risk-control goals of sentencing, especially with those persons diverted from prison or jail because of crowding.

The list of intermediate sanctions includes house arrest, electronic monitoring, and intensive supervision (*Federal Probation*, 1986; Petersilia,

1987). DuPont (1985) explicitly identifies a role for community residential facilities as an adjunct to traditional probation or parole supervision. Such facilities would serve to increase both the punitive severity and public safety of traditional community-based corrections.

In an era when both correctional costs and populations grow yearly, planners, practitioners, and policymakers have supported a wide range of correctional alternatives. As Guynes (1988) has observed, one effect of prison and jail crowding has been a dramatic increase in probation and parole populations. Further, Petersilia (1985), among others, suggests that these larger supervision populations are increasingly made up of more serious and more dangerous offenders. Community residential facilities have come to be seen as an important option for the management and control of these growing and more dangerous offender populations.

A result has been the redefinition of the role of community residential facilities. The traditional role of transitional placement for offenders, or as a response to special needs populations such as substance abusers, has been expanded. Residential placement has emerged as a correctional alternative in its own right.

Hicks (1987) observes that the use of residential placement as an alternative to incarceration or traditional community supervision has engendered some changes in operations and philosophy. She terms this a movement "toward supervision rather than treatment." Thus in many cases residential facilities provide little more than a place to live and access to community resources. The emphasis in these programs is upon custody and control rather than counseling and correction.

Prison on the Cheap?

Unable or unwilling to underwrite the costs of prison for large numbers of convicted offenders, several jurisdictions have supported community residential facilities. As Hicks (1987) notes, "Budget weary legislators often view halfway houses as an inexpensive lunch" (p. 7). Residential programs, they hope, will provide public safety as well as incarceration, but at a fraction of the cost. As substitute prisons, however, the atmosphere of these programs has changed.

Traditional halfway houses, where staff and programs are designed for the provision of direct services to residents, still continue. These programs provide counseling, substance abuse treatment, educational and vocational training, and a variety of social services. In other, newer programs, especially those operated by corrections departments, the atmosphere is closer to that of a minimum-security prison than a rehabilitative community.

This addition of residential programs as "bed space" to the traditional use of such programs as treatment modalities has led to a schizophrenic field of practice. In most facilities, rules and regulations are stricter, and enforcement more rigid, than in earlier days. Additionally, a number of "large" facilities, housing hundreds of residents, have been added. Typically "prerelease" centers, these larger facilities house prison inmates eligible for parole, or in the final months before their release.

The recent growth in community residential facilities has complicated the picture. These facilities serve a variety of clients, ranging from as-yet-unconvicted offenders diverted from court through prison inmates. Facility sizes range from those housing fewer than 10 residents to those with populations in the hundreds. Treatment services range from programs providing full services to those in which few, if any, direct services are available to residents. The one constant is that residents live in the facilities for a period of time, and are generally free to leave the facilities during approved hours, for approved purposes, without escort.

Residential Facilities in Contemporary Corrections

As the foregoing discussion illustrates, it is not possible to describe the average residential facility. Diversity in population, program, size, and structure is the rule. It is, unfortunately, also not possible to know for certain how many such facilities are in operation today, or the number of offenders served by them. As Hicks (1987) observes, "There are no national figures, only educated guesses" (p. 2).

The International Halfway House Association published a directory of residential facilities in 1981 that lists almost 2,300 facilities with a combined capacity of nearly 100,000 beds (Gatz & Murray, 1981). Not all of these facilities, however, serve correctional populations. Five years earlier, Seiter et al. (1977) estimated that approximately 400 facilities existed that served correctional populations, with a capacity of about 10,000 beds. In 1978, a survey of parole authorities revealed the existence of nearly 800 facilities, with almost 15,000 inmates being paroled to halfway house placements. More recently, the National Institute of Corrections supported a survey that identified 641 community corrections residential facilities. The identification was based on the characteristics of residents as under correctional supervision, among other criteria.

While the methods and definitions employed in these different studies varied considerably, the results are fairly consistent. Given these admittedly incomplete data, it is possible to estimate that there are in excess of 600 residential facilities in operation today. Further, it appears that the number of facilities has grown as much as 50% in the last decade.

It is not possible to estimate the number of offenders served by these facilities with any certainty. Length of residence is typically short, on the order of three to four months, meaning that a facility with 50 beds may serve 150 to 200 individuals annually. Based on the probability that a halfway house would serve three to four times as many residents as it has beds in each year, Allen and his colleagues (1978, p. 2) estimate that roughly 10,000 beds equals 30,000 to 40,000 residents each year. Further, many of those in residential facilities are included in the totals of other correctional population counts, such as the number of prison inmates or persons under parole supervision. Still, it is clear that the total number of residents in these facilities each year is substantial.[1]

Types of Facilities

The large number of facilities and their differing traditions, populations, and services render it difficult to assess the impact of residential programs. Beyond noting that these programs have played an important role in the provision of services to convicted offenders, and that their importance as alternatives to imprisonment has increased, the variety of facilities means that questions of effectiveness must be narrowly drawn.

Allen and his colleagues (1978), for example, have developed a four-class typology of halfway houses, using two dimensions to yield four possible types of facilities. Halfway houses can be either public or private, and they can be either interventive or supportive in program. Public or private, of course, relates to the organization of the facility as either a government entity or not. Program types are based on whether the services of the facility are designed to intervene in problem areas of the residents' lives, such as substance abuse counseling, or to provide a supportive environment in which residents use community resources.

This simple typology indicates that different facilities must be assessed differently. For example, a residential facility designed to provide supportive services would not be well evaluated on the basis of direct service provision. Similarly, a program aimed at intervention would not be well understood solely in terms of resident length of stay. Rather, the type of program offered in a facility must form an important base of any assessment effort.

What Do We Know
About the Effectiveness Question?

Despite the long tradition of residential community correctional programs, the research literature concerned with them is sparse and inconclusive. There appear to be a number of reasons that residential programs have been largely ignored by correctional researchers.

First, residential facilities represent a relatively small part of the correctional system, and, as mentioned above, it is often difficult to distinguish between residential facilities that serve only correctional clientele and those that serve a broader constituency. Second, many programs are operated by private entities, and are either unwilling or unable to facilitate research. Third, generalization is a problem, because these programs are often markedly different from locale to locale, in terms of both the treatment offered and the types of clients they accept. Finally, it is often difficult to develop an adequate comparison group and to conduct a follow-up of residents. Despite these obstacles, there have been some notable attempts to evaluate the effectiveness of residential programs.

As correctional interventions, residential community correctional programs seem to meet two objectives: a reduction in postprogram criminality (recidivism) and an increase in prosocial behavior on the part of clients. Outcome assessments of residential programs then should assess both of these dimensions of program effectiveness. The literature indicates that recidivism has generally been the focus of most outcome evaluations, with varying definitions of recidivism.

In the first systematic evaluation of correctional halfway houses, Allen et al. (1976) reviewed 35 studies of halfway houses. Of these, 17 used quasi-experimental designs in comparing postprogram recidivism rates, 2 utilized true experimental designs, and 16 relied on nonexperimental designs. Based on the experimental and quasi-experimental studies, the researchers concluded that the evidence was about equally divided between lower recidivism rates for halfway house residents and no difference in recidivism rates when compared with a control group. They also found no evidence that halfway houses improved socially acceptable adjustment behaviors of residents, but that they were cheaper to operate than prisons, while more expensive than parole and probation.

Focusing on parolees, Latessa and Allen (1982) reported on evaluations of halfway house programs providing an overview of evaluations of programs throughout the United States. They rated 44 such studies as being characterized by sufficient methodological rigor to allow assessment of postrelease outcome. Of these, only 2 studies were found to have employed true experimental designs, involving random assignment to either an "experimental" (halfway house placement) or "control" (incarceration or other placement) group. Neither study indicated that halfway house clients performed significantly better than did subjects in the control conditions. An additional 23 studies employed quasi-experimental designs. There were also 19 nonexperimental studies that reported outcome data.

In general, the results were mixed, with some reports showing significantly lower recidivism among halfway house residents, some showing no significant differences, and others showing that the halfway house clients did significantly worse on release than did their counterparts in the control groups. In their conclusions, Latessa and Allen suggest that the literature indicates that halfway house programs are at least as effective as parole, especially given that halfway house clients are generally characterized by having higher risk and greater needs than those in a traditional parole population. Similarly, Seiter et al. (1977) conclude that prior evaluations "suggest that halfway house programs may more effectively reintegrate prisoners returning to the community than direct release to parole" (p. 160).

In an attempt to compare "recidivism" rates, some research has indicated that certain social, demographic, and criminal history characteristics must be controlled. Those with less education, who are younger, and who have less successful employment records, longer prior criminal records, and generally less stability in their social and personal lives are more likely to recidivate (Beha, 1977; Beran, McGruder, & Allen, 1974; Donnelly & Forschner, 1984; Dowell, Klein, & Kirchmar, 1985; Moczydlowski, 1980; Moran, Kass, & Muntz, 1977; Seiter, Petersilia, & Allen, 1974).

In a recent study, Donnelly and Forschner (1987) used discriminant function analysis and found that a similar set of factors serve to distinguish between residents who completed or failed to complete a halfway house program. Thus it appears that in order to determine if a residential program has been effective it is necessary to ensure that any differences between the treatment and control groups on these dimensions are known.

In addition to recidivism, however defined, it is important that improved prosocial behavior or social adjustment be measured. One of the earliest examples of this type of measurement was done by Seiter et al. (1974), using a scale of social adjustment. This scale allowed a cumulative score of the subject's involvement in employment, education, residence, interpersonal relations, and the like to be computed. The scale yielded a continuous score for each subject, thereby allowing comparisons. Based on their measure of recidivism *and* social adjustment, Seiter et al. conclude in their study of Ohio halfway houses that "halfway houses are more effective at assisting ex-offenders in their reintegration to the community than traditional modes of assistance."

Several other studies of halfway house program effectiveness have also attempted to address this dimension of outcome. Beck (1979) evaluated federal community treatment centers (CTCs) with measures of both recidivism and social adjustment, measured as days employed and money earned. He concluded that CTC clients fared better in social adjustment than did control subjects. Toborg, Center, Milkman, and Davis (1978) report similar effects in social adjustment in their review and assessment of more than 250 community assistance programs.

Finally, as Donnelly and Forschner (1987) have observed, "The success or failure of a halfway house is often defined in terms of the number or percent of the residents who complete the halfway house program" (p. 5). While they note that completion of the program may not satisfy those who define the "real goal" of correctional intervention as reduced recidivism, they argue that program completion is both an important organizational goal of the halfway house agency and inversely related to recidivism. These characteristics of program completion, they suggest, make it an appropriate criterion of outcome.

In a recent study of halfway house programs that examined both recidivism and social adjustment, we studied 132 probationers who resided in three halfway houses during 1983 (Latessa & Travis, 1986). A comparison group was composed of a sample of 140 felony probationers selected from the county probation department. We conducted a three-year follow-up through the use of official criminal records.

The results of this study illustrate the similarities and differences between the two groups. While there were a number of similarities between the halfway house and probation samples with regard to demographics, criminal history, and special problems/needs, some notable differences existed. Those in the halfway house sample were less educated and less likely to have been married. Those in the probation group had more prior convictions, and the halfway house subjects exhibited more prior involvement in drugs, alcohol treatment, and psychiatric problems. These data support other studies that have found that residential populations are in need of more intensive treatment than regular probationers. We also found that the halfway house group received significantly more services and treatment than the probation sample. This was true in almost every area examined.

Finally, the factors examined for the follow-up showed no significant differences between the two groups in terms of new crime convictions or social adjustment. Simply stated, the halfway house group did no better and no worse than the probation sample with regard to convictions or positive adjustment.

In addition to the outcome analysis, we conducted a discriminant analyses of factors associated with outcome (both recidivism and program completion). The results revealed few surprises. Prior criminal history, measured by the number of prior adult convictions, filing of technical probation violations, and the presence of a drug problem predicted recidivism in expected ways. Similarly, the provision of employment training was associated with fewer new convictions. In regard to program completion, higher scores on a social adjustment scale, enrollment in an educational program, and the absence of drug or psychiatric problems were associated with success. The provision of group counseling, however, was associated with failure.

While further research is required if we are to understand the relationships fully, the data from our study and from the studies of other researchers tend to support the following observations:

(1) Residential community correctional groups display greater service needs than do regular probation or parole groups.

(2) Many of these needs, such as psychiatric and drug/alcohol abuse history, are related both to positive adjustment and to new criminal convictions.

(3) Offenders in residential facilities are more likely to receive a variety of treatment and counseling services.

(4) When these observations are combined with the finding of no significant differences in recidivism and social adjustment outcomes between
groups, the possibility of a treatment effect is raised. That is, from these
studies it would appear that halfway house residents receive services
commensurate with their needs.

(5) Based on group characteristics at intake, an a priori assumption that
the halfway house group would demonstrate a higher rate of recidivism and lower social adjustment seems reasonable. That, generally,
no such differences in outcome have been observed and that residential
groups have received considerably more treatment interventions may
indicate that program participation is beneficial for this group.

The obvious implication of these conclusions is that placement
into a residential program should be considered a dispositional
option for convicted offenders. A general assessment of risk alone,
however, may not adequately identify those most likely to benefit
from such placement. That is, rather than viewing residential placement as a punitive (more intrusive) or incapacitative (more controlling) sanction for convicted offenders, placement in a program should
be guided by an assessment of an offender's needs. It is possible that
residential intervention can reduce the likelihood of negative outcome through meeting the treatment needs of clients.

There is also little evidence that successful completion of a residential program is a prerequisite of successful completion of probation or parole. Indeed, this suggests that residential programs, perhaps by virtue of their more rigorous rules and expectations of
program participation, may not be appropriate for some offenders.

Most of the research has revealed that residential placement has
been used with those offenders presenting higher needs and a priori
risk, in general, than the regular probation/parole population. Even
among this group, however, such placement may not always be
necessary. Future research should address case classification issues.
Such efforts could help identify the types of features within this
high-risk/high-needs group who are most likely to benefit from
placement in a particular residential program.

As is clear from the evaluation studies summarized above, most
of the research on residential facilities has focused on halfway houses
or similar placements with an interventive design. As yet, little is
known about the use and effects of residential placements in facilities designed to provide closer surveillance of offenders, without
interventive treatments. For these programs, the primary criteria of
evaluation would appear to be protection of public safety and cost

considerations. Extrapolating from what we have learned about interventive programs, it is reasonable to expect that residents in such facilities will pose no greater danger to the community than those under probation or parole supervision. They are no more likely to "recidivate" than those who are imprisoned. And, when compared with imprisonment, residential facility costs should be lower.

The Future of Residential Facilities

What does the future hold for residential community correctional facilities? First, in many ways they will remain an enigma to correctional researchers. Residential facilities that evolved from traditional halfway houses are now becoming multiservice agencies. The evolution will continue, but, unfortunately, so will our lack of understanding of these facilities, their effectiveness, and their role in the correctional process.

Second, residential community correctional facilities will continue to grow and develop new programs. In large part this will be a response to the crowding of local and state correctional institutions. Many traditional residential facilities will seize the opportunity and will diversify and offer a wider range of programs and services, such as victim assistance programs, family and drug counseling, drunk driver programs, work release centers, and house arrest, electronic monitoring, and day programs for offenders.

Finally, while there has been an increase in public sector operation of residential facilities, particularly prerelease and reintegration centers, it will be the private sector that will continue to play a dominant role in the development and operation of residential correctional programs. A number of arguments support private provision of community-based correctional services. Principal among these is cost-effectiveness. Proponents argue that the private sector will contain costs and thus, for the same dollar amount, provide more, or at least better, service. Government agencies, it is suggested, cannot achieve the same level of cost-efficient operation as can private, especially for-profit, companies.

As Clear, Hairs, and Record (1982) succinctly summarize: "Due to 'domestication' (characterized by a lack of competition and critical self-assessment), corrections officials often are inadvertently rewarded by taking a budget-administration approach rather than a cost-management stance." The attraction of private involvement in community corrections is the promise of a free market, or, as Greenwood

(1981) put it, "They would be free to innovate, to use the latest technology and management techniques as in any profit service industry."

Another, perhaps more compelling, reason for the continued development of private community residential programs is that they can offer what Gendreau and Ross (1987) call "therapeutic integrity." That is, because of their accountability to the contractor and the possibility of competition, privately operated programs may provide more intensive and higher-quality service provision than might government agencies. Indeed, many who have studied public community correctional agencies have lamented the increasingly bureaucratic role of the change agent (Clear & Latessa, 1989), noting the large number of staff who are simply "putting in time" for retirement or who are encumbered by paperwork and red tape. It often seems that organizational goals outweigh concerns about effective treatment and service delivery.

Of course, this is really an issue of accountability that involves some nonmonetary value questions. This is one of the fundamental differences between the private and public sectors. Private enterprise often measures outcome in terms of profit, while the public sector measures it in terms of social value and benefits. While there is no empirical evidence that the private sector is "better" at providing services, reducing recidivism, and so forth, there is a growing sentiment that it ought to at least be given a chance. Privately run facilities may also be in a better position to lobby for more services, staff, and programs. One need only look at the typical adult probation department, where caseloads range from 150 to 300, to see how ineffective they have been in garnering additional resources. Private providers may, because of contractual agreements, be better able to advocate for additional support.

Of more importance than the simple dichotomy between public and private operation is the future evolution of the mission of community corrections residential facilities. The traditional halfway house had a charitable, quasi-volunteer, and service-oriented mission (Wilson, 1985). The contemporary multiservice community agency or department of corrections-operated facility is more formal, legalistic, and control oriented. As correctional agencies contract with both new private sector vendors and older, charitable programs, the emphasis in residential facilities may change from treatment to custody. Further, as the importance of correctional contracts for the support and spread of residential facilities grows, the "community" nature of these programs may increasingly be replaced by a more formal, governmental administrative style. That is, the forces that currently support the development of programs may ultimately change them in fundamental ways.

The traditional halfway house operated by a civic-minded reform group for the purpose of assisting offenders may be replaced by a for-profit or nonprofit contractor working for the government. Thus, rather than a focus on the needs and interests of the community and the offender, the emphasis may be placed on the needs of the correctional system for bed space.

Of course, it is also entirely likely that the current confusion in residential programs will continue. There will continue to be traditional halfway houses focused on the needs of residents, with deep roots in the community. There will also be a variety of custody and crowding-control facilities designed to provide minimal direct services. Only time will tell what the future of community corrections residential facilities will be. The one thing that is clear is that some form of such facilities will exist in the future.

Note

1. Estimating the size of the community corrections residential facility population is hazardous at best. In her 1987 article, however, Hicks reported interviews with representatives of California, Texas, and the Federal Bureau of Prisons. These officials estimated that by 1988, the combined total of offenders served in residential facilities for these three jurisdictions would exceed 7,000. Given that these numbers do not include probationers or misdemeanants in all three jurisdictions, a conservative extrapolation yields an estimated 70,000 offenders in residential facilities during 1988. This represents about 10% of the prison population for that year.

References

Allen, H. E., Carlson, E. W., Parks, E. C., & Seiter, R. P. (1978). *Program models: Halfway houses.* Washington, DC: U.S. Department of Justice.

Allen, H. E., Seiter, R. P., Carlson, E. W., Bowman, H. H., Grandfield, J. J., & Beran, N. J. (1976). *National Evaluation Program Phase I: Residential inmate aftercare, the state of the art summary.* Columbus: Ohio State University, Program for the Study of Crime and Delinquency.

Beck, J. L. (1979). An evaluation of federal community treatment centers. *Federal Probation, 43*(3), 36-40.

Beha, J. A. (1977). Testing the functions and effects of the parole halfway house: One case study. *Journal of Criminal Law and Criminology, 67,* 335-350.

Beran, N. J., McGruder, J. L., & Allen, H. E. (1974). *The community reintegration centers of Ohio: A second year evaluation.* Columbus: Ohio State University, Program for the Study of Crime and Delinquency.

Clear, T., Hairs, P. M., & Record, A. L. (1982). Managing the cost of corrections. *Prison Journal, 53,* 1-63.

Clear, T., & Latessa, E. J. (1989, March). *Intensive surveillance versus treatment.* Paper presented at the annual meeting of the Academy of Criminal Justice Sciences, Washington, DC.

Donnelly, P. G., & Forschner, B. (1984). Client success or failure in a halfway house. *Federal Probation, 48*(3), 38-44.

Donnelly, P. G., & Forschner, B. (1987). Predictors of success in a co-correctional halfway house: A discriminant analysis. *Journal of Crime and Justice, 10*(2), 1-22.

Dowell, D., Klein, C., & Kirchmar, C. (1985). Evaluation of a halfway house for women. *Journal of Criminal Justice, 13,* 217-226.

DuPont, P. (1985). *Expanding sentencing options: A governor's perspective.* Washington, DC: National Institute of Justice.

Federal Probation. (1986). Intensive probation supervision [Special issue]. Vol. 50, No. 2.

Gatz, N., & Murray, C. (1981). An administrative overview of halfway houses. *Corrections Today, 43,* 52-54.

Gendreau, P., & Ross, R. R. (1987). Revivification of rehabilitation: Evidence from the 1980's. *Justice Quarterly, 4,* 349-407.

Greenwood, P. (1981). *Private enterprise prisons? Why not?* Santa Monica, CA: RAND Corporation.

Guynes, R. (1988). *Difficult clients, large caseloads plague probation, parole agencies.* Washington, DC: U.S. Department of Justice.

Hicks, N. (1987). A new relationship: Halfway houses and corrections. *Corrections Compendium, 12*(4), 1, 5-7.

Keller, O. J., & Alper, G. (1970). *Halfway houses: Community centered correction and treatment.* Lexington, MA: D. C. Heath.

Latessa E. J., & Allen, H. E. (1982). Halfway houses and parole: A national assessment. *Journal of Criminal Justice, 10*(2), 153-163.

Latessa, E. J., & Travis, L. F. (1986, October). *Halfway houses versus probation: A three year follow-up of offenders.* Paper presented at the annual meeting of the Midwestern Criminal Justice Association, Chicago.

McCarthy, B. R. (Ed.). (1987). *Intermediate punishments: Intensive supervision, home confinement, and electronic surveillance.* Monsey, NY: Criminal Justice Press.

Moczydlowski, K. (1980). Predictors of success in a correctional halfway house for youthful and adult offenders. *Corrective and Social Psychiatry and Journal of Behavior Technology, Methods and Therapy, 26,* 59-72.

Moran, E., Kass W., & Muntz, D. (1977). In-program evaluation of a community correctional agency for high risk offenders. *Corrective and Social Psychiatry and Journal of Behavior Technology, Methods and Therapy, 23,* 48-52.

Petersilia, J. (1985). *Probation and felon offenders.* Washington, DC: U.S. Department of Justice.

Petersilia, J. (1987). *Expanding options for criminal sentencing* (Publication No. R-3544-EMC). Santa Monica, CA: RAND Corporation.

President's Commission on Law Enforcement and Administration of Justice. (1967). *Task force report: Corrections.* Washington, DC: Government Printing Office.

Rush, G. E. (1991). *The dictionary of criminal justice* (3rd ed.). Guilford, CT: Dushkin.

Seiter, R. P., Carlson, E. W., Bowman, H., Grandfield, H., Beran, N. J., & Allen, H. E. (1977). *Halfway houses.* Washington, DC: Government Printing Office.

Seiter, R. P., Petersilia, J. R., & Allen, H. E. (1974). *Evaluation of adult halfway houses in Ohio* (Vol. 2). Columbus: Ohio State University, Program for the Study of Crime and Delinquency.

Toborg, M. A., Center, L. J., Milkman, R. H., & Davis, D. W. (1978). *The transition from prison to employment: An assessment of community-based assistance programs.* (National Evaluation Program Phase I report). Washington, DC: U.S. Department of Justice.

Wilson, G. P. (1985). Halfway house programs for offenders. In L. F. Travis (Ed.), *Probation, parole, and community corrections* (pp. 151-164). Prospect Heights, IL: Waveland.

12. Punishing Labor: Unpaid Community Service as a Criminal Sentence

Douglas C. McDonald

In recent years, orders to give unpaid labor, or "community service," have become a common element in celebrity offenders' court-imposed punishments. Michael Milken, the "junk" bond dealer convicted of violating federal securities laws, was ordered to do charitable work full-time for three years, without pay, after he completes his term in a federal prison. Community service orders were handed out also to Oliver North, an aide to President Reagan who ran afoul of the law while running a covert operation in Nicaragua out of the White House, and to Zsa Zsa Gabor, a Hollywood celebrity and one-time actress, for breaking traffic laws and slapping the police officer who stopped her. Although community service sentences come into the public eye through cases such as these, thousands of unremarkable offenders convicted in the nation's criminal courts each year are also ordered to pay back their communities through a variety of ways, all involving unpaid labor.

To some, such sentences are "smart" because they advance a variety of penal purposes. They provide a means of extracting punishment from lawbreakers. The community is given something of value, which in some cases may seem a sensible alternative to footing the bill for incarcerating offenders in order to punish them. With any luck, the experience of serving the community may also inculcate a sense of allegiance to the society, moderating more predatory impulses that are given too free a rein by some offenders. Whether, and under what conditions, the imposition of community service actually serves the public interest is a question that deserves some scrutiny, however. The intelligent use of unpaid labor as a criminal sanction requires attention to how various purposes are best balanced.

This chapter explores the recent emergence of community service sentences, how they have been used, the purposes for which they have been imposed, and what we know about their effectiveness.

Bringing Community Service
Back Into the Criminal Law

Community service sentences owe their recent incarnation to several judges in California's Alameda County courts (Beha, Carlson, & Rosenblum, 1977; McDonald, 1986a). Alameda's judges faced a conundrum that judges have confronted for more than a century: Does it make sense to impose fines on poor people—in Alameda's case, women who violate traffic laws—only to have them jailed if they do not pay? Jailing poor women for default also has the unwanted effect of visiting punishment upon their children and others who depend upon them. Sending them to jail if their offenses warrant it is one thing; sending them to jail for not being able to afford fines is another. The solution the Alameda judges hit upon was to order these women to work without pay at projects that would benefit the public or for public charities. Within years, such sentences became a fixture in the Alameda courts and began to be used more broadly, for other types of offenders as well.

This was an innovative development. In recent history, such sentences were not countenanced by lawmakers. They hark back to much earlier customs and laws, however. Ancient Babylonian, Greek, Roman, and Jewish law all contained provisions for calculating compensation to be paid by offenders to their victims or their victims' kin (Schafer, 1970). In many societies that we call "primitive," offenders have been required to compensate their victims. Victim restitution fell into disuse when victims lost their central role in the penal process, a development that occurred when organized governments emerged and asserted their authority. Crimes became defined as crimes against the state, and officials in the employ of kings and their governments were given authority to administer the criminal law. Victims desiring compensation were referred to the civil courts. By the nineteenth century, restitution had vanished from criminal law and procedure in Western societies, although judges here and there may have continued to order, on occasion, restitution payments in conjunction with criminal penalties (McDonald, 1986b).

Community service orders also harked back to another earlier practice—that of requiring convicts to undertake uncompensated labor for their crimes as punishment. Roman offenders could be spared worse punishment if they performed hard manual labor on public projects (such as road building) or manned oars on galleys. From the early seventeenth century, criminals convicted in English courts of all but the most serious crimes could be impressed into the Royal Navy. They could also be transported to the colonies, where they could be required to work without pay, or be given a "ticket of leave," whereby they agreed to work as indentured servants to free settlers. With the end of impressment and transportation in the nineteenth century, the opportunities for extracting labor as a punishment ended in England (although inmates could still be forced to work behind prison walls). In North America, courts never relied upon impressment or transportation, and the practice of ordering unpaid labor as punishment was less established as a consequence.

In 1973, a few years after the Alameda judges brought unpaid community service back into modern criminal courts, the British government instituted systematic nationwide reform to introduce community service sentencing on a widespread scale. This demonstrated that judges would impose community service orders upon offenders convicted of relatively serious crimes, and that such sentences were feasible. In the United States, the practice began to be adopted by a number of criminal courts across the country, a development that was encouraged by federal policy. In 1976, the Law Enforcement Assistance Administration (LEAA), the federal agency created to funnel money to states and local governments for criminal justice reforms, actively promoted the use of the sanction. Indeed, federal funds provided about 60% of the seed money spent to create the formalized community service sentencing programs in the following few years (Krajick, 1982). The Office of Juvenile Justice and Delinquency Prevention, another federal agency, similarly undertook in 1978 a substantial initiative to stimulate program development in the juvenile courts, and spent about $30 million in 85 counties and states during the three years that followed (Schneider, Griffith, Schneider, & Wilson, 1982).

Because of the fragmented nature of our federal system of government—with governments at the national level, in 50 states, and in about 4,000 counties—court reforms more often than not have a kind of patchwork quality. In some jurisdictions, judges simply sentence persons without any dedicated organization to administer the programs, other than existing probation. In others, formal programs have been established. Regardless of whether dedicated administrative arrangements exist, judges have used the sentences for a wide variety of reasons, and for different types of offenders. Few surveys have been done, but one in 1977 found that about half of all juvenile courts polled imposed community service sentences without having any special institutionalized arrangements for administering them, other than existing probation departments (Schneider, Schneider, Reiter, & Cleary, 1977). Moreover, surveys in 1977 and 1978 counted 58 formally organized community service sentencing programs in the criminal courts and another 70 for juveniles (Hudson, Galaway, & Novack, 1980; Schneider et al., 1977).

No similar surveys have been reported since then (although one supported by the National Institute of Corrections is currently under way).[1] My impression, based on hearsay and unsystematic reporting, is that these sentences have become quite commonplace in many courts, especially at the lower levels, where misdemeanor and traffic cases are disposed of. The rising pressure on courts to sanction drunk drivers more seriously has probably resulted in many more persons being required to provide unpaid community service as punishment, often on weekends and days off. It is also my impression, however, that the proportion of such sentences to the total remains quite small, overwhelmed by the courts' continued reliance upon fines, jail, and probation. Lacking any national reporting system that tracks dispositions in these lower courts, it is difficult to do more than guess about the size of the population required to perform unpaid labor. In England, however, it appears that about 8% of all offenders sentenced for serious crimes are given community service orders (Morris & Tonry, 1990).

Why Impose Unpaid Labor as a Sentence?

Sentencing laws throughout most of the United States are more enabling than prescriptive. That is, they give judges the authority to impose various sanctions for specific categories of offenses, but are typically agnostic as to the purposes to be served at sentencing. Judges consequently follow their own sentencing philosophies more often than not. The result of this general tendency is that community service is imposed for a multiplicity of purposes.

In the 1970s, it was common to hear the sentence championed as a means of paying restitution. Indeed, it was often referred to as "symbolic restitution" and was seen as a close cousin to financial restitution. Rather than paying back a specific victim, the offender served the "community" instead. This link to restitution reflected community service's immediate ancestry in civil law.

It was also thought that imposing community service served other utilitarian purposes—principally, that it provided a means of rehabilitating offenders. Indeed, the British policy was motivated strongly by the hope that community service would provide a means of offender rehabilitation in the community. Reformers thought that if convicted criminals were to work alongside public-spirited citizens in voluntary organizations, they might acquire a greater sense of civic responsibility (Young, 1979). One of the early advocates of community service in the United States, Judge Dennis Challeen (1980), a Minnesota county court judge, argued on behalf of the sentences because "they require offenders to make efforts toward self-improvement, thus removing them from their roles as losers and helping them to address their personal problems and character defects that alienate them from the mainstream of society" (p. 7). Some of the scholarly advocates put it slightly differently:

> Restitution may be more rehabilitative than other correctional measures because it is rationally related to the amount of damages done, is a specific sanction which allows the offender to clearly know when requirements are completed, requires the offender's active involvement, provides a socially appropriate and concrete way of expressing guilt, and creates a situation in which an offender is likely to elicit a positive response from other persons. (Hudson et al., 1980, p. 19)

This language may seem a little dated to contemporary ears, in part because a sea-change took place in thinking about criminal sanctions in the 1970s and 1980s. Whereas criminal sentences had for decades been justified by appeals to rehabilitative rationales, the legitimacy of these rationales was eroding rapidly. Robert Martinson (1974), one of three authors who systematically assessed the findings of prison rehabilitation studies, summarized his view by declaring that "nothing works." Legal scholars such as Francis Allen (1964) had earlier attacked the rehabilitative ideal on other grounds—that it gave too much power to the state without adequate justification—and sought to limit state power in criminal sentencing procedures. These and other developments encouraged a return to a notion of basing sentences not on crime control objectives (whether rehabilitation, incapacitation, or deterrence), but on the principle that persons who violate the laws are deserving of punishment. This retributionist theory of sentencing has been given broadest circulation under the concept of "just deserts" (von Hirsch, 1976).

In this climate, community service began to be seen and justified more as a punishment, an "intermediate punishment," one that was less severe than incarceration (perhaps) but that could be more onerous than other lesser sanctions. Thus Norval Morris and Michael Tonry (1990) refer to community service as a "fine on the offender's time." Advocates of community service, such as those persons at the Vera Institute of Justice in New York City who ran one of the early demonstration projects, advertised the sanction to criminal court judges as a "punishment" suited for persons convicted of the sorts of offenses that would otherwise result in short jail stays, which were arguably imposed largely for punitive purposes, or for persons who were not being sufficiently punished by receiving other lesser sanctions (McDonald, 1986a).

Others see the community service sentence as an appropriate alternative to an imprisonment term. For some, this is a matter of principle; for others, it is a more bloodless assessment of costs and benefits. The principled argument takes a few different forms. One is based on what is essentially a desert-based rationale. That is, sentences should be scaled to the severity of the offense, rather than to the suspected dangerousness of the offender or to the perceived likelihood of his or her being rehabilitated. Graver crimes are deserving of more severe punishments, and lesser crimes of lesser penalties. Community service is therefore more appropriate than jail, as a matter of principle, for crimes not serious enough to warrant imprisonment (von Hirsch, Wasik, & Greene, 1989).

Another line of principled argument is that offenders should be given the "least restrictive sanction," which is often translated as "less than imprisonment." In the late 1960s, the American Bar Association (1969) promulgated standards for criminal sentencing, and one of the four general principles included the proposition that "a sentence not involving confinement is to be preferred to a sentence involving partial or total confinement in the absence of affirmative reasons to the contrary." This principle of inflicting the least harm was grounded partly on certain value-laden assumptions, most notably a preference for restraining coercive state power over individuals. It was grounded also on propositions that were more utilitarian: that community-based, nonincarcerative sanctions are generally more effective in promoting public safety than imprisonment. This proposition was expressed clearly in the influential 1973 report of the National Advisory Commission on Criminal Justice Standards and Goals, which declared that "the institutional model for corrections has not been successful in curbing potential crime." Indeed, in that report, prisons were seen as destructive.

> The effectiveness of prison as a school for crime is exaggerated, for the criminal can learn the technology of crime far better on the streets. The

damage the prison does is far more subtle. Attitudes are brutalized, and
self-confidence is lost. The prison is a place of coercion where compliance
is obtained by force. The typical response to coercion is alienation, which
may take the form of active hostility to all social controls or later a passive
withdrawal into alcoholism, drug addictions, or dependency. (p. 223)

These assumptions were converted into guidelines for funding by
the Law Enforcement Assistance Administration in subsequent years.
One LEAA publication describing its funding priorities, issued in
about 1976, declared that the agency "places a high priority on
community-based corrections—programs that appear to offer more
hope of rehabilitation because they keep certain types of offenders
in their community where they have family or social ties" (Law
Enforcement Assistance Administration, n.d.). Such beliefs did not
die in the 1970s. Federal District Judge Jack Weinstein wrote in 1987
that the federal courts sentenced probationers to work alongside
volunteers in public and private agencies for the purpose of rehabilitation, "an achievement that prison often fails in miserably, particularly when the prison population exceeds capacity" (p. 25).

Is Community Service a Useful Sanction?

Ultimately, the question of whether community service sentences
are in fact more effective, or more "cost-effective," than other sanctions in controlling crime is an empirical one that is capable of being
answered by research. (In contrast, whether it is a more appropriate
or just sanction for certain types of offenses is a normative question
that cannot be resolved through empirical research.) And its relative
effectiveness depends, obviously, upon what it is compared with.
Although there were several national assessments of community
service and restitution programs supported by the federal government in the 1970s, none really addressed the question of relative
effectiveness. Ken Pease (1985) reports that in England and Wales,
between 1979 and 1982, 10% of those given community service
sentences were reconvicted for new offenses. But whether offenders
would have been reconvicted at higher or lower rates had other
sentences been imposed was not determined.

My own research on the Vera Institute of Justice's community
service sentencing project did attempt to estimate the relative crime
control effects of the sanction (McDonald, 1986a). In 1979, the institute formally organized a project in the Bronx criminal court, where

misdemeanor convictions are taken; within a few years, the project had grown to include the criminal courts of Manhattan, Brooklyn, and Queens. The purpose of the project was to provide judges an option to short jail terms (terms of 90 days or less) that was imposed on chronic property offenders largely for the purpose of punishing them. In addition, the sentence—a 70-hour obligation that was to be served full-time for two weeks—was to be used in equal measure for enhancing the sanction visited upon persons who were thought to be escaping sufficient punishment because jail cells were in short supply, because the offenders were seen as too poor to pay fines, and because probation is not designed to provide punishment. In other words, it was to be both an "alternative" to a jail sentence and a means of punishing more people who would otherwise escape the net of social control and punishment.

The labor these offenders provided was undoubtedly burdensome, but was not designed to humiliate them. They worked in crews led by foremen on staff at the Vera Institute, and they were given tasks that involved painting senior citizens' centers and community-owned nursing homes, cleaning neighborhood lots, and preparing ghetto buildings for renovation and conversion to low-income housing.

A sample of those who were given community service orders by the courts was followed for six months after they had been ordered to perform the service. Between 39% and 51% had been rearrested, depending upon the borough, typically for a variety of property crimes. A sample of comparable persons given short jail sentences instead of community service was also followed, and the proportion rearrested within six months of release from jail in each of the boroughs was identical to the sample sentenced to community service. These findings give no support to the idea that community service either rehabilitates offenders better or deters further crime more effectively than a short jail term.

Community service does yield other benefits, however, although calculating their worth is not without difficulties. I estimated that approximately 60,000 hours of labor were donated to the community during 1984, which would have been worth about $200,000–$270,300 if someone had paid between minimum wage and $4.50 per hour for the time. Some of the work would not have been done at all in the absence of the donated service, so it didn't show up as a savings on anybody's budget, and especially not the city government's budget. Given that jail in New York City is expensive—approximately $38,500 per year for operating costs alone during 1984—it may seem at first blush that avoiding its use and imposing community service instead would reap a substantial savings. But this depends upon having the courts actually employ community service as a substitute for jail terms rather than for other nonincarcerative sentences. Using a statistical model of sentencing decisions, I estimated that judges in two of the three original courts having the community service option used it as a jail alternative in only about one-fifth to one-fourth of the cases. When the program's operation was redesigned, and the agreement with the courts and prosecutors renegotiated, the project met its target in all borough courts—that is, community service was imposed half the time as an alternative to jail. In even these circumstances, however, the project did not result in direct savings to the city's budget for jail operations.

I estimated that in 1982, the average cost of operating the Vera Institute's project was about $1,077 per offender sentenced to community service, and that it declined about $100 during the following year. I further estimated that use of the sanction averted use of jail cells that amounted to about 102 total prisoner/years in 1984. Although the average cost of operating the jails that year was $38,500 per prisoner/year, saving 102 prisoner/years of jail time did not yield a dollar savings that amounted to 102 times $38,500 per year. This is because jails incur only *marginal* savings for each person not imprisoned, and not the per capita average. Most costs of jailing (especially staff salaries) are quite fixed; those costs are merely spread across a somewhat smaller number of prisoners rather than being reduced proportionately. (In New York City, emptying a few cells by use of community service merely created vacancies for other prisoners, for the demand for jail cells there, as in many other places, far outstrips the available supply.)

This illustrates an important point, not only for community service sentences but for many other nonincarcerative sanctions that aim to lighten the demand for jail cells. Expanding their use may not reduce overall costs to the government unless certain conditions are met. Their use must be expansive enough to permit a reduction in the number of prison or jail facilities in operation; this is the only real way of reducing operating costs of jails and prisons. Or their expanded use must avert expenditures for building new cells. (In New York, which was expanding its jail capacity, the steady reduction of the demand for cells by use of community service might have been translated into a decision to build fewer new cells, at $71,000 apiece.) The option of driving down the cost of administering community service sentences is limited if one wants to retain any real ability to supervise labor and to enforce nonperformance.

There is another cost not often reckoned with: additional crime that may result from not imposing more restrictive sanctions. Even though a jail sentence may not rehabilitate or deter chronic property offenders any better than a term of community service, it does keep these people off the streets and away from other people's property and persons for a period of time. That is, jail "incapacitates" offenders for the time that they are behind bars. By placing these offenders in the community instead, the incapacitative benefits that jail yields are lost. How substantial that loss is depends upon what kinds of offenders are given community service instead of jail, how long they would have been behind bars, and how much crime they actually commit that would have been averted by a jail sentence. Knowing precisely who would have gone to jail and for how long in the absence of a particular intermediate sanctioning option is difficult to estimate (and attempts to do so have often been distorted seriously by institutional or ideological interests in claiming large success), but my own estimates of forgone incapacitation benefits in the New York City project give some indication of how one might go about calculating it. Using statistical models of sentencing decisions, I estimated the percentage of those offenders given community service who would have gone to jail, and the average number of days they would have served. The project also tracked all offenders given community service and recorded the dates and natures of their arrests. This permitted us to develop an estimate of the number of arrests that would have been averted by the use of jail had the community service option not been available to the courts: about 15 arrests per 100 persons sentenced to community service during the period of our evaluation.

One could attempt a finer calculation of cost and benefit trade-offs, estimating the value of the losses inflicted by these crimes, and the marginal savings incurred by the use of community service, variously administered, but putting dollar values on crimes committed is not entirely satisfactory, especially for violent crimes. It also points to the larger problem of trying to justify the use of community service sentences in strictly utilitarian terms: The net gain, if there is any, is not all that clear in many instances. My own view is that a more compelling reason for considering community service, as well as other intermediate sanctions, is that it provides a means of more finely matching deserved punishments with the severity of offenses. This suggests the importance of developing guidelines to determine how much unpaid labor, and of what sort, should be given for crimes of differing severity, although there may be compelling practical reasons for preferring a fixed "dose" of hours or days to be served by all, as the Vera Institute's administrators concluded (McDonald, 1986a).

Finally, there are a host of other important issues that cannot be addressed here for lack of space. These include the crucial questions of how programs might be designed to accomplish different penal purposes, the advantages and disadvantages of placing community service administration in public or private agencies, how to design opportunities for unpaid labor that do not threaten the jobs of government employees, the extent to which other support services are needed by persons deemed too poor to pay fines, whether it makes penological sense to stack community service obligations onto other criminal sanctions, and whether special procedures are needed to enforce these obligations. Readers interested in these matters should turn elsewhere (see, e.g., McDonald, 1986a; Morris & Tonry, 1990; Pease, 1985; Pease & McWilliams, 1980; Young, 1979).

Note

1. This survey is being conducted by Alan Harland, a criminologist at Temple University.

References

Allen, F. A. (1964). *The borderland of criminal justice.* Chicago: University of Chicago Press.

American Bar Association. (1969). *Standards relating to sentencing alternatives and procedures.* New York: Project on Standards for Criminal Justice.

Beha, J., Carlson, K., & Rosenblum, R. H. (1977). *Sentencing to community service.* Washington, DC: Government Printing Office.

Challeen, D. A. (1980). Turning society's losers into winners [Interview]. *Judges' Journal, 19.*

Hudson, J., Galaway, B., & Novack, S. (1980). *National assessment of adult restitution programs: Final report.* Duluth: University of Minnesota, School of Social Development.

Krajick, K. (1982, October). The work ethic approach to punishment. *Corrections Magazine.*

Law Enforcement Assistance Administration. (n.d.). *A partnership for crime control.* Washington, DC: Author.

Martinson, R. (1974). What works? Questions and answers about prison reform. *Public Interest, 35,* 22-54.

McDonald, D. C. (1986a). *Punishment without walls: Community service sentences in New York City.* New Brunswick, NJ: Rutgers University Press.

McDonald, D. C. (1986b). *Restitution and community service* (Crime File study guide). Washington, DC: National Institute of Justice.

Morris, N., & Tonry, M. (1990). *Between prison and probation: Intermediate punishments in a rational sentencing system.* New York: Oxford University Press.

National Advisory Commission on Criminal Justice Standards and Goals. (1973). *Corrections.* Washington, DC: Government Printing Office.

Pease, K. (1985). Community service orders. In M. Tonry & N. Morris (Eds.), *Crime and justice: An annual review of research* (Vol. 6). Chicago: University of Chicago Press.

Pease, K., & McWilliams, W. (Eds.). (1980). *Community service by order.* Edinburgh: Scottish Academic Press.

Schafer, S. (1970). *Compensation and restitution to victims of crime* (2nd ed.). Montclair, NJ: Smith Patterson.

Schneider, P. R., Griffith, W. R., Schneider, A. L., & Wilson, M. J. (1982). *Two-year report on the national evaluation of the Juvenile Restitution Initiative: An overview of program experience.* Eugene, OR: Institute of Policy Analysis.

Schneider, P. R., Schneider, A. L., Reiter, P., & Cleary, C. (1977). Restitution requirements for juvenile offenders: A survey of practices in American juvenile courts. *Juvenile Justice, 28,* 47.

von Hirsch, A. (1976). *Doing justice: The choice of punishments.* New York: Hill & Wang.

von Hirsch, A., Wasik, M., & Greene, J. (1989). Punishments in the community and the principles of desert. *Rutgers Law Journal, 20,* 595-618.

Weinstein, J. B. (1987). A trial judge's first impression of the federal sentencing guidelines. *Albany Law Review, 52,* 1-31.

Young, W. (1979). *Community service orders.* London: Heinemann.

13. The English Experience: Intermediate Treatment With Juveniles

J. Robert Lilly

This chapter offers a brief overview of the English experience with intermediate treatment (IT) for juveniles. Although the English experience with IT will not be compared with juvenile justice and IT in the United States directly, comparisons will be used when illustrative. Discussion of the current status of juvenile IT is necessarily preceded by a general review of criminal justice in England. After a clarification of terms, IT is examined within its sociopolitical context. The conclusions focus on the future of "juvenile justice" in England.

Setting: The 1980s

PRISON POPULATION PATTERNS

When in 1934 Sutherland wrote, "Prisons are being demolished and sold in England because the supply of prisoners is not large enough to fill them" (p. 800), the prison population had been declining steadily since 1908. At that time the prison population for England and Wales was 22,000, a 20-year high. By 1915, the number had been halved, and it remained at the 11,000-12,000 level throughout the 1920s and 1930s. The imprisonment rate per 100,000 population for England and Wales was 30, below Sweden at 38 and below the modern paragon of penal tolerance, the Netherlands, which had a rate of 57 (Rutherford, 1989, p. 27).

The decline of prison populations reversed with a steady increase in the 1950s and 1960s. The growth rate surged in the 1980s. During

Mrs. Thatcher's first year as prime minister, the average daily prison population was more than 45,000. By spring 1988, the number had grown to approximately 50,000, and projections for 1996 put the total between 63,000 and 69,000 (Rutherford, 1989, p. 27). As also occurs in the United States, overcrowding conditions are severe; sometimes as many as 1,000-1,500 people are held in police cells that "are totally unsuitable for the task" (Rutherford, 1989, p. 27). One news account reported that one in five prisoners is held in a police or court cell because of prison overcrowding ("Law Society Leads Move," 1988).

Comparatively, English jail and prison overcrowding in the 1980s was worse in some ways than in the United States because of problems almost unknown in the United States. Some older English prisons, for example, still have "slopping out," that is, the practice of using plastic buckets for toilets. Plans do not call for eliminating this practice completely for another seven years ("Action on Jail Slops Practice," 1989; *Dundee Evening Telegraph,* February 21, 1989; "End Slopping," 1989; "Jail 'slopping' attacked," 1989; "Slopping Out Move," 1989). Until then, inmates in some of the older prisons will continue to rely on plastic buckets. In the late 1980s, 6,500 cells in England were reported to need access to nighttime toilets.[1]

SENTENCING PATTERNS

The 1980s prison population reflected increases in sentence lengths. Between 1976 and 1986 the proportion of adult male indictable offenders sentenced to immediate custody rose from 16% to 21%. And the length of the crown court's sentences alone increased from 17 months in 1980 to 18.9 months in 1987.[2] The trend continued into the late 1980s, when it was reported that increasingly tougher sentences were being given for violent offenses. According to one report, for example, between 1985 and 1987 the jail sentence in England and Wales for using firearms to resist arrest increased 95%, to 6.7 years. Other increases in crown court sentencing are presented in Table 13.1.

For men age 21 and over sentenced to immediate punishment for indictable offenses at all courts, the average sentence rose from 11.9 months in 1984 to 14 months in 1986, and then to 15.1 months in 1987. Only 4,000 juveniles were sentenced to immediate custody in 1987, compared with 6,800 in 1983. For young adults (ages 17-20), the figure was 21,300 for 1987, compared with 23,100 in 1983 ("Stiffer Jail Sentences," 1988).

TABLE 13.1 Increases in Crown Court Sentencing

	1984	Average: Adult Male 1987	Increase (%)
Using firearms to resist arrest	3.4	6.7	95
Rape	3.8	6.2	63
Robbery			
with firearms	5.7	7.0	22
without firearms	3.1	3.8	21
Indecent assault on a female	2.0	2.3	15
Manslaughter	4.9	5.5	11

SOURCE: *Criminal Statistics* (1987).

SENTENCING REFORMS

Official reports beginning in 1978 and 1979 repeatedly stressed that prison sentences in England and Wales were used "more frequently and for longer terms than can be justified on grounds of proportionality or crime control" (Ashworth, 1988, p. 726). The logic of this conclusion was based on the observation that increased reliance on imprisonment to protect the public was questionable (a) because the crown court dealt with no more than 7% of all crimes committed and (b) because 60% of those released from prison are convicted of another offense within two years. Imprisonment reduces offending only for a limited period.

But it was not until 1989 that calls for sentencing reform experienced support from places ordinarily opposed to it. Support for such reforms was heard from senior judges in mid-1989, for example. They asked for more guidance to ensure that fewer nonserious offenders were sent to prison and to maintain sentencing consistency throughout England and Wales. And even the right-wing Centre for Policy Studies lent its support for an independent sentencing commission ("Judges Call," 1989). The crown court judges, however, were firmly opposed to this idea.

By the beginning of the 1990s, the Conservative government was proposing new court procedures to curtail what it was calling the excessive use of imprisonment. These measures were intended to create a new style of social inquiry report before passing a sentence and a noncustodial package of community punishment selected by probation officers to suit the circumstances of each offender ("Law Reform Set," 1990). Judges and magistrates who nonetheless imposed prison sentences would, according to the proposal, be obliged to explain their rejection of the noncustodial option.

The proposal was aimed at both crown court judges and magistrates. Douglas Hurd, then Home Office secretary, strongly rebuked the magistrates for sentence disparity. He called for fewer jail sentences, and claimed that magistrates in the North of England were more punitive than those in the South. He also stated that in view of the high proportion of ethnic minority members in prison, magistrates should watch out for racial discrimination and unconscious bias in their sentencing ("Cut Down," 1989). Although the effectiveness of the proposal will not be known for some time, Whitehall[3] proclaimed it the most serious postwar attempt to reform the criminal justice system.

PRIVATIZATION AND CRIMINAL JUSTICE

In the 1980s, the New Right government joined disenchanted liberals in a reformulation of criminal justice. Influenced by both Thatcher's and Reagan's penchant for an unregulated marketplace, this new alliance promoted the privatization and deregulation of punishment. This happened in a highly charged atmosphere in which a radical change had taken place in the ownership and management of a number of ("nationalized") public utilities, including water, gas, steel, electricity, and British Telecom. The "break-even" philosophy/policy of the state as the natural provider was replaced with the profit motive.[4] This development threatened several time-honored beliefs, two of which included "Only in America could such a thing transpire" and "Only the state has a monopoly on the use of legitimate power." Of more immediate concern to the Right was the belief that privatization would reduce the level of state expenditures for "law and order."[5]

Specific privatization proposals have included not only "private prisons" and for-profit immigration detention centers, but also the transportation of the accused and convicted between cell and court room. Each suggestion has been greeted with strong opposition from unions, some if not all of which, it is often said (with good reason), the Right government wants to destroy.[6] When the Home Office announced in 1989, for example, that it was introducing stricter noncustodial penalties for persistent offenders that would combine elements of probation and community service and possibly electronic monitoring, delegates at the annual meeting of the National

Association of Probation Officers (NAPO) "endorsed a motion pledging them to fight any attempt to privatize their work" ("Stricter Non-Jail," 1989). Reportedly, NAPO feared the government's plans would transform association members into compliant "community punishers." NAPO judged the contracting out of probation work to be obscene, illogical, and unworkable.

Terms

The term *intermediate treatment* (IT) was first introduced by a Home Office (1968) white paper, *Children in Trouble*. It referred to a wide range of provisions for young people at risk and in trouble (Nellis, 1989, p. 173). By the early 1970s it took the form of low-intensity preventive social work. Toward the end of the decade and in the early 1980s, a group of scholars/researchers from the University of Lancaster led an unusually successful and controversial attempt to restrict it to high-intensity alternatives to residential care and custody.

In broad terms, IT for juveniles is part of a wide assortment of tasks, sentences, and dispositions under the rubric of alternatives to custody. Because there is no single definition of *alternatives to custody*, proposals include virtually anything that involves crime prevention, punishment, or control outside custodial institutions. Alternatives to custody can include many diverse activities, ranging from sentencing choices following conviction to pretrial decisions and broader policies of preventing risk groups—that is, juveniles—from experiencing formal justice and control (Vass, 1990, p. 1). Examples of such community programs include

> neighborhood crime prevention schemes; bail; police cautioning; intermediate treatment projects for juveniles; probation orders (with or without special requirements); fines and fixed penalties; conditional discharge orders; tracking schemes; tagging; supervision orders with special requirements; suspended sentences; parole; deferred sentences; compensation orders; binding over; attendance centre orders; suspended sentence supervision orders; and community service orders. (Vass, 1990, p. 1)

Over the years these "programs" have been described by various labels reflecting not only professional ethos but political ideology as well. They have been called community-based dispositions, community care programs, community corrections, community correctional programs, noncustodial penal measures, diversionary penal measures, decarceration, deinstitutionalization, humane punishment, supervision in the community, and, more recently, punishment in the community (more about this later). The lack of specificity plagued the use of IT with juveniles, and from the "mid-eighties it . . . was considered too serious an impediment to good public relations . . . and a number of areas—by no means all—abandoned it, without there being any clear consensus as to what it should be replaced with" (Nellis, 1989, p. 173).

IT's History

IT AS TREATMENT

IT is difficult to describe, but the practice does have definite features. First, after the 1968 white paper, IT was initiated by the Children and Young Persons Act (1969). It contained a liberal interest in creating a broad range of preventive work for young people under the age of 16. Some of it was to be available voluntarily, some as diversion from court, and some as a formal request from a supervision order. When sufficient intermediate treatment became available, two existing measures for juvenile attendance and detention centers were to be phased out. IT had a quasi-medical flavor because it was concerned with "behavioral disorders" and "treatment" as well as alternative forms of education for youth at risk. Second, it was the result of a long-standing Home Office interest in creating a measure between ordinary probation and removal from home. And by the mid-1970s, when residential care was becoming expensive and unfashionable, IT was the beneficiary of significant government spending and local government support. "IT officers" were created by the Social Service Department (SSD); they were not probation officers per se but they were used by the courts. IT officers followed a social services/welfare orientation, as did the governmental approach to juvenile issues in the 1960s.[7] Perhaps the most significant power of the Children and Young Persons Act (1969) was found in its provisions that allowed for additional requirements to be added to supervision orders for juvenile offenders. These additional requirements were known to juvenile social workers as "intermediate treatment."

By the mid- to late 1970s, the broad approach to IT was repudiated by professionals because of its generality and critiques of the medicalization of deviance/crime. The IT focus on preventiveness was generally replaced with more specific concerns. This new focus did not see a total elimination of preventive concern, however; some professionals still thought preventive work was worthwhile. Eventually most of this support gave way to an emphasis by social workers on "youth social work" and "juvenile justice" concerns. There were other developments, as well.

Between 1969 and 1982, the magistrate courts did not respond fully to the government's hope that the 1969 provisions would be implemented. In fact, when the Conservatives came to power in 1970, they refused to implement the relevant sections of the 1969 law. Later, during another Conservative era, the relevant sections of the 1969 act actually were repealed by the Criminal Justice Act of 1982. Indeed, part of the momentum leading to some of the 1982 changes was the fact that in the intervening years since the 1969 act, magistrates were reported to have responded to the IT provisions with fits of nervous giggles and pejorative comments that IT was "treats" for offenders (Rutherford, 1989, p. 30). The 1982 changes were also endorsed by some social workers who supported the new provisions; they reasoned that an increase in youth tariffs would eventually make it easier to eliminate some forms, if not all, of youth custody.

The new provisions created two distinct forms of IT. *Discretionary IT* permitted the courts to give juvenile supervisors the power to require supervised juveniles to comply with "directions." *Stipulated IT* allowed the court itself to give directions as part of the supervision order. In some instances both were used to work out a program or "package" of activities of "treatment" that was viewed as "intermediate" between removal from home and routine supervision (Gibson, 1989, p. 1241). These orders were sometimes referred to as a "90-day order" because this represented the maximum number of days of the supervision order that could be specified by the court for purposes of IT. The period of supervision allowed by the 1982 revision could last up to three years, irrespective of age. Viewed cynically, the new provisions were created as much to placate magistrates, who could now control IT if they wished, "as to occupy any logical place in the sentencing tariff" (Gibson, 1989, p. 1241).

In retrospect, the 1970s was a transition period in which hopes and aspirations for a welfare approach were greatly eroded by research and public disillusionment. The decline in care orders for residential provisions of local authorities demonstrates this point quite clearly. In 1969, when the Children and Young Persons Act was implemented, there were approximately 7,500 young people in Community Homes with Education (CHE). However, at that time, there were fewer than 100 long-term secure places for young people. By 1980 the situation had changed (and is still changing). Then there were fewer than 5,500 young people in CHE, and the number of long-term security places for children and young people had increased to 300. The early 1980s witnessed an era in which the government rejected a welfare model for juveniles for a more rigid, judicial model for coping with offenders (Tutt, 1982). The new model was more rigid in theory than in practice, however.

New Penal Mood in the 1980s

Although accounts of juvenile justice social work vary, the broad patterns of developments in the late 1980s are easily recognized. Beginning with the 1982 Criminal Justice Act, professional social workers' emphasis shifted away from IT's focus on "preventive work" of the 1970s. The new focus, sponsored by the University of Lancaster, was on "systems management"; it stressed monitoring and controlling the way young offenders were processed by juvenile justice agencies, with particular emphasis given to diversion from court (Nellis, 1991b). Attention was also given to the provision of care and custody, such as intensive 90-day programs for groups or individuals.

The success of the systems management/alternative to custody varied across England. Significant increases occurred in the number of youth cautioned (written warnings from the police), and this too varied by region of the country. There was an overall national reduction in the use of custody for juveniles from a high of 7,900 in 1981 to a low of 2,400 in 1989. Official statistics indicated that since 1982 there actually had been a slight but nonetheless surprising and significant decline in total court proceedings and the number of persons sentenced for indictable offenses. And 1980-1986 data indicated that there had been a shift away from custody for juveniles 14-16 years old, in contrast to the practices of the previous decade (Rutherford, 1989, p. 27).

While it is true the government had provided funds in 1983 for IT projects to reduce the use of care and custody, these initiatives cannot distract from other forces of change at work. Rutherford (1989) identifies five features that characterize the "sea-change . . . [of] juvenile justice in the mid-1980s" (p. 29):

(1) *Local nature of reform:* The point here is that while reforms were initiated by the national government, they could be translated into practice only

at the local level. This latter development was highly problematic, as witnessed by the rather widespread opposition by youth workers against custody throughout England and Wales.

(2) *Reform thrust:* The primary thrust for change against custody was made by local social work practitioners whose enthusiasm for change was aided by the newly created Association for Juvenile Justice (1983).

(3) *Process versus programs:* Many early IT projects were criticized for neglecting issues related to the "juvenile justice context within which they were located" (Rutherford, 1989, p. 29). Consequently, greater attention was later given by practitioners to providing credible alternatives to custodial sentences. This eventually resulted in some local courts recognizing that viable custody options existed.

(4) *Interagency collaboration:* The crux of this element of reform against juvenile custody was a variety of new forms of collaboration involving statutory and nonstatutory agencies. These brought together various organizations within the juvenile justice system, and provided a basis of a consensus approach to the whole issue of juvenile crime.

(5) *Anticustody ethos:* The above developments helped to create a powerful anticustody climate in some sections of England and Wales. It was initiated at the local level by social workers working with young offenders. In some parts of the country it resulted in persuading magistrates to create "custody free zones," where custody was not used for a 12-month period.

Juvenile Justice: Recent Developments

The Children and Young Persons Act (1969) intended that penal custody for juvenile offenders 14-16 years of age be phased out. However, in addition to opposition from the Magistrates Association, the Conservative party never accepted this idea. Still, some social work practitioners in the juvenile justice system felt that the late 1980s ended on a high note:

> The 1980s have seen a revolution in the way the juvenile justice system operates in England and Wales. There are few areas of criminal justice practice and policy of which we can be proud but this is an exception. While there is no room for complacency there is a core of good practice and interagency cooperation that can be built upon in the 1990s. Many notions that once seemed totally unrealistic, such as the abolition of juvenile imprisonment, are now viewed as achievable. (Jones, 1989, p. 1)

Optimism of this type in the late 1980s could turn sour.

IT AS PUNISHMENT

The 1988 green paper strategy for young adults had a different philosophy and terminology/rhetoric than was found in previous strategies with youth. Now the government insisted that any new measures taken to reduce imprisonment for youth be described as "punishment" rather than IT. This represented a significant change because throughout most of the 1980s it did not look as though punishment in the community would affect juveniles as such (Nellis, 1991b). In fact, Nellis (1991b) indicates that within professional discussions optimism actually prevailed that custody for 14-16-year-olds would be eliminated; the government proposals inadvertently appeared to make such a change more feasible. This change in focus was not, however, entirely the result of government initiatives.

Some practitioners who had subscribed to preventive work thought it should be discarded. They reasoned that it was apparently ineffective as a means of reducing crime because it apparently increased the likelihood of youngsters' receiving more severe sentences. Indeed, "after a spell of prevention, they still appeared in court" (Nellis, 1991, p. 6).[8] It is perhaps worth noting that the call to stop preventive work failed somewhat, nonetheless it did not become the exclusive preserve and rallying call of the "grossly underfunded youth services" (Jeffs & Smith; quoted in Nellis, 1991b, p. 6). Within some social service departments there is still interest in social work crime prevention.

As Nellis (1991b, p. 1) notes, paradoxically, the Conservative government at the same time actually shared this type of sentiment as witnessed by the green paper *Punishment, Custody and the Community* (Home Office, 1988).[9] This position permitted the government to take some credit for the practices successfully sponsored in the recent past by the University of Lancaster, but not the *terms* of IT. Yet it did not hamper the government's late-1980s goal of wanting, with the aid of previously successful IT practices, to again call for a reduction in crime and the number of young adult offenders sentenced to custody. In essence, the government was interested in the rhetoric of punishment and the successful results of IT, even though it had not previously endorsed IT. It must be made clear that the late-1980s government still saw "alternatives" as options in a system that retained custody, rather than as replacements for custody itself (Nellis, 1991b). This position nonetheless is significant because it demonstrates that the government was beginning to see alternative sentences as important. This is different from the Conservative government's position on juvenile justice at the time of the 1970 general election, when "short, sharp shock" was the juvenile justice battle cry (Nellis, 1991b). Within one decade the government's position dramatically shifted from emphasizing custody to advocating alternatives to custody, albeit with the rhetoric of punishment.

Three important additional factors helped move the government toward its new position. First is the high cost of imprisonment. In November 1987, for example, the government announced that six extra prisons were to be built in England and Wales as part of the continuing priority given to law and order. The cost of adding 4,200 new cells was reported to be £59.5 million in 1988-1989, with an increase to £92 million in 1989-1990. Home Office expenditures also were announced to go up by £360 million to a total of £6.06 billion in 1988-1989, with another increase up to £6.4 billion scheduled for 1990-1991 ("Six New Jails," 1987).[10]

Second, the government's determination to cut public expenditures clashed with its equal determination to restore "law and order" by repressive means. Suggestive of this sentiment is the fact that at the same time the government announced plans for new prisons, it also announced it would increase the Metropolitan Police by 300 and the provincial police forces by 500 for 1989-1990 at an increase of approximately £240 million for 1988-1989 alone. Statistics on ethnic minorities in prison are more indicative of the government's repressive "law and order." According to the Prison Reform Trust's 1989 figures, Afro-Caribbean people in Britain were nearly eight times more likely to be sent to prison than white people ("Black Jail Figures," 1989).[11]

Third, another factor pushing the government to its new position is its European League record of imprisonment rates; increasingly these have become a source of political embarrassment for the United Kingdom. With an imprisonment rate of 95.8 per 100,000, more people are imprisoned in the United Kingdom than in any other country in the European Community ("UK Prison Numbers," 1988). As a deputy undersecretary at the Home Office stated:

> International comparisons show Britain has a proportionately higher prison population than most other European countries. The position is particularly stark with respect to young offenders. Comparison of ourselves with broadly similar European neighbors—France and Germany— shows that both countries have a young offender custodial population that is only about half the British figure. (Faulkner, 1988, p. 3)

JUVENILE JUSTICE AND CHANGING TIMES

As Nellis (1991b, pp. 3-4) comments, times can quickly change, and now there are many more factors to consider than when Jones (1989) described the "successful revolution" in juvenile justice. The government's white paper on community care, for example, substantially changed the basis on which authorities provide social services and affected the organizational climate in which juvenile justice develops (Department of Health, 1989). The same applies, according to Nellis (1991), to the impact of the Criminal Justice Act of 1988 and the Children Act 1989. Furthermore, the changes discussed in the 1988 green paper *Punishment, Custody and Community* have been developed further in a white paper (Home Office, 1990) and in a new Criminal Justice Bill introduced in November 1990.

Although the government has agreed to abolish custody for 14-year-olds, there is no doubt that the 1988-1990 developments make it clear that punishment is the new ethos of work with juveniles, no less than with adults. As Nellis (1991b) remarks, "The Bill is less about *building on* the measures that have been successful with juveniles in the 1980s, and more about *toughening them up,* and among other things it includes provision for electronically monitored curfews for 16-17 year olds" (see also Nellis, 1990, 1991a).

One additional factor is changing the context of English juvenile justice policy and practice. Some practitioners have begun to take note of the government's late-1980s mass crime prevention effort. This represents a significant shift, because practitioners have had a protracted period of antagonism toward the Conservative government's calls for preventive work of any kind. Practitioners are beginning to consider that preventive work may provide an overall framework for their future work with juveniles. Juvenile justice in the 1990s is thus developing what was earlier called "a vortex of changing systems" (Cooper, 1983, p. 96).

Conclusions

Whatever the "vortex of changing systems" might come to mean, it is clear at this point that the government is interested in "toughening up" existing measures for older juveniles, 16-17-year-olds. This observation is supported by examining that portion of the white paper *Crime, Justice and Protecting the Public* (Home Office, 1990) that deals with young offenders. In a move consistent with changing demographics and a 1980s trend that witnessed an increasing number of 14-year-olds being cautioned, the white paper proposes that the juvenile court be reconstituted as a *youth court*, with an upper age limit of 18. This presents a major new challenge to the SSD because it paves the way for it to see "whether the lessons of juvenile justice can be transferred to an older age group, both in regard to cautioning and in the use of alternatives to custody" (Nellis, 1991b, p. 13).

This development assumes that the SSD will have success in reducing the use of custody for older youths (young adults) that it had with 14-16-year-olds. It is, however, at this point that the "toughening up" process, especially for 17-year-olds, appears in bold relief. The measures that applied to 17-year-olds when they were in adult court are not only being retained in the newly reconstituted youth court, they also are being extended to 16-year-olds (Nellis, 1991b, p. 3). This is essentially a "transfer down" of adult penalties that had been mooted in the 1988 green paper *Punishment, Custody and the Community* proposal for a variable jurisdiction with 16-20-year-olds. This represents a substantial toughening-up process, and, as Nellis (1991b) notes, "it is no surprise that the government now wants the new measures—IT and supervised activities as well—to be characterised as 'punishment in the community,' the same as it is (or will be) for the young adults" (p. 14).

A "toughened flexibility" for the new youth court also was proposed by the white paper as seen in an inordinately complex set of arrangements for supervision and probation orders. The proposed legislation would permit the youth court to select *either* a supervision order *with* IT/supervised activity or a probation order with a day center requirement "according to the maturity of the offender and the arrangements available locally" (Home Office, 1990, para. 8, 17). The toughening-up process is further evidenced by the proposal that "both 16 and 17 year olds will be eligible for the new *combined* probation and community service order . . . in the *same* way as those over 17" (Home Office, 1990, para. 8, 18; emphasis added). While the government is using the discarded rhetoric of IT, its proposed policies speak otherwise. The future of juvenile justice in England and Wales appears to be headed toward less treatment and more punishment.

Notes

1. See Billy Bragg's song "Rotting on Remand," on his *Workers Playtime* album (1988), for a popular culture account of the living conditions in remand prisons. This

comparison to U.S. prisons/jails is not to suggest that overcrowding and "slopping out" are problems created by the Conservative government, but it must be recognized that it has had more than a decade to solve these problems.

2. Crown courts have trials by jury with full-time judges with legal qualifications who are appointed for life. Magistrate courts do not have juries, and the part-time judges are local dignitaries usually recommended by justices of the peace. They are usually without legal qualifications.

3. *Whitehall* refers to the British civil service administration, as distinct from the party government.

4. Matthews (1989) states that the range of powerful responses ranged from "messianic acclamation on one side to violent resistance on the other" (p. 1). He states further that the severity of these responses reflects the degree to which the process of privatization marked a major transformation in the nature of contemporary social and political relations.

5. As in the United States, the Right in England claims to be the "law and order" party. And also as in the United States, the crime and prison overcrowding problems worsened in England after more than a decade of Conservative government.

6. All types of public employment in England are unionized to a far greater extent than in the United States.

7. While the welfare approach to juvenile offenders is often portrayed as an invention of the 1960s, it has a long and respectable history in legislation and action going as far back in England as 1790, when the Philanthropic Society was established. Its purposes included the rescue of destitute infants, the care of children of convicts, and the reform of young criminals. And in 1908 the Children's Act aimed at establishing a more child-oriented legal system (Tutt, 1982, p. 7).

8. This process is called "uptariffing" (see Nellis, 1987, p. 7).

9. See Lilly (1990) for a discussion of this green paper and the Conservative government's interest in using electronic monitoring and home confinement in the community.

10. In terms of early 1991 exchange rates, the British pound is worth approximately 1.94 U.S. dollars, so £92 million for prison construction equals approximately $182,360,000. This means it would cost approximately $43,420 per cell, a cost only slightly influenced by prisoners' rights issues and cell standards. As in the United States, these figures vary by region of the country. According to the National Association for the Care and Resettlement of Offenders, keeping a prisoner in a police station cell in London costs £201 per night, or approximately $390.

11. The Prison Reform Trust calculates that if whites were jailed at the same rate, the total prison population would exceed 300,000; in August 1989 the white prison population was about 50,000. Because of a number of confirmed reports in the mid- and late 1980s of police corruption, brutality, mismanagement, and falsification of evidence, public confidence in the police may be at an all-time low ("Skepticism Over Change," 1989). One official response has included efforts to create a new image of the Metropolitan Police as a "service" ("How Police Force Plans," 1989). Despite these problems, Britain's police in 1989 were given one of the highest public pay settlement raises at 9.25%, a full 2.5% higher than the pay offered to 500,000 local government white-collar employees ("9.25 pc Police Rise," 1989).

References

Action on jail slops practice. (1989, February 21). *Yorkshire Post* (Leeds).

Ashworth, A. (1988). Crime and punishment: Towards a national sentencing policy. *New Law Journal, 7*, 726-727.

Black jail figures "would shame South Africa." (1989, August 7). *Independent*, p. 3.

Cooper, J. (1983). *The creation of the British personal social services 1962-1974.* London: Heinemann.

Criminal statistics, England and Wales. (1987). London: HMSO.

Cut down on jail sentences, Hurd tells magistrates. (1989, July 29). *Daily Telegraph*.

Department of Health. (1989). *Caring for people.* London: HMSO.

End slopping, says prison report. (1989, February 21). *Eastern Daily Press* (Norwich).

Faulkner, D. (1988). Introduction. In National Children's Homes, *Roundtable consultation on strategy for reduction in the use of custody for young adult offenders (17-20 year olds)* (pp. 3-4). London: National Children's Homes.

Gibson, B. (1989). Intermediate treatment. *Law Society Gazette, 1*, 1241-1242.

Home Office. (1968). *Children in trouble.* London: HMSO.

Home Office. (1988). *Punishment, custody and the community.* London: HMSO.

Home Office. (1990). *Crime, justice and protecting the public.* London: HMSO.

How police force plans to be reborn as a service. (1989, November 27). *Independent*, p. 6.

Jail "slopping" attacked. (1989, February 21). *Scotsman*.

Jones, D. (1989, March 30). The successful revolution. *Community Care* (suppl.), pp. i-ii.

Judges call for new sentencing guidelines. (1989, July 11). *Independent*, p. 2.

Law reform set to curb jailings. (1990, January 2). *Guardian*, p. 1.

Law Society leads move to ease remand cell "squalor." (1988, October 31). *Times*, p. 7.

Lilly, R. J. (1990). Tagging reviewed. *Howard Journal, 29*, 229-245.

Matthews, R. (1989). Privatization in perspective. In R. Matthews (Ed.), *Privatizing criminal justice* (pp. 1-23). London: Sage.

Nellis, M. (1987). The myth of uptariffing in IT. *ADJUST, 12*, 7-12.

Nellis, M. (1989). Juvenile justice and the voluntary sector. In R. Matthews (Ed.), *Privatizing criminal justice* (pp. 157-177). London: Sage.

Nellis, M. (1991a). Electronic monitoring: Grounds for resistance. In J. R. Lilly & J. Himan (Eds.), *The electronic monitoring of offenders* (Vol. 2). Leicester, England: Leicester Polytechnic.

Nellis, M. (1991b). The last days of "juvenile justice"? In P. Carter, T. Jeffs, & M. Smith (Eds.), *Social work and social welfare yearbook 3.* Milton Keynes: Open University Press.

9.25 pc police rise fuels fear of pay spiral. (1989, July 26). *Daily Telegraph*.

Rutherford, A. (1989). The mood and temper of penal policy: Curious happenings in England during the 1980s. *Youth and Policy, 27*, 27-31.

Six new jails proposed with 4,200 extra places. (1987, November 4). *Times*, p. 5.

Skepticism over change of success. (1989, November 27). *Independent*, p. 6.

Slopping out move. (1989, February 21). *Western Mail* (Cardiff, Wales).

Stiffer jail sentences "act as yellow card" to violent criminals. (1988, October 26). *Times*, p. 5.

Stricter non-jail penalties planned. (1989, October 14). *Times*, p. 6.

Sutherland, E. H. (1934). The decreasing prison population of England. *Journal of Criminal Law and Criminology, 24*, 880-900.

Tutt, N. (1982). Justice or welfare? *Social Work Today, 14*(7), 6-10.

UK prison numbers "shameful." (1988, October 19). *Independent*, p. 2.

Vass, A. A. (1990). *Alternatives to prison.* London: Sage.

PART V

Issues and Controversy

14. Scaling Intermediate Punishments: A Comparison of Two Models

Andrew von Hirsch

We have been punishing by extremes in this country. Either offenders are incarcerated or they are put on probation—often, where caseloads are large, with perfunctory supervision. Intermediate sanctions have largely been lacking. Those who commit crimes of middling seriousness thus are punished too much or too little.

Now, however, interest in intermediate sanctions is growing. A variety of sanctions are being tried—day fines, community service, intensive supervision, home detention, and the like. However, not much thought has been given to the scaling of these penalties: They are fashioned largely ad hoc, and applied to whatever heterogeneous groups of offenders seem most convenient. With the creditable exception of the Vera Institute's day-fine experiments (Greene, 1988), there have been few attempts to decide who should receive what types (and how much) of the new sanctions, for what kinds of offenses.

In the growing body of literature on intermediate sanctions, only two efforts have been made to address the scaling of such penalties in systematic fashion. One, authored by Martin Wasik, Judith Greene, and myself, attempts to scale noncustodial sanctions according to desert principles (von Hirsch, Wasik, & Greene, 1989). The other, by Norval Morris and Michael Tonry (1990), offers somewhat different scaling principles, and is based on a hybrid rationale that embodies

AUTHOR'S NOTE: I am indebted to Lisa Maher for detailed suggestions and supporting research. I would also like to thank James Byrne, Judith Greene, Uma Narayan, Martha Jane Smith, and Michael Tonry for their helpful comments.

preventive as well as retributive elements. This chapter compares the two approaches.

The two schemes share certain ideas. Both recognize that intermediate penalties must be considered sanctions in their own right, not mere substitutes for incarceration. Both recognize that such sanctions are *punishments*, because they involve the deprivation and censure that characterize a punitive response. Both recognize that— because the deprivations involved are by definition substantial— there needs to be explicit guiding principles to scale these penalties rationally and fairly. Finally, both favor the development of explicit standards for the use of intermediate penalties—standards the construction of which would be guided by the principles the authors' propose. Whether those standards should take the form of statewide numerical sentencing guidelines or more broadly worded legal norms for judicial decision would depend on the particular jurisdiction.[1]

If the scaling of intermediate penalties is as important as the two groups of authors contend, the critical question becomes, How good are the proposed scaling principles? This is the question I examine here. I will begin with von Hirsch et al.'s (1989) desert-based scheme and its apparent advantages, and then examine Morris and Tonry's (1990) reasons for rejecting desert as the primary scaling principle. Next, I will consider the merits of Morris and Tonry's own proposals. How defensible are the scaling principles these authors offer? How useful are their principles when applied to several problems facing intermediate sanction policy today—problems such as the potential overuse of revocation? If Morris and Tonry's proposals seem wanting, could more helpful scaling principles be developed that still rely on a hybrid rationale for sentencing?

Desert-Based Scaling
and Its Apparent Advantages

Desert can serve as the main guiding principle in scaling noncustodial penalties. The von Hirsch et al. (1989) model follows this approach, with the following elements resulting:

- Noncustodial sanctions would be graded according to the seriousness of the crime of conviction and, to a lesser extent, the criminal record. Intermediate sanctions, being by definition of middle-range severity, would thus be employable chiefly for crimes of medium and upper-medium seriousness. Lesser crimes would have to receive middle responses (pp. 600-606).

- Substitution would be permitted among sanctions of comparable onerousness, but with policy-based limitations on how extensive that substitution may be (pp. 604-606).
- There would be stringent limits on the severity of the backup sanctions that could be used against offenders who violate the conditions of an intermediate punishment. Imprisonment could be employed only for the most serious breaches (pp. 609-610).

Such a scheme would have a number of apparent advantages. First, it would restrict the use of imprisonment. Incarceration, especially for significant periods, is a severe punishment. It is thus appropriate only for crimes of a serious nature. Offenses of intermediate or lesser seriousness—such as most property crimes—would generally require less severe, nonincarcerative responses. Because such crimes—for example, burglaries in California—are so often punished at present by imprisonment (von Hirsch & Mueller, 1984, p. 266), the resulting reduction in the use of the prison sanction could be substantial.

Second, the scheme would require that penalties of intermediate severity (for example, substantial fines or community service)[2] be used for crimes that are of at least intermediate gravity. One would not see such penalties used, as they are so often today, upon persons who have committed the least serious felonies, merely because such persons seem potentially "cooperative."

The scale of punishments would also be reasonably simple, because there would be limits on interchangeability of penalties. For each band of severity, one type of sanction would normally be recommended: for example, day fines in the middle range, day attendance for the upper middle. Substitution of sanctions of equivalent onerousness would be permitted, if there were special reasons—for instance, the defendant's inability to perform the tasks of the normally recommended punishment (see von Hirsch et al., 1989, pp. 604-605). However, free substitution would be barred,[3] as would the piling up of multiple sanctions on particular defendants.

Finally, and perhaps most important, the revocation sanction would be brought under control. It is a disturbing fact today that, in large penal systems such as those in Texas and California, a substantial percentage or even the bulk of those committed to prison enter via parole or probation revocation (Messinger & Berecochea, 1990). Intermediate sanctions could aggravate this tendency if imprisonment

is routinely resorted to as the breach sanction. Under a desert rationale, imprisonment could be invoked only for more reprehensible
kinds of conduct[4]—for example, breaches that are comparable (or
nearly comparable) in gravity to criminal conduct that would warrant incarceration in the first place.

Morris and Tonry's Rejection of
Desert as the Guiding Principle

Morris and Tonry nevertheless reject such a model. In their scheme,
desert would have a less central role in grading offenses and substitutability would be much more permissive. Why the downgrading
of desert? Morris and Tonry (1990) offer three reasons—none, in my
judgment, especially convincing.

First, Morris and Tonry claim that desert cannot be the main basis
for ordering punishments. It is merely a limiting principle that tells
us what extremes of leniency and severity would be *un*deserved for
a given type of offense. Within those extremes, they say, it is entirely
proper to fix the sentence for a particular offender on the basis of
crime prevention concerns, including deterrence, incapacitation, and
treatment (pp. 105-106; see also Morris, 1982, chap. 5). (Unless otherwise noted, all page numbers cited in discussion of Morris and
Tonry's scheme refer to their 1990 book.)

To what extent, however, is desert readily indeterminate? It is true
that it gives only limited guidance in setting the anchoring points of
the penalty scale (see von Hirsch, 1985, chaps. 4, 8). However, desert
is more than a mere limit when deciding on the scale's internal
structure—that is, the ordering of penalties relative to one another.
Punishing one crime more severely than another expresses greater
disapproval for the former crime, and hence is justified only to the
extent that crime is more serious. This is why penalties should be
scaled comparatively according to the seriousness of offenses. Ordinal desert *is* infringed when criminal acts of comparable gravity are
punished differently on crime prevention grounds, and this holds
even if the differences are kept within given bounds (von Hirsch,
1985, 1990b).

Morris and Tonry allude to this distinction between anchoring the
penalty scale and deciding comparative punishments, but then brush it
aside. They reiterate their original claim that desert provides mere
limits, and then assert (amazingly, for a work devoted to principles)
that one should not bother too much about philosophizing (pp. 87-89).

Second, Morris and Tonry contend that desert is inherently a draconian philosophy—that its adoption inevitably would lead to harsher penalties. This view is not easy to square with the following features of the desert model:

- The leading desert theorists have urged a substantial scaling down of penalties and, particularly, a reduction of the use of imprisonment (see, e.g., Singer, 1979; von Hirsch, 1976). Indeed, I have proposed a penalty scale in which terms of imprisonment would seldom exceed five years even for serious felonies (von Hirsch, 1976, chap. 16).

- Desert theory is consistent with a substantial deflation of penalties. Provided that penalties are ordered according to crimes' comparative seriousness, the penalty scale can be anchored so that only the most serious offenses—such as acts of actual or threatened violence to the person—are punished by incarceration (von Hirsch, 1976; von Hirsch et al., 1989, pp. 615-616).

- Desert-oriented schemes, as actually enacted, have not been more severe than those that give desert merely a peripheral role (von Hirsch, 1990a, pp. 400-405). In fact, the more sophisticated schemes that rely significantly on desert, such as Minnesota's sentencing guidelines, appear to have helped slow down increases in prison populations (see von Hirsch, Knapp, & Tonry, 1987, chap. 8).

- Desert bars the singling out of offenders with "bad" criminal or social histories. The more desert constraints are relaxed, the more penalties for such persons can be escalated—as in selective-incapacitation schemes (see von Hirsch, 1984, pp. 1105-1107).

Such points would need to be addressed and explained away if Morris and Tonry are to sustain their claim about desert and severity. Instead, they resort largely to rhetorical arguments. They begin by asserting that desert demands eye-for-an-eye punishments, so that— in a country with more than 10,000 homicides annually—there would have to be a comparable number of executions (p. 106). The obvious rejoinder is that modern desert theory calls for *proportionate* sanctions, not for sanctions as injurious as the offending conduct.[5] Morris and Tonry next reluctantly concede that point, but assert that even proportionate sanctions would be unduly severe—because the rule maker would rely on the "worst case" of each kind of crime in setting the penalty (p. 106). Yet this surely is not the way to design desert-based guidelines. Such guidelines, as Tonry himself admits elsewhere, would base the normally recommended sanction on the typical instance of the crime, and leave the worst cases to be dealt with as aggravated circumstances (see von Hirsch et al., 1987, chap. 2). The

Minnesota guidelines, for example, are actually constructed this way (see von Hirsch et al., 1987, chap. 5).

Third, Morris and Tonry argue that desert-based scaling cannot be achieved because of the difficulty of comparing penalties (pp. 94-97). Each person will suffer differently from any penal deprivation, depending on his or her age, sensitivities, and so on. In Morris and Tonry's words, "a year [in prison] often is not a year" (p. 94), depending on the character of the prison and the degree of resilience of the person.

The law, however, generally works with standard cases—and allows limited deviations for certain unusual situations. Why should the desert model not follow this paradigm? Notwithstanding the fact that individuals experience penalties differently, we can still gauge and compare the *characteristic* of onerousness of various sanctions (von Hirsch, 1990c, pp. 547-548; von Hirsch et al., 1989, pp. 609-610). We might then deviate from those standard judgments in special situations (say, of illness or advanced age) that give the penalty an uncharacteristic bite.[6]

It seems a non sequitur on Morris and Tonry's part to assert that—because the onerousness of penalties cannot be compared precisely in individual cases—we need not even compare it approximately in standard cases. Relying on approximate severity judgments surely will produce more commensurable penalties than abandoning the desert model and relying extensively on nondesert criteria, as Morris and Tonry propose.

The arguments Morris and Tonry offer against desert-based scaling of penalties scarcely seem impressive. Why then, their rejection of a desert model? Their real reason, as far as I can discern, reflects certain value preferences. They wish to provide more scope for introducing crime control concerns, and for substituting among different penalties, than a desert model would permit.

A desert model rests on a particular set of value judgments. It emphasizes punishment's censure-conveying role; calls for penalties to be distributed proportionately, according to their censuring implications; and gives proportionality precedence over preventive concerns (von Hirsch, 1990b). Someone who does not share these preferences may favor an alternative conception of sanctioning.

If Morris and Tonry do prefer such an alternative conception, so be it. Their analysis would have been more illuminating, however, had they denominated that preference for what it is—a *value* preference. The real issue is neither the imagined harshness of desert nor the supposed impossibility of scaling deserved punishment. It is what kind of fairness constraints—and of how stringent a nature— we should observe in punishing criminals.

Morris and Tonry's Scheme for
Scaling Intermediate Punishments

Morris and Tonry's main idea is that of interchangeability of "equivalent" sanctions. They propose "establishment of 'exchange rates' to achieve, for appropriate cases, principled interchangeability between prison and non-prison sentences and among different non-prison sentences" (p. 93). This conception raises the question: Equivalent by what standard?

Equivalence, Morris and Tonry emphasize, does *not* mean equality, or even approximate equity, in the severity of the sanctions involved. (That standard of equivalence, they say, would be suited to a desert scheme.) They would permit substitutability among penalties of significantly *differing* severity. The onerousness of the sanction thus would not define equivalence, but merely invoke outer desert constraints—that no penalty involved be disproportionate in leniency or harshness to the gravity of the conduct (pp. 104-105).

Instead, Morris and Tonry speak of equivalence of *function*. One penalty may be substituted for another (within certain desert bounds, as just noted) if both serve the same penological ends in the circumstances. In their words:

> Equivalence of function . . . plays an essential role in the sentencing calculus, guiding or giving sentencing choices within the bounds of not undeserved punishments. If in an individual case the governing purposes at sentencing are retributive and deterrent, a short period of incarceration or a substantial fine may equally well achieve those functional purposes at sentencing. Similarly, if the retributive and incapacitative functions of punishment seem most apposite at sentencing of a drug-using repetitive thief, confinement or house arrest subject to electronic monitoring and frequent unannounced drug testing may be equivalent. (p. 104)

I submit that neither of Morris and Tonry's proposed standards—that is, neither their suggested desert limits nor their notion of "equivalence of function"—are helpful, in the form the authors state them.

DESERT LIMITS

Morris and Tonry admit, as noted, that there should be certain desert-based constraints on the use of intermediate punishments. One proposed constraint is that interchangeability should not be permitted for offenses presumptively punished by imprisonment of 24 months' duration or more (p. 79). The idea seems to be that such offenses are too serious to warrant intermediate sanctions, and that for such offenses interchangeability would lead to too great disparities—between lengthy confinement for some offenders and much more modest community sanctions for others. This limit, however, says nothing about what should happen below 24 months.

A further desert-based constraint is offered, namely, that the penalty must *neither depreciate the crime and record, nor impose suffering in excess of that justified by the crime and record* (p. 101). In short, the penalty should be neither too tough nor too lenient, relative to the character of the conduct. Morris and Tonry offer no gloss, however, on the meaning of this vague standard. Would it, for example, be permissible—for an offense of intermediate gravity—to imprison some offenders for up to a year and subject others to a monetary penalty equivalent (say) to 30 days' earnings? One cannot tell.

Morris and Tonry might reply that no precise formula can be supplied: The desert limits would have to vary with other features of the system, such as the breadth of the various offense categories and the number of seriousness gradations. What is troublesome about Morris and Tonry's formulation, however, is not that it lacks precision (what penal theory can be precise?), but that it provides virtually no guidance concerning the weight that should be given to crime seriousness in deciding punishments.

If desert is treated as setting limits only, as Morris and Tonry would have it, the critical question is whether those constraints make desert integral or merely peripheral to the penalty structure.[7] Thus:

- From an "integral" view, desert limits would substantially shape (albeit not fully determine) the gradation of penalties. One might, for example, classify noncustodial penalties into several bands according to their degree of punitiveness—say, into "mild," "intermediate," and "onerous." Substitutions would then be permitted within a given band (even if those penalties differ somewhat in punitive bite), but would be restricted among different bands. Thus short prison terms and home detention might be interchangeable as both are fairly onerous, albeit not equally severe; but such prison terms could not be interchanged with moderate financial penalties, because the disparity in punitiveness would be too large.
- From a "peripheral" view, the scaling of noncustodial penalties would be determined mainly by preventive considerations, and desert would be invoked only to bar *manifest* disproportion. Limits of this kind would serve mainly as a supplement to the statutory maxima. The statute, for

example, might authorize up to 90 days' jail for petty misdemeanors. The principle against "excessive" punishment might bar imprisonment for such offenses, as the disproportion involved would be so blatant. For less trivial offenses, however, almost any combination of intermediate sanctions would be permissible.

Which of these two views, the integral or the peripheral, do Morris and Tonry support? It is not easy to tell. They speak approvingly of Minnesota-style sentencing guidelines and, in some passages, refer to their proposals as ways of improving such guidelines and extending their reach to noncustodial penalties (chap. 3). Since Minnesota's guidelines prescribe rather narrow ranges of permitted punishment and emphasize the gravity of the offense, this would suggest support of the "integral view"—as, more explicitly, does an earlier article by Tonry (1987, pp. 407-411). On the other hand, the (earlier-discussed) passages in the book attacking desert theory convey a rather different message. If desert is severe or unworkable, as Morris and Tonry claim it is, should not its constraints be diluted very considerably?

Whatever Morris and Tonry's intentions might be, their book supplies no *principled* discussion of the breadth of proportionality constraints. It is difficult to tell whether these constraints are to be wide or narrow because the authors tell us so little about why these constraints should exist or how they are to be ascertained.

INTERCHANGEABILITY OF FUNCTION

Morris and Tonry's main suggested criterion for interchanging penalties is that they be equivalent in "function." This, however, can be no substitute for adequate, well-delineated desert constraints. The criterion does not necessarily concern justice at all, since the assumed functions or aims being compared may be those of crime control. Penalty A's "functional equivalence" with Penalty B may consist of no more than its believed ability to incapacitate (or deter) with comparable efficiency.

The criterion also seems scarcely usable. To decide whether Penalty A is functionally equivalent to Penalty B, one would have to be capable of ascertaining, first, what the appropriate aims or functions of the sentence are, and, second, how well different penalties can achieve those functions. Is this possible?

The aims or functions of the sentence are largely indeterminate under Morris and Tonry's theory. They say, for example, that where the governing purposes of the sentence are "retributive and deterrent," a short stint of incarceration and a substantial fine might be functionally equivalent (p. 104). How does one tell, however, when those are the appropriate purposes? The reference to a retributive purpose is puzzling, because Morris and Tonry have just finished explaining that desert provides only broad limits and little or no guidance in deciding the particular sentence. The deterrent purpose is equally uncertain, because they provide no suggestion about how to decide when this—rather than some other aim—is the desired purpose. In Morris and Tonry's theory, the judge is supposed to decide the aims of sentence in the particular case. Alas, if the judge is uncertain on the choice of aims, he or she receives no guidance.

Even if the function of the sentence were specified, one seldom could tell how well various penalties achieved it—for the requisite knowledge of penalties' preventive effects is usually lacking (see, e.g., National Academy of Sciences, 1978, pp. 19-90). In Morris and Tonry's just-cited example, suppose the aim of the sentence is assumed to be deterrence, and one is trying to decide whether a prison term or a fine is "functionally equivalent." That would require one to gauge whether imprisonment or the fine deterred about equally well. When can one do that with any confidence?

Applying Morris and Tonry's Model

How well would Morris and Tonry's proposed scheme fare in practice? Let us try it out on three problems that have been troubling intermediate sanction policy.

The first problem is that of using intermediate sanctions for lesser crimes. The sponsors of "alternatives" are understandably concerned about the public credibility of their programs, and credibility is enhanced through high rates of program completion and low rates of breach of program conditions. This prompts the recruitment of more tractable offenders as participants, as they tend to have modest crimes and criminal records. (This has been occurring in several much-touted intensive supervision programs, for example; see, e.g., Clear & Hardyman, 1990, pp. 48-53.) The result is merely to increase punishment levels for less serious cases.

How is recruitment from the shallower end of the offender pool to be prevented? In a desert-based scheme such as von Hirsch et al.'s (1989), intermediate-severity sanctions would be barred in principle for offenders with lesser crimes and modest records (pp. 615-616). How about Morris and Tonry's scheme? It is impossible to tell, given the uncertain nature of its desert limits. An "integral" interpretation of those limits, as noted earlier, would restrict using the more substantial noncustodial sanctions to punish lesser felonies. However, a "peripheral" interpretation would not, because the disproportionality involved would not be obvious and manifest.

A second problem is sanction stacking: imposing multiple sanctions on a given offender, such as day fines *and* community sanctions *and* something else. Sanction stacking makes the severity of penalties difficult to gauge, as it is hard to assess the onerousness of a heterogeneous smorgasbord of penalties. Stacking also makes compliance more complicated, and thereby increases the likelihood of breach and possible revocation. While the offender may abide by the conditions of a particular sanction, the more different kinds of things he or she is expected to do, the less likely it is the offender will do them all.

The von Hirsch et al. (1989) proposal would largely bar sanction stacking through its restrictions on the multiplication of sanctions (pp. 604-606, 618). Morris and Tonry offer no such restrictions. Provided the loose interchangeability criteria are met, the judge would be free to choose any of a variety of intermediate penalties, to invent new variants, and to pile several such sanctions on particular offenders.

Moreover, the judge, in making such choices, would be free to determine the purpose the particular sanction would serve (Morris & Tonry, 1990, pp. 77-78, 90-91). Giving judges wide leeway to choose the "purpose at sentencing" raises the question of how unsupported judgments are to be kept in check. Consider the judge who harbors the supposition that "short, sharp shocks" have a marvelous deterrent effect. How free should that judge be to adopt deterrence as the purpose at sentencing, and to invoke short stints of jail as the preferred deterrent?

Last, and perhaps most problematic, is the question of revocation. Offenders receiving intermediate sanctions have more extensive requirements to fulfill than those put on probation, and their compliance tends to be more thoroughly monitored. Frequent violations will thus be uncovered. Easy resort to revocation may well mean that *more* such offenders will end up in prison than would have had the sanction not existed at all.

When someone violates the conditions of his or her punishment, the breach can be seen as involving three distinct elements:

(1) The offender has not yet completed the original punishment, and still "owes" the uncompleted portion in some comparable form.

(2) The act of breach, arguably, is itself conduct of a moderately reprehensible character, calling for some added punishment.

(3) The breach, if more than a technical violation, may involve new criminal conduct.

With these three elements identified, it is apparent why a desert rationale would restrict the severity of breach sanctions. Element 1 would not call for any added severity at all; Element 2 would call only for a modest addition, given the not-so-great degree of reprehensibleness of the act of breach; and Element 3 would warrant substantial added severity only if the conduct were of a seriously criminal character (see von Hirsch et al., 1989, pp. 609-610). Under Morris and Tonry's model, such arguments for restricting breach sanctions weaken, because the desert constraints are so much more uncertain.

Can Morris and Tonry's "equivalence of function" criterion help? Not much. A defendant who breaches the terms of noncustodial punishment may be perceived as presenting a higher degree of risk. Imposing greater restrictions thus would seem warranted on preventive grounds. Severe breach sanctions, such as imprisonment, may be seen as an effort to pursue the preventive goal of the sanction by more restrictive means, the initial milder response having failed.

Morris and Tonry suggest a "soft in-out line," which would allow interchange between brief jail or prison terms and other intermediate penalties (pp. 54-55). This seems sound enough in principle. Short periods of confinement are comparable with the more onerous intermediate punishments, such as home detention. Permitting such interchanges, however, makes it even more important to have them governed by a clear rule. From a desert rationale, that rule would permit such interchanges only when the penalties involved are of comparable severity (see von Hirsch et al., 1989, p. 605). If desert constraints were relaxed somewhat, the rule on interchanges could be more permissive: One might permit substitutions between brief prison terms and the more substantial noncustodial penalties even when the latter penalties are not quite so severe as imprisonment.

How much interchangeability is permitted in Morris and Tonry's scheme? It is impossible to tell, because the model's desert constraints are indeterminate. Until the limits on interchangeability are more clearly specified, a "soft" in-out line is hazardous. We could end up where we are today: with wide variation in the response to common misdemeanors and lesser felonies, ranging from probation through intermediate sanctions to imprisonment.

In sum, I doubt how helpful Morris and Tonry's principles are, in their present form, for scaling noncustodial penalties. They offer insufficient limits on the practice of mixing and matching at will—of responding with varying severity to similar offenses, stacking sanctions,[8] or invoking imprisonment for breaches.

Can Fuller Guidance Be Provided, With Mixed Penal Aims?

The question raised by Morris and Tonry's book, but not satisfactorily answered, is whether it is possible to provide meaningful guidance for the choice of noncustodial penalties, while adopting a hybrid set of sentencing aims. This is possible, but only through more stringent constraints on the choice of sanctions than the authors have been prepared to suggest. Some of those constraints might be as follows.

First, penal equivalence should mean approximate equivalence in penal bite, that is, in severity. Penalties that are significantly different in onerousness are simply not "equivalent" in any ordinarily understood sense of the term. Based on a desert rationale, substitution among penalties of differing severity would not be permitted; on a mixed rationale, it might be. Even according to the latter rationale, however, there should remain an important moral difference between (a) replacing a sanction with another equally severe one and (b) replacing it with, say, a substantially more severe one. The former—substitution by a comparably severe sanction—stands less in need of special justification, because neither the offender's suffering nor the extent of the implicit censure alters. That difference should not be obliterated by speaking of penalties that diverge in severity as "equivalent" (see also von Hirsch et al., 1989, p. 617).

Second, to the extent that substitution among penalties of differing onerousness is permitted, there must be *meaningful* limits—and not just vague ones—on the extent of the permitted difference. While a hybrid model may have less stringent proportionality constraints than a desert model, it still differs from a wholly or primarily utilitarian rationale in that proportionality remains an important consideration. Vague formulations of the appropriate desert limits, such as are found in Morris and Tonry's book, just will not help—for the reasons already elaborated.

Could meaningful limits on permitted differences in severity be supplied? Conceivably, yes—as illustrated by the "integral" view referred to earlier. However, such limits, to be helpful, should be significant enough so that they would (a) sharply limit the use of intermediate sanctions for crimes of less than medium seriousness[9] and (b) similarly restrict the escalation of the penal response for violations of conditions attached to penalties.

Third, there should also be certain other, policy-based, limitations. Proliferation and stacking of sanctions should be restricted. Even within the applicable constraints on severity, moreover, there should be some guidance concerning the kinds of reasons a judge may rely upon in choosing the sanction. Rather than the unfettered freedom to decide the "purpose at sentence" that Morris and Tonry suggest, there should be some way of scrutinizing the rationality of that purpose and its achievability in situations at hand.

What Can Noncustodial Sanctions Deliver?

A desert model, we have seen, can scale noncustodial sanctions with some degree of coherence. The alternative, a hybrid set of aims, would require considerable clarification before it is helpful at all. Which approach, then, is preferable? The answer depends, in part, on what intermediate sanctions are capable of achieving.

Intermediate penalties are doubtless capable of delivering punishment. They involve significant deprivations of liberty or comfort, visited in a manner that conveys censure. Their degree of onerousness can be adjusted to reflect the gravity of the criminal conduct. The sanctions are thus well suited for being scaled according to a desert model.

A hybrid model, such as the one just discussed, would nevertheless relax ordinal desert constraints in order to give added scope to crime preventive concerns. It presupposes that significant amounts of extra prevention can thereby be delivered. For intermediate punishments, is that presupposition realistic? Could the partial relaxation of desert constraints be expected to enhance the preventive effects of these sanctions? I doubt it.

Let us begin with deterrence. It is notoriously difficult to gauge the magnitude of deterrent effects. Insofar as we understand deterrence at all, it appears that crime rates are not particularly sensitive to moderate variations in the punishments for various crime categories (see, e.g., National Academy of Sciences, 1978, pp. 19-90). Yet moderate variations in severity are all that such a model should allow.

What of incapacitation? Imprisonment for substantial durations is at least conceivably capable of delivering a substantial incapacitative pay-off. That is what has given the selective-incapacitation debate its edge. Does selective incapacitation breach desert requirements to an unacceptable degree? How great are its preventive benefits, and how well can they be estimated? The proponents of selective incapacitation and its critics (including myself) have disagreed sharply on these issues.[10]

For intermediate punishments, however, the prospects for incapacitation diminish: Such sanctions are seldom capable of restraining illegal behavior much. Most routinely administrable intermediate penalties—such as day fines or community service—leave the offender free to commit further offenses. Short periods of incarceration can have only a limited incapacitative effect, because the offender returns so soon to the community. To enhance the incapacitative impact, one might resort to sanctions having longer periods of intervention, stringent surveillance conditions, and rigorous default penalties (e.g., home detention of lengthy durations). Such sanctions, however, tend to be of more than intermediate onerousness, and their default penalties could well increase, not reduce, reliance on the prison.

What of rehabilitation? Despite extensive efforts to develop more effective treatments during the last decade, there remains considerable dispute over what works, and how well.[11] Yet even if one accepts that some therapies can succeed, one might question whether intermediate sanctions are their most promising vehicle. Morris and Tonry speak, for example, of placing drug-using offenders in supervised treatment programs to alleviate their use of drugs and its associated criminality (chap. 7). However, a recent survey of drug treatments by Anglin and Hser (1990) suggests that it is primarily the more onerous treatments—those of lengthy duration, involving residential treatment or close outpatient monitoring—that have much prospect of alleviating drug dependence. Such drastic rehabilitative interventions, like the similar incapacitative ones, stand at the high end of the spectrum of intermediate sanctions, and scarcely seem suited for most middle-level offenses.

Even if relaxing desert constraints would not enhance crime prevention, might it be defended in the name of "parsimony"—as permitting a reduction in levels of intervention without sacrifice of such preventive efficacy as exists already? Norval Morris (1982, chap. 5) has so claimed, but with little supporting argument. It is not apparent why watering down desert requirements will diminish overall punishment levels. Widening the permissible range of punishments might permit reduced responses for persons deemed favorable risks, but it will at the same time allow *escalated* responses to those deemed potential recidivists (see von Hirsch, 1984, pp. 1105-1107). Parsimony can better be achieved by moving the penalty scale's anchoring points downward—that is, by proportionate penalty reductions, not selective ones.

Ultimately, the choice between a desert model for sentencing and a hybrid model is an ethical one. If a departure from ordinal desert constraints can yield substantial crime control payoffs, the choice is not easy: One must decide whether the preventive benefits would justify the sacrifice in equity involved. Given that choice, I would opt for preserving the desert constraints, except, perhaps, in extraordinary circumstances (see von Hirsch, 1987a, 1988b; see also Robinson, 1987); others might well be more ready to pursue the preventive goals. The smaller the prospective crime prevention benefits are, however, the easier that choice becomes. Even those who adhere less determinedly than I do to retributive principles might still be reluctant to sacrifice ordinal proportionality in order to achieve small or dubious crime control benefits. That, then, is the practical argument in favor of a more desert-oriented approach to scaling noncustodial penalties: It is fairer, and little would be achieved by doing otherwise.

Notes

1. For a comparison of numerical guidelines and legal standards couched as guiding principles, see von Hirsch et al. (1987, chap. 3).

2. I am referring here to community service involving significant rather than perfunctory work requirements. For community service as involving a spectrum of severity, see von Hirsch et al. (1989, pp. 611-612).

3. The von Hirsch, Wasik, and Greene scheme's rules on limited substitution do not derive directly from desert constraints. As the article points out, one could create a desert-based penalty grid that allows extensive substitution among comparably severe penalties. Instead, a number of policy considerations are suggested for restricting substitution; for example, that proliferation of sanctions makes it more difficult to compare penalties' onerousness (see von Hirsch et al., 1989, pp. 602-606).

4. Little has been written on the scaling of breach sanctions under a desert model. For a simple suggested formula, see von Hirsch et al. (1989, pp. 609-610). For somewhat less stringent proposed limits on revocation, designed for a framework statute on sentencing principles, see Wasik and von Hirsch (1990, p. 514).

5. See, for example, von Hirsch (1985, chap. 5). I am, incidentally, opposed to the death penalty altogether (see von Hirsch, 1985, p. 26).

6. Besides aggravating/mitigating factors that address the gravity of the conduct in unusual circumstances, a desert rationale would also permit consideration of special factors that make the penalty more severe than it characteristically is. Illness or age would be such factors. (See von Hirsch, 1987b, p. 188.)

7. For a comparable discussion of this difference, see von Hirsch (1985, pp. 141-145).

8. See also the discussion of "tailor-made" penalties for particular offenders in von Hirsch (1988a).

9. Such crimes should, of course, receive mild penalties instead.

10. For a summary of that debate and my contentions in it, see von Hirsch (1985, chaps. 9-11; 1988b).

11. For an indication of how sharp the disagreement over treatment effectiveness skill is, see Lab and Whitehead (1988, 1990), Whitehead and Lab (1989), and Andrews et al. (1990a, 1990b).

References

Andrews, D. A., Zinger, I., Hoge, R. D., Banta, J., Gendreau, P., & Cullen, F. T. (1990a). Does correctional treatment work? A clinically relevant and psychologically informed meta-analysis. *Criminology, 28,* 369-404.

Andrews, D. A., Zinger, I., Hoge, R. D., Banta, J., Gendreau, P., & Cullen, F. T. (1990b). A human science approach or more punishment and pessimism: A rejoinder to Lab and Whitehead. *Criminology, 28,* 419-429.

Anglin, M. D., & Hser, Y. (1990). Treatment of drug abuse. In M. Tonry & J. Q. Wilson (Eds.), *Drugs and crime* (pp. 393-460). Chicago: University of Chicago Press.

Clear, T., & Hardyman, P. (1990). The new intensive supervision movement. *Crime and Delinquency, 36,* 42-60.

Greene, J. A. (1988). Structuring criminal fines: Making an "intermediate penalty" more useful and equitable. *Justice System Journal, 13,* 37-50.

Lab, S. P., & Whitehead, J. T. (1988). An analysis of juvenile correctional treatment. *Crime and Delinquency, 34,* 60-83.

Lab, S. P., & Whitehead, J. T. (1990). From "nothing works" to "the appropriate works": The latest stop on the search for the secular grail. *Criminology, 28,* 405-417.

Messinger, S., & Berecochea, J. (1990). *The prison population and the corrections process.* Sacramento: California Bureau of Criminal Statistics.

Morris, N. (1982). *Madness and the criminal law.* Chicago: University of Chicago Press.

Morris, N., & Tonry, M. (1990). *Between prison and probation: Intermediate punishments in a rational sentencing system.* New York: Oxford University Press.

National Academy of Sciences. (1978). Report of Panel on Research on Deterrent and Incapacitative Effects. In A. Blumstein, J. Cohen, & D. Nagin (Eds.), *Deterrence and incapacitation: Estimating the effects of criminal sanctions on crime rates* (pp. 1-90). Washington, DC: Author.

Robinson, P. (1987). Hybrid principles for the distribution of criminal sanctions. *Northwestern Law Review, 82,* 19-42.

Singer, R. G. (1979). *Just deserts: Sentencing based on equality and desert.* Cambridge, MA: Ballinger.

Tonry, M. (1987). Prediction and classification: Legal and ethical issues. In D. M. Gottfredson & M. Tonry (Eds.), *Prediction and classification* (pp. 397-413). Chicago: University of Chicago Press.

von Hirsch, A. (1976). *Doing justice: The choice of punishments.* New York: Hill & Wang.

von Hirsch, A. (1984). Equality, "anisonomy," and justice: A review of *Madness and the criminal law. Michigan Law Review, 82,* 1093-1112.

von Hirsch, A. (1985). *Past or future crimes: Deservedness and dangerousness in the sentencing of criminals.* New Brunswick, NJ: Rutgers University Press.

von Hirsch, A. (1987a). Hybrid principles in allocating sanctions: A response to Professor Robinson. *Northwestern Law Review, 82,* 64-72.

von Hirsch, A. (1987b). Principles for choosing sanctions: The proposed Swedish statute. *New England Journal on Criminal and Civil Confinement, 13,* 171-195.

von Hirsch, A. (1988a). Punishment to fit the criminal. *The Nation, 246,* 901-902.

von Hirsch, A. (1988b). Selective incapacitation reexamined: The National Academy of Sciences' report on "criminal careers" and "career criminals." *Criminal Justice Ethics, 7,* 19-35.

von Hirsch, A. (1990a). The politics of "just deserts." *Canadian Journal of Criminology, 32,* 397-413.

von Hirsch, A. (1990b). Proportionality in the philosophy of punishment: From "Why punish?" to "How much?" *Criminal Law Forum, 1,* 259-290.

von Hirsch, A. (1990c). Why have proportionate sentences? A reply to Professor Gabor. *Canadian Journal of Criminology, 32,* 547-549.

von Hirsch, A., Knapp, K. A., & Tonry, M. (1987). *The sentencing commission and its guidelines.* Boston: Northeastern University Press.

von Hirsch, A., & Mueller, J. (1984). California's indeterminate sentence: An analysis of its structure. *New England Journal on Criminal and Civil Confinement, 10,* 253-300.

von Hirsch, A., Wasik, M., & Greene, J. A. (1989). Punishments in the community and the principles of desert. *Rutgers Law Journal, 20,* 595-618.

Wasik, M., & von Hirsch, A. (1990). Statutory sentencing principles: The 1990 white paper. *Modern Law Review, 53,* 508-517.

Whitehead, J. T., & Lab, S. P. (1989). A meta-analysis of juvenile correctional treatment. *Journal of Research in Crime & Delinquency, 26,* 276-295.

15. From Net Widening to Intermediate Sanctions: The Transformation of Alternatives to Incarceration From Benevolence to Malevolence

Dennis J. Palumbo

Mary Clifford

Zoann K. Snyder-Joy

Over the last 25 to 30 years, there has been a great turnaround in the way alternatives to prison have been justified and legitimized. In the 1960s and early 1970s, they were supposed to provide a means for helping offenders become law-abiding members of the community. That purpose of these programs was best expressed by the President's Commission on Law Enforcement and Administration of Justice (1967):

> Although most inmates of American correctional institutions come from metropolitan areas, the institutions themselves often are located away from urban areas and even primary transportation routes.... Remoteness interferes with efforts to reintegrate inmates into their communities and makes it hard to recruit correctional staff, particularly professionals. (p. 4)

> The general underlying premise for the new directions in corrections is that crime and delinquency are symptoms of failures and disorganization of the community as well as of individual offenders. In particular, these failures are seen as depriving offenders of contact with the institutions that are basically responsible for assuring development of law-abiding conduct: sound family life, good schools, employment, recreational opportunities, and desirable companions, to name only some of the more direct influences. (p. 6)

During the 1970s, a number of states (Colorado, Connecticut, Kansas, Minnesota, and Oregon) adopted community corrections programs based on these principles. The belief was that there were a large number of inmates in prison—anywhere from 30% to 70% (Lauen, 1988)—who did not belong there and who could be rehabilitated much more effectively in community corrections programs. However, beginning in the mid-1970s, most states moved in the opposite direction. Pronouncing rehabilitation dead, they enacted harsh criminal codes (Arizona enacted one in 1978) that included mandatory sentencing provisions based on "just deserts" and "get tough" premises.

By the mid-1980s, the high cost of incarceration forced a reexamination of the "get tough" approach. Alternatives to incarceration were adopted and promoted again, but this time for different reasons. One reason was the belief that, at least in some locations, felony offenders who were a threat to public safety were being placed on regular probation. These were offenders who were "too antisocial for the relative freedom that probation now offers, but not so seriously criminal as to require imprisonment" (Petersilia, Turner, Kahan, & Peterson, 1985, p. ix).

Thus was born the idea of "intermediate punishments" (McCarthy, 1987; Petersilia, 1987). Officials, such as judges, no longer have to choose between prison and probation, because now they have several other options they can use. Moreover, some supporters of the intermediate punishment position believe that a certain class of offenders have problems that require the controls available through alternatives, such as intensive probation supervision, home arrest, electronic monitoring, and shock incarceration. For example, some parole officers and parole board members in Arizona whom we interviewed in our research believe that some offenders have few vocational and social skills and have trouble controlling their behavior and meeting schedules, and therefore need extra controls. In reporting on her study of probation in California, Petersilia (1987) concludes that "today's probationers, who appear to pose a more serious threat to public safety than in the past, should have more supervision, not less" (p. 107). As we shall show below, the argument is that these offenders have shown through their behavior that they cannot be placed on regular probation or parole, but at the same time their crimes are not serious enough to warrant prison sentences. Hence alternatives are the perfect solution for them, according to this perspective (Binder, 1987). As Byrne, Lurigio, and Baird (1989) state, "These intermediate sentences are expected to provide safe and acceptable alternatives to prison, while also serving as attractive centerpieces for the new 'get tough' probation image" (p. 7).

In addition to this construction of alternatives, conservative legislators began to support intermediate measures in the belief that they are cost-effective; they are supposed to reduce costs while at the same time providing greater control over offenders who might be out on regular probation. In addition, however, these recent developments have led to a state of confusion about a number of issues, including whether or not these alternatives widen the net of social control, are really more cost-effective than other measures, are punitive enough, and sufficiently protect public safety. It is not likely that alternatives will be able to achieve all the goals their proponents claim. As Clear, Flynn, and Shapiro (1987) note:

> Commonly, IPS [intensive probation supervision] is expected to reduce prison crowding, increase public protection, rehabilitate the offender, demonstrate the potential of probation, and save money. Even a skeptic is bound to be impressed. (pp. 10-11)

However, "by promising too much to too many, IPS program developers may be guaranteeing their failure in much the same way as did the proponents of the 'scared straight' program" (Byrne et al., 1989, p. 11). The confusion about the goals of alternatives is especially bothersome when one is evaluating an alternative, such as home arrest, because it is not clear which goals should be used to assess effectiveness (Decker, 1985). We were faced with this problem when we evaluated the home arrest program in Arizona.

We will describe the operation of one alternative in Arizona— home arrest with electronic monitoring—and discuss what impact it has on these issues.[1] We will argue that alternatives to incarceration inevitably lead to net widening and are not cost-effective. Hence they cannot achieve all of the goals they are supposed to. Moreover, the confusion about which goals should be paramount often leads to poor policy design during the legislative stage, as well as problems during implementation. Until the goal confusion is cleared up, these programs will not be successful. We begin with a description of home arrest in Arizona that we use as our case study. Although it is just a "case study," we believe that the general conclusions we reach apply as well to most other alternatives in most states.

Home Arrest in Arizona

Arizona passed its home arrest bill during the 1988 legislative session, and it became law in July 1988. According to the bill's sponsors, the principal reasons for passing the bill were that it might reduce correctional costs because it would be less costly than keeping the same offenders in prison, and it might be beneficial to offenders because they could maintain family ties, be employed, and perhaps become responsible members of the community.[2]

The home arrest bill was the third law dealing with alternatives to incarceration passed in Arizona during the 1980s. This is somewhat surprising, because the state has been among the leaders in the "get tough on crime" movement of the 1980s. It has emphasized incarceration and has added a large number of prison beds over the last 10 years. Arizona has the third-highest incarceration rate in the country, and since 1978 it has had one of the harshest criminal codes as well. As a result, the state's corrections budget increased by about 900% over a 10-year period, from $25 million in 1976-1977 to $246 million in 1988-1989, and its prison population went from 3,813 in 1980 to 13,400 in 1990. But because of the high cost of corrections, the state also adopted intensive probation in 1983 and community punishment in 1987.

The home arrest program in Arizona is a modest one; it is a parole release program rather than a sentencing alternative, and is staffed to handle only 130 inmates at any one time. (It has never reached this level, for reasons we will explain below.) To ensure that an inmate remains confined at home, he or she wears an anklet that emits an electronic signal that is transmitted through the inmate's telephone lines to a central computer. If the inmate is not in the home when he or she is supposed to be, a violation is recorded and a parole officer is dispatched to the residence to investigate.

During its first year of operation, the program expended $654,185, which is a drop in the bucket compared with the total corrections budget of $246 million.

The bill stipulates that an inmate is eligible for home arrest if he or she

(1) was convicted of committing a Class 4, 5, or 6 felony not involving the intentional or knowing infliction of serious physical injury or the use or exhibition of a deadly weapon or dangerous instrument;

(2) was not convicted of a sexual offense;

(3) was not previously convicted of any felony;

(4) violated parole by the commission of a technical violation that was not chargeable or indictable as a criminal offense; and

(5) has been certified as eligible for parole under the emergency release provisions of Arizona Revised Code, Section 31-233I, and served one year of his or her sentence.

This last provision is important. The emergency release provision of the Arizona Revised Criminal Code allows the director of the Department

TABLE 15.1 Ethnic Origin of Home Arrestees

Ethnic Background	Males	Females	Total Number	Percentage
Caucasian	70	9	79	45.1
Black	34	5	39	22.3
Hispanic	42	11	53	30.3
Indian	3	0	3	1.7
Other	1	0	1	0.0
Total	150	25	175	100.0

of Corrections to release inmates on regular parole who meet the criteria in Items 1 through 4 whenever the prison population exceeds 95% of its rated capacity. In other words, individuals who are eligible for release on home arrest *are the same* as those eligible for release on regular parole whenever the prison population exceeds 95% of its rated capacity, which it has done for a number of years.

The typical inmate placed on home arrest during its first year of operation was a black or Hispanic 29-year-old male convicted of a drug, burglary, or theft offense (see Tables 15.1-15.3). The median sentence received was four years and the average amount of time served prior to release to home arrest was 10 months. There are many who would question whether or not these kinds of offenders should be sent to prison in the first place, and many who would say that they should be released on regular parole. However, except for the fact that the prison population exceeds the capacity of the system, it is unlikely that they would be released on regular parole in Arizona.

TABLE 15.2 Felony Class of Home Arrestees

Felony Class[a]	Males	Females	Total Number	Percentage
2	5	1	6	3.4
3	10	0	10	5.7
4	98	20	118	67.4
5	17	0	17	9.4
6	18	3	21	12.0
Old code	2	1	3	1.7
Total	150	25	175	100.0

NOTE: a. Felony classes in Arizona range from 1 through 6, with 1 being the most serious (i.e., murder, rape, aggravated assault) and 6 being the least serious (i.e., theft, possession of drugs).

TABLE 15.3 Offense Categories of Home Arrestees

Category	Males	Females	Total Number	Total Percentage
Homicide	0	1	1	.6
Kidnapping	2	0	2	1.1
Robbery	12	1	13	7.4
Aggravated assault	8	1	9	5.1
Burglary	32	3	35	20.0
Theft	19	2	21	12.0
Forgery	2	1	3	1.7
Fraud	0	2	2	1.1
Stolen property	9	0	9	5.1
Drug offense	52	14	66	37.7
Family offense	2	0	2	1.1
Escape	1	0	1	.6
Obstruction	2	0	2	1.1
DWI/traffic offense	9	0	9	5.1
Total	150	25	175	100.0

Legislative and Implementation Problems

At the time the home arrest bill was passed, the Arizona State Legislature was controlled by Republicans, particularly by conservative Republicans who had been strong supporters of the "lock 'em up" position. In addition, the state attorney general and his chief assistant, who had been one of the main architects of the tough 1978 Criminal Code, would not support any bill that appeared to be "soft on criminals" or that released offenders from prison before their maximum release date. In order to get the hard-liners' support for *any* alternative to incarceration, it had to be sold as a means of reducing the cost of corrections while at the same time protecting public safety and constituting adequate punishment. Thus the community corrections bill that was passed in 1987 had to be called "community punishment." In regard to home arrest, the chief assistant attorney general insisted that eligibility be limited to those convicted of Class 4, 5, or 6 felonies and that those convicted of Class 1, 2, or 3 felonies (which are mostly violent crimes) should not be included, even though the Department of Corrections recommended in favor of including these classes. Thus, by legislative design, eligibility for home arrest was limited to those who probably would be released under the emergency release provisions of Section 31-233I if home arrest did not exist. This is because the eligibility provisions for release under 233I are identical to those for release under home arrest. In other words, the seeds of net widening were built into the legislation in order to placate the conservatives who felt that public safety and punishment were paramount concerns. And this was done even though the goal of reducing costs and prison populations might be defeated if net widening occurred, because home arrest is more expensive than regular parole. These contradictions did not seem to bother the hard-liners, perhaps because they did not care if the program was deemed a failure anyway; this would give them an excuse to kill the legislation next time around.

Additional complications developed during implementation. The Board of Pardons and Paroles (BPP), which had the authority to decide which inmates would be released to home arrest, was reluctant to place many inmates on home arrest. The Arizona BPP is appointed by the governor, and its members are political insiders who tend to be wary of making pardon and parole decisions that will result in public hue and cry. The first inmates were not placed on home arrest until December 1988, five months after the bill was passed, and then only 7 inmates were placed in the program. This increased to 14 in January 1989 and 17 in February 1989, but dropped back to just 2 in March 1989. During the first year of operation, only 175 inmates were placed on home arrest. Because the program was staffed so that it could handle 130 inmates at any one time, the average cost per inmate per day for the first 11 months was far greater than the cost per inmate per day in prison ($127 compared with $46) (Palumbo, 1990).[3] Thus the politically appointed BPP practically guaranteed that the program would be deemed a failure when cost-effectiveness was used as an evaluation criterion, because not enough inmates were released to the program.

More important, the perception began to develop among members of the BPP and among home arrest parole officers that there is a class of offenders who *need* the controls that the system provides. These are offenders who had previously violated probation or parole rules, who had drug abuse problems, who had committed fairly serious offenses,[4] or who had a number of write-ups for bad behavior while in prison. In the view of these officials, these inmates needed the controls that home arrest provided because they had shown that they could not control themselves. In this view, costs were not important. As one parole officer said, "Some of these guys lack elementary social skills, such as paying their bills on time, being on schedule, and relating to others." The officials viewed home arrest as a good way for these "dysfunctional" inmates to get some structure and discipline in their lives.

The BPP would not release anyone to home arrest who

had a history of violence,
had an extensive arrest history,
had several institutional write-ups,
had substance abuse history,
had committed a serious offense,
had prior probation of parole violations, or
was not close to his or her provisional release date.

Thus, for some parole board members and parole officers, the main goal of the program was to provide some structure and training for inmates in the hope that this would help them better adjust to life outside of prison. Costs and reducing the number of inmates in prison are secondary goals at best from this perspective.

In summary, the politics of policy formation and the implementation structure of the program made it likely that there would be net widening and that the program would therefore not be cost-effective. The overriding concern for public safety of the conservatives in the legislature and of the BPP made it likely that the inmates placed on the program would be low-risk, nonviolent offenders who could and probably would have been supervised on regular parole. At the same time, the program was supposed to be cost-effective, but how could this occur if there indeed was net widening?

Cost-Effectiveness

It is very difficult to determine whether or not the home arrest program is cost-effective. The simple, straightforward method is to divide total expenditures for the program by the total number of bed days[5] that inmates spend in the program for a specific period to get a per day cost for each inmate. If this figure is lower than the cost per day for inmates in prison, the program might be said to be cost-effective. But this method can be considered accurate only if several things also occur: (a) The program is implemented at full capacity, (b) the inmates placed in the program would not have been placed on regular parole under provisions of 233I (i.e., stronger nets), (c) the program does not return a large proportion of inmates to prison for technical violations, and (d) the prison beds made available through home arrest are not immediately filled with new inmates (i.e., larger nets). We will now discuss each of these in turn.

FULL IMPLEMENTATION

If the home arrest program in Arizona operated at full capacity of 130 inmates per day for a year, the number of bed days for the program would be $130 \times 365 = 47,450$. Since the total expenditures for the program during its first year were $654,185, the cost per inmate per day would be $654,185 \div 47,450 = \$13.78$. Since the Arizona Department of Corrections estimates that the cost per inmate per day in prison is $46.00, the home arrest program would appear to be very cost-effective. But because of the problems created by the BPP, the program never operated at full capacity, so the actual cost per day was $127, which is more than the cost of prison. Even if the program did operate at full capacity, in order for it to be cost-effective the following three factors would also have to be considered.

STRONGER NETS

Costs will be increased if the inmates placed on home arrest are those who would have been put on regular parole if home arrest did not exist. As an illustration of what this aspect of net widening would add to the cost, assume that 40% of the inmates placed on home arrest under full implementation would have been placed on regular parole, that the per day cost of regular parole is $4.00, and that an inmate was on home arrest for six months on average and would have served the same amount of time on regular parole in the absence of home arrest. There would have been 260 inmates on home arrest over the course of a year under this assumption (i.e., 130 inmates each six months); 40% of this is 104. Without home arrest the cost of regular parole for these 104 would be $104 \times \$4 \times 183 = \$76,128$. But since they were put on home arrest, the actual cost was $104 \times \$13.78 \times 183 = \$262,260$. Thus there was an added cost for these inmates of $186,132. Consequently, the actual per inmate per day cost of home arrest under the assumption that there was a 40% net widening is $654,185 + 186,132 \div 47,450 = \$17.70$, rather than $13.78. The added cost for an assumption of 40% net widening is therefore $3.93. Notice also that this still is *less* costly than incarceration in prison.

INCREASED TECHNICAL VIOLATIONS

The costs will increase if the percentage of inmates being sent back to prison for technical violations is greater for those on home arrest than for those on regular parole. This is usually the case for alternatives, and it is the case for home arrest. The proportion who fail on home arrest for technical violations in Arizona is 34%; for those on regular parole it is 15%. Assume that the 19% more who failed in home arrest (because of its closer monitoring) would spend on average four months more in prison than they would have in the absence of home arrest; the costs for these are $260 \times .19 \times \$46 \times 120 = \$272,688$. This must be added to the total costs of home arrest (as well as the stronger net-widening costs), so the costs now are $\$654,185 + \$186,132 + \$272,688 = \$1,113,005$, and the cost per day is thus $\$1,113,005 \div 47,450 = \$23.46$. The added cost of the increase in technical violations is thus $5.76. Note that this still is about half the cost of prison incarceration.

LARGER NETS

The costs will be greater if the prison beds made available through releases to home arrest are filled immediately with new inmates because the beds are available. Let us assume that the 130 beds made available due to home arrest are filled with new inmates rather than left empty, and that they are filled because judges know that there is room available. The costs here amount to $\$46 \times 130 \times 365 = \$2,182,170$. When this is added to the previous costs, the costs of home arrest now amount to $\$1,113,005 + \$2,182,700 = \$3,295,705$, and the per inmate per day cost is $\$3,295,705 \div 47,450 = \$69.46$. The added cost for this factor is $46.00. Notice that now the cost of home arrest is greater than the cost of prison and that the larger net factor adds the most to the overall costs.

It is now clear that the program is not cost-effective if (a) it is not fully implemented, (b) there are stronger nets, (c) the failure rate due to technical violations is higher than for regular parole, and (d) the alternative makes it possible simply to expand the prison population. It is also clear that the last factor has a greater impact on cost than stronger nets and increases in technical violations combined. If an alternative is *not* used as a way of reducing the total number of prison beds in use, or to eliminate some of these institutions, then alternatives to incarceration cannot be cost-effective.

Alternatives to incarceration can widen the net in more than one way. They can widen the net in the sense that they move an inmate from regular parole (or probation) to an alternative that has more controls (i.e., stronger nets), and they can widen the net in the sense that they simply increase the overall use of prisons because the space is made available (i.e., larger nets).

In summary, net widening and implementation problems both add greatly to the costs of an alternative such as home arrest. But even if implementation problems are overcome, the programs will not be cost-effective if there is net widening. Thus it is crucial to determine whether or not net widening does in fact occur.

Net Widening

Net widening is a complex concept that is very difficult to measure. A number of different dimensions have been identified by various researchers. For example, Austin and Krisberg (1981) identify wider, stronger, and different nets. We will focus on stronger nets (i.e., an offender is placed on intensive probation who would have been on regular probation if the former did not exist) and larger nets (i.e., the existence of alternatives facilitates expansion of the prison population).

In addition, whether or not net widening is a malevolent or benevolent outcome depends on the social construction given it by the various stakeholders in the system (Guba & Lincoln, 1989). Those who argue that there are some offenders who are so antisocial that they need more control than is afforded by regular probation or parole would see net widening as benevolent, or at least as a sanguine outcome. To them, it is really a form of "net mending," because existing nets are allowing too many offenders to slip through to more freedom than they should have (presumably because they are a threat to public safety).

It is difficult to tell when the net-widening concept originated, but one of its early connotations arose in connection with juvenile diversion programs in the 1960s and community corrections programs in the 1970s. These programs, as we said above, were targeted at offenders who were prison bound (in the case of community corrections) or who were going to be labeled as "criminals" (in the case of juvenile offenders). The purpose of alternatives was to rehabilitate these individuals. Some researchers argued that, instead, the programs were putting some juveniles under supervision in diversion programs who would have been released if the programs did not exist, and some adult offenders were being put in community corrections programs who would have been given lesser sentences if the former did not exist (Austin & Krisberg, 1981; Scull, 1984). Some researchers have estimated that approximately 25% of adult offenders in community corrections programs are in this category (Covey & Menard, 1984; Decker, 1985; Winterfield, 1983). Such outcomes were viewed as malevolent.

However, as we have shown here, this stronger net dimension does not detract from the cost-effectiveness of the programs. Moreover, if the intermediate punishments construction is correct, the outcome is not malevolent because the ones these new nets are catching may need the extra control.

The second dimension of net widening—larger nets—has not gotten as much attention as has the dimension of stronger nets, but it is much more significant. As Duffee notes, prison populations will grow more rapidly under alternatives unless there are guidelines so that "those possessing characteristics which would normally imply incarceration are transferred to a noninstitutional setting, *and* the prison space set aside for these offenders is not filled with other offenders. Generally, this does not happen" (in Duffee & McGarrell, 1990, p. 16; see also Vass, 1990).

We have shown above that it is the larger nets dimension that has the greatest impact on costs. As long as the principal outcome of alternatives to incarceration is to make room available so that more and more drug and property offenders—most of whom are minority group members—can be incarcerated, then alternatives greatly increase the overall costs of the system. Moreover, because it is mostly minority offenders (i.e., blacks and Hispanics) who are caught up, in proportions that are 15 times greater than their representation in the general population, net widening gains back much of its original malevolent connotation.

Have alternatives facilitated the increase in the number of people being put under some form of correctional supervision? In order to answer this question, it would be necessary to separate out the impact that tougher criminal codes and increases in arrest, conviction, and incarceration rates have had from those that alternatives have had. To our knowledge, there has been no research to date that has tried to do this. The facts that the prison population has expanded at a more rapid rate than those in alternatives and that there has been an overall increase in the numbers under some form of correction supervision at the same time there has been an increase in new alternatives indicates that the latter has contributed something to the former. But, as Vass (1990, pp. 15-17) points out, there are other factors involved besides alternatives in the rapid expansion of prison populations.

Promising Too Much to Too Many

Perhaps some net widening is desirable in the sense that there is a need for stronger nets for some offenders and that these offenders can be supervised more economically outside of prison. But there is a great deal of confusion about just what the goals of intermediate punishments should be. As long as the prison beds made available are not retired from service, intermediate punishments very likely add to the overall costs of corrections because they make it possible to increase the total number of people being put under correctional supervision. They may be cost-effective in the sense that it is less costly to supervise offenders under home arrest or intensive probation than in prison, but they are *not* cost-effective when total corrections expenditures are a part of the equation.

Also, there is the question of whether public safety should be emphasized over treatment. The programs are being sold to the public, and supported by conservative legislators, through the arguments that they provide greater controls for dangerous felons who otherwise would be on regular probation or parole and that they are cost-effective. If treatment is included, it is done as an "add-on" rather than as the main reason. Under these conditions, there is likely to be little if any real treatment actually provided.

A key question that needs to be addressed is, What kinds of offenders are being put in prison and what kinds are placed in these alternative programs? As the data on home arrest presented above show, the major categories are burglary and drug offenders (and the two are highly related).[6] This brings us back to problem definition and policy design. The prison crisis is a crisis about policy, and this involves politics and economics.

A key element of the policy problem is the way we define the problem (Dery, 1984; Palumbo, 1989). Control over definition of social problems is tantamount to control over policy prescriptions aimed at solving the problems. And since a large proportion of the people who are being put in prison (and placed in alternative programs) are drug/property offenders, a large part of the policy problem is how we define the drug issue.

If it is defined as a health/economic problem, then there is a need for treatment centers and job opportunities rather than home arrest, intensive probation, or prison. If it is defined as a criminal problem, then there seems to be a need for these alternative programs, not because they are cost-effective or because they will reduce prison populations, but because these "offenders" are in need of control, discipline, and punishment. Scientific facts cannot settle this question, because it is a matter of political ideology.

Conclusions

The main reason for adopting home arrest (and other alternatives) in Arizona (and in other states as well) is the assumption that it will help reduce the skyrocketing costs of corrections. However, there are conflicting constructions and perceptions about what is most important in such programs. The theoretical assumption that seems to guide the operation of home arrest and other contemporary alternatives is that there is a class of offenders who need the greater degree of control that such options afford. Moreover, conservative legislators demand that public safety be a paramount concern in such programs. Consequently, the only offenders who are eligible for the programs are those who have committed relatively minor felony offenses. Moreover, during implementation, because of the stress on public safety, a large proportion of offenders are sent back to prison for technical violations. As a result, it is unlikely that these programs actually reduce costs. Particularly if the beds that may be made available by the programs are immediately filled rather than "decommissioned," it is likely that these alternatives will significantly increase the costs of corrections rather than reduce them.

Does that mean alternative programs are failing? Yes, if costs are the main impetus for their adoption, because the programs are not reducing costs. The question of whether or not the alternatives are successful by other measures revolves around the correctness of the theory that is developing about the need for such options (McCarthy, 1987; Petersilia, 1987). And the answer to this is a matter of how we define and construct the problem; this is a matter of values and ideology. The typical offender in most alternative programs is a black or Hispanic male in his mid-20s who was arrested and convicted of a drug offense, burglary, or theft. The latter two crimes are likely to be related to the offender's drug problem. If this problem is defined as a public health or social issue rather than a criminal one, then, of course, the theory that is developing about the need for intermediate sanctions for a certain class of offenders is really a way to justify what the state is doing as it increases its control over minority populations. From one political perspective, this is a malevolent outcome. It is minorities—blacks and Hispanics—who are being sentenced to prison and also to the newer alternatives in proportions far greater than their representation in the overall population. This is *not* benevolence, as the developing justification would have us believe. As Byrne et al. (1989) succinctly write:

> As more revenue is devoted to corrections, less will be available to educate our children, preserve our natural resources, house our poor, or combat abuse, neglect, and other social ills. We are clearly at a crossroads in the United States, a national point of reckoning. The current course toward increased use of incarceration will bankrupt

programs that are needed to deal with complex social problems, and it will do little to increase public safety. (p. 41)

We add here that the increased use of alternatives to incarceration will do little to alter this; in fact, these alternatives are likely to increase the costs of corrections and accelerate the crises in education, housing, and other social ills, because in increasing corrections budgets they leave fewer resources for addressing social problems. What is needed are major changes in sanctioning policies. This entails not only a reevaluation of mandatory and harsh sentencing codes (as is being done in Arizona), but also putting a cap on incarceration rates. The emphasis on mandatory sentencing and the "drug crisis" will simply aggravate rather than solve social ills. Alternatives to incarceration should be used to alleviate the prison crisis brought on by the "war on drugs" and the "crime problem." If they are used instead as intermediate *punishments*, they are likely to add to the crisis.

Notes

1. We conducted an evaluation of home arrest in Arizona during February-May 1990. The senior author also prepared a *Report to the State Legislature of Arizona on Home Arrest* during September 1989 through January 1990. These two studies provide the empirical basis for this chapter.

2. We interviewed four state legislators about the bill. While the bill's chief sponsor emphasized the community ties aspects, the other legislators were more impressed by the economic aspects.

3. Of course, the start-up costs are expected to be higher as the program irons out problems, but the home arrest program never achieved its full operating capacity during the first year. At the same time, it should be noted that the average cost per inmate did decline each month and reached a low of $27 per day by October of 1989.

4. Although inmates *convicted* of violent offenses were not eligible for the program, some of these inmates had committed violent crimes, but were sentenced for lesser offenses through plea bargaining.

5. "Bed days" are computed by adding the number of days that inmates spend in the program over a specific period of time.

6. Although we present data for home arrest only, the same categories of offenders are being put on intensive probation in Arizona and probably in other states as well.

References

Austin, J., & Krisberg, B. (1981, January). Wider, stronger and different nets: The dialectics of criminal justice reform. *Journal of Research in Crime & Delinquency*, pp. 165-196.

Binder, A. (1987). A systematic analysis of Decker's "A systematic analysis of diversion: Net widening and beyond" [includes Decker's rejoinder]. *Journal of Criminal Justice, 15*, 255-263.

Byrne, J. M., Lurigio, A. J., & Baird, S. C. (1989). *The effectiveness of the* new *intensive supervision programs* (Research in Corrections, No. 5). Washington, DC: National Institute of Corrections.

Clear, T., Flynn, S., & Shapiro, C. (1987). Intensive supervision in probation: A comparison of three projects. In B. R. McCarthy (Ed.), *Intermediate punishments: Intensive supervision, home confinement, and electronic monitoring.* Monsey, NY: Criminal Justice Press.

Covey, H. C., & Menard, S. (1984). Community corrections diversion in Colorado. *Journal of Criminal Justice, 12,* 1-10.

Decker, S. (1985). A systematic analysis of diversion: Net widening and beyond. *Journal of Criminal Justice, 16,* 207-216.

Dery, D. (1984). *Problem definition in policy analysis.* Lawrence: University of Kansas Press.

Duffee, D., & McGarrell, E. (Eds.). (1990). *Community corrections: A community field approach.* Cincinnati, OH: Anderson.

Guba, E., & Lincoln, Y. (1989). *Fourth-generation evaluation.* Newbury Park, CA: Sage.

Lauen, R. (1988). *Community managed corrections.* Washington, DC: American Corrections Association.

McCarthy, B. R. (Ed.). (1987). *Intermediate punishments: Intensive supervision, home confinement, and electronic monitoring.* Monsey, NY: Criminal Justice Press.

Palumbo, D. (1989). *Public policy in America.* San Diego, CA: Harcourt Brace Jovanovich.

Palumbo, D. (1990, January). *Home arrest in Arizona: Report to the state legislature on the operation of the Home Arrest Program during its first year.* Tempe: Arizona State University.

Petersilia, J. (1987). *Expanding options for criminal sentencing* (Publication No. R-3544-EMC). Santa Monica, CA: RAND Corporation.

Petersilia, J., Turner, S., Kahan, J., & Peterson, J. (1985). *Granting felons probation: Public risks and alternatives* (Publication No. R-3186-NIJ). Santa Monica, CA: RAND Corporation

President's Commission on Law Enforcement and Administration of Justice. (1967). *Task force: Corrections.* Washington, DC: Government Printing Office.

Scull, A. T. (1984). *Decarceration: Community treatment and the deviant—a radical view* (2nd ed.). Cambridge: Basil Blackwell/Polity.

Vass, A. A. (1990). *Alternatives to prison: Punishment, custody, and the community.* Newbury Park, CA: Sage.

Winterfield, L. (1983, February). *Colorado community corrections: A case of not widening the net* (Research report). Netherland, CO: Timberline Associates.

16. Intermediate Sanctions and the Female Offender

Robin A. Robinson

> State dollars now spent warehousing women who could have been sentenced safely and more cheaply to alternative rehabilitative punishments in the community would be better spent on helping them overcome poverty, drug addiction and victimization—the major pathways to crime for women.
>
> TRACY HULING,
> Public Policy Director,
> Correctional Association of New York

The nature of women's crime in the United States has been, historically, at odds with the nature of punishment. Scholars of female criminality have postulated that women's crime has been subsumed under the broader mantle of crime in general. Female offenders have been sentenced to sanctions that are determined by aggregate crime rates and trends, although implemented subject to gender role stereotypes by correctional officers (see, for example, Daly & Chesney-Lind, 1988; Erez, 1989; Simpson, 1989). Recent scholarship has suggested that women's crime is, with few exceptions, the product of an etiology that is unique to women (Harris, 1977; Simpson, 1989). Women's crime may tend to be reactive rather than proactive in the motivation behind the act, and, at that, reactive to life crises or prolonged disadvantage that the women seek to alleviate (see, for example, Chesney-Lind & Rodriguez, 1985; Gilfus, 1987; Simpson, 1991). Some factors in the etiology of criminality may be common to both males and females, but there are a few factors that appear to be

AUTHOR'S NOTE: My thanks to Anthony Braga for his valuable assistance in the preparation of the data, and to Jim Byrne for helpful discussions leading to the development of this chapter. The responsibility for the content herein is my own.

specific to women, and therefore relevant to programs for female offenders, including domestic violence (battering of women), single motherhood, and history of sexual abuse. Further, race and class differences distinguish between the crimes of white women and black women (Hill & Suval, 1988; Laub & McDermott, 1985; Simpson, 1991); distinctions among racial and ethnic groups beyond the white/black dichotomy show still other differences, and warrant further research (Simpson, 1991).

Women's crime is most often crime of an economic nature: credit card fraud, welfare fraud, shoplifting, check writing on insufficient funds, forgery, prostitution. Women's violent crime (11.4% of all U.S. violent crime; Federal Bureau of Investigation, 1989) represents a very small amount of crime overall, and is often in response to domestic abuse (Browne, 1987). Of all women sentenced to incarceration, less than 11% were sentenced for violent offenses (U.S. Department of Justice, 1990). Of all women sentenced to probation, approximately 8% were sentenced for violent crimes (U.S. Department of Justice, 1990). The great majority of women convicted of violent crimes have no prior criminal history (78%), underscoring the situational nature of the crime and the lack of threat such women pose to community safety (American Correctional Association, 1990; Gilfus, 1987).

The very low proportion of women in the overall prison population—5.2% of state and federal prisoners, 8% of probationers (Clear & Cole, 1990), and about 15% of all offenders in correctional control (U.S. Department of Justice, 1990)—suggests that women have never been a large enough part of the criminal population to have been considered uniquely in the determination and design of sanctions. As noted in the introductory quote above, most women's crime derives from desperation brought about by conditions of poverty, chemical dependencies, and victimization, both current abuse and childhood abuse, such abuse including physical, emotional, and/or sexual abuses, and their initial and long-term effects (see, for example, American Correctional Association, 1990; Browne, 1987; Chesney-Lind & Rodriguez, 1985; Daly & Chesney-Lind, 1988; Figueira-McDonough, Inglehart, Sarri, & Williams, 1981; Goetting & Howsen, 1983; James, 1976; James & Myerding, 1977). Victimizations and conditions of poverty among female offenders, among other factors, are illustrative of the incidental nature of crimes as social events in the life course (Elder, 1985; Hagan & Palloni, 1988).

Another result of the relatively low number of women in the offender population is the dearth of program resources dedicated to the particular needs of women in the criminal justice system. For example, most states have only one prison for women, with all levels of custody classification (maximum, medium, and minimum) housed in close proximity or intermingled in one prison population (Clear & Cole, 1990). Some states house women prisoners in a section of a two-sex facility (Clear & Cole, 1990). In most states, programs for women inside prison walls, and certainly in jails, are constrained by limited fiscal resources that are most often directed toward the more dangerous, more violent, and more visible male offenders. Prison industry and education programs are most often designed to address the needs and control of male prisoners (Clear & Cole, 1990). Visiting areas and living areas are similarly organized around the needs of the vast majority that is the male offender population (Baunach, 1985), though some programs are being developed to aid in maintaining family units (Neto & Bainer, 1983).

An argument that has been raised relative to the expansion of intermediate sanctions is that prison crowding problems are forcing the development of intermediate sanctions in the direction of noninstitutional or reduced institutional surveillance, and away from treatment components, and for the wrong reasons—that is, to reduce prison crowding rather than to reduce recidivism (Byrne, 1990). This argument is particularly germane to the development of intermediate sanctions for female offenders. The issues that need to be addressed relative to female offenders extend the argument to one not only of surveillance versus treatment, but also of surveillance versus help in the broader sense. Design criteria in the development of intermediate sanctions for women should address treatment components for the women themselves, as well as ensure the least possible disruption and trauma to the minor children for which female offenders are often the sole providers (Clear & Cole, 1990). There is a caveat here relative to the importance of intermediate sanctions that can be tailored to the needs of individual offenders. Clear and O'Leary (1983) warn that programs that do not address offender needs and allow failure may actually result in the offender serving more time under correctional control than if the offender had served a term of incarceration. Programs that allow community failure may disrupt the families of female offenders more by bouncing mothers in and out of the correctional system.

This chapter reviews the four principal intermediate sanctions currently employed around the country, relative to their use with women: intensive probation supervision (IPS), shock incarceration or split sentence (a period of incarceration followed by probation), house arrest, and electronic monitoring. The discussion will begin

with a state-by-state summary of the use of each of the sanctions—
which are available, which are used with women, and to what extent
they are used with women—followed by possible implications of the
use of each sanction with women relative to generalized life issues
and circumstances of female offenders. The chapter concludes with
a history and description of a model community corrections program
located in Portland, Oregon, designed and implemented by a female
ex-prisoner for the particular life issues, needs, and family responsibilities of women offenders, and under contract to the Oregon Department of Corrections as an alternative to incarceration since 1989.

State-by-State Summary
of Intermediate Sanctions

The four most common intermediate sanctions in use in the United
States today are intensive probation supervision, shock incarceration (a period of incarceration, often on a military boot camp model,
followed by probation), house arrest (confinement to home, with or
without electronic monitoring), and electronic monitoring. All may
be used as components of IPS.

Data compiled from all 50 states and the District of Columbia show
that the intermediate sanctions considered here are available to both
males and females. Data on intermediate sanctions were collected by
surveying the states as to the availability of programs, program components, and gender availability. The data reviewed here were compiled from two analyses published in 1990 (Byrne, 1990; U.S. General
Accounting Office, 1990). The availability is summarized in Table 16.1.
States reporting the availability and use of intermediate sanctions reported 110 programs nationwide, with 52 of the programs, or 48%,
available to both males and females. Of the 52 programs that are
available to both males and females, 28 were IPS programs, 10 were
house arrest programs, 10 were electric monitoring programs, and 4
were shock incarceration programs. The remainder of the programs did
not specify availability by gender in their reports.

A total of 17 states provided data to indicate the gender distribution for IPS programs; these are summarized in Table 16.2. Sufficient
data were not available for the other intermediate sanctions discussed here. Braga (1991) notes that the mean female representation
in the 17 IPS programs providing data on gender distribution reflects
the overall proportion of women in correctional control nationwide,
about 15%. He notes further that the data on gender distribution do

TABLE 16.1 Program Availability, by Gender of Offender

State	IPS	M/F	HA	M/F	EM	M/F	SI	M/F
Alabama	X	Y	X	N	X	N	X	N
Alaska	X	N						
Arizona	X	Y					X	M
Arkansas	X	N	X	N				
California	X	Y	X	N	X	Y		
Colorado	X	Y	X	Y				
Connecticut	X	N	X	N	X	N	X	N
Delaware	X	N	X	N	X	N		
Florida	X	Y	X	Y	X	Y		
Georgia	X	Y	X	N	X	N	X	N
Hawaii	X	Y	X	N	X	Y		
Idaho	X	Y	X	Y				
Illinois	X	Y						
Indiana	X	N	X	N				
Iowa	X	Y						
Kansas	X	Y	X	N	X	N		
Kentucky	X	Y	X	Y	X	Y	X	Y
Louisiana	X	Y	X	N			X	Y
Maine	X	Y						
Maryland	X	N	X	N	X	N		
Massachusetts								
Michigan			X	Y	X	Y	X	N
Minnesota								
Mississippi	X	Y	X	Y			X	N
Missouri	X	Y	X	N	X	N	X	N
Montana	X	Y	X	N	X	Y		
Nebraska	X	Y	X	Y				
Nevada			X	N				
New Hampshire	X	Y	X	Y	X	Y		
New Jersey	X	Y						
New Mexico	X	Y	X	Y	X	N		
New York	X	Y					X	Y
North Carolina	X	N						
North Dakota								
Ohio	X	Y						
Oklahoma			X	Y	X	N	X	Y
Oregon	X	N	X	N	X	N		
Pennsylvania								
Rhode Island								
South Carolina	X	N					X	N
South Dakota	X	N	X	N				
Tennessee	X	Y						
Texas	X	Y	X	N	X	Y	X	N
Utah	X	N			X	N		
Vermont								

continued

TABLE 16.1 Continued

State	IPS	M/F	HA	M/F	EM	M/F	SI	M/F
Virginia	X	Y	X	N				
Washington	X	N						
West Virginia	X	Y	X	Y	X	Y		
Wisconsin	X	Y						
Wyoming	X	Y	X	N	X	Y	X	N
Washington, DC	X	Y	X	N	X	N	X	N
Totals								
51	41		30		24		15	
110 programs	28 Y (68%)		10 Y (33.3%)		10 Y (41%)		4 Y (26%)	
52 Y (48%)	13 N (32%)		20 N (66.6%)		14 N (59%)		10 N (66%)	
							1 M (8%)	

SOURCE: U.S. General Accounting Office (1990) and Byrne (1990). Table prepared by Anthony Braga, Rutgers University.
NOTE: IPS = intensive probation supervision; X = program currently in use; HA = house arrest; Y = available for males and females; EM = electronic monitoring; N = no gender distinction in state data; SI = shock incarceration; M = males only; M/F = male/female availability.

not provide information on the equity of program components, or on the characteristics of males and females sentenced to the programs, including instant offense. The data do not include items to measure equity of treatment of male or female probationers while they are in the program. Clearly, these are areas for further study.

The data available on program function do not reveal program components or assistance available to women who must provide for their children while serving their sentences, or whose domestic lives are disrupted in other ways, including circumstances related to their crimes, such as domestic abuse. Programs appear to have been developed in many cases without considering the characteristics and life-course events of the offenders enrolled in them.

Implications of Female Offenders' Serving Sentences in Intermediate Sanction Programs

The life issues and circumstances that have been associated with female criminality in the findings of recent research may extend to the use of the intermediate sanctions under discussion here. While less than 5% of all offenders under correctional control are sentenced to intermediate sanctions (Byrne, 1990), the number is likely to increase

TABLE 16.2 IPS Participation of Female Offenders in 17 States

State	Percentage	Number in IPS	Total Female Offenders
California			
Contra Costa County	20.0	34	170
Ventura County	15.0	25	168
Los Angeles County	15.0	24	157
Colorado	10.2	17	168
Florida	14.7	N/A	N/A
Georgia	11.0	288	2,622
Illinois	14.0	306	2,187
Iowa	11.9	12	101
Kentucky	7.0	94	1,337
Massachusetts	10.6	24	227
Mississippi	26.0	14	54
Missouri	15.9	N/A	N/A
New Jersey	9.0	36	400
Ohio	14.4	57	399
South Carolina	12.0	77	641
Tennessee	16.0	75	466
Texas	17.0	1,436	8,446
Virginia	11.3	39	346
Washington, DC	14.0	25	181
Totals	mean = 15.3	2,583	18,070

SOURCE: Braga (1991).

over the next decade, with the explosion of prison crowding and various social mandates to control new kinds of behaviors leading to new kinds of criminalization. Since women offenders appear to be proportionally represented in, at least, IPS programs, and are subject to sentences in intermediate sanctions, the array of such sanctions should be scrutinized for the impacts they may have on the lives of women offenders relative to the intents of the programs. If the intent is surveillance with punishment as both the motive and the only expected outcome, the accomplishment of control may suffice. If the intent is rehabilitation or rehabilitative control, the goal reduced recidivism and habilitation, then the uses of certain intermediate sanctions with female offenders demand examination.

Women offenders are highly likely to be mothers (American Correctional Association, 1990); a community corrections program for women in Oregon counts 70% of its population to be mothers (Our New Beginnings, 1988). Further, women offenders are likely to be the sole supporters of minor children. They are highly likely to be impoverished heads of households, to be victims and/or survivors of physical and/or sexual violence, and to have histories and current habits of heavy drug and/or alcohol use (American Correctional Association, 1990; Immarigeon, 1987). They are likely to have interrupted their education early, to have limited job skills (Figueira-McDonough et al., 1981), and to have borne their children at an early age. Many stay in relationships with men in which they are habitually physically abused, or have one physically abusive relationship after another (American Correctional Association, 1990; Browne, 1987). They often commit crimes to survive, unaware or uncaring of the possible consequences (see, e.g., Browne, 1987; Miller, 1986). In light of this profile of women offenders, the four intermediate sanctions mentioned above are considered.

Intensive probation supervision is the most commonly employed intermediate sanction in the United States (Byrne, Lurigio, & Baird, 1989). Table 16.1 shows that women are represented, on the average, in proportion to the percentage of women under correctional control nationwide. Though the effectiveness of IPS is questionable relative to recidivism reduction and continues to fall under scrutiny, it may contribute to a reduction in prison crowding, and may be cost-effective when compared with prison. The elements of intermediate sanctions need further analysis as well. There is a continuing debate on these issues (see Byrne, 1990; U.S. General Accounting Office, 1990). Just what the cost-effectiveness of IPS is in consideration of other intermediate sanctions is not known, as little is known about house arrest, electronic monitoring, and shock incarceration (Byrne, 1990). Traditional consideration of cost-effectiveness takes into account actual program costs of administration, surveillance, and treatment components.

The use of IPS with women offenders bears other considerations relative to cost-effectiveness, recidivism reduction, and diversionary impact. As discussed above, most crimes by women are of an economic nature, for means of survival, to support their children, or to support drug habits, and are committed often with or for male partners. Violent crimes by women are highly likely to be committed in response to situations of domestic violence. The use of IPS with women demands scrutiny relative to the integrity of the family unit and care of the children, and the availability of supports and treatment components to alleviate the factors attributable to crimes committed by most women offenders.

The economic factors that lead women to commit the crimes of fraud, forgery, theft, and prostitution must be considered in the IPS model when used with women. To expect women to continue to support their children, often alone, in absence of treatment components to help ameliorate the poverty prompting the crimes is to contribute to program failure. The lack of job skills and the lack of child care to enable employment are factors that cannot be ignored if the goal is to prevent the commission of repeat crimes of the same nature. Indeed, IPS programs that include components to target such issues can be complemented by implementing, in tandem, community services to prevent such crimes. At the least, women serving time on IPS should be provided with program components to promote economic self-sufficiency, including safe and reliable organized child care, skills training, and education.

Violent crimes of a domestic nature may contribute further to the economic and emotional issues with which women on IPS may have to contend. A domestic relationship that is disrupted by violence may lead to economic hardship for a woman and her children, particularly if the partner who leaves has provided significant financial support to the household. If the woman is the offender—that is, if she committed a violent act against her abuser, a not uncommon type of female crime—and receives a sanction that keeps her in the community with inadequate counseling and program assistance, she may be inclined or forced to rely on often inadequate public income supports. Welfare assistance in disrupted families and child-care costs related to job training or related employment issues are rarely calculated as costs in evaluations of community corrections programs; the particular circumstances of female offenders warrant such consideration.

Alcohol and/or other drug habits, often begun early in life in response to physical and/or sexual abuse, may contribute to women's crime (American Correctional Association, 1990; Clear & Cole, 1990; Miller, 1986); 74% of female offenders begin alcohol and/or drug use between the ages of 13 and 14 (American Correctional Association, 1990). The use of intensive probation can work to help alleviate these problems in the lives of women offenders if the programs are structured specifically to provide support in these areas of need. In fact, these elements are not at the forefront of program design in IPS. More common are "blaming the victim" platitudes and "get tough" policies that may mean little to women who have been victimized from an early age, feel stigmatized and marginal to the community, and have been conditioned to expect punishment and harm as a fact of life. Further, the common use of such features as curfew, house arrest, and electronic monitoring as part of IPS (Byrne, 1990) may mean danger to women who are suffering domestic abuse by keeping them in their homes, with few opportunities to seek outside support or other living arrangements. Such fear can perpetuate or aggravate established alcohol and/or other drug habits, and threaten the success of such women under intensive probation supervision with drug and/or alcohol monitoring, two common features.

A less common but nevertheless controversial feature of IPS is shock incarceration, used with IPS as a split sentence. An equity issue relative to sentencing practices involving intermediate sanctions arises here. Women offenders may well be tempted to "choose" such programs over straight sentences of several or more years (sometimes there is a choice between shock and straight-time incarceration) because they will return to the community and to their children much sooner. Incarcerated women offenders, regardless of sentence length, who have been victims of physical and/or sexual abuse as children often self-castigate and worry that their children are enduring the same abuses they suffered as children, in foster care or other living arrangements pending the end of the sentence. The anguish of separation from their children is a common theme of prison mothers' stories (Baunach, 1982, 1985; Datesman & Cales, 1983; McGowan & Blumenthal, 1976), and the temptation to choose a "short" shock sentence over a straight-time sentence seems considerable.

Shock incarceration typically involves a short sentence in an institutional, often paramilitary, program emphasizing discipline, self-control, and unquestioning obedience. Such design and elements may militate against program success for women offenders for a few reasons. First, most women offenders have endured violent control tactics from others in their domestic relationships, as children and/or as adults. The tyrannical, impersonal, military "boot camp" drill sergeant prototype on which the shock incarceration programs are often founded may resemble closely the abusive homes and partners of which female offenders have been so fearful. While the women may be conditioned to capitulate to authority under threat of punishment, the long-range effect may be to prolong the sense of powerlessness that contributed to their instant and prior offenses.

Second, individuals who have suffered abuse in their lives, especially sexual abuse, usually progress through initial and long-term effects of powerlessness and stigmatization, among others (Finkelhor & Browne, 1986). They may have little or no confidence in their ability to protect themselves against future harm, have a propensity for self-harm, and may have difficulty accepting the value of their individual talents, skills, or abilities to survive. The nature of a paramilitary regimen may exacerbate the clinical aftereffects of such abuse. The wearing of uniforms, the preclusion of decision making, "rock moving"-type punishments, and barracks-type living may further threaten an already fragile sense of the ability to discern constructive life choices.

Third, women's violent crime is less often preceded by a criminal history (22%) than property crime (39%) (American Correctional Association, 1990), and much of women's nonviolent crime is motivated by women's economic hardship (Chesney-Lind & Rodriguez, 1985; Daly & Chesney-Lind, 1988). The precepts of shock incarceration do not address specifically either of those particular characteristics of women's crime, and raise equity issues that underscore the mismatch of punishment, crime, and individual criminal.

Overall, while the intermediate sanctions that are discussed here may be preferable to straight sentences in traditional institutions by providing women with the opportunity to serve their sentences more or less in the community, the same program deficits that prison holds for women are replicated in great part in the "alternative" sentencing practices. In some cases, intermediate sanctions may be worse, by keeping women in dangerous domestic situations or allowing program failure that may result in extended time under correctional control. If scarce resources are to be spent to design and implement alternative sanctions to prison, the particular characteristics of women offenders should be addressed in the design of programs to which they will be sentenced.

Our New Beginnings:
A Model for Women's Sanctions

Our New Beginnings (ONB) is an alternative to incarceration designed, administered, and implemented by Carole Pope since 1981 in Portland, Oregon. Pope, herself an ex-prisoner who spent four years in the Oregon Women's Correctional Center for theft and forgery in the late 1970s, created the program from a litany of needs she either observed or experienced as a woman in prison. Pope, a classical pianist with a master's degree in music, who speaks freely of her own early sexual abuse, alcoholism, and descent into self-destructive behaviors, learned from many women in prison that they shared many life-course events, if not socioeconomic backgrounds. When Pope was paroled she had not dealt with the life crises to which she now attributes her self-destructive behaviors and crimes, and, without support in the community, she quickly violated her parole and returned to prison. By the time she was released, she had organized a small group of women prisoners who were also returning to the community, and together they began the fledgling support program for women offenders that would become the current alternative sanction for women, which holds contracts with the state of Oregon, known as Our New Beginnings.

ONB was founded on the theme of the life course of women offenders. The organization has as its tenets issues that were empirically derived by its founder and others from their own experiences. ONB addresses a staggering array of general services for the women who are sentenced there, including, but not limited to, housing, mental health, drug and alcohol counseling, child care, maternal education, literacy tutoring, job placement, life skills training, anger counseling, advocacy for children, job training, incest/abuse counseling, prenatal care, other medical care including AIDS education and support, and an addicted mothers' program with an on-site residential facility for drug-addicted mothers and their children. With 72% of the women at ONB reporting mental health issues, the mandatory mental health assessment and available services are essential (Our New Beginnings, 1988), a reflection of the serious mental health needs of the aggregate population of women offenders (American Correctional Association, 1990).

Besides the plethora of services available to the women who are sentenced to ONB, either as 1 of 27 residents or as 1 of about 65 day-treatment probationers, ONB is notable for its location in an expansive, renovated Victorian house in the community, run, in part, by other ex-offenders. The program was originally designed to work with women coming out of prison, but in 1989 it received its first contract from the state of Oregon as a "front-end" alternative to the Women's Correctional Center. Women who serve time at Our New Beginnings are placed there for federal (1%), state (21%), and county (78%) sentences. Their offense categories include felonies (53%) and misdemeanors (47%). From 1984 to 1987, the program provided services, both resident and nonresident, to 693 women, 64% of whom successfully completed the program—that is, did not return to jail or prison. Strict house rules and rules of personal care are enforced through drug and alcohol monitoring, prohibition against driving, monitoring of personal responsibility and adherence to individual program plans, and rules of group living. Infringement or violation of house rules or terms of probation results in swift return to incarceration. Some 36% of the women fail to complete their sentences at ONB and are returned to traditional institutions.

The program benefits from community support, with about 60% of its funding coming from contracts and 40% from private grants. A major concern of policymakers and administrators is always cost-effectiveness, and ONB seems to be viable on that criterion as well. Pope reports that the cost of caring for women prisoners in Oregon breaks down as follows: $80 a day in the Justice Center jail, $56 a day in the Oregon Women's Correctional Center, an average of $38 a day for all state facilities, and $32 dollars a day for ONB (McCarthy, 1988). Because the components of surveillance and treatment are not measured, the comparison may be simplistic; this issue requires more detailed study. Another factor in comparing costs would be to ascertain the number of ONB participants who, in absence of ONB, would have been sentenced to probation and the number who would have been jail or prison bound.

ONB reports that 71% of the women sentenced there are unskilled, and that 78% have not been employed for a year prior to program entry. The response to this need was the development of an expansive offering of job training programs, with support and direct training coordinated with the assistance of private and public sector employment services and business and industry councils throughout the area. Literacy and other education programs are provided, along with job preparation and job training, to provide a foundation for ongoing and future employment. Women who need them receive transportation and child care to work at jobs in the community while serving their time at ONB. Further, postsecondary education is encouraged and supported programmatically, unlike many traditional institutional sanctions for women.

An important theoretical premise underlies the treatment component of ONB. The life-course events that are often neglected in traditional institutional programs, and in intermediate sanctions designed for the aggregate population of offenders, have become the focus of programs for the women at ONB. Incest and other child abuse, domestic violence issues, and other issues characteristic of the aggregate of female offenders are shared experiences at ONB, and the stigmatization that most women had felt hitherto is to some extent diminished by understanding, counseling, both group and individual, and strategies to cope with such victimization. An aftercare component supports women in the community after they have served their time, to help ameliorate the "bouncing" effect, in and out of the system, that may otherwise extend the original time to which an offender is sentenced.

Summary and Conclusion

The emergence of intermediate sanctions has been, with few exceptions, in keeping with the proclivity of criminal justice systems and departments of corrections to plan for the majority of offenders, male, and fit the small minority of offenders, female, into the larger plan. The nature of women's crime argues against such a system for women of punishment by default—that is, punishments created for males. The design of a few intermediate sanctions that are gaining in popularity around the country may be, in fact, particularly harmful, or in any case not helpful, to the intended outcomes of rehabilitation for women: reduced recidivism, the amelioration of life issues that may have contributed to their crimes, and deterrence. These intermediate sanctions include shock incarceration on the "boot camp" model, house arrest, and electronic monitoring.

While intermediate sanctions as alternatives to incarceration have provided recourse for thousands of offenders, many caveats remain in the use of these sanctions with female offenders. Intensive probation supervision, electronic monitoring, house arrest, and shock incarceration present to female offenders many of the same constraints and punitive program elements that women face in traditional institutional settings. The potentially positive aspects of the most common intermediate sanctions, those of keeping offenders in the community at less cost to the state and less disruption to the offender's life, may be contraindicated for women whose lives in the community are fraught with poverty, abuse, and mental illness.

A model currently exists that has used anecdotal and empirical evidence of issues in the life courses of female offenders to develop a comprehensive program for female offenders, at the "front end" and "back end" of the correctional system. Efforts should be made by state departments of corrections to establish programs that address directly and specifically the individual needs of women offenders. Further, such efforts should recognize the differences that exist among women offenders relative to race and class, thus avoiding the overgeneralization of female offender characteristics that may militate against program success. The replication of such programs around the country would address the traditional concerns of corrections: reducing recidivism by alleviating conditions contributory to women's crime; cost-effectiveness, as suggested in the Oregon model by what may be the less than one-half of incarceration cost per woman; possible diversionary impact; and community safety through rehabilitative surveillance and individual development.

Community safety means not only protection of the community from criminal acts, but contributions to the community by individual women who have received services to better the lives of themselves and their children. What kinds of programs can we create to move toward that goal? What social responses can we make to women who have offended, once we have an informed understanding of the lives behind the crimes? The development of individual program plans tailored to individual women, comprising treatment components responsive to their particular life-course characteristics, present the strongest model for intermediate sanctions for female offenders.

References

American Correctional Association. (1990). *The female offender: What does the future hold?* Laurel, MD: Author.

Baunach, P. J. (1982). You can't be a mother and be in prison . . . can you? Impacts of the mother-child separation. In B. R. Price & N. J. Sokoloff (Eds.), *The criminal justice system and women.* New York: Clark Boardman.

Baunach, P. J. (1985). *Mothers in prison.* New Brunswick, NJ: Transaction.

Braga, A. (1991, March). *The availability and effectiveness of intermediate sanctions: A reexamination.* Paper presented at the annual meetings of the Academy of Criminal Justice Sciences, Nashville.

Browne, A. (1987). *When battered women kill.* New York: Free Press.

Byrne, J. M. (1990, March). *Assessing what works in the adult community corrections system.* Paper presented at the annual meetings of the Academy of Criminal Justice Sciences, Denver.

Byrne, J. M., Lurigio, A. J., & Baird, S. C. (1989). *The effectiveness of the new intensive supervision programs* (Research in Corrections, No. 5). Washington, DC: National Institute of Corrections.

Chesney-Lind, M., & Rodriguez, N. (1985). Women under lock and key: A view from the inside. *Prison Journal, 63*(2), 47-65.

Clear, T. R., & Cole, G. F. (1990). *American corrections.* Pacific Grove, CA: Brooks/Cole.

Clear, T. R., & O'Leary, V. (1983). *Controlling the offender in the community: Reforming the community-supervision function.* Lexington, MA: D. C. Heath.

Daly, K., & Chesney-Lind, M. (1988). Feminism and criminology. *Justice Quarterly, 5,* 497-538.

Datesman, S. K., & Cales, G. L. (1983). "I'm still the same mommy": Maintaining the mother/child relationship in prison. *Prison Journal, 63*(2).

Elder, G. (1985). *Life course dynamics.* Ithaca, NY: Cornell University Press.

Erez, E. (1989). Gender, rehabilitation, and probation decisions. *Criminology, 27,* 307-327.

Federal Bureau of Investigation. (1989). *Crime in the United States, 1988.* Washington, DC: Government Printing Office.

Figueira-McDonough, J., Inglehart, A., Sarri, R., & Williams, T. (1981). *Females in prison in Michigan, 1968-1978.* Ann Arbor: University of Michigan, Institute for Social Research.

Finkelhor, D., & Browne, A. (1986). Initial and long-term effects: A conceptual framework. In D. Finkelhor (Ed.), *A sourcebook on child sexual abuse.* Beverly Hills, CA: Sage.

Gilfus, M. E. (1987). *Seasoned by violence, tempered by love: A qualitative study of women and crime.* Unpublished doctoral dissertation, Brandeis University.

Goetting, A., & Howsen, R. M. (1983). Women in prison: A profile. *Prison Journal, 63*(2).

Hagan, J., & Palloni, A. (1988). Crimes as social events in the life course: Reconceiving a criminological controversy. *Criminology, 26,* 87-100.

Harris, A. R. (1977). Sex and theories of deviance: Toward a functional theory of deviant type-scripts. *American Sociological Review, 42,* 3-16.

Hill, G. D., & Suval, E. M. (1988). *Women, race and crime.* Paper presented at the annual meetings of the American Society of Criminology, Chicago.

Immarigeon, R. (1987). Few diversion programs are offered female offenders. *Journal of the National Prison Project, 12,* 9-11.

James, J. (1976). Motivations for entrance into prostitution. In L. Crites (Ed.), *The female offender.* Lexington, MA: Lexington.

James, J., & Myerding, J. (1977). Early sexual experiences as a factor in prostitution. *Archives of Sexual Behavior, 7*(1), 31-41.

Laub, J. H., & McDermott, M. J. (1985). An analysis of serious crime by young black women. *Criminology, 23,* 81-98.

McCarthy, N. (1988, February 21). Program of hope is starved for funds. *Oregonian,* p. B3.

McGowan, B. G., & Blumenthal, K. L. (1976). Children of women prisoners: A forgotten minority. In L. Crites (Ed.), *The female offender.* Lexington, MA: Lexington.

Miller, E. M. (1986). *Street woman.* Philadelphia: Temple University Press.

Neto, V. V., & Bainer, L. M. (1983). Mother and wife locked up: A day with the family. *Prison Journal, 63*(2).

Our New Beginnings, Inc. (1988). [Program description and information materials]. Portland, OR: Author.

Simpson, S. S. (1989). Feminist theory, crime, and justice. *Criminology, 27,* 605-631.

Simpson, S. S. (1991). Caste, class, and violent crime: Explaining differences in female offending. *Criminology, 29,* 115-135.

U.S. Department of Justice. (1990). *Sourcebook of criminal justice statistics 1989.* Washington, DC: Government Printing Office.

U.S. General Accounting Office. (1990). *Intermediate sanctions: Their impacts on prison crowding, costs, and recidivism are still unclear.* Washington, DC: Government Printing Office.

17. The Development of Intermediate Punishments at the Federal Level

Jody Klein-Saffran

Crisis in Corrections and the Pressure for Alternatives

Federal corrections continues to face unprecedented growth in inmate population. Between September 1981 and September 1990, the federal prison population virtually doubled in size—from about 26,000 to about 58,000. There are various reasons for this dramatic increase, primarily related to changing trends in the conviction population, sentencing structure, and public policy.[1] This chapter explores the development of intermediate punishments and their impact on the federal criminal justice system as the system strives to manage the growing number of convicts without jeopardizing public safety.

During the last decade, the number of criminal cases filed in U.S. district courts has increased by more than 56%. This trend, in large part, reflects the number of drug cases filed and drug defendants sentenced. Between 1980 and 1990, the number of drug cases filed increased by 302%—from 3,127 to 12,592 cases (Judicial Conference of the United States, 1989). This increase is due mainly to the trend in recent legislation, which, in addition to making sentencing changes, authorized additional criminal justice resources specifically related to drug crime interdiction and prosecution (e.g., the Comprehensive Crime Control Act of 1984; the Anti-Drug Abuse Act of 1986; the

AUTHOR'S NOTE: Opinions expressed here are my own, and do not necessarily reflect the policies or procedures of the Federal Bureau of Prisons. I would like to thank James Byrne, Gerry Gaes, and Judy Gordon.

Anti-Drug Abuse Act of 1988, section 1005[c]; and the White House's "National Drug Control Strategy" of September 1989).

Changes in sentencing structure have affected the amount of time an offender must serve in prison for particular offenses. For example, a comparison of the average time served for drug offenders sentenced prior and subsequent to implementation of both the Comprehensive Crime Control Act of 1984 and the Anti-Drug Abuse Act of 1986 shows a 170% increase in expected length of stay, from 18.3 months to 49.4 months (Federal Bureau of Prisons, Office of Research and Evaluation, 1989). In addition, the Anti-Drug Abuse Acts of 1986 and 1988 require mandatory minimum federal sentences for specific drug offenses. Independent of the anti-drug abuse legislation, sentencing guidelines promulgated by the U.S. Sentencing Commission (1989) reduced the use of straight probation, resulting in more commitments and further affecting the growth in the federal prison population.

One way to measure prison crowding involves the examination of the average daily population versus the rated capacity. The Federal Bureau of Prisons (1986a) bases rated capacity on available space in permanent housing, excluding hospital/infirmary, segregation, and administrative detention. Once computed, this rating can be compared with correctional standards. The average year-end population and rated capacity between 1981 and 1989 and the projected average daily federal prison population between 1990 and 1995 are presented in Table 17.1, which also includes the number of drug offenders in the prison population—a figure that has more than tripled in this period. The Bureau of Prisons projects that by 1995, 66% of federal inmates will be drug offenders (Federal Bureau of Prisons, Office of Research and Evaluation, 1989). Moreover, within the next six years, prison population projections estimate the federal inmate population will double, reaching heights of more than 100,000 (U.S. Sentencing Commission, 1989). If these projections are accurate, legislators and administrators must act now or face even more serious crowding problems in the near future.

Assessing Options

One response to the expanding prison population is to build more prisons. However, even if such construction were completed in a timely manner, it would not eliminate crowding, but would simply lower the crowding rate (U.S. General Accounting Office, 1989). Thus, even if prisons could be built quickly enough in response to

TABLE 17.1 Prison Population, Capacity, and Projections 1985-1995

Year	Prison Population[a]	Capacity[b]	% Crowded	Drug Offenders[c]	% Drugs
1981	26,195	23,648	11	5,527	21
1982	28,079	24,072	17	5,871	21
1983	30,115	23,936	26	7,671	25
1984	32,238	24,874	30	8,307	26
1985	35,959	25,638	41	9,482	26
1986	41,444	27,785	49	12,036	38
1987	44,285	27,614	59	14,354	42
1988	44,295	30,748	57	15,473	45
1989	51,152	31,727	61	19,615	50

Low Growth Projections

Year	Projections[d]	Capacity[e]	% Crowded	Drug Offenders	% Drugs
1990	56,400	35,574	59	30,800	53
1991	62,450	39,789	57	38,400	58
1992	69,500	47,932	45	45,400	62
1993	77,000	56,424	36	51,900	65
1994	85,600	71,664	19	57,600	67
1995	95,100	75,144	27	62,400	66

NOTES: a. Based on total federal prison population at fiscal year end.
b. Based on year-end rated capacity.
c. Figures for 1981-1986 are from Federal Bureau of Prisons (1986b); for 1987-1989, from the Key Indicators Strategic Support System data base; and for the 1990-1995 low growth projections, from Federal Bureau of Prisons, Office of Research and Evaluation (1989).
d. Projections as reported in Federal Bureau of Prisons (1991), based on average daily population projections.
e. Projections for 1992 to 1995 are based on planned changes to rated capacity as reported in Federal Bureau of Prisons (1991).

the rising prison population, there would be a host of other problems affecting prison operations, including a lack of trained correctional staff, limited recreation and training space for institutional programs, and exorbitant operating costs that would exceed the initial building costs (U.S. General Accounting Office, 1989).

Another strategy for coping with crowded prisons has been the development of intermediate punishments. These sanctions provide a host of punishments that can range in severity from restitution to residential community corrections centers, with a variety of options in between (e.g., fines, community service, intensive probation supervision, house arrest, electronic monitoring, and intermittent confinement). The intent of intermediate punishment is to provide judges with an entire range of meaningful sanctions rather than just a bifurcated prison/no prison option. Morris and Tonry (1990) argue that a comprehensive sentencing system should include the interchange-ability of sentences, thereby authorizing choices among equivalent incarcerative and nonincarcerative punishments for certain types of offenders. According to Morris and Tonry, community-based pun-ishments would fill the void between ordinary probation and incar-ceration. In the last few years, there have been several forms of intermediate, community-based punishments available to federal judges that may be less costly than prison and that afford public protection. Some correctional professionals believe that the public can be better protected via closer community supervision of offend-ers (Baer, 1987; Nidorf, 1988). And by maximizing the number of individuals being supervised in the community, prison bed space can be saved for more serious offenders.

Prior to the enactment of the current federal sentencing guidelines, intermediate punishments were used by federal judges in certain cases to divert convicted individuals from incarceration. This prac-tice is frequently referred to as a "front-door" approach because it happens at the start of an individual's sentence. Intermediate punish-ment is also used at the last portion, or "back door," of an individual's sentence. For example, a prisoner might serve the last two to six months of his or her sentence in the community under some form of community-based corrections, which could include home confine-ment, community corrections centers (halfway houses), or intensive supervision. However, due to federal mandatory minimum sentenc-ing laws and the limited use of intermediate punishments in the current sentencing guidelines, many of these punishments are no longer available for use, even for nonviolent offenders. As a result, there is a movement among correctional professionals to establish credible, punitive nonprison sentences that can substitute for or supplement more traditional sanctions. By doing so, and by educat-ing the public on these punishments, these individuals hope to facilitate changes in the guidelines to make intermediate punish-ments more available as a sentencing option (Committee on Com-munity Corrections, 1988).

The Role of Intermediate Sanctions in the Federal Sentencing Guidelines

The Sentencing Reform Act is included in Chapter II of the Com-prehensive Crime Control Act of 1984. The sentencing act established the U.S. Sentencing Commission as an independent agency in the judicial branch; its primary purpose is to promulgate sentencing guidelines for the federal criminal justice system (Hutchinson & Yeller, 1989). This legislation has a direct and profound impact on the use of intermediate sanctions in federal sentencing because judges' sentencing options depend on the parameters established by these guidelines.

In October 1985, President Reagan appointed seven people to serve full-time as the first commissioners on the U.S. Sentencing Commission (Nagel, 1990). The 1984 legislation instructed the U.S. Sentencing Commission to create categories of offense behavior, offender characteristics, and guideline ranges that specify an appropriate sentence for each convicted offender. According to the Sentencing Commission (1989), "The Comprehensive Crime Control Act of 1984 foresees guidelines that will further the basic purposes of criminal punishment, i.e., deterring crime, incapacitating the offender, providing just punishment, and rehabilitating the offender" (p. 1.1). When Congress enacted the sentencing law, it sought to achieve "truth in sentencing" to attack problems of disparity, dishonesty, and "unwarranted" discretion (Nagel, 1990). Hence three objectives—honesty, uniformity, and proportionality—provide the underlying rationale for the guidelines. The guidelines are intended to aid federal judges in sentencing federal offenders nationwide to comparable punishments (Nagel, 1990) for committing similar offenses. In 18 U.S.C. sec. 3551, Congress identified three modes of sanctions that could be used for an individual found guilty of an offense: probation, fines, and imprisonment. In some cases the court may impose, as an addition to the sentence, a sanction of a fine, forfeiture, or restitution.

In determining sentencing ranges, the Sentencing Commission based its decisions on examinations of average sentences that had been served by offenders prior to the guidelines for each offense category and of specified sentences for particular crimes as contained in federal statutes, parole guidelines, and other relevant sources (Hutchinson & Yeller, 1989). Table 17.2 depicts the sentencing matrix established by the Sentencing Commission, which represents 43 offense levels and 6 criminal history categories. Each level overlaps the preceding and succeeding levels and categories so that if the court is unsure of a particular offense level or category, one level change will not necessarily make a difference in the sentence that a judge imposes (Hutchinson & Yeller, 1989). The vertical axis represents the offense level, otherwise known as the severity of the offense

TABLE 17.2 Sentencing Table (in months of imprisonment) Criminal History Category (Criminal History Points)

Offense Level	I (0 or 1)	II (2 or 3)	III (4, 5, 6)	IV (7, 8, 9)	V (10, 11, 12)	VI (13 or more)
1	0-6	0-6	0-6	0-6	0-6	0-6
2	0-6	0-6	0-6	0-6	0-6	1-7
3	0-6	0-6	0-6	0-6	2-8	3-9
4	0-6	0-6	0-6	2-8	4-10	6-12
5	0-6	0-6	1-7	4-10	6-12	9-15
6	0-6	1-7	2-8	6-12	9-15	12-18
7	1-7	2-8	4-10	8-14	12-18	15-21
8	2-8	4-10	6-12	10-16	15-21	18-24
9	4-10	6-12	8-14	12-18	18-24	21-27
10	6-12	8-14	10-16	15-21	21-27	24-30
11	8-14	10-16	12-18	18-24	24-30	27-33
12	10-16	12-18	15-21	21-27	27-33	30-37
13	12-18	15-21	18-24	24-30	30-37	33-41
14	15-21	18-24	21-27	27-33	33-41	37-46
15	18-24	21-27	24-30	30-37	37-46	41-51
16	21-27	24-30	27-33	33-41	41-51	46-57
17	24-30	27-33	30-37	37-46	46-57	51-63
18	27-33	30-37	33-41	41-51	51-63	57-71
19	30-37	33-41	37-46	46-57	57-71	63-78
20	33-41	37-46	41-51	51-63	63-78	70-87
21	37-46	41-51	46-57	57-71	70-87	77-96
22	41-51	46-57	51-63	63-78	77-96	84-105
23	46-57	51-63	57-71	70-87	84-105	92-115
24	51-63	57-71	63-78	77-96	92-115	100-125
25	57-71	63-78	70-87	84-105	100-125	110-137
26	63-78	70-87	78-97	92-115	110-137	120-150
27	70-87	78-97	87-108	100-125	120-150	130-162
28	78-97	87-108	97-121	110-137	130-162	140-175
29	87-108	97-121	108-135	121-151	140-175	151-188
30	97-121	108-135	121-151	135-168	151-188	168-210
31	108-135	121-151	135-168	151-188	168-210	188-235
32	121-151	135-168	151-188	168-210	188-235	210-262
33	135-168	151-188	168-210	188-265	210-262	235-293
34	151-188	168-210	188-235	210-262	235-293	262-327
35	168-210	188-235	210-262	235-293	262-327	292-365
36	188-235	210-262	235-293	262-327	292-365	324-405
37	210-262	235-293	262-327	292-365	324-405	360-life
38	235-293	262-327	292-365	324-405	360-life	360-life
39	262-327	292-365	324-405	360-life	360-life	360-life
40	292-365	324-405	360-life	360-life	360-life	360-life
41	324-405	360-life	360-life	360-life	360-life	360-life
42	360-life	360-life	360-life	360-life	360-life	360-life
43	life	life	life	life	life	life

SOURCE: U.S. Sentencing Commission (1989).
NOTE: A = probation available (see 5B1.1[a][1])43; B = probation with conditions of confinement available (see 5B1.1[a][2]); C = new "split sentence" available (see 5C1.1[c][3],[d][2]);

behavior. There are 43 categories of offense severity designated. For each offense category the Sentencing Commission has weighted the offense behavior and arrived at an offense level. The horizontal axis represents the criminal history category, which is defined as the offender's record of past criminal conduct (U.S. Sentencing Commission, 1989, sec. 4.1). Specific factors included in the criminal history score, while not systematically researched, are "consistent with the extant empirical research assessing the correlates of recidivism and patterns of career criminal behavior" (sec. 4.1). A guideline range is provided for each combination of offense level and criminal history category.

By examining Table 17.2, one can assess the use of intermediate sanctions in the U.S. Sentencing Commission guidelines. For example, as presented in the table, when the minimum number of months equals zero, the sentencing court has a variety of sentencing options. The court can sentence the offender to probation, incarceration, community confinement, intermittent confinement, or home detention. In this category, community confinement, intermittent confinement, or home detention can be imposed in lieu of incarceration. In addition, if the offender is sentenced to probation, the judge can impose a variety of probation conditions in the form of community confinement, home detention, or intermittent confinement. However, the use of "exchange rates" (or interchangeability concepts) has yet to become part of the federal sentencing guidelines.

As the minimum number of months of imprisonment increases, sentencing options become more punitive. For example, if the minimum number of months of imprisonment ranges between 1 and 6, the court can impose a sentence of probation only in conjunction with a condition or combination of conditions requiring a period of community confinement, home detention, or intermittent confinement (U.S. Sentencing Commission, 1989).

Table 17.2 illustrates that with each offense level increment, the minimum number of months of confinement also increases. Furthermore, as the guidelines and months of imprisonment increase, the availability of sentencing options decreases. As shown in the sentencing grid, the offense levels marked off by C indicate that if the minimum number of imprisonment months ranges between 8 and 10, the court can impose a "split sentence." But the split sentence would consist of imprisonment for one-half of the minimum number of guideline months and supervised release with the condition of community confinement or home detention for the remaining portion of the sentence. For example, an offender who receives guidelines of

8-14 months must serve 4 months of that sentence incarcerated. After satisfying that part of the sentence, the offender would be able to complete the rest of the sentence through an alternative consisting of either community confinement or home detention as a condition of supervised release. In no case do the guidelines allow fines, restitution, or community service to be imposed in lieu of incarceration when the latter is mandated. Moreover, the guidelines treat fines, restitution, and community service as part of the sentence and not as independent sentences (U.S. Sentencing Commission, 1989).

As previously indicated, recent implementation of the sentencing guidelines, as well as other mandated sentencing legislation, has increased the penalties attached to certain offenses. These changes preclude the use of straight probation for many offenses that previously were subject to this form of punishment. In addition, both "front-door" and "back-door" uses of intermediate sanctions have been restricted. The use of intermediate sanctions for most nonviolent offenders is now limited, and the numbers of short-term commitments, intermittent confinements, and community confinements have increased, as has, consequently, the overall prison population.

The impact of the above-described guidelines on sentencing and corrections is difficult to assess, in large part because the guidelines themselves are constantly being reviewed and revised. Currently, an advisory committee is researching the available array of intermediate punishments. This advisory group was formed (in 1990) by a U.S. sentencing commissioner who will make recommendations to the full Sentencing Commission regarding the use of intermediate punishments in the guidelines. Until this process is completed, the form and content of intermediate sanction programs can be expected to vary both within and across the federal court system.

Field Tests of Various Intermediate Sanctions in the Federal System Interagency Efforts

Between 1986 and 1990, the Federal Bureau of Prisons, U.S. Parole Commission, and Federal Probation System initiated a number of pilot projects to test intermediate sanctions in lieu of incarceration or other community-based programs. Each agency had a specific role in the projects. For example, the Federal Bureau of Prisons screened the applicants, the U.S. Parole Commission advanced parole dates for the release of applicants, and the Federal Probation System provided community supervision. The pilot programs described below include a "reparative" work project, special curfew parole, and a community control project.

REPARATIVE WORK PROJECT

In cooperation with the Bureau of Prisons and the National Institute of Justice, the Parole Commission in March 1985 initiated an experimental program in which selected inmates had their parole dates advanced by up to 60 days if they volunteered to complete 400 hours of "reparative work" (Baer & Klein, 1987), which was defined as unpaid volunteer work for public agencies or nonprofit private agencies. The purpose of the project was to develop an alternative form of punishment that returns something of value to the community and, simultaneously, saves prison bed space.

During the first phase of the project, 100 inmates completed the required 400 hours of reparative work while residing in halfway houses in selected cities. These inmates performed 38,481 hours of unpaid reparative work that otherwise would have cost the participating agencies more than $168,000 to contract out. In return, release dates were advanced by a total of 5,538 days, representing a significant savings in prison bed space. The first phase of the project was ended in 1986; paradoxically, budgetary constraints required the Bureau of Prisons to curtail the amount of time offenders could stay in halfway houses.

SPECIAL CURFEW PAROLE

Over the last few years the Federal Bureau of Prisons has been faced with increasingly crowded prisons and limited space in its Community Correction Centers. To help ease the crowding and provide smooth transition into the community, the U.S. Parole Commission, with the assistance of the U.S. Probation System, implemented a program (in March 1986) that provides a substitute for Community Correction Center residence for the 60-day period preceding the otherwise scheduled parole release date. This program is designed for prisoners who would otherwise qualify for Community Correction Center residence, but who have acceptable release plans and do not require the support services provided by the Community Correction Center. Under this program, with the approval of a parole commissioner, selected inmates have their release dates advanced up to 60 days on the condition that they remain at their places of residence between curfew hours of 9 p.m. and 6 a.m.

Intensive supervision of the parolee during the special curfew parole period includes at least one weekly contact with the parolee as well as monitoring of this special condition by random telephone contacts. The Bureau of Prisons reports that the project has saved approximately $4 million since 1986 and has requested that the program be extended indefinitely. Approximately 4,000 offenders have participated in this program and very few problems have been reported. Less than 3% have been revoked for violations while on curfew parole and no serious offenses appear to have been committed during program participation (U.S. Parole Commission, 1988).

COMMUNITY CONTROL PROJECT

In January 1988, the Federal Bureau of Prisons, the U.S. Parole Commission, and the Federal Probation System initiated a pilot program in the Los Angeles and Miami areas to test the feasibility of confining offenders in their homes and monitoring their whereabouts electronically. The program, the Community Control Project, is generally restricted to releasees who have stable residences and reasonable employment prospects and who would otherwise be released to halfway houses to relieve prison crowding. Program participants are paroled directly into the community between 60 and 180 days prior to their previously scheduled release dates instead of being released through halfway houses. During this period of early release, offenders abide by a curfew monitored through electronic surveillance.

How effective is the program as a community control strategy? As of February 28, 1990, 358 parolees had been released on supervision with a special condition of home detention enforced through the use of electronic monitoring. Of these, 310 completed the program. The 48 individuals who failed to complete (13%) were returned to prison as the result of a revocation from supervision. This violation rate is comparable with that of other house arrest programs using electronic monitoring (see Baumer & Mendelsohn, 1988, as well as chap. 4, this volume; also see Jolin, 1987).

Several conclusions can be drawn from the pilot project at this point. First, by using electronic monitoring equipment it is possible to confine offenders in their residences with reasonable assurance that unauthorized absences from the home will be discovered immediately (Beck & Klein-Saffran, 1989). Second, electronic monitoring is very labor-intensive. In order to provide needed services, it appears that a caseload of no more than 25 parolees per officer is essential. Third, home confinement can be cost-effective. The Probation System has estimated the cost of home confinement to be approximately $15 per day, including equipment and all other supervision costs. (By comparison, placement in a halfway house costs about $35 per day.) Fourth, electronic monitors alone cannot enforce a viable home confinement program. Supervising agents need to have personal involvement with offenders to ensure compliance with parole conditions (Beck & Klein-Saffran, 1990).

Thus far, the results of this project are encouraging, and expansion of the project began in October 1990. Eligible inmates with release plans showing residence in the following areas may be considered for inclusion in the program: Atlanta, Georgia; Baltimore, Maryland; Brooklyn, New York; Cleveland, Ohio; Columbia, South Carolina; Dallas and Houston, Texas; Denver, Colorado; Detroit, Michigan; and Washington, D.C. An additional two areas (Nebraska and Idaho) will be included in the home confinement project without the use of the electronic monitoring.

Federal Probation Initiatives
in Intermediate Punishments

In the past, there have been a number of programs developed by probation departments to provide judges with alternative sentencing options. Today, many of these program initiatives are impeded by changing sentencing laws. As mentioned earlier, the sentencing guidelines have particularly affected the probation system at the lower range of the guidelines. At this range, the guidelines have made probation a sentence with very specific conditions. Because of the now limited allowable use of probation in felony offenses, many of the past initiatives are no longer viable options. Judges in many cases are no longer allowed to sentence federal offenders to alternatives in lieu of incarceration unless the offenders are within the lowest guideline range. Departure from the guidelines is made only under special circumstances and then the judge must give specific reasons for the departure. Three probation-based program initiatives that have been used prior to the implementation of the guidelines and have subsequently been modified to take into account current sentencing practices are discussed below: intensive supervision, home confinement, and community service.

INTENSIVE SUPERVISION

Federal probation classifies cases into high- or low-activity levels of supervision. The main purpose of this classification system is to allocate officers' time to offenders who are more likely to pose a risk in the community (Meierhoefer, 1988). Certain high-activity supervision cases, additionally, are deemed to be in need of intensive supervision, which involves closer oversight than high-activity cases. Intensive supervision is used as a management tool and involves smaller caseloads, stringent release conditions, and greater emphasis on surveillance and control (Petersilia, 1987; von Hirsch, Wasik, & Greene, 1989).

Several programs that fall under the rubric of intensive supervision have the following elements in common: team supervision, caseloads of no more than 25, high rate of poor-risk offenders, and substance abuse testing. Three federal probation programs that have made unique contributions as intensive supervision projects are described below.

Hyattsville Project

This program began in July 1988 as a cooperative study between the U.S. Probation Office for the District of Maryland and the U.S. Parole Commission. The program examines the feasibility of using a supervision team to provide more services and intensive supervision coverage than is typically possible with the resources available to the U.S. probation system. There are more personal contacts and home visits combined with assistance for the parolee as required. The program's stated goals are to deter misconduct through closer supervision and to aid the transition into the community through support services. If deterrence and assistance fail, misconduct is discovered more readily and sanctioned earlier due to the intensive level of supervision. Either way, public protection is enhanced.

The program includes only higher-risk cases, such as those with a history of drug abuse and extensive prior criminal behavior. As of the program's inception, 80 offenders entered the project. Out of the 80 participants, 34% (27) were revoked for technical violations and 11% (9) were revoked for new arrests (Michael Suser, U.S. probation officer, District of Maryland, personal communication, May 15, 1990). Some of the accomplishments of the intensive supervision project include increased surveillance activities, averaging 18 contacts per case per month, and increased assistance in support services, such as referrals to alcohol and drug treatment programs and counseling services. The probation officers assisted in job placement for about half of the parolees in the project. Of these poor parole risks, 55% remained incident free in the community as of October 1990. The program is being evaluated using a matched control group to assess program performance and rate of flow of offenders back into prison. It is hoped that replication of projects like this could reduce the number of offenders returning to prison.

Northern District of Ohio

Modeled after the District of Maryland's Hyattsville Project, an intensive supervision program was begun in the Northern District of Ohio's Cleveland, Akron, and Toledo offices. The objective of the intensive supervision program in this district is the strict enforcement of "high-risk" case supervision conditions. Officials in the district believe that strict enforcement of supervision will enhance public protection, and that either offenders will be discouraged from criminal conduct or any criminal conduct they do commit will be discovered immediately and acted upon.

To meet Northern Ohio's high-risk criterion, an offender placed on intensive supervision must have an extensive criminal record, be considered a poor risk according to the Parole Commission's salient factor score, or fall under the sentencing guidelines' criminal history category of V or VI (see Table 17.2). From its inception in August 1989 until May 1990, a total of 87 cases were placed in the program. An additional 70 cases were expected to be accepted by December 1990 (John Pete, U.S. probation officer, Northern District of Ohio, personal communication, May 7, 1990). Outcome data are not available at this point.

Southern District of Florida

In spring 1990, the Southern District of Florida initiated an intermediate sanction program within its intensive supervision unit. According to the district's 1990 program statement, there are two main purposes of the intensive supervision unit: to provide an immediate consequence for drug use and to provide intensive investigation to determine whether an offender who has illegally used drugs under supervision is involved in other violations. The new program will include every offender who has a positive EMIT test result for cocaine or a positive PharmChem confirmation for marijuana or any other drug. One positive drug test will result in transfer of supervision to this intensive supervision unit. Each participant will pass through various program phases, and each phase will provide graduated sanctions dependent upon the negative behavior exhibited. Thus the supervision planning process is tailored to fit each participant's life and the particular problems he or she experiences. The sanctions increase in severity as the negative behavior increases within a given phase of treatment. This sanction-based system allows the probation officer to revoke the supervised individual as a last resort, only after all other options are exhausted. According to program developers, consistent application of the sanction system allows the probation officer to build a case, which increases the likelihood of the court's not denying revocation in cases that warrant this action. In addition, the second goal, that of promoting positive behavior, is pursued by a system of rewards such as positive written and verbal reinforcement, reduced supervision, and permission to travel.

HOME CONFINEMENT

For the last few years, home confinement has been used as an intermediate sanction by the federal courts to sentence offenders in lieu of incarceration. It has been also been used as an early-release method by the U.S. Parole Commission since 1986 as part of the special curfew parole program. There are many types of home confinement programs, ranging from imposition of late-night curfew conditions to 24-hour continuous detention. Enforcement techniques vary as well, from random contacts by a supervising officer to continuous electronic monitoring (Hofer & Meierhoefer, 1987). The use of electronic monitoring devices to enforce home confinement conditions has grown rapidly due to crowded federal prisons and the technique's apparent cost-effectiveness. However, we still know very little about the actual effectiveness of these programs. Early descriptions of home confinement programs presented uncritical accounts of individual programs, and most of the early academic literature focused on ethical and constitutional issues (del Carmen & Vaughn, 1986). More recently, empirical studies have been undertaken that will facilitate an understanding of the theoretical and practical implications of such systems, enabling policymakers to make informed decisions based on research (see Baumer & Mendelsohn, chap. 4, this volume).

COMMUNITY SERVICE

Prior to the implementation of the U.S. Sentencing Guidelines, community service was a sanction used as an alternative to imprisonment. Since the 1960s, U.S. federal courts have often chosen to suspend sentences and impose special conditions of probation that include directing offenders to perform community service for public or nonprofit agencies (Maher & Dufour, 1987). In the past, community service orders have been used as an intermediate sanction, and many well-structured community service programs have focused on the offender's need for resocialization and on community protection.

Provisions of the Sentencing Reform Act encourage the use of community service and recognize that community service can serve many purposes of punishment (Administrative Office of the U.S. Courts, Division of Probation, 1988). The U.S. Sentencing Guidelines allow community service to be ordered as a condition of probation or supervised release. In addition, if the offender is convicted of a felony and sentenced to probation, the court must order one or more of the following sanctions: a fine, restitution, or community service (U.S. Sentencing Commission, 1989, sec. 5F1.3). Despite the U.S. Sentencing Commission's approval of using community service as an addition to probation or condition of supervised release, community service orders are not used in lieu of incarceration.

Many U.S. federal districts have experimented with the use of community service programs and have developed such programs based on strict discipline and public protection. In general, these programs have stringent requirements, and probation officers, offenders, and recipients of community service work together closely. Unfortunately, most of the programs have not been evaluated, and only a few programs have kept statistical records. One program that received extensive publicity is located in Atlanta, Georgia (Northern District of Georgia). In the early 1980s this district implemented its Community Service Order program. The program was fully implemented between 1985 and 1986, a time when the number of offenders sentenced to the program increased. According to the district's 1986 annual report, during 1986 the program coordinator made 118 placements into the program, resulting in 23,500 hours of supervised community service. By 1989, 469 placements were made and approximately 104,800 hours of community service performed. With the advent of the U.S. Sentencing Guidelines, the Northern District of Georgia's annual report showed a decrease in the number of program placements. This decrease had been anticipated, given that the guidelines reduced the court's opportunity to use community service work as an alternative to incarceration (Richard Maher, U.S. probation officer, Northern District of Georgia, personal communication, May 7, 1990).

Federal Bureau of Prisons Initiatives

In addition to the programs described to this point, the Federal Bureau of Prisons is currently expanding its institutional capacity by building new correctional facilities and expanding its community-based corrections programs. Two new types of community-based programs have been initiated: intensive confinement centers (or boot camps) and home confinement programs.

INTENSIVE CONFINEMENT CENTERS

Boot camp prisons are prison programs modeled after military boot camps (MacKenzie & Parent, 1990). These programs are designed to confine inmates for a short period of time in a highly regimented program of strict discipline, military drill and ceremony, and physical exercise. Boot camps, commonly known as "shock incarceration," are programs that often operate as separate entities within larger correctional institutions. It is intended that brief confinement in such programs will "shock" participants into an awareness of the harsh realities of prison life without subjecting them to long prison sentences (Karacki, 1989). An underlying program assumption is that physical exertion and military-style discipline will both improve the physical condition of offenders and instill order and discipline in their lives.

The Federal Bureau of Prisons' Intensive Confinement Center (ICC) at Lewisburg, Pennsylvania, began to accept participants in November 1990, and the first training cycle, involving 42 inmates, started on January 28, 1991. As of March 1992, 219 participants had graduated from the ICC.

The ICC is designed to incarcerate 192 adult male federal offenders. Like all Bureau of Prisons facilities, its mission is to maintain custody of inmates in an environment that is safe, secure, and humane. It offers a specialized program that involves a highly structured environment consisting of a daily regimen of vocational training, life skills training programs essential to a successful postrelease return to mainstream community life, and substance abuse counseling. Each training cycle lasts 180 days. Participation is voluntary, and the incentive for inmates who successfully complete the program is the opportunity to serve the remainder of their sentences, a portion greater than otherwise would be possible, in a community-based program.

HOME CONFINEMENT AND ELECTRONIC MONITORING

Home confinement is another community corrections option that can be used effectively to sanction nonviolent offenders. By allowing offenders to leave home only to work, the court can require them to support their families, pay restitution, and even pay the costs of their own supervision (Federal Bureau of Prisons, 1989). Home confinement programs are often combined with electronic monitoring as a supervision tool. In these programs, offenders are required to wear electronic devices that monitor their presence in particular locations. As of late 1990, home confinement and electronic monitoring programs had expanded to include 14 federal judicial districts, and plans for systemwide expansion were under way.

Future Directions in Intermediate Punishments at the Federal Level

While the demand for prison cells is increasing, the available resources to house these offenders are limited. Therefore, politicians, corrections administrators, researchers, and the general public are becoming more attracted to less expensive intermediate punishments for nonviolent offenders. In response to this demand, more programs offering punishment and control within community settings are emerging as intermediate sanctioning alternatives throughout the country, and we can expect to see these program initiatives flourish during the 1990s. Many of these new intermediate punishment programs may somewhat resemble the "alternatives to incarceration" that emerged during the 1970s, but they differ fundamentally in ideology. The fundamental aims of current intermediate sanction programs are punishment, control, and public safety, while earlier initiatives were based on individual offender rehabilitation and treatment. This distinction is important. Another difference between current efforts and earlier ones is technological. Advances in technology have provided corrections officials with new ways to monitor some offenders effectively without restricting them to institutional settings.

If these program initiatives are to make a difference in the 1990s, it is important that the field of corrections continues to develop a "total systems" approach to the "crisis" it is experiencing. Interagency cooperation with regard to these programs has been facilitated due to limited resources and other problems facing the corrections system, and continued cooperation is needed for these programs to be effective. No agency can or should work alone to solve the "crisis in corrections."

Furthermore, evaluation of these new initiatives must be an integral component of their operations. The federal corrections system has developed many new intermediate punishment initiatives that have provided valuable information for future program efforts. We know, for example, that by using electronic monitoring equipment it is possible to confine offenders in their residences with reasonable assurance that unauthorized absences from the home will be discovered quickly. Thus far, it also appears that recidivism has been low for intensive probation supervision programs (Petersilia & Turner, 1990). These results suggest that programs can control high-risk offenders effectively in the community without jeopardizing public safety. However, many programs lack measurable outcomes because of poor record keeping and the fact that evaluation components were not included during program development. Without continued research and evaluation, program success cannot be measured adequately.

Finally, intermediate punishments cannot be developed merely as a response to prison crowding and political policy. Instead, such programs must also reflect the primary functions of corrections, such as fairness, risk management, and accountability and justification for the use of punishment. These programs and initiatives need to grow with a clear underlying sense of purpose. Without clear articulation of policies regarding punishment, control, treatment, and use of resources, new programs will not be effective (Byrne, Lurigio, & Baird, 1989). The knowledge and available resources in the federal corrections system today, combined with the system's need to pursue strategies for coping with its growing population, make it a natural laboratory in the effort to develop intermediate sanction programs that embody these fundamental values and goals. It is time now to evaluate these federal initiatives systematically, and to determine what works and with whom. The results of this evaluation effort could then be used to expand the sentencing options available under the current federal sentencing guidelines.

Note

1. For a more complete review, see the reports recently released by the U.S. General Accounting Office (1989, 1990) on prison crowding and intermediate sanctions.

References

Administrative Office of the U.S. Courts, Division of Probation. (1988, October). *Community service: A guide for sentencing and implementation* (Publication No. 108).

Anti-Drug Abuse Act of 1986. (P.L. No. 99-570, 100 Stat. 3207).

Anti-Drug Abuse Act of 1988. (P.L. No. 100-690, 102 Stat. 4181).

Baer, B. F. (1987, Winter). Abolish parole? *Perspectives, 11,* 24-25.

Baer, B. F., & Klein, J. R. (1987). Reparative work programs benefit communities and offenders. *Corrections Today, 49*(7), 84-86.

Baumer, T., & Mendelsohn, R. (1988). *Correctional goals and home detention: A preliminary empirical assessment.* Paper presented at the annual meeting of the American Society of Criminology.

Beck, J. L., & Klein-Saffran, J. (1989). *Community control project* (Research Unit Report No. 44). Chevy Chase, MD: U.S. Parole Commission.

Beck, J. L., & Klein-Saffran, J. (1990). *Home confinement and the use of electronic monitoring: A federal pilot project.* Unpublished draft report.

Byrne, J. M., Lurigio, A. J., & Baird, S. C. (1989). *The effectiveness of the new intensive supervision programs* (Research in Corrections, No. 5). Washington, DC: National Institute of Corrections.

Committee on Community Corrections. (1988, June). *Charter.* Unpublished manuscript.

Comprehensive Crime Control Act of 1984. (P.L. No. 98-473, 98 Stat. 1837, title II).

del Carmen, R. V., & Vaughn, J. (1986, June). Legal issues in the use of electronic surveillance in probation. *Federal Probation, 50,* 60-69.

Federal Bureau of Prisons. (1986a). *Program statement 1061.7.* Washington, DC: Author.

Federal Bureau of Prisons. (1986b). *Statistical report fiscal year 1986.* Washington, DC: Author.

Federal Bureau of Prisons. (1989). *State of the bureau.* Washington, DC: Author.

Federal Bureau of Prisons. (1991). *Budget and finance report to Congress.* Washington, DC: Author.

Federal Bureau of Prisons, Office of Research and Evaluation. (1989, May). *Projecting the Bureau of Prisons population through 1995.* Washington, DC: Author.

Hofer, P., & Meierhoefer, B. (1987). *Home confinement: An evolving sanction in the federal criminal justice system.* Washington, DC: Federal Judicial Center.

Hutchinson, T., & Yeller, D. (1989). *Federal sentencing law and practice.* Saint Paul, MN: West.

Jolin, A. (1987). *Electronic surveillance program: Clackamas County Community Corrections Oregon evaluation.* Oregon City: Clackamas County Community Corrections.

Judicial Conference of the United States. (1989). *Impact of drug related criminal activity on the federal judiciary.* Unpublished report to the U.S. Congress.

Karacki, L. (1989). *Shock incarceration: An alternative for first offenders.* Washington, DC: Federal Bureau of Prisons, Office of Research and Evaluation.

MacKenzie, D. L., & Parent, D. (1990). *Shock incarceration and prison crowding in Louisiana.* Unpublished draft report.

Maher, R., & Dufour, H. (1987, September). Experimenting with community service: A punitive alternative to imprisonment. *Federal Probation, 51,* 22-27.

Meierhoefer, B. S. (1988). *Community supervision of federal offenders.* Unpublished report, U.S. Probation System.

Morris, N., & Tonry, M. (1990). *Between prison and probation: Intermediate punishments in a rational sentencing system.* New York: Oxford University Press.

Nagel, I. (1990). Structuring sentencing discretion: The new federal sentencing guidelines. *Journal of Criminal Law and Criminology, 80,* 883-943.

Nidorf, B. (1988). Sanction-oriented community corrections: Sale job? sellout? or response to reality? *Perspectives, 12,* 6-8.

Petersilia, J. (1987). *Expanding options for criminal sentencing* (Publication No. R-3544-EMC). Santa Monica, CA: RAND Corporation.

Petersilia, J., & Turner, S. (1990), Comparing intensive and regular supervision for high-risk probationers: Early results from an experiment in California. *Crime and Delinquency, 36,* 87-111.

U.S. General Accounting Office. (1989, November). *Prison crowding: Issues facing the nation's prison systems.* Washington, DC: Government Printing Office.

U.S. General Accounting Office. (1990, September). *Intermediate sanctions: Their impacts on prison crowding, costs, and recidivism are still unclear.* Washington, DC: Government Printing Office.

U.S. Parole Commission. (1988). *Curfew parole evaluation.* Washington, DC: U.S. Parole Commission, Research Unit.

U.S. Sentencing Commission. (1989, November). *Guidelines manual.* Washington, DC: Author.

von Hirsch, A., Wasik, M., & Greene, J. (1989). Punishments in the community and the principles of desert. *Rutgers Law Journal, 20,* 595-618.

18. The Effectiveness Issue: Assessing What Works in the Adult Community Corrections System

James M. Byrne

April Pattavina

Do We Have Time to Find Out What Works?

Let us begin by stating the obvious: We have serious crowding problems in both the institutional and community corrections systems in the United States. Jankowski (1991) recently reported that the adult correctional population in this country "reached a new high of over 4.3 million [in 1990], an increase of about 7% since 1989 and 44% since 1985" (p. 1). The correctional system has not expanded quickly enough to absorb this influx of offenders, leading to unprecedented levels of crowding both in our institutions and in our community corrections programs. As a short-term response to the crowding problem, federal, state, and local decision makers have attempted to develop a range of new, surveillance-oriented intermediate sanctions, with names such as intensive supervision, shock incarceration, and house arrest. The question we raise here is simple: Do these new intermediate sanctions "work," in terms of cost-effectiveness, diversionary impact, and recidivism reduction? To answer this question, we have reviewed all the available evaluation research on this new wave of intermediate sanctions.

AUTHORS' NOTE: We would like to thank Anthony Braga, Rutgers University, and Tara Denno, University of Massachusetts at Lowell, for their assistance in the compilation of the program review and evaluation summary data included in this chapter.

There are some who argue (a) that the search for *effective* community-based sanctions is a waste of time and (b) that we should simply continue to expand the *current* array of "get tough" intermediate sentencing options available to judges across the country (see, e.g., Conrad, 1991). The assumption seems to be that although *academics* continue to criticize the quality of evaluation research in community corrections, policymakers and program managers already know which programs are effective and the real issues are how, when, and where to expand these programs. While it is difficult to disagree with the notion that the correctional crowding problem demands immediate attention, the danger in this approach is that we may be moving the community corrections system in the wrong direction (i.e., toward surveillance and away from treatment) for the wrong reasons (i.e., to ease crowding, rather than to reduce recidivism).

In this chapter, we provide a review of the available research on the effectiveness of both traditional probation supervision and the new wave of surveillance-oriented intermediate sanctions, such as intensive probation supervision (IPS), house arrest, electronic monitoring (EM), and shock incarceration. Since the majority of recent evaluations have examined IPS programs, only cursory summaries of the research literature in the other areas are provided. Focusing on IPS evaluation research, four questions are addressed:

(1) Are IPS programs cost-effective?
(2) Do IPS programs divert offenders from prison and jail?
(3) Do IPS programs protect the community (i.e., reduce recidivism)?
(4) Which specific elements of IPS programs have the greatest impact on adult offenders (in terms of recidivism reduction)?

The answers to these questions, when viewed in conjunction with the assessments of research on other intermediate sanctions, suggest that the successful community corrections programs of the 1990s will bear little resemblance to their surveillance-oriented 1980s counterparts.

Data and Method

In the spring of 1989, the Program Evaluation and Methodology Division of the U.S. General Accounting Office (GAO) conducted a survey of state correctional administrators, requesting recent program descriptions and evaluation reports for a range of intermediate sanctions programs.[1] As a consultant for GAO, the first author initially reviewed these materials in the summer and fall of 1989. In addition to the materials collected in the 1989 GAO survey, we have reviewed the published evaluation research on this subject, as well as the research reviews on intensive supervision (Byrne, 1990a; Byrne, Lurigio, & Baird, 1989; Morris & Tonry, 1990); house arrest, with and without electronic monitoring (Petersilia, 1987; Tonry & Will, 1988); shock incarceration (Parent, 1989; U.S. General Accounting Office, 1988; see also MacKenzie & Parent, chap. 7, this volume); fines (Cole, chap. 9, this volume); and residential community corrections (Byrne & Kelly, 1989; Latessa & Travis, chap. 11, this volume). We should emphasize that the following review is based on our own summary and assessment of these materials; it does not reflect the position of the U.S. General Accounting Office on the effectiveness of these sanctions.[2]

THE EFFECTIVENESS OF TRADITIONAL PROBATION

There were 2,670,234 adult offenders on probation at the end of 1990, a 6% increase over the previous year. Despite the "get tough" rhetoric of the 1980s, probation continues to be the sanction of choice in the United States. But does it work as an offender control strategy? Ted Guest offered the dominant perspective on probation effectiveness in the February 1990 issue of *U.S. News & World Report*:

> As the gap between prison space and inmate population widens, a massive class of criminals—roughly 1 in 75 adult Americans—is now being handled outside the walls under "supervision." In principle, they are being monitored by authorities. In practice, that is a farce. Most roam the streets with impunity, many committing new crimes or violating release conditions. (pp. 23-24)

The problem with this view of probation effectiveness is that it is simply incorrect. The vast majority (more than 80% nationwide) of the offenders placed on probation complete their terms successfully, with no new criminal arrests or convictions. Indeed, a strong argument can be presented in favor of developing *nonsupervision* alternatives (e.g., day fines) for many of these offenders (see Byrne, 1990b; von Hirsch, Wasik, & Greene, 1989). Apart from the fact that we place *too many* people on probation, it is difficult to argue against the overall effectiveness of traditional probation supervision. This basic point has been ignored by many intermediate sanction advocates, who invariably begin their appeal for these "new" sanctions with a quick dismissal of current probation practices.

Of course, any overall assessment of effectiveness can at times be misleading. Despite the general success of probation in terms of offender control, there is certainly a subgroup of offenders who will commit many new crimes while on probation (see Petersilia, Turner, Kahan, & Peterson, 1985). As a result, probation administrators across the country have developed risk classification strategies to identify offenders who have characteristics (e.g., extensive priors, drug dependency, unemployment, family problems) that would make them "high risks" to recidivate. The assumption is that, given limited resources and large caseloads, it is this subgroup of offenders that should be most closely supervised. Byrne and Kelly (1989) estimated that about 10% of the offenders under probation supervision in the United States fell into this high-risk category, and that approximately 6 of 10 high-risk offenders would be rearraigned within one year of the date their probation began. More recently, Langan and Cunniff (1992) completed the most comprehensive survey of *felony* probationers conducted to date in the United States. A sample of 79,000 felons placed on probation in 32 counties across 17 states was identified, representing about one-fourth of the 1986 felony probationer population ($N = 306,000$). Approximately 10% of these probationers were classified and supervised as high-risk, intensive supervision cases. Within three years, 56% of these felons were *rearrested* on felony charges (compared with an overall failure rate of 43%, using felony arrest as the criterion). "High-risk" felons were more likely than other felony probationers to have had prior felony convictions (39% versus 26%) and to have drug abuse problems (75% versus 53%). It seems safe to say that traditional probation supervision does not work very well with such offenders, but it is not clear *why* this is the case. Is it simply a question of inadequate resources? Or do we need to rethink our supervision strategy for this subgroup of offenders? Unfortunately, probation researchers have all but ignored these fundamental questions (see Gottfredson & Gottfredson, 1988).

THE CURRENT AVAILABILITY OF INTERMEDIATE SANCTIONS

Table 18.1 presents an overview of the availability, as of spring 1989, of intermediate sanctions for adult offenders in the United States (aggregated by state, with Washington, D.C.). At that time, 40 states and Washington, D.C., had IPS programs in place, and 26 states, and Washington, D.C., operated separate house arrest programs

TABLE 18.1 An Overview of the Current Availability of Intermediate Sanctions for Adult Offenders

State	IPS	House Arrest	Electronic Monitoring	Shock Incarceration/ Split Sentencing	Other Sanction?
Alaska	x	—	—	—	—
Alabama	x	x	x	x	C
Arkansas	x	x	x	—	—
Arizona	x	—	—	x	D
California	x	x	x	—	—
Colorado	x	x	—	—	—
Connecticut	x	x	x	x	A,D
Delaware	x	x	x	—	—
Florida	x	x	x	x	—
Georgia	x	x	x	x	A
Hawaii	x	x	x	—	—
Idaho	x	x	—	—	—
		(awaiting approval)			
Illinois	x	x	—	—	—
Indiana	—	x	x	—	—
Iowa	x	—	—	—	—
Kansas	x	x	x	—	E
Kentucky	x	x	x	x	—
Louisiana	x	x	—	x	F
Maine	x	—	—	x (split)	—
Maryland	x	x	x	—	—
Massachusetts	—	—	—	—	D
Michigan	—	x	x	x	—
Minnesota	—	—	—	—	D
Mississippi	x	x	—	x	—
Missouri	x	x	x	x	—
Montana	x	x	x	—	—
Nebraska	x	—	x	—	—
Nevada	—	—	—	—	—
New Hampshire	x	x	x	—	—
New Jersey	x	—	—	—	—
New Mexico	x	x	x	—	—
New York	x	—	—	x	—
North Carolina	x	—	—	—	—
North Dakota	—	—	—	—	—
Ohio	x	—	—	—	—
Oklahoma	—	x	x	x	—
Oregon	x	x	x	—	—
Pennsylvania	—	—	—	—	—
Rhode Island	—	—	—	—	—
South Carolina	x	—	—	x	—

continued

TABLE 18.1 Continued

State	IPS	House Arrest	Electronic Monitoring	Shock Incarceration/ Split Sentencing	Other Sanction?
South Dakota	x	—	—	—	—
Tennessee	x	—	—	—	—
Texas	x	x	x	x	—
Utah	x	—	—	—	—
Vermont	—	—	—	—	—
Virginia	x	—	—	—	—
Washington	x	—	—	x	—
West Virginia	x	x	x	—	—
Wisconsin	x	—	—	—	—
Wyoming	x	x	x	—	—
Washington, D.C.	x	x	x	x	A,B
Total number of states	41	27	24	16	
%	80	55	47	31	

NOTE: These figures are based on a GAO survey of intermediate sanctions conducted by the Program Evaluation and Methodology Division in the spring of 1989. A distinction has been made between house arrest programs generally and the subset of house arrest programs with EM components. Other forms of intermediate sanctions (including community service, restitution, and fines) are also available in many jurisdictions. With the exception of Florida's Community Control program, all IPS programs use the title "intensive supervision." In this table, a dash indicates that no program is currently in place. A = community work/service program; B = weekend sentence; C = supervised intensive restitution; D = day reporting centers now being developed; E = residential community corrections; F = community rehabilitation center.

(with and without electronic monitoring components). Of these states, 23 (plus Washington, D.C.) had house arrest programs *with* EM components. Shock incarceration and/or split sentencing could be found in 16 states, while some other form of intermediate sanction (e.g., day reporting centers, community rehabilitation centers, supervised intensive restitution) was identified by corrections administrators in 10 states. Obviously, intermediate sanctions represent one of the major "growth areas" in the field of corrections, but it is important to keep in mind that only a small proportion (less than 5%) of all convicted offenders will be placed in one of these programs in a given year. According to Jankowski (1991), there were 55,000 offenders on intensive supervision (and 7,000 under electronic monitoring) in 1990, representing about 2% of the 1990 adult probation population.

THE CHARACTERISTICS OF IPS PROGRAMS

The most detailed program model descriptions were provided for IPS programs. Tables 18.2 and 18.3 provide state-by-state breakdowns of their key components. As can be seen, there is considerable interstate variation in the design of IPS programs. Moreover, the overlap among/between sanctions is apparent: 82% of the IPS programs included a curfew/house arrest component, 56% had an EM component, and 32% utilized a period of shock incarceration.[3] It should be clear by this point that any overall assessment of the effectiveness of this new wave of intensive supervision programs must take into consideration not only the types of offenders placed in the program (and the types of probation officers providing supervision), but also the variation in key program features highlighted here.

To most observers, *intensive supervision* connotes close contact between the offender and his or her probation officer. But what does *close* actually mean? The answer to this question varies from state to state, and sometimes within states as well. Our examination of minimum monthly contact levels revealed that the *intensity* of supervision provided by IPS programs was not uniform (see Figure 18.1). For example, six states developed IPS programs that required probation officers to contact offenders *25 or more times* per month, while three states developed IPS programs with minimum contact standards of one contact (or less) per week. The *types* of contacts required (face-to-face, collateral, curfew checks, and so on) also varied from program to program. Despite these interstate variations, it is obvious that increased levels of surveillance are an important element of most IPS programs in this country. The question is, Can this emphasis on surveillance be justified as an effective strategy of offender control?

EFFECTIVENESS OF INTENSIVE PROBATION SUPERVISION

Only 18 of 41 states with IPS programs provided any form of evaluation data to the General Accounting Office.[4] Of these 18 evaluations, 14 included an assessment of recidivism, 9 measured cost-effectiveness, and 9 examined diversionary impact (see Table 18.4). Before we review these evaluations, it is important to assess the extent to which this subgroup of evaluated programs is comparable to the entire population of IPS programs. We found that the *evaluated* IPS programs were less likely to include curfew/house arrest

TABLE 18.2 Interstate Comparison of the Key Components of Intensive Probation Supervision Programs

State	Component													
	1	2	3	4	5	6	7	8	9	10	11	12	13	14
Alaska	NA	NA	NA	NA	NA	NA	NA	NA	NA	NA	NA	NA	NA	NA
Alabama	NA	NA	NA	NA	NA	NA	NA	NA	NA	NA	NA	NA	NA	NA
Arkansas	NA	NA	NA	NA	NA	NA	NA	NA	NA	NA	NA	NA	NA	NA
Arizona	x	x		x	x	x	x	x			x	x	x	
California	x	x	x	x	x	x	x		x			x	x	
Colorado	x	x			x	x	x					x	x	
Connecticut	x	x					x		x					
Delaware							x				x			
Florida	x	x	x		x	x	x	x	x		x			
Georgia	x	x		x	x	x	x	x			x	x	x	
Hawaii	x	x		x	x	x	x				x	x	x	
Idaho	x			x	x	x	x		x		x	x	x	x
Illinois	x		x				x				x	x		
Indiana[a]	—	—	—	—	—	—	—	—	—	—	—	—	—	—
Iowa	x		x		x	x					x	x		
Kansas	x	x	x			x	x							x
Kentucky	x				x	x	x	x	x		x			x
Louisiana	x			x	x	x	x		x			x	x	
Maine	x			x	x	x			x					x
Maryland	NA	NA	NA	NA	NA	NA	NA	NA	NA	NA	NA	NA	NA	NA
Massachusetts[b]		x						x				x	x	
Michigan[a]	—	—	—	—	—	—	—	—	—	—	—	—	—	—
Minnesota	—	—	—	—	—	—	—	—	—	—	—	—	—	—
Mississippi	x			x	x		x	x			x	x	x	x
Missouri	x					x	x	x		x	x			
Montana	x	x				x	x	x				x		x
Nebraska		x				x	x	x	x					x
Nevada[a]	—	—	—	—	—	—	—	—	—	—	—	—	—	—
New Hampshire	x	x		x	x	x								
New Jersey	x	x	x		x	x	x		x	x	x	x	x	x
New Mexico	x	x			x	x	x				x	x	x	
New York									x			x	x	x
North Carolina	NA	NA	NA	NA	NA	NA	NA	NA	NA	NA	NA	NA	NA	NA
North Dakota[a]	—	—	—	—	—	—	—	—	—	—	—	—	—	—
Ohio					x	x	x				x	x	x	x
Oklahoma[a]	—	—	—	—	—	—	—	—	—	—	—	—	—	—
Oregon		x										x	x	
Pennsylvania	NA	NA	NA	NA	NA	NA	NA	NA	NA	NA	NA	NA	NA	NA
Rhode Island[a]	—	—	—	—	—	—	—	—	—	—	—	—	—	—
South Carolina	x		x		x	x	x				x			
South Dakota	NA	NA	NA	NA	NA	NA	NA	NA	NA	NA	NA	NA	NA	NA
Tennessee	x	x	x		x	x	x	x			x			
Texas	x	x							x			x	x	

continued

TABLE 18.2 Continued

State	1	2	3	4	5	6	7	8	9	10	11	12	13	14
							Component							
Utah	x	x					x				x	x	x	
Vermont[a]	—	—	—	—	—	—	—	—	—	—	—	—	—	—
Virginia	x			x	x	x	x					x	x	
Washington	NA	NA	NA	NA	NA	NA	NA	NA	NA	NA	NA	NA	NA	NA
West Virginia	x	x			x	x								x
Wisconsin					x	x								
Wyoming	x	x		x	x	x				x				x
Washington, D.C.	x	x		x	x	x	x				x			
Total (N = 34)	28	19	10	12	26	25	23	9	12	2	17	19	19	12
% with feature	82	56	29	35	76	74	68	26	35	6	50	56	56	35

NOTE: NA indicates that an IPS program exists, but no detailed program description was available for review. The total number of states with IPS programs is 41. Components are as follows: 1 = curfew/house arrest; 2 = electronic monitoring; 3 = mandatory (high needs) referrals/special conditions; 4 = team supervision; 5 = drug monitoring; 6 = alcohol monitoring; 7 = community service; 8 = probation fees; 9 = split sentence/shock incarceration; 10 = community sponsors; 11 = restitution; 12 = objective risk assessment; 13 = objective needs assessment; 14 = court costs/fees.
a. No current IPS program (N = 8).
b. No current IPS program, but data available on characteristics of previously evaluated program (N = 1).

TABLE 18.3 Key Features of IPS Programs in 34 States

Program Feature	Number	Percentage
(1) Curfew/house arrest	28	82
(2) Electronic monitoring	19	56
(3) Mandatory referrals for treatment/special conditions	10	29
(4) Team supervision	12	35
(5) Drug monitoring	26	76
(6) Alcohol monitoring	25	74
(7) Community service	23	68
(8) Probation fees	9	26
(9) Split sentence/shock incarceration	12	35
(10) Community sponsors	2	6
(11) Restitution	17	50
(12) Objective risk assessment	19	56
(13) Objective needs assessment	19	56
(14) Other court costs/fees	11	32

NOTE: A total of 41 states have IPS programs, according to the GAO nationwide survey conducted in spring 1989. Detailed program description data were unavailable for 8 states. Although there is currently no IPS program operating in the state of Massachusetts, this table includes descriptive data from the previously evaluated Massachusetts program. Thus a total of 34 states provided GAO with the information summarized here.

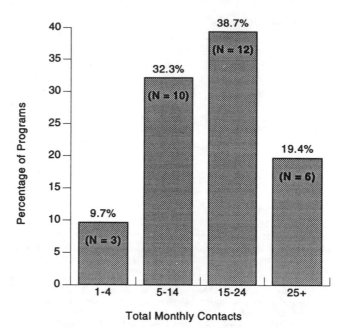

Figure 18.1. Number of Monthly Contacts for 31 States With IPS Programs

NOTE: Monthly contact data were unavailable for 12 states, while 8 states did not have IPS programs at the time of this review. Intrastate variation was identified in at least 5 states. When this occurred, the minimum contact level was reported.

components, electronic monitoring, and shock incarceration, but more likely to have mandatory treatment referrals, objective risk/need assessment, and probation fees. We should also point out that since these programs are constantly changing, the program models we were forwarded in the spring of 1989 may not match the models in place at the time of the *evaluations*. Policymakers need to keep this in mind if they attempt to replicate the "successful" models implemented in other states.

The essential characteristics of the 18 evaluations, included in our review of IPS effectiveness, are presented in Tables 18.5 and 18.6. A summary of the outcome of these evaluations (i.e., recidivism, cost, and diversionary impact) is provided in Table 18.5. Because of the generally poor quality of these evaluation designs (e.g., only one randomized field experiment, compared with nine nonexperimental and eight quasi-experimental designs),[5] an *overall* summary of these research findings is difficult. Nonetheless, some basic findings about recidivism, cost-effectiveness, and diversionary impact can be presented and discussed.

TABLE 18.4 Interstate Variation in the Development and Evaluation of Intensive Probation Supervision Programs

State	IPS Program	IPS Evaluation (Date Completed)	Type of Evaluation Diversion	Cost	Recidivism
Alaska	yes	no			
Alabama	yes	no			
Arkansas	yes	no			
Arizona	yes	yes (87)	x	x	x
California	yes	yes (90)	—	—	x
Colorado	yes	yes	x	—	x
Connecticut	yes	no			
Delaware	yes	no			
Florida	yes	yes (89)	x	—	—
Georgia	yes	yes (87)	x	x	x
Hawaii	yes	yes (88)	—	x	—
Idaho	yes	no			
Illinois	yes	yes (88)	—	x	x
Indiana	no	no			
Iowa	yes	yes (88)	—	x	x
Kansas	yes	no			
Kentucky	yes	yes (87)	—	x	x
Louisiana	yes	no			
Maine	yes	no			
Maryland	yes	no			
Massachusetts	yes (85-87 only)	yes (89)	—	—	x
Michigan	no	no			
Minnesota	no	no			
Mississippi	yes	yes (no date)	—	—	x
Missouri	yes	no			
Montana	yes	no			
Nebraska	yes	no			
Nevada	no	no			
New Hampshire	yes	no			
New Jersey	yes	yes (87)	x	x	x
New Mexico	yes	no			
New York	yes	yes (89)	—	—	x
North Carolina	yes	yes/NA	NA	NA	NA
North Dakota	no	no			
Ohio	yes	yes (87)	x	x	—
Oklahoma	no	no			
Oregon	yes	yes (87)	x	—	—
Pennsylvania	no	no			
Rhode Island	no	no			
South Carolina	yes	no			
South Dakota	yes	no			

continued

TABLE 18.4 Continued

State	IPS Program	IPS Evaluation (Date Completed)	Type of Evaluation Diversion	Cost	Recidivism
Tennessee	yes	no			
Texas	yes	no			
Utah	yes	no			
Vermont	no	no			
Virginia	yes	yes (88)	x	—	x
Washington	yes	no			
West Virginia	yes	no			
Wisconsin	yes	yes (89)	—	—	x
Wyoming	yes	no			
Washington, D.C.	yes	yes (89)	x	x	x
Total	41/51	18/41	9/18	9/18	14/18
% with feature	80	44	50	50	78

NOTE: NA indicates that no evaluation was available for review. Following are notes concerning only those states with available IPS evaluation data.

Arizona: See the final report by Haynes (1987; recidivism data, pp. 32-37; diversionary impact, p. 29; cost-effectiveness, pp. 37-45, Tables 3-6).

California: Petersilia and Turner (1990) present six-month follow-up recidivism data for three counties only (Contra Costa, Ventura, and Los Angeles).

Colorado: Diversion results are summarized by Mande (1988, p. 60). Mande also presents recidivism data (pp. 13-15) and evaluation design information (p. 48, Table 17).

Florida: Diversion results are summarized in Baird (1989) and Baird and Wagner (1990, pp. 112-125).

Georgia: Erwin (1987) presents diversion results (pp. 61-62), assessment of cost-effectiveness (pp. 63-66; see, in particular, Tables 14-15), and recidivism results (pp. 38, 43, 45-52, 53-60; see, in particular, Table 7).

Hawaii: See the evaluation of IPS by the First Circuit Court, Adult Probation Division (1987; overall probation recidivism data, pp. 118-126; cost-effectiveness, pp. 96-98).

Illinois: Although the stated purpose of the program is diversion, actual evaluation data are presented only on cost (see Conti, 1988, pp. 5-8) and recidivism (see Conti, 1988, p. 4).

Iowa: Grossheim and Bucklew (1988) present recidivism (pp. 11-18) and cost (p. 22) data for both probationers and parolees on intensive supervision.

Kentucky: "Year Two" evaluation results are summarized by Wilson, Denton, and Williams (1987). A total of 72% of the IPS cases were parolees (see p. ii). Wilson et al. present cost comparisons (pp. 55-57) and recidivism results (pp. 41-53; see, in particular, Tables 21, 25).

Massachusetts: See Byrne and Kelly (1989, chap. 6) for results of a recidivism study.

Mississippi: A small (N = 83), one-jurisdiction evaluation of an intensive supervision program, including *both* probationers and parolees, was conducted. See the report by the Mississippi Department of Corrections (n.d.; data provided on revocations only, p. 31, Table 13).

New Jersey: The most recent findings from New Jersey's IPS program are found in Pearson and Harper (1990). See also the summary of Pearson's original 1987 evaluation by Byrne et al. (1989, pp. 27-32).

New York: A statewide implementation evaluation was conducted by Lockhart and Wheeler (1989; recidivism results, pp. 58-60, 62-74).

Ohio: See the evaluation of Ohio's community corrections act, which includes an intensive diversion program (Austin, Quigley, & Cuvelier, 1989; diversionary impact, pp. 19-20; cost-effectiveness, pp. 20-21).

Oregon: See the discussion of diversionary impact in Clear, Flynn, and Shapiro (1987).

Virginia: Recidivism results are presented in a report by Jenkins and Jones (1988, pp. i, 25, 42). Diversion results are summarized in the same report (p. 41).

Wisconsin: Evaluation results reported by the Wisconsin Department of Health and Social Services (1989) include both intensive probation and parole, with a focus on assaultive offenders (pp. 1, 6). Recidivism results are summarized in the executive summary of that report (see also pp. 8-11).

Washington, D.C.: Evaluation findings are presented in the program's 1989 annual report (Schumann & Bailey, 1989; diversionary impact, p. 18; cost-effectiveness, pp. 19-22; recidivism results, pp. 15-17).

TABLE 18.5 Characteristics of Evaluations of Intensive Probation Supervision Programs in 18 States

State	Evaluation (year)	Evaluation Design Type[a]	IPS Sample Size[b]	Comparison or Control Group[c]	Primary Recidivism Criterion[d]	Length of Follow-Up[e]
Arizona	Haynes (1987)	nonexperimental	(multisite) 948	regular probationers	rearrest	variable
California	Petersilia and Turner (1990)	experimental	3 sites, approximately 240 IPS offenders	regular probationers; CRMT; ESP, regular probationers	rearrest	6 months
Colorado	Mande (1988)	quasi-experimental	(5 judicial districts) 168	residential community corrections offenders	rearrest	variable
Florida	Baird and Wagner (1990)	quasi-experimental	(statewide) 1,500	3 comparison groups: probation, county jail, and prison	N/A	N/A
Georgia	Erwin (1987)	quasi-experimental	(13 pilot courts) 200	2 comparison groups: probation and prison	rearrest	18 months
Hawaii	First Circuit Court, Adult Probation Division (1987)	N/A	N/A	N/A	N/A	N/A
Illinois	Conti (1988)	nonexperimental	1,425	none	rearrest	variable

continued

TABLE 18.5 Continued

State	Evaluation (year)	Evaluation Design Type[a]	IPS Sample Size[b]	Comparison or Control Group[c]	Primary Recidivism Criterion[d]	Length of Follow-Up[e]
Iowa	Grossheim and Bucklew (1988)	quasi-experimental	4 districts 521 (101 probationers, 958 parolees)	offenders on regular probation or parole	rearrest	variable
Kentucky	Wilson et al. (1987)	nonexperimental	11 districts, 1,337 (378 probationers, 958 parolees)	first-year vs. second-year participants	reconviction	1 year
Massachusetts	Byrne and Kelly (1989)	quasi-experimental	13 sites (227)	high-risk, maximum-supervision cases from control courts	rearraignment	1 year
Mississippi	Department of Corrections (1988)	nonexperimental	1 jurisdiction, 39 (29 probationers, 10 parolees)	2 matched groups: probationers and parolees	technical revocations	variable
New Jersey	Pearson (1987), Pearson and Harper (1990)	quasi-experimental	(statewide) 554	matched sample of prisoners/parolees (N = 122)	rearrest	6 months, 1 year, 18 months, 2 years
New York	Lockhart and Wheeler (1989)	nonexperimental	(statewide) 3,189	non-ISP felony probation cases	rearrest	variable

Ohio	Austin et al. (1989)	quasi-experimental	Intensive Diversion Unit (IDU), 399	three comparisons: prison, felony probation, CCP	N/A	N/A
Oregon	Clear et al. (1987)	nonexperimental	unclear	N/A	N/A	N/A
Virginia	Jenkins and Jones (1988)	nonexperimental	491	3 comparison groups: prison, probation violators, parole violators	reconviction	variable
Wisconsin	Department of Health and Social Services (1989)	nonexperimental	64 (probationers and parolees)	"hypothetical" comparison group created	return to prison for a conviction	1 year
Washington, D.C.	Schumann and Bailey (1989)	nonexperimental	181	N/A	rearrest	variable

NOTE: N/A = not applicable.
a. Three evaluation design types were identified: Experimental designs involved random assignment to treatment and control groups, quasi-experimental designs included some type of matched group design (usually posttest only), and nonexperimental designs included a range of studies with no control groups and/or pre/post comparisons.
b. Many studies present findings across a number of sites. Each site may have developed its own version of IPS; the total number of IPS offenders is included in this table, along with the number of test sites.
c. In some states (e.g., California), comparison groups varied somewhat from site to site. If multiple comparison groups were used, they are listed here. In all but one of the quasi-experimental design evaluations (Massachusetts), no statistical controls were used to adjust for known differences between treatment and control groups.
d. The source of outcome data varied from study to study. In some studies (e.g., Colorado), rearrest data were garnered from termination summaries for those offenders who had their probation revoked. In other states (e.g., Massachusetts, New Jersey, Georgia), the criminal behavior of all offenders was examined, using either state or local criminal history records.
e. Invariably, evaluators have focused on in-program behavior during a specified period (e.g., 6 months, 1 year). However, some evaluators (e.g., in Colorado, Illinois, and Arizona) simply recorded whether an offender had been rearrested prior to completion of his or her probation term, regardless of actual time at risk.

TABLE 18.6 Outcomes of IPS Evaluations in 18 States: Recidivism, Cost, and Diversion

State	Recidivism Rate (%)[a]	Recidivism Reduction?	Cost-Effectiveness Cost	Cost-Effectiveness Effective?	Diversionary Impact Claimed?
Arizona	8	no	$13.72/day	yes	yes
California	20	no	N/A	N/A	N/A
Colorado	1.8	no	N/A	yes	yes
Florida	N/A	N/A	N/A	N/A	yes
Georgia	40.0	unclear	$4.37/day	yes	yes
Hawaii	N/A	N/A	$30.00/day	N/A	N/A
Illinois	14.6	N/A	$6.30/day	yes	N/A
Iowa	11.9	yes	$5.44/day	yes	N/A
Kentucky	3.0	no	$6.37/day	yes	N/A
Massachusetts	56.6	yes, by level of implementation	N/A	N/A	N/A
Mississippi	44.0	no	N/A	N/A	N/A
New Jersey	10.8 (1 year)	yes	$16.56/day	yes	yes
New York	21.2	no	N/A	N/A	N/A
Ohio	N/A	N/A	estimates only (hypothetical)		yes
Oregon	N/A	N/A	N/A	N/A	unclear
Virginia	unclear	unclear	N/A	N/A	yes
Wisconsin	5.0	yes	N/A	N/A	N/A
Washington, D.C.	6.0	N/A	$7.44/day	yes	yes
Total (valid *n*)	—		—		
Number with effect		4/12		8/8	8/9

NOTE: N/A= not available.
a. Recidivism data are included only to highlight the differences among evaluations; they cannot be compared directly for two reasons. First, the criterion measures used by evaluators varied. The primary recidivism criteria identified in Table 18.5 were used here. Second, length of follow-up also varied (see Table 18.5).

Recidivism Reduction

The majority of IPS program evaluations do *not* support the notion that "intensive" supervision significantly reduces the risk of offender recidivism. One possible explanation for this finding is found in a review of the basic characteristics of these programs. Although offender treatment was certainly an important feature of most (if not all) IPS programs, *at least in theory*, the day-to-day emphasis of these programs was on offender surveillance, utilizing a variety of techniques (e.g., drug and alcohol testing, electronic monitoring, curfew checks). In fact, these programs changed their approach to both offender surveillance *and* control (i.e., stricter revocation policies), while maintaining existing treatment strategies. This certainly suggests that the current emphasis on surveillance and control is misplaced and that we should be focusing our attention on improving the quantity and quality of treatment if we really want to change the (criminal) behavior of adult offenders.

Evidence to support this position is found in the preliminary results of the first randomized field experiment of an IPS program model. Petersilia and Turner (1990) highlighted their findings from three California test sites (Ventura, Los Angeles, and Contra Costa counties) in the January 1990 issue of *Crime and Delinquency*. According to the authors, there were

(1) significantly higher levels of surveillance for the experimental groups, but

(2) no significant differences in the percentage of offenders *employed* in experimental versus control groups across all three sites, and

(3) no significant differences between experimental and control groups in the percentage of offenders in counseling for two of the three sites.

Significantly, the authors found that after six months, there were no significant differences in arrest rates between experimental and control groups at all three sites. Further analyses conducted after a one-year follow-up support this initial finding. Would the results have been different if the emphasis of these three programs had been on *treatment*, rather than surveillance and control? Or is it possible that *all three elements* (treatment, surveillance, control) must be in place before we can expect any significant recidivism reduction effects?

The results of the evaluation of the Massachusetts Intensive Probation Supervision program appear to support the latter proposition (Byrne & Kelly, 1989). Among IPS offenders, it was initial *employment change* (i.e., stable employment at four-month reassessment, because the offender either got a job or continued previous employment) that was the best predictor of success (e.g., no rearraignment during a one-year follow-up period). But, importantly, it appears that the effect of the *surveillance* component (i.e., contacts) of the Massachusetts IPS program was indirect, through its effect on the offender change measures (in employment, substance abuse, and marital/family problems). These results underscore the "interaction" between surveillance and treatment, which suggests to us that future IPS program development efforts must include *both* higher contact levels and more intensive treatment provision efforts. Unfortunately, we were unable to measure treatment availability and treatment quality directly in the Massachusetts evaluation. This is perhaps the single most neglected area in community corrections research today (Palmer, 1992). It is our hope that the next wave of intermediate sanction evaluations will include direct measures of treatment availability and quality, along with information on surveillance (contacts, drug tests, curfew checks, and so on) and control (i.e., response to offender noncompliance with program rules). It is only by including all three measures in a single evaluation that we can begin to disentangle their effects.

Cost-Effectiveness and Diversionary Impact

Unlike the recidivism assessments, assessments of IPS cost-effectiveness and diversionary impact found evaluators in agreement (in their conclusions) that the IPS programs they evaluated were (a) cost-effective, in comparison with incarceration,[6] and (b) providing *true diversion* from prison and/or jail. Unfortunately, there were limitations both in the *designs* used in these studies and the *techniques* employed to measure both outcomes. As a result, we do not yet know the answers to these two important questions about the effectiveness of IPS programs.

EFFECTIVENESS OF OTHER INTERMEDIATE SANCTIONS

Local, county, state, and federal decision makers have developed a number of "intermediate" sanctions in the last few years, largely in response to our correctional crowding crisis. While the *stated* purposes of these programs are similar to those of IPS programs (i.e., community protection, cost-effectiveness, diversionary impact), we know much less at this point about whether these programs actually work. (For more detail on the effectiveness issue, see the reviews of each of these sanctions included in this volume.)

House Arrest and Electronic Monitoring

House arrest programs are currently being operated in 26 states and Washington, D.C., either at the state (e.g., Florida) or local (e.g., California) level. In many respects, these programs can be distinguished from IPS programs only by their names. They have many of the same features as the IPS programs described earlier. Florida's Community Control program, for example, has been described in the literature as *both* an intensive supervision program and a "house arrest" program. The "name game" can be taken one step further when we consider electronic monitoring. Some states refer to their "house arrest" programs as electronic monitoring programs, perhaps due to the public's attraction to new technology. Regardless of *what* these programs are called, it is impossible to assess their overall effectiveness at this point because the necessary evaluation research on the use of house arrest programs as front-end intermediate sanctions has not been completed. (For a detailed review of the effectiveness issue, see Baumer & Mendelsohn, chap. 4, this volume.)

Shock Incarceration

As of the spring 1989 GAO survey, shock incarceration programs were operational in 16 different states. Since the time of this review, several other states have developed shock incarceration programs. There are two basic types of shock incarceration programs: (a) programs that simply combine a period of incarceration with a period of probation supervision, and (b) programs that introduce offenders to a "boot camp," which may or may not be followed by a period of probation supervision. We know remarkably little about the effectiveness of either form of shock incarceration, and what evidence we do have does *not* suggest that these programs should be expanded (see Byrne & Kelly, 1989; Latessa & Vito, 1988; Parent, 1989). A September 1988 review of the effectiveness of boot camp programs by the U.S. General Accounting Office (1988) concluded that "the State boot camp programs are relatively new, and it is too early to tell whether they will offset prison overcrowding, reduce prison costs, or reduce recidivism" (p. 1). Given this basic lack of information, it seems incredible that shock incarceration has been advanced as one of the primary correctional tools for young adult offenders in the coming decade. As MacKenzie and Parent (chap. 7, this volume) emphasize, we need to know much more about the effectiveness of various types of boot camps before we expand such programs any further.

Residential Community Corrections Programs and Day Reporting Centers

Two other types of intermediate sanction programs have recently come into vogue: residential community corrections (or halfway houses) and day reporting centers. The results of nationwide reviews of the numbers and types of offenders in both these types of programs are now available.[7] Unfortunately, there is little research evidence to date on the effectiveness of these sanctions (but see the chapters on both sanctions included in this volume).

Day Fines and Other Intermediate Sanctions

A variety of other intermediate sanction options have been proposed, most notably "day fines" and labor/community service. Cole (1989) has reviewed the available research on the effectiveness of fines as an intermediate sanction, and concludes that we simply "don't know" what their effectiveness is. Most reviews of the fines option focus only on the issue of collections/enforcement; little is currently known about the impact of fines on the subsequent behavior of offenders. McDonald (chap. 12, this volume) has reviewed the available evaluation research on community service as a stand-alone intermediate sanction. His findings do *not* suggest that policymakers should expect these programs to be cost-effective or to reduce recidivism.

Concluding Comments:
Why Do We Need Evaluation Research?

It should be clear by this point that we have continued to expand the use of intermediate sanctions even though the basic evaluation research on the implementation and impact of these programs has not been completed. In the short run, it certainly makes good sense to do *something* to address the current institutional crowding problem. However, it is time now to assess these programs, expanding on the features of the programs that work while changing (or deleting) those features that do not. The above review of IPS research reveals why this is critical: The available evidence points toward a renewed awareness of the importance of offender treatment as a recidivism reduction strategy and the futility of simply increasing the level of offender surveillance and/or control.

Notes

1. We would like to thank George Silberman, assistant director of the Program Evaluation and Methodology Division, U.S. General Accounting Office, for providing these survey results to us.

2. A report on the results of this survey was released by the GAO in the fall of 1990. For a comparison of the findings from both our review and the GAO survey, see Braga (1991).

3. Shock incarceration involves a "split" sentence (i.e., a period of incarceration followed by a period of probation supervision). The duration of both the shock and the subsequent supervision varies from state to state. More detailed summaries of the tables included in this chapter can be found in Byrne (1990a) and Braga (1991).

4. Subsequent reviews of the professional literature, as well as follow-up calls to several sites, revealed that the paucity of evaluation reports was not a function of the survey; these programs have simply not been evaluated to date.

5. The Hawaii evaluation was not really an evaluation at all, but a review of the available research on IPS programs, with some discussion of the *potential* impact of such a program in Hawaii.

6. The estimated *cost* of an IPS program varied from $4.37 per day in Georgia to $30.00 per day in Hawaii. Only the New Jersey evaluator attempted to estimate the cost of subsequent reincarceration for either new crimes or technical violations. Typically, *diversionary impact* assessments were based on an assessment of whether an offender was prison bound.

7. The National Institute of Corrections is currently completing a nationwide survey of residential community corrections programs (see Schmidt, 1988, for an overview), and Dale Parent has recently completed a nationwide survey of day reporting centers for the National Institute of Justice.

References

Austin, J., Quigley, P., & Cuvelier, S. (1989, December). *Evaluating the impact of Ohio's community corrections program on public safety and costs: Final report.* San Francisco: National Council on Crime and Delinquency.

Baird, S. C. (1989). *Analysis of the diversionary impact of the Florida Community Control program.* San Francisco: National Council on Crime and Delinquency.

Baird, S. C., & Wagner, D. (1990). Measuring diversion: The Florida Community Control program. *Crime and Delinquency, 36,* 112-125.

Braga, A. (1991, March). *The availability and effectiveness of intermediate sanctions: A reexamination.* Paper presented at the annual meeting of the Academy of Criminal Justice Sciences, Nashville.

Byrne, J. M. (1990a, March 16). *Assessing what works in the adult community correction system.* Paper presented at the annual meeting of the Academy of Criminal Justice Sciences, Denver.

Byrne, J. M. (1990b). The future of intensive probation supervision and the new intermediate sanctions. *Crime & Delinquency, 36,* 6-41.

Byrne, J. M., & Kelly, L. (1989). *Restructuring probation as an intermediate sanction: An evaluation of the Massachusetts Intensive Probation Supervision program.* Final report to the National Institute of Justice, Research Program on the Punishment and Control of Offenders.

Byrne, J. M., Lurigio, A. J., & Baird, S. C. (1989). *The effectiveness of the new intensive supervision programs* (Research in Corrections, No. 5). Washington, DC: National Institute of Corrections.

Clear, T. R., Flynn, S., & Shapiro, C. (1987). Intensive supervision in probation: A comparison of three projects. In B. R. McCarthy (Ed.), *Intermediate punishments: Intensive supervision, home confinement, and electronic surveillance* (pp. 31-51). Monsey, NY: Criminal Justice Press.

Cole, G. F. (1989). Fines can be fine—and collected. *Judges' Journal, 28*, 2-6.

Conrad, J. P. (1991). The pessimistic reflections of a chronic optimist. *Federal Probation, 55*(2), 4-9.

Conti, S. (1988). *Intensive probation supervision: Statewide summary*. Springfield: Administrative Office of the Illinois Courts.

Erwin, B. S. (1987). *Evaluation of intensive probation supervision in Georgia: Final report*. Atlanta: Georgia Department of Corrections.

First Circuit Court, Adult Probation Division [Hawaii]. (1987). *Report to the Fourteenth State Legislature*. Honolulu: Author.

Gottfredson, M. R., & Gottfredson, D. M. (1988). *Decision making in criminal justice: Toward the rational exercise of discretion*. New York: Plenum.

Grossheim, P., & Bucklew, J. (1988). *Evaluation of Iowa's intensive supervision program: Final report*. Des Moines: Iowa Department of Corrections.

Haynes, P. (1987). *Adult intensive probation supervision program: Evaluation report*. Phoenix: Arizona Criminal Justice Commission.

Jankowski, L. (1991, November). Probation and parole. *Bureau of Justice Statistics Bulletin*.

Jenkins, T. L., & Jones, M. A. (1988). *Intensive supervision program: Client characteristics and supervision outcomes—a caseload comparison*. Richmond: Virginia Department of Corrections, Research and Evaluation Unit.

Langan, P., & Cunniff, M. (1992, February). *Recidivism of felons on probation, 1986-89* (Special report). Washington, DC: Bureau of Justice Statistics.

Latessa, E. J., & Vito, G. F. (1988). The effects of intensive supervision on shock probationers. *Journal of Criminal Justice, 16*, 315-330.

Lockhart, P. K., & Wheeler, D. (1989). *Initial report on implementation and operation of the intensive supervision program*. Albany: New York Division of Probation and Correctional Alternatives.

Mande, M. J. (1988). *An evaluation of Colorado's intensive supervision probation program*. Denver: Colorado Judicial Department.

Mississippi Department of Corrections, Community Services Division. (n.d.). *Drug I.D. program: An evaluation report*. Greenwood: Author.

Morris, N., & Tonry, M. (1990). *Between prison and probation: Intermediate punishments in a rational sentencing system*. New York: Oxford University Press.

Palmer, T. (1992). *The reemergence of correctional intervention*. Newbury Park, CA: Sage.

Parent, D. (1989). *Shock incarceration: An overview of existing programs*. Washington, DC: National Institute of Justice.

Pearson, F. S. (1987). *Final report of research on New Jersey's intensive supervision program*. New Brunswick, NJ: Rutgers University, Institute for Criminological Research.

Pearson, F. S., & Harper, A. G. (1990). Contingent intermediate sentences: New Jersey's intensive supervision program. *Crime & Delinquency, 36*, 75-86.

Petersilia, J. (1987). *Expanding options for criminal sentencing* (Publication No. R-3544-EMC). Santa Monica, CA: RAND Corporation.

Petersilia, J., & Turner, S. (1990). Comparing intensive and regular supervision for high-risk probationers: Early results from an experiment in California. *Crime & Delinquency, 36*, 87-111.

Petersilia, J., Turner, S., Kahan, J., & Peterson, J. (1985). *Granting felons probation: Public risks and alternative.* Santa Monica, CA: RAND Corporation.

Schmidt, L. (1988). Profiling the residential community corrections industry: The NIC survey of residential community corrections programs. *Perspectives, 12*(12), 18-19.

Schumann, A. M., & Bailey, C. R. (1989). The intensive probation supervision program annual report (November 1, 1987-October 31, 1988). Washington, DC: Superior Court, Social Services Division.

Tonry, M., & Will, R. (1988). *Intermediate sanctions: Preliminary report to the National Institute of Justice.* Washington, DC: National Institute of Justice.

U.S. General Accounting Office. (1988). *Prison boot camps: Too early to measure effectiveness* (Briefing report to the Honorable Lloyd Bentsen, U.S. Senate). Washington, DC: Government Printing Office.

U.S. General Accounting Office. (1990). *Intermediate sanctions: Their impacts on prison crowding, costs, and recidivism are still unclear.* Washington, DC: Government Printing Office.

von Hirsch, A., Wasik, M., & Greene, J. A. (1989). Punishments in the community and the principles of desert. *Rutgers Law Journal, 20,* 595-618.

Wilson, D. G., Denton, J. L., & Williams, C. E. (1987). *Intensive supervision program evaluation: Year two.* Frankfort: Kentucky Corrections Cabinet, Planning and Evaluation Branch.

Wisconsin Department of Health and Social Services, Office of Policy and Budget. (1989). *Reducing criminal risk: An evaluation of the High Risk Offender Intensive Supervision Project.* Madison: Author.

PART VI

A Look at the Future

19. The Long Road From Policy Development to Real Change in Sanctioning Practice

Donald Cochran

How to develop effective sanctioning policies and implement real change is one of the most serious, but also often ignored, questions facing criminal justice in the United States. According to the Bureau of Justice Statistics, in 1990 the United States reached a record 755,425 inmates in prisons, some 400,000 in jails. In addition, there are 2.5 million individuals on probation and more than 400,000 on parole in the United States. The problem of figuring out what to do with 4 million offenders is overwhelming for both policymakers and practitioners. The panic around crime and corrections has created a situation in which every faddish half-baked idea and/or quick-fix solution imaginable has been put forward under the guise of innovation.

If we ever expect to work our way out of the current criminal justice morass, we will need a well thought out, well-structured, and well-funded information-driven system of alternative sanctions. This is much easier said than done, because all the actors in the system, either as policymakers or practitioners, are going to have to let go of their pet theories about offenders, communities, sentencing practices, and other issues. Policies and practices are going to have to accommodate paradigms that may be far removed from the way we are doing business today. The present problems associated with moving policy to actual practice are overwhelming. Nevertheless, they are usually ignored in the current discussion of intermediate sanctions.

Because of the potentially dangerous consequences associated with inappropriate policies and practices in corrections, there is a critical need to understand and overcome problems in moving policy to practice and to minimize conflicts before the entire correctional system becomes totally paralyzed. In this chapter, I offer opinions about how the present problems in moving policy to practice have been created and some perspective on issues that need to be addressed if we are to resolve the problems.

Organizational Analysis Model

In order to frame my analysis and suggestions for solutions to problems associated with policy and practice, I draw from a 1986 work by Lee Boleman and Terrence Deal in which the authors discuss approaches to understanding and managing organizations. They point out that in any organization there are four different ways of looking at problems and opportunities.

First, there is the structural perspective built on the belief that organizations are designed as rational systems. The core issue for this school of thought is how to meet the organization's purpose through design and structure.

Second, there is the human relations frame of reference, where the emphasis is on the conflict in organizations. It is believed that conflict comes about because of the mismatch between the needs of the organization and the needs of individuals.

A third perspective is the political view, which sees an organization as an arena housing a complex variety of individuals and interest groups competing for always limited resources.

Finally, there is the symbolic perspective, which emphasizes ambiguity and uncertainty and fosters a belief in the idea that what matters is not what really happens regarding policy and practice in the organization, but how people interpret what happens.

Policy Development Pressures

Boleman and Deal argue that effective organizations have to deal with the complexity of bringing together all four of these perspectives. Most organizations have not been able to create a marriage of all four. In the area of criminal justice policy and practice, we have been unable to establish a relationship, let alone a marriage.

The present schism between policy and practice in criminal justice exists because executive and legislative policymakers have tended to emphasize the political and symbolic perspectives and practitioners have tended to retreat to the perspectives of structural and human relations problems. In the political sphere, most elected policymakers have come into office during the past decade on a platform of "no new taxes" and "get tough on crime," two concepts not easily reconcilable. In addition, they are faced daily with a variety of constituencies who expect their individual problems and interests to receive priority status.

Some of the funding issues faced by elected policymakers include how to fund new prisons, new roads and bridges, schools, early childhood programs, programs for the elderly, drug abuse programs, mental health programs, public housing, Medicaid programs, programs for people with AIDS, programs for the homeless, and more. These issues are endless. These same elected officials are also well aware that changes in our nation's economy have led to the exportation of many of our unskilled jobs, that our population is aging, that the federal government and more than 40 states started the decade of the 1990s with serious fiscal problems, that local cities and towns are going bankrupt, and that our underclass is expanding due to the ravages of children in poverty, unemployment, and adult illiteracy. All of the above problems require money to solve, money that does not exist at the local or state level. At the same time, the federal government has cut back its fiscal commitment in the area of criminal justice as well as other human service areas. Everyone wants an ever-increasing piece of a constantly shrinking fiscal pie.

How have most legislative bodies dealt with these enormous problems? In the area of corrections, they have instituted policies that are currently built mostly on the sands of illusion. Because of the complexity of the problems confronting policymakers, there has been a tendency to emphasize policies that are driven by symbolism rather than substance. Given the lack of research and reliable information behind the new intermediate sanctions, policies and practices are generally based on political considerations accompanied by the buzzwords *punishment* and *innovation.* Programs such as house arrest, electronic monitoring, intensive supervision, boot camps, and mandatory sentences are usually sold through the promise of punishment and public safety. In addition, because of the public's anger over taxes, these programs generally carry financial penalties in the form of fees to be paid by offenders. Because these programs really cannot be paid for by offenders, there is a tendency to raise funds through bond measures, thus selling our children's future.

Most of the current intermediate sanction models are built on the general premise of creating jail cells in the community. The fact that communities are open systems where people have considerable freedom of movement, and not closed-system total institutions (as are prisons), is conveniently ignored by policymakers. Programs such as house arrest and electronic monitoring cannot offer the same level of temporary safety that a prison can offer. It is a mistake to imply that probation and parole sanctions can equal prison in safety for the community. In the meantime, if a pet program suffers a setback, the response is generally a more punitive policy. If a highly publicized crime occurs, the legislature simply responds by passing another specific-offense mandatory sentence law. There have been only limited efforts to analyze the criminal justice system's actual capacity to respond to the expectations raised by alternative sanction policies. (For more on alternative sanctions in general, see Byrne, Lurigio, & Baird, 1989; Clear & O'Leary, 1983; Cochran, Corbett, & Byrne, 1986; Corbett, Cochran, & Byrne, 1987; Erwin, 1990.)

Community corrections agencies are clearly increasing their levels of program activity and visibility, but often this activity is nothing more than mindless operationalism sold as accountability. Our criminal justice policies are being built on a foundation of quicksand. Symbolism over substance simply requires that policies be adapted as fast as the next crisis occurs. The key is that laws and policies have to be passed at a rate faster than the public's awareness of how fast criminal justice agencies are sinking.

Policy to Practice Problems

After laws and policies are established, the community corrections managers in the system are expected to move the policies to practice by creating programs that are expected to be risk free in many communities that continue to be resource poor. These miracles are expected to be carried out by administrative systems generally not structured to commandeer the technology and other resources necessary to implement new programs, or to overcome bureaucratic inertia and institutional rigidity, or to ensure that a system for producing a desired result is actually in place and working.

With the present penchant for downsizing government, and continuous tax-cutting proposals gaining the headlines, the daily reality of a community corrections manager is far removed from the rhetoric. The Massachusetts probation system, for instance, still has to deal on a daily basis with 140,000 offenders, including a high-risk group that is 40% functionally illiterate, 93% unemployed, and more than 90% substance abusers. These offenders live in communities lacking adequate resources to deliver needed rehabilitative services. According to Barry Nidorf, chief probation officer in Los Angeles County, 66,000 probation cases have to remain unsupervised in that county because funding has been reduced at the same time that increased demands have been placed on the system. The Massachusetts and Los Angeles probation systems are not alone in dealing with these problems. Probation agencies in many jurisdictions are confronted with a Catch-22 situation of reduced resources and an increasing offender population on probation for offenses that in any rational system would result in incarceration.

Managers are expected to be forceful, dynamic leaders in systems that continue a tradition of operating as "street-level bureaucracies" without defined tasks, agreed-upon goals, performance standards, a consistent chain of command, or adequate information systems. Many community correction systems lack reliable information about how the routine work in the organization is being performed, let alone how quality and innovative work could be performed. Lacking adequate and reliable computerized information systems, community corrections agencies are operating blindly, without reliable research relating to sanctioning outcomes.

The paucity of reliable information systems leads to correctional policy decisions based primarily on political considerations. In addition, the lack of adequate dialogue among judges, legislators, prosecutors, and probation officials, accompanied by lack of information and research, leads to continued organizational role confusion and squandering of already strained physical, fiscal, and human resource in the criminal justice arena.

Managers are also confronted with considerable human relations problems as they try to move intermediate sanctions policy to practice. First, many of our organizations work on the idea of the "germ theory" approach to change. Bureaucracies seem to attack anything new. Change is treated as a noxious agent attacking the body of the organization.

The management of change is made more complex for the manager on a human relations level because not all resistance to change is irrational and regressive. Certainly some people operate on "automatic pilot" and are not about to change. However, if we assume that all resistance to change comes from the "Neanderthals" in the system, we are missing a substantial reality.

Effective organizations do not shut out constructive criticism. It is clear from experience that any organization is better off whenever leaders are able to create situations in which some people's preferences can be satisfied without making other people worse off. In the public sector there is a long history of elected and appointed leaders who have achieved significant changes by purposively crafting public visions of what is desirable and possible for agencies to do. These leaders have fostered ideas, developed visions of programs, focused public and agency attention, and ultimately mobilized talent and resources to implement the emerging new programs. These leaders have succeeded by building coalitions that have attempted to build win-win situations for all parties involved.

In today's world of instantaneous electronic polling and sophisticated marketing techniques it is not difficult to discover what people might want. However, it is a quite different and more challenging problem to engage the public, legislators, judges, correctional officials, and line workers in a process of rethinking how criminal justice problems are defined, how alternative solutions can be envisioned, and how responsibilities for action can be allocated. Effective policy has to be more than discovering what people want; it has to entail the creation of contexts in which people can critically evaluate and revise what they believe.

With many politicians running for office or protecting their jobs by being critical of and condescending to public service and by passing laws and creating policies that do not create a context that involves the people expected to carry out the programs, it is little wonder that new political policies are not always received with overwhelming enthusiasm in community corrections agencies.

Because many policies are being established based on the latest media headlines, rarely taking into account an agency's capacity to carry them out, there is considerable role confusion resulting in substantial stress among probation and parole workers. Along with a lack of resources, an officer's reward for successfully working with a dangerous offender is that he or she can expect to be assigned an increasing number of dangerous offenders. With the lack of prison and jail cells, a community corrections officer who takes the rhetoric of public safety seriously and proposes the revoking of a person's probation or parole will be labeled a failure for clogging up the prison system. Officers who came into the probation field a generation ago with the belief that they could make a difference in people's lives through effective enforcement of reasonable sanctions and good casework supervision are, naturally, going to be resistant to the degrading of their skills and beliefs through the introduction of a mechanical and deskilled approach to probation. People who were asked to make a commitment to the profession of community corrections and to work in that system for a decade or more, expecting to move eventually into roles that would involve increased organizational influence might reasonably be expected to resist policies and practices that move away from valuing their knowledge and skills.

The problem of moving policy to practice in order to institute realistic intermediate sanctions is not unsolvable. The management strategies used to develop and institute alternative sanctions have to be adjusted. This is a complex problem, carried out in complex communities and complex organizations. Our strategies have to acknowledge these complexities.

The new sanctioning policies are not being created in a vacuum. They are being introduced into environments that have long histories, with existing goals, strategies, structures, activities, resources, and cultures in place. The introduction of expanded sanctioning options requires careful planning if the goal is successful implementation. The key issue in the planning process is how to manage expectations in the implementation of an expanded sanctions menu. The ability to manage the interaction between policy expectations and the criminal justice system's operational capacity to institute programs will be the key element that separates successful and unsuccessful programs. We are at a critical stage in the development of alternative sanctions. We have come to a point of very high policy expectations and generally low organizational capacity to deliver effective programs.

As prisons became more crowded during the 1980s, probation and parole agencies generally went through the decade in a state of stagnation. In many jurisdictions, it was a decade in which there were low policy expectations and equally low organizational capacity to deal with community corrections problems. The problem with the present situation of high policy expectations and continued low organizational capacity is that we are in the process of moving from stagnation to an equally unproductive point of organizational gridlock. The gridlock will occur as long as the driving force behind alternative sanctions is to punish people cheaply. If policy expectations continue to outdistance the resources being applied to the problem, community corrections agencies will have little or no hope of meeting the expectations, and we will end up with organizational gridlock. The process of moving policy to practice will require the stretching of people's expectations, accompanied by the introduction of resources that allow the agencies to catch up with expectations.

The Role of Information Technology

Intelligent, effective, and efficient use of information technology (IT) will be a key ingredient in the dynamic process of balancing policy expectations and organizational capacity building in community corrections. Probation and parole agencies will be able to create a perception of public value to their practices only when they get to the stage of using information to create new services and to solve formerly intractable problems. A management information system (MIS) is one of the most basic and important tools available to community corrections managers today. It has the greatest potential to aid management in integrating structural, human resource development, political, and symbolic changes in the organization.

The strategic goal of IT is consistent with a good alternative sanctions program, namely, to move from experience-based guesswork toward better service and individual case outcomes through reliance on computers, work-load accounting, and research-validated offender classification systems. The structure of the organization will be enhanced along with the operational management process by the development of improved managerial planning, oversight, evaluation, and accountability. One of the reasons community corrections has been subject to every harebrained idea imaginable, always under the guise of innovation, is that probation and parole systems have not advanced along the path of using applications of computer technology for managers. We can no longer afford either deliberate or accidental ignorance in community corrections. The practice of developing policies and programs based on anecdotes rather than information and knowledge must cease.

Probation and parole systems are going to have to be structured in such a way that they routinely make use of computerized criminal offender records that are complete, timely, and accurate in their content. Computers are going to have to be used to empower the frontline workers in the organization. On-line risk/need systems are important, along with up-to-date arrest data, conviction data, and prior probation, corrections, and parole offender case management information, as well as information about prior probation and parole revocation history and institutional disciplinary history.

This risk information is essential in order to avoid the ever-present danger of using alternative sanctions as a net-widening program instead of a risk management program. Organizations are going to need computerized work-load staffing systems to be sure that limited personnel resources are being used in such a way that all of the activities of the organization complement one another.

Although the policy to practice problems in probation and parole are generally dealt with at a macro level, ultimately, if we expect to overcome these problems, we are going to have to use management information and decision support systems (DSS) to be sure that we develop practices and solve problems on a micro level—one jurisdiction, one problem, one program, one officer, and one offender at a time.

Information as a Strategic Resource

The strategic use of MIS and DSS will change the whole process of individual and organizational accountability and responsibility. Combined with good communication systems, IT will widen the manager's span of control: flattening organizational hierarchies by making information more readily available to all levels of the organization, reducing delays in implementing new programs, and helping to reduce costs, while still retaining managerial oversight and control. Managers will be clued into key indicators and exception reports measuring what is actually going on in the organization at both quality and quantity levels.

Key indicators and exception reports will help focus everyone's attention on the desired organizational practices, by encouraging more frequent and accurate review of the actual effects of various alternative sanctions. Information technology makes it possible to introduce more sophisticated operational research methodologies, such as survival analysis. Within a very short period of time, probation and parole agencies will be able to know whether or not a new program and/or practice is attaining the outcome desired. Probation and parole agencies will be able to review long-standing programs to determine whether or not they are still appropriate.

Over a short period, with the structural development of on-line data bases, researchers using tools such as survival analysis will be able to develop "critical success factors" and make the monitored program outcome results available to managers through automated executive support systems. This structural emphasis on measurable outcome—the public sector's version of the bottom line—will allow for real innovation (not the usual fads) and experimentation about how even more effective outcomes can be achieved through improved practices.

This structural strategy has the potential to solve a long-term organizational dilemma: how to balance the organization's needs with the needs of individual employees. IT allows for the empowering of the frontline employee and has great potential for reducing resistance to change. Along with a comprehensive training program for upgrading each employee's survival skills, the distribution of timely, accurate, and meaningful information to those frontline workers who are in the middle of the action will increase the organization's flexibility to respond to crisis situations in a timely and intelligent manner. IT can be used to enrich the jobs of probation and parole officers by effectively matching up the knowledge and skills of long-term officers with offender needs, as well as by identifying the knowledge and skills new officers need to bring to the job today.

Quality research, effective training, and a comprehensive system of getting information to those practitioners who have a need to know will go a long way toward reducing resistance to change from long-term employees. Nobody wants to be set up to look like a fool. Yet, historically in public service, especially in probation and parole, long-term employees have often been subject to such abuse. Changes have been constantly foisted upon them without analysis of the organization's capacity to handle the new assignments. The new assignments were rarely accompanied by adequate explanations or training programs for individual workers. If expanded and improved information and knowledge are made available to frontline workers, the worst of them will be less threatened by changes brought about through alternative sanctions; the best of them will translate the knowledge into improved offender and organizational outcomes.

Information is a strategic organizational resource. Unlike every other resource, when information is used, the supply of information is not depleted. The opposite is actually true: The more information is distributed, the more it is enriched and augmented. This is a crucial point for today's public manager, especially in the political sphere, where fiscal resources are going to continue to be scarce. Accurate, timely, and meaningful information has the potential of to put community corrections managers in a position of power they have never before experienced. As long as the battles are going to be over the use of limited resources, probation and parole administrators are going to have to be able to use information intelligently as they argue for their personnel, programs, and budgets.

With federal, state, and local governments in fiscal crisis, and citizens generally disenchanted with the government, elected officials are not always able to make adequate resources available to criminal justice agencies. Probation and parole administrators will need the ability to use information to determine accurately what work needs to be done, what outcomes their agencies will produce if resources are added, and what will probably happen to program outcomes and organizational practices if resources continue to be reduced.

Probation and parole agencies have historically lacked political clout because, among other reasons, their budgets generally lack capital outlay requirements, they lack computer information systems, and they work with clientele no one cares about. Therefore, the agencies have generally lacked any kind of power base when it came to budget negotiations. However, agencies that develop reliable information systems will be in a new arena. Information- and knowledge-driven alternative sanction programs can and will be funded. This will happen whether jails and prisons continue to be overcrowded or not. The preliminary research in both Georgia and Massachusetts probation is showing that when these programs contain a balance between risk control and risk reduction they are proving to be more effective. Past public perception problems encountered by probation and parole agencies can be addressed by a balanced risk management program through more flexible and effective use of limited government resources. The cost, humaneness, and success of alternative sanction programs that prove to be effective will make them politically palatable.

Finally, IT is crucial for administrators to move policy to practice in the symbolic sphere. Agencies will need to emphasize risk control strategies such as 24-hour surveillance, daily criminal record checks, prompt probation revocation hearings for noncompliance with court-ordered sanctions, and modern drug monitoring practices to be sure that limited treatment resources are not wasted on unmotivated offenders. All of these strategies need to become standard community corrections practice. In addition, risk reduction programs such as mandatory drug treatment, employment training programs, adult literacy, violence reduction, and other behavior change programs will also need to become standard elements of community corrections.

The process of offender supervision, surveillance, and enforcement of organizational standards and court orders will lead to better case outcomes. When community corrections organizations have adequate risk control and risk reduction resources available and are able to hold both agency staff and offenders accountable, public support for probation and parole will increase because of the new professional competence and effectiveness.

Community corrections agencies that make effective use of IT can develop programs and practices that will improve the agencies' relationships with the general public. Present attitudes notwithstanding, people want to believe in the effectiveness of their government agencies. By developing practices that are information driven, structurally sound, employee sensitive, and politically palatable, community corrections agencies will be able to strengthen both government's ability to represent the interest of its people and the people's trust in government's ability to do so.

References

Boleman, L., & Deal, T. (1986). *Modern approaches to understanding and managing organizations.* San Francisco: Jossey-Bass.

Byrne, J. M., Lurigio, A. J., & Baird, S. C. (1989). *The effectiveness of the* new *intensive supervision programs* (Research in Corrections, No. 5). Washington, DC: National Institute of Corrections.

Clear, T. R., & O'Leary, V. (1983). *Controlling the offender in the community: Reforming the community-supervision function.* Lexington, MA: D. C. Heath.

Cochran, D., Corbett, R. P., Jr., & Byrne, J. M. (1986). Intensive probation supervision in Massachusetts: A case study in change. *Federal Probation, 50,* 32-41.

Corbett, R. P., Jr., Cochran, D., & Byrne, J. M. (1987). Managing change in probation: Principles and practice in the implementation of an intensive probation supervision program. In B. R. McCarthy (Ed.), *Intermediate punishments: Intensive supervision, home confinement, and electronic surveillance.* Monsey, NY: Criminal Justice Press.

Erwin, B. S. (1990). Old and new tools for the modern probation officer. *Crime & Delinquency, 36,* 61-74.

20. The Future of Intermediate Sanctions: Questions to Consider

Todd R. Clear

James M. Byrne

Intermediate Sanctions as Panacea

No one can question that the huge growth in the correctional industry of the 1970s and 1980s has permanently changed the face of corrections in the United States. As we move into the 1990s, the corrections systems in most states confront entrenched crises in which the number of new prisoners added each month routinely exceeds the number released and overwhelms even the most ambitious new construction programs. For some states, the problem of correctional crowding begins its second decade; others—the lucky ones—are faced with a relatively new problem and gifted with the examples of numerous jurisdictions from which to learn.

There are, however, few success stories to emulate. The states of Washington and Minnesota were widely touted as able to avoid the crises of crowding through careful sentencing legislation—yet these, too, have recently joined the ranks of the overcrowded in what seems at times an inexorable march toward ever-increasing prison populations. That states cannot "build their way" out of the crowding crisis has become a catchphrase of modern correctional planning. For example, the state of California, perhaps the nation's leader in the single-minded pursuit of new prison construction, recently "blinked." After a decade of wholesale prison growth, the California Blue Ribbon

AUTHORS' NOTE: We would like to thank Anthony Braga of Rutgers University for his assistance in the preparation of this chapter.

Commission on Inmate Population Management (1990) recently concluded that it is neither feasible nor wise to maintain the expansion policy. California is only the most dramatic example of the now commonplace realization that some other approach is required (see New Jersey Management Review Commission Task Group on Corrections, 1990).

The intermediate sanctions movement is a product of the search for a new strategy for corrections. Much is promised: Legislators, judges, and corrections officials can respond to the public call for serious sanctions for criminal acts without breaking the public bank. The message could not be more timely, and a host of conservative and liberal reformers alike have coalesced behind the idea (see McCarthy, 1987; Van Ness, 1989). The 1990s shape up truly as the decade of the intermediate sanction.

Correctional movements run in fairly dependable cycles. First there is the call for reform, followed by changes designed to implement reform, followed by criticism of the changes and new calls for reform. This is the pattern that preceded the intermediate sanction movement of the 1990s; it is also the pattern that will follow it. As states move toward the adoption of widespread intermediate sanctions, it is prudent to bear in mind that the seeds of future criticism are contained in the current design of the reforms. For this reason, it is important now to examine carefully the potential for intermediate sanctions' being viewed as another in a long line of failed panaceas. In our view, the ultimate "success" of intermediate sanctions will depend on how local, county, state, and federal policymakers respond to each of the five questions raised below.

What Are the Intermediate Sanctions Trying to Do?

Boiled to its basic core, the intermediate sanction argument is this: Many offenders now in prison can be adequately managed in settings less intrusive (and expensive) than traditional prisons. Many offenders under traditional probation supervision receive wholly inadequate amounts of supervision, given their circumstances. The gap between traditional prison and traditional probation is much too wide to fit well the variety of offenders under correctional control. Intermediate options are needed that will allow a much more carefully calibrated assignment of offenders to correctional programs that fit their circumstances (Morris & Tonry, 1990; Petersilia, 1987).

This argument combines three separable suggestions. First, the seriousness of many offenders' crimes calls for a response in between traditional probation and imprisonment. Second, the level of risk many offenders represent is too much for probation, but not enough for prison. Third, the extensive growth in imprisonment can be avoided through intermediate sanctions. These suggestions no doubt have merit, and plausible cases have been made for each. The more troubling question is whether they are compatible.

The frank bottom line for the intermediate sanction movement must be whether it is able to reduce overcrowding in corrections. The corrections field cannot afford an "innovation" that exacerbates crowding, and it is counterproductive to concentrate energy on a package of programs irrelevant to that need. Crowding, of course, is as endemic to probation as it is to prison, so if an intermediate sanctions package is to be of use, it must draw offenders from each group.

Doing so can be tricky. The main reason offenders are unsuitable for probation is that their risk to the community surpasses probation's control capacity. By contrast, prison is unsuitable when offenders' crimes are not serious enough to warrant such an extreme loss of freedom. The dilemma is the familiar schizophrenia of corrections— it seeks both to punish the offender and to protect the community. Often, however, those who commit serious crimes are not a danger, and those who persistently victimize commit crimes of questionable seriousness. Finding a large group of offenders who fit a profile requiring both moderate punishment and moderate risk control may be difficult (Clear & Hardyman, 1990).

Intermediate sanctions have generally sought to dramatize their "toughness" from a risk control standpoint. Electronic monitoring, drug testing, and intensive supervision are staples of surveillance programs, designed for watching people closely and keeping careful track of their activities. Such methods are a waste of resources when applied to offenders who constitute little risk. Yet that is precisely what has happened in several intermediate sanction programs. Notable by example are the intensive supervision programs of Georgia (Erwin, 1987) and New Jersey (Pearson, 1988). Under pressure to divert offenders from prison, these programs have selected offenders whose profiles are not markedly different from many clients on traditional probation, applying a quantum increase of control. The control may assuage public worry concerning offenders released from incarceration, but the confidence is falsely placed, because the offenders represent a limited risk in the first place. That is why evaluations of these programs find low rearrest rates. When offenders fail in these programs, it is most often because of their inability to live within the stringent program requirements (in particular, to abstain from drug use).

By contrast, intensive supervision programs that focus on high-risk offenders—as illustrated by the Bureau of Justice Assistance's intensive supervision experiments—appear to have very high failure rates (Petersilia & Turner, 1990). These programs have selected the highest failure-risk cases from regular supervision for close monitoring and control. It should be no surprise that they do often fail. Yet the high failure rate, combined with the high costs of intensive supervision, means these programs actually add to the costs of corrections (Petersilia & Turner, 1990).

One solution to the "goals dilemma" is to focus on regular probation failures. This group is composed of offenders who have demonstrated their risk to the community and are destined for incarceration. Providing intermediate sanctions for this group meets the aims of both increased public safety and reduced corrections costs. However, it is debatable whether the number of probation failures suitable for intermediate sanctions is large enough to reduce overcrowding in any meaningful way. And even if the target group is *potentially* large enough to have such an impact, it may simply result in a "name change" as probation violators become intermediate sanction violators who are returned to prison.

A more plausible solution is to disentangle the various types of intermediate sanctions and differentiate them in terms of the aims they may readily serve. For example, surveillance programs are really risk management programs, and they ought to be reserved for the highest-risk offenders in the system. To use New Jersey as an example, it is precisely the "worst" risks who ought to be released from prison to intensive supervision programs, not the "best," as is now the practice. If our goal is diversion from traditional prison, there are many programs that contain a punitive emphasis that meets the need many policymakers feel for retribution. Home detention, day reporting centers, day fines, community service, and restitution centers are examples of programs that provide cost-effective losses of freedom short of traditional imprisonment.

The fact remains that there is a fundamental contradiction in the aims that intermediate sanctions programs seek. There is a possibility that the 1990s will see the development of a hodgepodge of programs with multiple, often conflicting, aims. Experience suggests that offender eligibility criteria for new programs tend to reflect political considerations rather than any careful assessment of sanctioning goals and the programs that serve them. If this is the case, intermediate sanctions will find it difficult to justify their value.

What Is the Professional Base
for Intermediate Sanctions Workers?

The organizational placement of intermediate sanctions programs has symbolized the goal conflicts they face. When corrections agencies run them, they tend to be designed primarily as population reduction mechanisms. When run by the courts (through probation), they are more frequently established to enhance probation options. Independent agencies tend to be much more careful about program eligibility criteria than programs run by traditional corrections agencies, because these independent systems are often subject to greater public scrutiny. The natural tendency is for organizations to run intermediate sanction programs in ways that facilitate meeting broader organizational goals.

Buried under these goal struggles is a subtle but important question about the disciplinary underpinning of intermediate sanctions: What is the discipline of knowledge that defines the operation of these programs, and to what educational background should program developers look for staff?

The long-standing tradition in corrections has been that the fields related to human behavior—psychology, social work, and counseling—are the educational basis for "professional" workers who involve themselves with offenders' problems. Those who merely "watch" offenders, such as guards, require only high school diplomas, for they are "nonprofessionals."

The intermediate sanctions movement has brought the ideas of surveillance and control into the traditionally professional jobs of "working with" offenders. What is the appropriate educational basis for this type of work? One answer might be that undergraduate criminal justice programs can serve as a higher-education feeding system for these jobs. Certainly, this has frequently been the case in many areas across the country. The first postcollege job for many criminal justice majors is that of probation officer or prison counselor.

The training focus of most criminal justice programs at the undergraduate level is decidedly not oriented toward the behavioral sciences. It is a bit difficult to characterize the emphasis of these programs fully, but it is not too far afield to call them procedural, semilegal, and bureaucratic in their focus. The natural parent discipline might actually be public administration, which is traditionally offered as an interdisciplinary, graduate level of education.

There may be important implications to this shift in educational expectations. The premium traditionally placed on technical expertise about people, with appropriate allowances for discretion, is replaced by an emphasis on what might be called "good judgment" operating within closely prescribed policy boundaries. The staff of intermediate sanctions programs are less "experts on offenders" than they are "operators of supervision programs."

There are those who will applaud this shift. By all accounts, the human behavior focus has supported considerable mayhem being practiced on offenders under the rubric of "changing their behavior" (McCleary, 1974; Stanley, 1975). Rules and procedures for correctional programs have increased the amount of elementary fairness with which offenders are managed outside of the prison context.

Yet it would be naive to believe that the special problems of compulsive sex offenders and habituated drug users, for example, do not require special understanding. There are plenty of examples of tragic errors in judgment made by correctional professionals because they had a poor understanding of the behavioral dynamics of special types of offenders. They knew well how the system works, but did not have equal understanding of the complexities of its clients. It is in this respect that the movement toward increased surveillance and control is problematic, because it implies that we can lower job requirements in the area of "treatment" skills in favor of a background in "policing" skills.

The struggle over the professional orientation of the new corrections staff is more than a conflict over the philosophy of offender management; it is a sorting out of the professional identity of the field. Already, corrections leaders recognize their allegiance to the fields of management and administration more than to the behavioral sciences. The shift in knowledge base is merely flowing deeper into the agencies themselves.

Some would say this is a watering down of professional expectations for the field. They have a point, for if a guard is qualified to "watch people" with only a high school diploma, why must the staff for electronic monitoring programs have more training? As Corbett and Marx (chap. 6, this volume) point out, such line staff "deskilling" is a likely consequence of our continued attraction to the technology of control.

Today, the educational identification of corrections is a mixture of several fields. The entry of the current brand of intermediate sanctions into the system coincides with a rethinking of the corrections professional. So long as no single education or certification approach is accepted as valid for the workers of the field, the idea of the corrections professional will be more a vision than a reality.

How Will the Traditional Methods of
Nonincarcerative Corrections Be Changed by Shifts
From "Soft" to "Hard" Technologies?

The most serious problem faced by the corrections field is the general problem of "technical uncertainty" (Thompson, 1967), because the methods of correctional work have effects that are not very reliable. To a certain extent, the problem is intractable because it is caused by the uncertainty of human behavior, which cannot be eliminated.

The traditional methods of corrections have been technically quite "soft" and also quite uncertain. The techniques of counseling, empathy, insight, life structuring, feedback, and reality testing—for a long time the mainstays of the corrections worker—are quite fragile in several respects. They appear to work only marginally well, their operation is heavily dependent upon individual skills (and is therefore quite idiosyncratic), and the offender plays a dominant role in their operation.

The technologies of the intermediate sanctions movement have been developed with the express aim of reducing uncertainty. These technical components are "hard" in that they are not easily altered by the vagaries of human uncertainty. Electronic monitors, paper-driven classification rules, and random drug testing are designed to reduce the human element of correctional management.

However, it is still *people* who must decide how to respond to the information generated by these new technologies (e.g., violation of curfew reports, positive drug tests, the identification of "high risk" offenders). Managers of intermediate sanctions programs must recognize that while these hard technologies eliminate some types of error, they build in others (Clear, 1988).

The advent of hard technologies seems already to have affected the field. New approaches are often implemented in the face of strong staff resistance, probably because staff resent the encroachment on their discretion. Those workers who pride themselves on their skills in traditional "people work" are sometimes seen by their peers to have an outmoded perspective on the job. In many agencies, there is a growing value placed on "enforcement" that has replaced the idea of problem solving when offenders violate program rules. The logic of intermediate sanctions relies heavily on the idea of rules enforcement.

Civil liability has reinforced the need to harden the technical base of corrections. When the clients of the system commit gruesome crimes while under correctional control—and it must be emphasized that technical uncertainty leads inevitably to such events—litigators increasingly seek to find a culprit in the system who can be held accountable. The powerful benefits of hindsight are that decisions that were reasonable at the time lay exposed, after the fact, as plainly incompetent. Soft technologies, with their lack of rules, are extremely vulnerable to post hoc evaluations, and they can prove to be quite costly to the system. The harder techniques, with their rules and prescribed practices, provide a foundation for a defense in the face of inevitable failure.

The ability to defend against attack is critical for the survival of intermediate sanctions. Advertised as alternatives to prison (though often they are not), these programs are often hard to sell to public policymakers in the first place. The rhetoric of "tough" corrections helps a cautious public to relax, and the prominent display of strict program rules goes far to help outsiders understand that the program can be intrusive in ways a prison cannot. When clients fail, public demonstrations of program strictness will counter troubled public reactions. The hard technical core emerges as a crucial component of intermediate sanctions, for all these reasons.

As soft techniques become rarer in the correctional field, there must be an accompanying change in the job satisfaction structure of the work. Old-time corrections professionals, when asked what they like about their jobs, often say something like, "Seeing how my efforts help someone to make it." The new breed of correctional worker will have to find new sources of pride in work well done. Will they replace the former change agenda with a new appreciation for enforcement, as in making a "quality arrest" (Harris, Clear, & Baird, 1989)?

What Empirical Basis Exists
for Intermediate Sanctions?

The traditional literature in behalf of intermediate sanctions is not promising. Early studies of intensive supervision, for example, did not seem to show promise (Banks, Porter, Rardin, Silver, & Unger, 1977). Offenders given intensive supervision often did worse than their counterparts receiving less attention. Remarkably, intensive programs often failed to become really intensive—clients in smaller caseloads were seen no more frequently than those in the comparison large caseloads (Niethercutt & Gottfredson, 1974).

Likewise, studies of attempts to divert offenders have often shown that the programs actually serve to widen the net of social control in two ways: Either they directly select clients from lesser levels of control or they so heavily sanction their program participants that there is a secondary effect of increased control (Austin & Krisberg, 1982).

This is not a secret literature—indeed, these studies are well known to criminologists and public policymakers alike. It is curious, then, that they seem to have had so little impact on the design of the new generation of alternatives (Clear & Hardyman, 1990).

Advocates of the intermediate sanctions movement have touted the emphasis on control and the hard technological base as the main differences of these new programs. Nevertheless, the evaluations of these programs to date are consistent and not encouraging. Intensive supervision programs seem to increase the chances of return to prison, mostly as a result of offenders' inability to abide by program rules, not as a result of new crimes (Byrne & Kelly, 1989; Erwin, 1987; Pearson, 1988; Petersilia & Turner, 1990). Even the most successful diversion programs suffer from secondary net-widening problems. Electronic monitoring programs similarly seem to be not much better than human contact, especially when used for long durations (Baumer & Mendelsohn, chap. 4, this volume).

Ironically, just as the field is eschewing the soft technical approaches and the goals they infer, a data base grows supporting these techniques. Recent studies have supported the value of structured case management approaches with emphasis on the specification of behavioral goals in both prisons and the community (Austin & Baird, 1990; Markley & Eisenberg, 1986). A summary of research on treatment programs gives reason to believe that rather substantial gains can be made through emphasizing offender change in tightly structured programs assigned to carefully selected offenders (Gendreau & Ross, 1987; Palmer, 1992). This is true even for drug offenders, who were previously thought to be immune to treatment intervention (Anglin & Speckart, 1988).

Overall, this is not a very promising picture in support of the popular new intermediate approaches, though it must be remembered that the research base is thin. Whether the picture will change, or whether the field will move to incorporate the softer techniques into these programs, remains to be seen.

What Reforms Can Be Expected in the Intermediate Sanctions Themselves?

There are three common ways in which correctional programs fail. First, they are poorly managed and as a result lose credibility with the public they serve. Second, they experience dramatic client failures that cause them to be shut down. Third, they grow to be perceived as inadequate or untimely, given public sentiments for change.

The new intermediate sanctions are not immune from any of these concerns. The programs described in early studies appear to have been very well run, but that is often the case with experiments. The growth of intermediate sanctions has been so rapid that even advocates wonder whether they are being sufficiently well planned. As the numbers of offenders in these programs grows—thousands are under electronic monitoring in Florida and Michigan each day, for example—the chance that administration will slip in quality increases. The credibility problems experienced by traditional probation can be attributed in great part to the lack of consistently good management. As the alternatives to probation grow, will the leaders of these programs evolve toward the same lax practices?

In the 1988 presidential election, the case of Willie Horton was a dramatic illustration of the reality every correctional program administrator knows: A single client can bring down any program, no matter how well established. Technical uncertainty guarantees that intermediate sanctions will have their Willie Hortons. For reasons previously cited, this is an especially difficult problem for these new, high-profile programs.

There seems to be no fail-safe way to deal with the Willie Horton problem. Luck and timing seem to be factors, as are good public relations prior to such an incident. Every local jurisdiction has its stories of such incidents, and they leave an imprint on correctional practice. The threat of the "dramatic incident" encourages program administrators to be very selective of offenders early in a program's history. As pressures build for a program to help overcome system crowding, the selection of offenders often becomes less cautious, as it should, and the odds begin to favor the "rare event." Time will provide its Willie Horton stories for the "new corrections."

Perhaps the most complicated questions have to do with the way the intermediate sanctions fit within the system's current array of programs, and how the critical public—the funding decision makers—view them. The integration of intermediate sanctions has something of a shotgun wedding feel to it. With such impossible crowding, leaders seem to have few choices but to try these new approaches. Often, they do so with ambivalent enthusiasm and a critical eye. Scholars have already criticized the new programs as contributing to disparity (von Hirsch, Wasik, & Greene, 1989), and such criticism can become a core rallying point for liberals and conservatives alike. With the exception of boot camps, federal support for these programs has been lukewarm (see Klein-Saffran, chap. 17, this volume), reflecting an entrenched skepticism about anything that smacks of being "soft on crime." As evaluations continue to fuel questions about these programs, they may become targets of even more fundamental criticism.

Perhaps this is a worst-case scenario. It is hard to imagine that any intermediate sanction will be eliminated if it has become a critical part of a more balanced correctional array of programs—especially if it demonstrably reduces the use of prison. Yet the crescendo of voices calling for intermediate sanctions is supported by a thin history and an even thinner intelligence base. Even a small set of circumstances may dramatically quiet this chorus.

Concluding Comments

This chapter has presented critical discussion of the intermediate sanctions movement in corrections. We have suggested that there are some unanswered questions about this popular new concept in corrections. It would indeed be remarkable if it were otherwise, for the problems of contemporary corrections are complex and the idea of intermediate sanctions is new. The answers to all these questions begin with clarity about the goals of the new programs. They have often seemed to style themselves as unabashedly "tough," and they have achieved this to the degree that, in some settings, offenders would rather be in prison than in the new programs. But simply "being tough" is not a philosophy, nor is it a program that works as an offender control strategy. This orientation leaves unaddressed concerns ranging from the professional identity of the staff to the effectiveness of the technical base of the field. Yet it cannot be denied that the decade of the 1990s will be the decade of intermediate sanctions, for a host of very good reasons. It is equally apparent that the new strategies of intermediate sanctions, taken as a package, offer more promise to the embattled field of corrections than anything else in recent experience. But it remains to be seen whether we can move beyond the "get tough" rhetoric and develop programs that can address the reality of offender control in the community.

References

Anglin, D., & Speckart, G. (1988). Narcotics use and crime: A multisample, multi-method analysis. *Criminology, 26,* 197-232.

Austin, J., & Baird, S. C. (1990). *The effectiveness of the client management classification system for prison classification.* San Francisco: National Council on Crime and Delinquency.

Austin, J., & Krisberg, B. (1982). The unmet promise of alternatives to incarceration. *Crime and Delinquency, 28,* 374-409.

Banks, J., Porter, A. L., Rardin, R. L., Silver, T. R., & Unger, V. E. (1977). *Summary phase I evaluation of Intensive Special Probation Project.* Washington, DC: National Institute of Law Enforcement and Criminal Justice.

Byrne, J. A., & Kelly, L. (1989). *Restructuring probation as an intermediate sanction: An evaluation of the Massachusetts Intensive Probation Supervision Program.* Final report to the National Institute of Justice, Research Program on the Punishment and Control of Offenders.

California Blue Ribbon Commission on Inmate Population Management. (1990). *Final report to the legislature.* Sacramento: State of California.

Clear, T. R. (1988). Statistical prediction in corrections. *Research in Corrections, 1*(1), 1-40.

Clear, T. R., & Hardyman, P. M. (1990). The new intensive supervision movement. *Crime and Delinquency, 36,* 42-60.

Erwin, B. S. (1987). *Evaluation of intensive probation supervision in Georgia.* Atlanta: Georgia Department of Corrections.

Gendreau, P., & Ross, R. R. (1987). Revivification of rehabilitation: Evidence from the 1980s. *Justice Quarterly, 4,* 349-408.

Harris, P. M., Clear, T. R., & Baird, S. C. (1989). Have probation officers changed their attitudes toward their work? *Justice Quarterly, 6,* 233-246.

Markley, G., & Eisenberg, M. (1986). *The Texas Board of Pardons and Paroles case management system.* Austin: Texas Board of Pardons and Paroles.

McCarthy, B. R. (Ed.). (1987). *Intermediate punishments: Intensive supervision, home confinement, and electronic surveillance,* Monsey, NY: Criminal Justice Press.

McCleary, R. (1974). *Dangerous men.* Beverly Hills, CA: Sage.

Morris, N., & Tonry, M. (1990). *Between prison and probation: Intermediate punishments in a rational sentencing system.* New York: Oxford University Press.

Niethercutt, M. G., & Gottfredson, D. M. (1974). *Caseload size variation and differences in probation/parole performance.* Washington, DC: National Center for Juvenile Justice.

New Jersey Management Review Commission Task Group on Corrections. (1990). *Corrections in New Jersey: Choosing the future.* Report to the Management Review Commission, Princeton, NJ.

Palmer, T. (1992). *The re-emergence of correctional intervention.* Newbury Park, CA: Sage.

Pearson, F. S. (1988). Evaluation of New Jersey's intensive supervision program. *Crime and Delinquency, 34,* 437-448.

Petersilia, J. (1987). *Expanding options for criminal sentencing* (Publication No. R-3544-EMC). Santa Monica, CA: RAND Corporation.

Petersilia, J., & Turner, S. (1990). Comparing intensive and regular supervision for high-risk probationers: Early results from an experiment in California. *Crime and Delinquency, 36,* 87-111.

Stanley, D. (1975). *Prisoners among us.* Washington, DC: Brookings Institution.
Thompson, J. D. (1967). *Organizations in action.* New York: McGraw-Hill.
Van Ness, D. (1989). *Restorative justice.* New York: Prison Fellowship.
von Hirsch, A., Wasik, M., & Greene, J. A. (1989). Punishments in the community and
    the principles of desert. *Rutgers Law Journal, 20,* 595-618.

Index

About the Authors

Terry L. Baumer is Associate Professor at the Indiana University School of Public and Environmental Affairs. He received his Ph.D. in sociology from Loyola University of Chicago. He has written in such diverse fields as the fear of crime, retail security, the robbery of financial institutions, and community corrections. He is currently engaged in the evaluation of several electronically monitored home confinement programs.

James M. Byrne is Professor in the Department of Criminal Justice at the University of Massachusetts at Lowell, and Director of the University's Center for Criminal Justice Research. He received his undergraduate degree in sociology from the University of Massachusetts at Amherst and his M.A. and Ph.D. in criminal justice from the School of Criminal Justice, Rutgers University. He has served as principal investigator for a number of evaluations in the community corrections area, including a nationwide review of the effectiveness of intermediate sanctions, a recent assessment of gender bias in the classification of juvenile offenders, and a field experiment on the most effective strategy for the location and apprehension of absconders from probation. He currently acts as a consultant to a variety of local, county, state, and federal agencies on community corrections issues.

Todd R. Clear, Ph.D., is Professor in the School of Criminal Justice, Rutgers University. He is author of numerous articles and books on correctional policy, including *Controlling the Offender in the Community*, *American Corrections*, and *The Presentence Investigation Report*. In 1986, he received the Cincinnati Award of the American Probation and Parole Association for his work on case management systems. His current research interests include community supervision of offenders, classification and prediction systems, and evaluation of penal policy.

344

Mary Clifford is a Ph.D. candidate in justice studies at Arizona State University. She has an M.S. in criminal justice from Northeastern University and a B.S. from Oklahoma State University in social aspects of law.

Donald Cochran is currently the Massachusetts Commissioner of Probation. He has been a teacher, coach, probation officer, and residential drug treatment program director. He holds a B.A. in history as well as four graduate degrees, including a doctorate degree in organizational behavior from the University of Massachusetts at Lowell. He is an Adjunct Professor of Criminal Justice at the University of Massachusetts at Lowell and a consultant to the National Institute of Corrections, the National Institute of Justice, the National Center for State Courts, the National Judicial College, and a number of correctional systems. He is also currently President of the National Association of Probation Executives and a board member of the American Probation and Parole Association and the Correctional Association of Massachusetts. He was selected the 1990 Probation Executive of the Year by the National Association of Probation Executives and Sam Houston University. He has published in the areas of organizational development, probation management, computer information systems, intermediate sanctions, adult and juvenile case classification, and case management, and is a frequent speaker at regional and national criminal justice conferences.

George F. Cole is Professor of Political Science at the University of Connecticut. A specialist on the administration of criminal justice, he has published extensively on such topics as prosecution, the courts, and corrections. His research over the last decade has focused on the use of monetary sanctions. In addition to his scholarly publications, he is the author of the widely used textbooks *The American System of Criminal Justice* (6th ed., Brooks/Cole, 1992) and, with Todd Clear, *American Corrections* (2nd ed., Brooks/Cole, 1990).

Ronald P. Corbett, Jr., is Director of Field Services for the Massachusetts Probation Department, where he directs all field operations, agency training, and program development. He is an adjunct faculty member at the University of Massachusetts at Lowell, where he teaches both undergraduate and graduate courses, and has published articles in a variety of journals, including *Federal Probation* and *Corrections Today*. He is a past recipient of the Haskell Memorial Distinguished Teaching Award (University of Massachusetts at

Lowell, 1990) and the Sam Houston State University Award (American Probation and Parole Association, 1990).

Elizabeth Piper Deschenes is a consultant to the RAND Corporation's Criminal Justice Program. Currently she is evaluating experimental correctional programs for adults and juveniles. As Co-Principal Investigator, with Susan Turner, she is investigating the effectiveness of intensive supervision programs for different types of drug offenders. With Peter Greenwood, she is evaluating residential and intensive aftercare programs for juvenile delinquents. She worked previously at UCLA as Co-Principal Investigator for two NIJ-funded projects studying the effects of civil commitment, probation, and parole on the drug use and criminal behavior of narcotics addicts. Her prior research at the URSA Institute in San Francisco involved the evaluation of experimental programs for violent juveniles and waiver to adult court. Her most recent publications include two articles on the effectiveness of legal supervision with narcotics addicts and another article on the waiver of juveniles to adult court; a forthcoming publication deals with drug treatment for juvenile offenders. She is a member of the American Society of Criminology, the Western Society of Criminology, and the Association for Criminal Justice Research in California.

Daniel Glaser is Senior Research Associate at the Social Science Research Institute and Professor Emeritus of Sociology at the University of Southern California. He is Past President of the American Society of Criminology and has been a recipient of that organization's Sutherland and Vollmer awards.

Judith A. Greene is Director of Court Programs for the Vera Institute of Justice in New York City. She is responsible for planning and developing programs designed to improve the functioning of the court in pretrial release, sentencing, and administration of intermediate criminal penalties. Her current activities include planning and management of not-for-profit bail bond agencies in Nassau and Bronx Counties, New York, and Essex County (Newark), New Jersey, which provide release from jail and close community supervision for selected pretrial detainees. She established the pilot project in Staten Island, New York, to introduce the European day-fine system to the American courts, and is now providing technical assistance to a network of jurisdictions around the country that are seeking to implement the day-fine concept. Prior to her work at Vera, she served as Director of the National Institute for Sentencing Alternatives at Brandeis University, and as Director of the Women's Resources Center of the San Francisco Sheriff's Department.

Sally T. Hillsman is Vice President for Research at the National Center for State Courts. She was previously Associate Director of the Vera Institute of Justice in New York City and has been Director of its Research Department since 1979. She has conducted research in a wide range of criminal justice areas, including intermediate sanctions, case processing, prosecution and court delay, pretrial diversion, and policing. Recently, she has completed research on fining practices in the United States and Western Europe, and has been working with jurisdictions across the country that are considering ways to implement the European day-fine concept in American courts. She holds a Ph.D. in sociology from Columbia University.

Jody Klein-Saffran is a Senior Research Analyst at the Federal Bureau of Prisons. She is a doctoral candidate in criminology at the University of Maryland, Institute of Criminal Justice and Criminology. Her research interests have been in the area of community corrections and intermediate sanctions.

Edward J. Latessa is Professor and Head of the Department of Criminal Justice at the University of Cincinnati. He received his Ph.D. in 1979 from Ohio State University. He has written extensively in the areas of correctional policy and treatment and evaluation research. He is coauthor of *Probation and Parole in America* (1985), *Introduction to Criminal Justice Research Methods* (1988), and *Statistical Applications in Criminal Justice* (1989). He is Past President of the Academy of Criminal Justice Sciences.

J. Robert Lilly is Professor of Criminology and Adjunct Professor of Law at Northern Kentucky University, and Visiting Scholar in the Department of Sociology and Social Policy, University of Durham, in Durham, England. He received his Ph.D. from the University of Tennessee in 1975. His research interests include juvenile delinquency, home confinement and electronic monitoring, and comparative criminology and criminal justice. He has published approximately 50 articles and book chapters, including contributions to *Criminology, Crime and Delinquency, Social Problems, Legal Studies Forum, Northern Kentucky Law Review, Journal of Drug Issues, The New Scholar, Adolescence, Qualitative Sociology, Urban Life, Federal Probation, International Journal of Comparative and Applied Criminal Justice, The Angolite,* and the *Howard Journal of Criminal Justice.* He has coauthored several articles and chapters with Richard A. Ball, and is coauthor of *House Arrest and Correctional Policy: Doing Time at Home* and *Criminological Theory: Context and Consequences.* He currently is doing research on the emerging national and international "commercial corrections complex."

Arthur J. Lurigio, a social psychologist, is currently Associate Professor of Criminal Justice at Loyola University, Research Associate at Northwestern University, and Director of Research for the Cook County, Illinois, Adult Probation Department. He received his doctorate from Loyola University of Chicago in 1984. His research interests include community crime prevention, criminal victimization and victim services, intermediate punishments, monetary sanctions, decision making in sentencing, crime and mental disorders, and AIDS in the criminal justice system.

Doris Layton MacKenzie is Associate Professor in the Institute of Criminal Justice and Criminology, University of Maryland, currently working as a Visiting Scientist at the National Institute of Justice, U.S. Department of Justice. She graduated from the Pennsylvania State University with a Ph.D. in psychology. Prior to joining the Maryland faculty, she was an Associate Professor at Louisiana State University with a joint appointment in the Department of Experimental Statistics and the Department of Criminal Justice. Her research has focused on corrections and offenders. She has published papers in the areas of inmate adjustment, recidivism, prison crowding, and classification, and is coeditor of two books, *The American Prison: Issues in Research and Policy* and *Measuring Crime: Large-Scale, Long-Range Efforts.* She has directed studies in classification, prison programs, and prison population prediction models. Currently she is director of a multisite study of shock incarceration examining nine shock programs. As an authority in the new boot camp prisons, she has been consultant to states considering initiating such programs, and has testified before committees of the U.S. House and Senate.

Gary T. Marx is Professor of Sociology at the University of Colorado and Director of the Center for the Social Study of Information Technology. He is the author of *Protest and Prejudice* and *Undercover: Police Surveillance in America.*

Jack McDevitt is Associate Director of the Center for Applied Social Research at Northeastern University. His past research in the area of community corrections includes an evaluation of the Hampden County day reporting center, an analysis of Massachusetts's probation classification system concerning gender bias, and consultation on a number of projects regarding community corrections alternatives. He is also a member of the Governor's Task Force on Alternatives to Incarceration and Community Corrections. His other research interests include the characteristics of hate crimes and the impact of crime on small businesses in Boston. He has published several articles and reports on alternatives to incarceration and hate-motivated crime.

Douglas C. McDonald is a Senior Social Scientist at Abt Associates Inc., a policy research organization headquartered in Cambridge, Massachusetts. Among his principal interests are criminal sentencing policies and practices, intermediate sanctions, drug policy, correctional financing, and privatization. Among his publications are three books: *Private Prisons and the Public Interest* (Rutgers University Press, 1990), which he edited; *Punishment Without Walls: Community Service Sentencing in New York* (Rutgers University Press, 1986); and *The Price of Punishment: Public Spending for Corrections in New York* (Westview Press, 1980).

Robert I. Mendelsohn is Associate Professor at Indiana University in the School of Public and Environmental Affairs at Indianapolis. Since 1986, he and Terry Baumer have been conducting field experiments on electronic monitoring. He has written and given presentations on local legal systems, court management, and police training. He is former Director of the Center for Criminal Justice Training at Indiana University, and is currently Special Assistant to the Associate Vice Chancellor for Undergraduate Education at Indiana University/Purdue University Indianapolis.

Robyn Miliano is Research Associate at the Center for Applied Social Research at Northeastern University. She has coauthored an article on day reporting centers published in the journal *International Association of Residential and Community Alternatives*. Also, in conjunction with the Crime and Justice Foundation, she completed an evaluation of the Hampden County day reporting center and presented the findings at the American Society of Criminology meetings in November 1990. Her other areas of research interest include evaluating the impact of crime on small businesses in Boston, analyzing crime trends in Boston, and researching gang activity. She holds a master's of science degree in criminal justice from Northeastern University.

Dennis J. Palumbo is Regents' Professor of Justice Studies and Political Science at Arizona State University. His most recent publications include *Public Policy in America* and *Implementation and the*

Policy Making Process. He has been editor of the *Policy Studies Review* and has authored or coauthored several articles on community corrections programs. He is currently coediting, with Rita Kelly, a series on controversial issues in public policy for Sage Publications.

Dale G. Parent is a Senior Analyst in Law and Public Safety with Abt Associates, a research firm in Cambridge, Massachusetts. At Abt, he has conducted studies on boot camp prison programs, day reporting centers, offender fee payments, and crime victim compensation programs for the National Institute of Justice. In addition, he conducted an assessment of community corrections, probation, and parole for the Oregon Governor's Task Force on Corrections Planning, and a management review of juvenile justice services in Jefferson Parish, Louisiana. Currently, he is directing an NIJ study of state practices to structure probation and parole revocations and to apprehend and punish absconders, as well as a national assessment of conditions of confinement in secure juvenile facilities for the Office of Juvenile Justice and Delinquency Prevention. Previously, he was Deputy Director of the National Institute for Sentencing Alternatives at Brandeis University, where he worked with policymakers and correctional officials in more than 20 states to develop nonconfinement sentencing programs. He also directed a national technical assistance program for residential community corrections programs for the National Institute of Corrections. During the 1982-1983 academic year he was a Guggenheim Fellow at the Yale Law School, where he participated in seminars on sentencing reform and wrote *Structuring Criminal Sentences,* a book about Minnesota's experience with sentencing guidelines. From 1978 to 1982, he directed Minnesota's Sentencing Guidelines Commission, the first such body in the nation. As a staff member at the Minnesota Department of Corrections, he developed, implemented, and evaluated the nation's first state parole decision-making guidelines.

April Pattavina is a doctoral candidate at the Institute of Criminal Justice and Criminology, University of Maryland. Her interests include community corrections and the relationship between urbanism and crime.

Joan Petersilia, Ph.D., is Director of the RAND Corporation's Criminal Justice Program. She has directed several major studies in the areas of policing, sentencing, career criminals, corrections, and racial discrimination. Most recently, her work has focused on the effectiveness of probation and parole, evaluating intensive probation and parole programs in 14 jurisdictions. Her most recent publication is *Intensive Supervision for High-Risk Probationers: Findings From Three California Experiments* (1990). Her other major publications include *Expanding Options for Criminal Sentencing* (1987), *Police Performance and Case Attrition* (1987), *The Influence of Criminal Justice Research* (1987), *Prison Versus Probation in California* (1986), and *Granting Felons Probation* (1985). In 1989-1990, she was President of the American Society of Criminology. She is a Fellow of both the American Society of Criminology and the Western Society of Criminology. She has received awards for her research from the American Probation and Parole Association and the California Probation, Parole, and Corrections Association.

Marc Renzema is Professor of Criminal Justice at Kutztown University, a unit of the Pennsylvania State System of Higher Education. He began his criminal justice career as a prison psychologist in 1969 and held a variety of practitioner and research positions before beginning college teaching in 1977. He holds a Ph.D. in criminal justice from the State University of New York at Albany as well as an M.A. in psychology from Temple University and a B.A. from Johns Hopkins University. In 1987, he founded *Offender Monitoring*, a newsletter he edited and published until 1989, when it became the *Journal of Offender Monitoring*. He has been following the development of electronic monitoring since the initial experiments at Harvard in the late 1960s.

Robin A. Robinson is an Assistant Professor at Rutgers University in the School of Social Work, New Brunswick. She received her Ph.D. in social welfare policy from Brandeis University, Florence Heller School for Advanced Studies in Social Welfare. Before undertaking her doctoral work, she was employed for many years as a public services librarian in inner-city neighborhoods in Massachusetts, where she coordinated interagency efforts to provide social services. Her current research interests include the relationship between sexual abuse history and deviant behaviors, correctional control of women, classification of prisoner risk and need, and community-based mental health services. She is currently at work on a book on changing perceptions of female deviance and crime.

Zoann K. Snyder-Joy is a doctoral candidate in the School of Justice Studies, Arizona State University. She is currently researching the perceptions of federal Indian policy held by American Indian women involved in education and school administration.

Lawrence F. Travis III is Professor of Criminal Justice at the University of Cincinnati. He received his Ph.D. in criminal justice in 1982 from the State University of New York at Albany. He has written extensively in criminal justice and is author of *Introduction to Criminal Justice* (1990) and editor of *Probation, Parole and Community Corrections* (1985). He is currently a Trustee-at-Large of the Academy of Criminal Justice Sciences.

Susan Turner is a social psychologist in the RAND Corporation's Criminal Justice Program. Her research has included work on the effectiveness of alternative correctional programs in both adult and juvenile arenas. She is currently collaborating with Joan Petersilia on the evaluation of intensive supervision probation and parole in 14 jurisdictions across the country. She has just completed *Intensive Supervision for High-Risk Probationers: Findings From Three California Experiments* (1990), with Joan Petersilia. Her other publications include *Diverting Prisoners to Intensive Probation: Results of an Experiment in Oregon* (1990), *Racial Equity in Sentencing* (1988), *Post-Release Criminal Behavior of San Diego Juveniles Placed in VisionQuest: An Evaluation of Treatment Effects* (1987), *Selective Incapacitation Revisited: Why the High Rate Offenders Are Hard to Predict* (1987), and *Guideline Based Justice: Implications for Racial Minorities* (1985). She is Past President of the Association for Criminal Justice Research (California) and a member of the American Society of Criminology and the Western Society of Criminology.

Andrew von Hirsch is Professor at the School of Criminal Justice, Rutgers University. He is also Research Fellow in Criminal Law at Uppsala University, Sweden. He has written extensively on sentencing theory and policy. His books include *Doing Justice* (1976), *Past or Future Crimes* (1985), and, with Kay Knapp and Michael Tonry, *The Sentencing Commission and Its Guidelines* (1987). He is now working on a volume titled *Censure and Sanctions*, dealing with punishment theory and noncustodial sentences.

Ronald K. Watts is Research Associate at the Social Science Research Institute, University of Southern California. He is concerned with evaluation issues in applied criminology, and has also done research on alcoholism, the social determinants of fertility, and conservation of electricity.